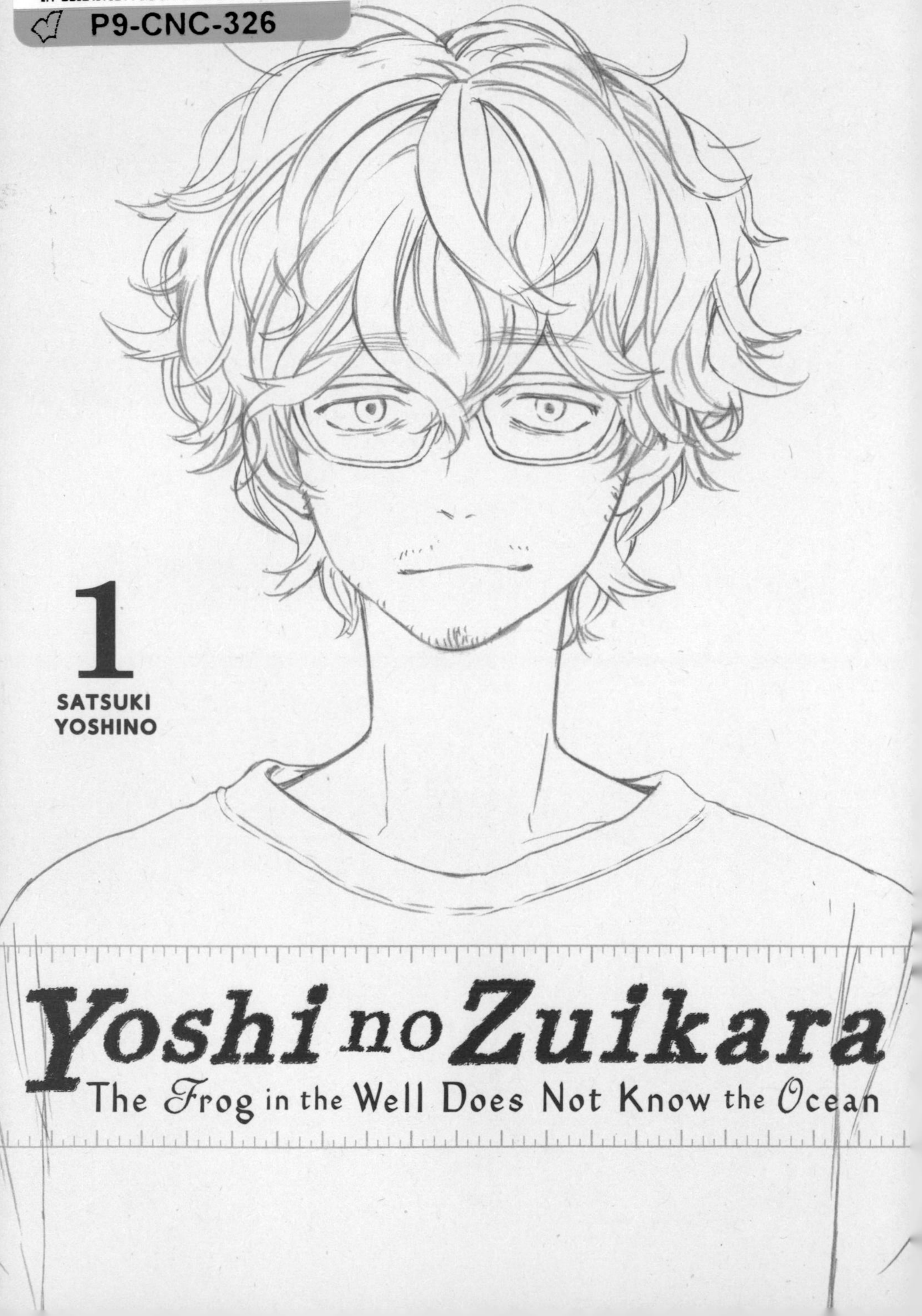

1

SATSUKI
YOSHINO

Yoshi no Zuikara

The Frog in the Well Does Not Know the Ocean

CONTENTS

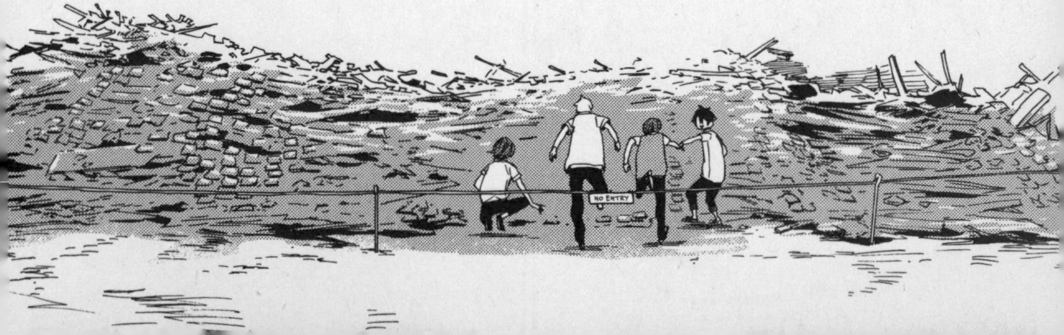
NO ENTRY

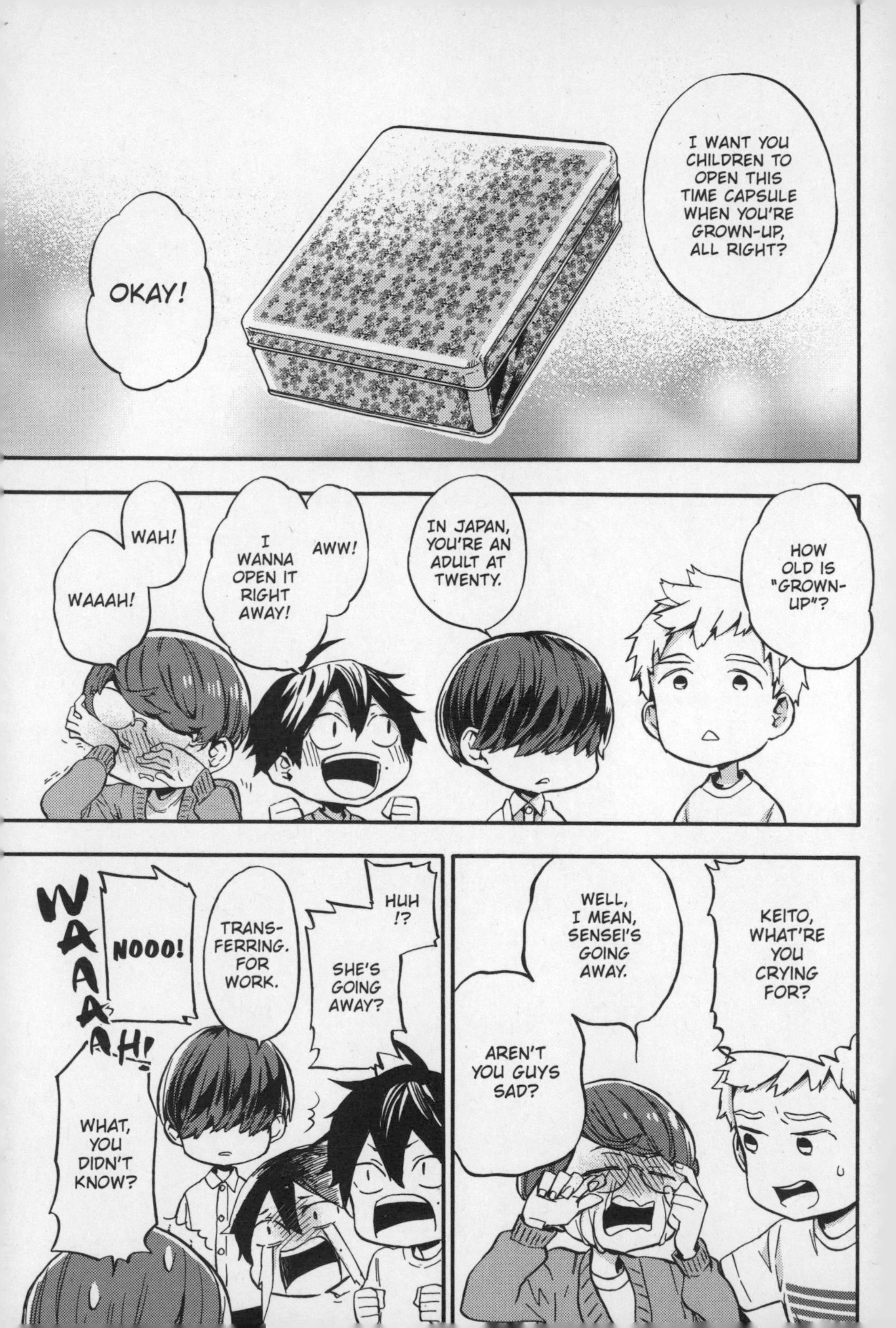
I WANT YOU CHILDREN TO OPEN THIS TIME CAPSULE WHEN YOU'RE GROWN-UP, ALL RIGHT?
OKAY!
HOW OLD IS "GROWN-UP"?
IN JAPAN, YOU'RE AN ADULT AT TWENTY.
AWW!
I WANNA OPEN IT RIGHT AWAY!
WAH!
WAAAH!
KEITO, WHAT'RE YOU CRYING FOR?
WELL, I MEAN, SENSEI'S GOING AWAY.
AREN'T YOU GUYS SAD?
HUH!?
SHE'S GOING AWAY?
TRANS-FERRING. FOR WORK.
NOOO!
WAAAAAH!
WHAT, YOU DIDN'T KNOW?

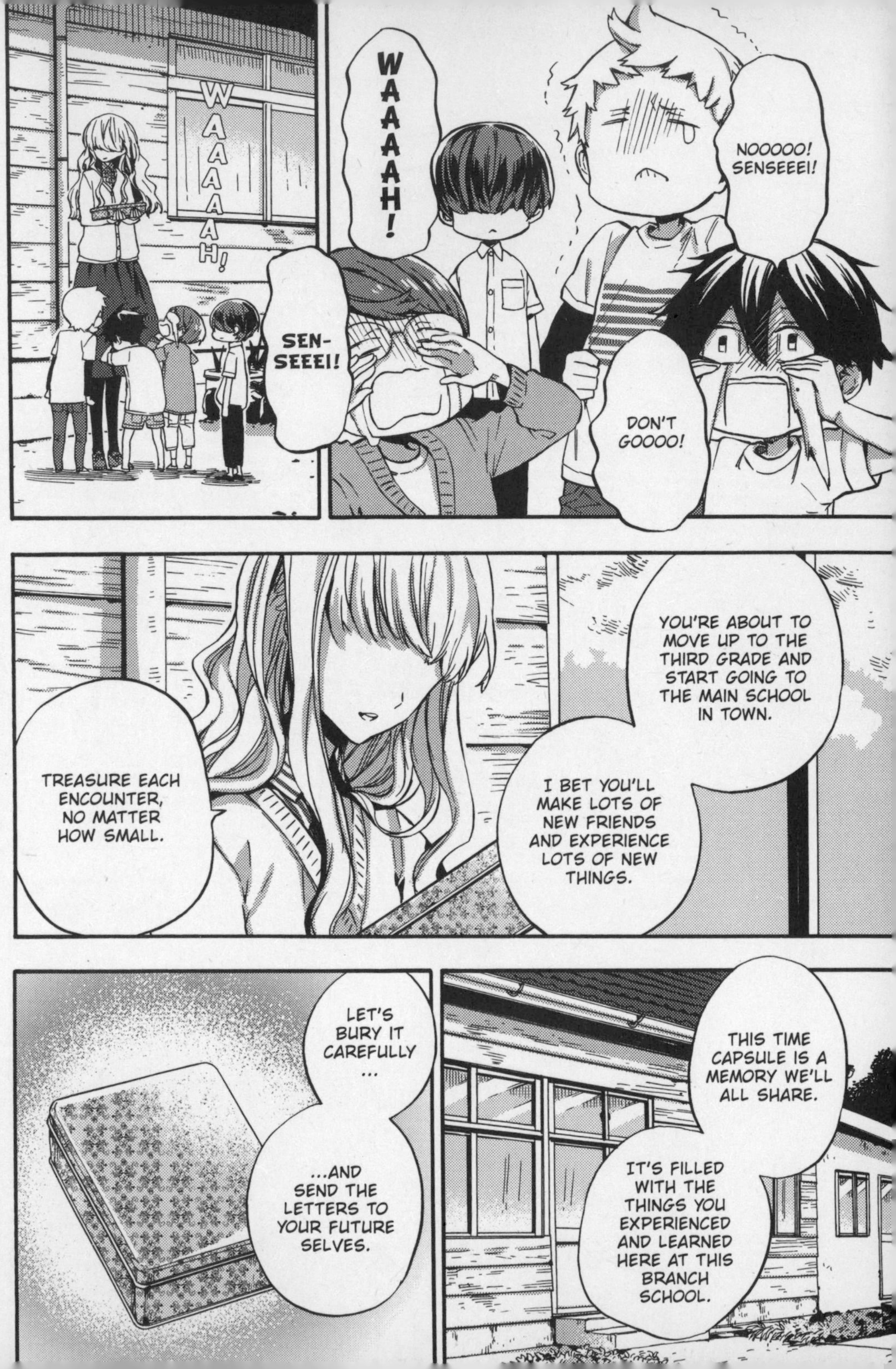
NOOOOO! SENSEEEI!
WAAAAAH!
SEN-SEEEI!
DON'T GOOOO!
WAAAAAH!
YOU'RE ABOUT TO MOVE UP TO THE THIRD GRADE AND START GOING TO THE MAIN SCHOOL IN TOWN.
I BET YOU'LL MAKE LOTS OF NEW FRIENDS AND EXPERIENCE LOTS OF NEW THINGS.
TREASURE EACH ENCOUNTER, NO MATTER HOW SMALL.
THIS TIME CAPSULE IS A MEMORY WE'LL ALL SHARE.
IT'S FILLED WITH THE THINGS YOU EXPERIENCED AND LEARNED HERE AT THIS BRANCH SCHOOL.
LET'S BURY IT CAREFULLY...
...AND SEND THE LETTERS TO YOUR FUTURE SELVES.

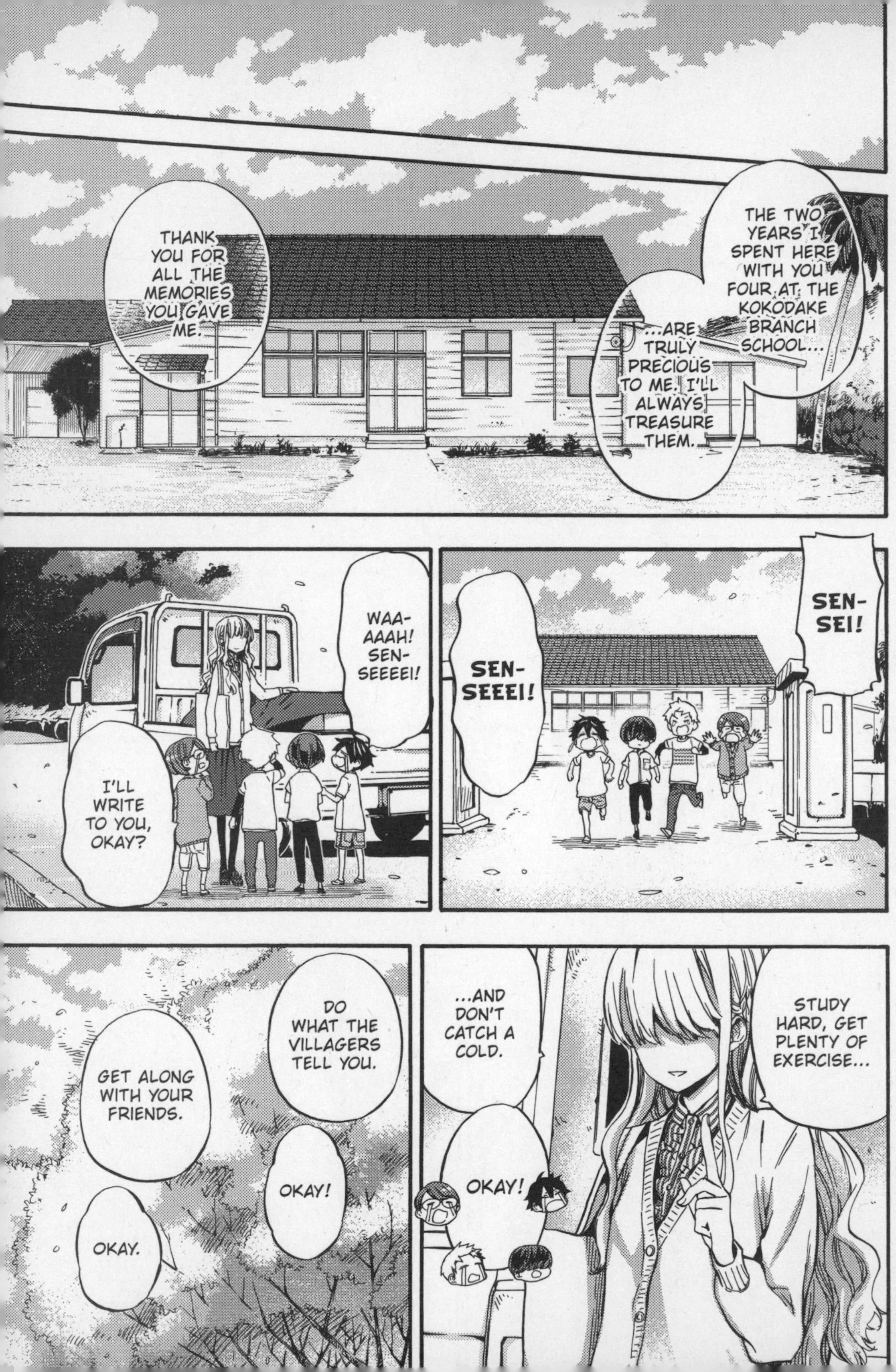
THE TWO YEARS I SPENT HERE WITH YOU FOUR AT THE KOKODAKE BRANCH SCHOOL...
...ARE TRULY PRECIOUS TO ME. I'LL ALWAYS TREASURE THEM.
THANK YOU FOR ALL THE MEMORIES YOU GAVE ME.
SEN-SEI!
SEN-SEEEI!
WAA-AAAH! SEN-SEEEEI!
I'LL WRITE TO YOU, OKAY?
STUDY HARD, GET PLENTY OF EXERCISE...
...AND DON'T CATCH A COLD.
OKAY!
DO WHAT THE VILLAGERS TELL YOU.
GET ALONG WITH YOUR FRIENDS.
OKAY!
OKAY.

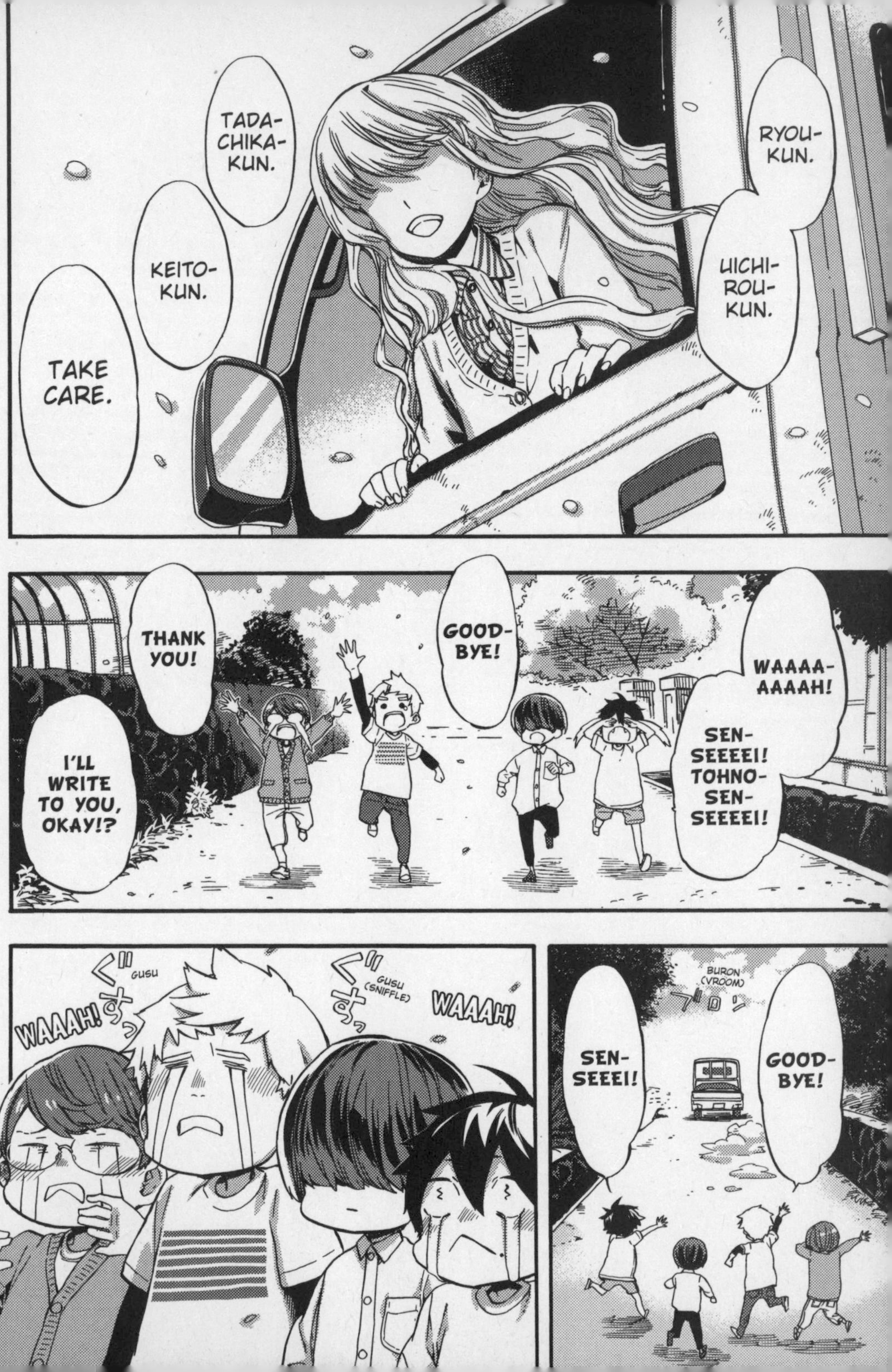
RYOU-KUN.
UICHI-ROU-KUN.
TADA-CHIKA-KUN.
KEITO-KUN.
TAKE CARE.
WAAAA-AAAAH!
SEN-SEEEEI! TOHNO-SEN-SEEEEI!
GOOD-BYE!
THANK YOU!
I'LL WRITE TO YOU, OKAY!?
BURON (VROOM)
GOOD-BYE!
SEN-SEEEI!
WAAAH!
GUSU (SNIFFLE)
GUSU
WAAAH!

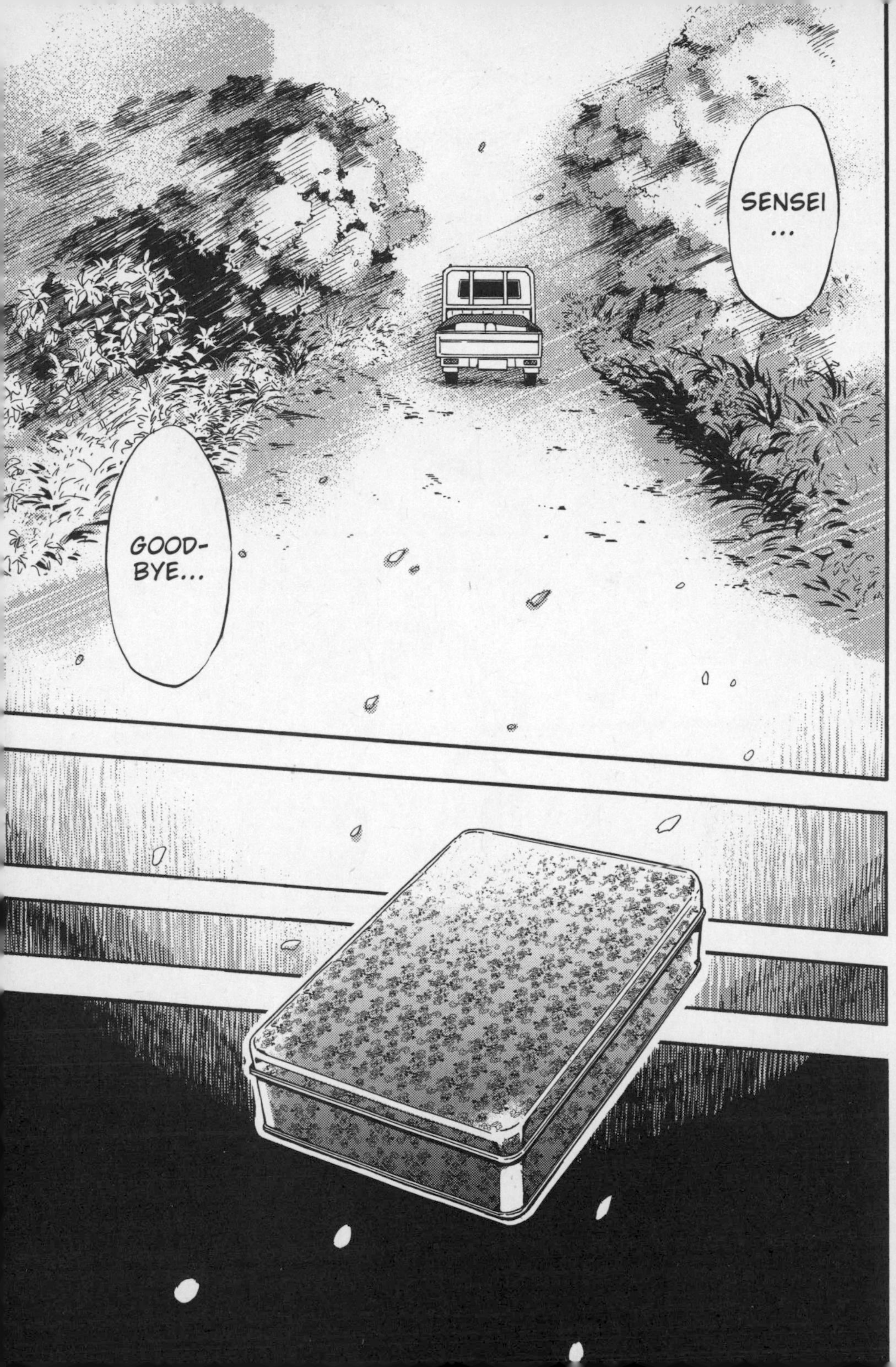
SENSEI ...
GOOD-BYE...

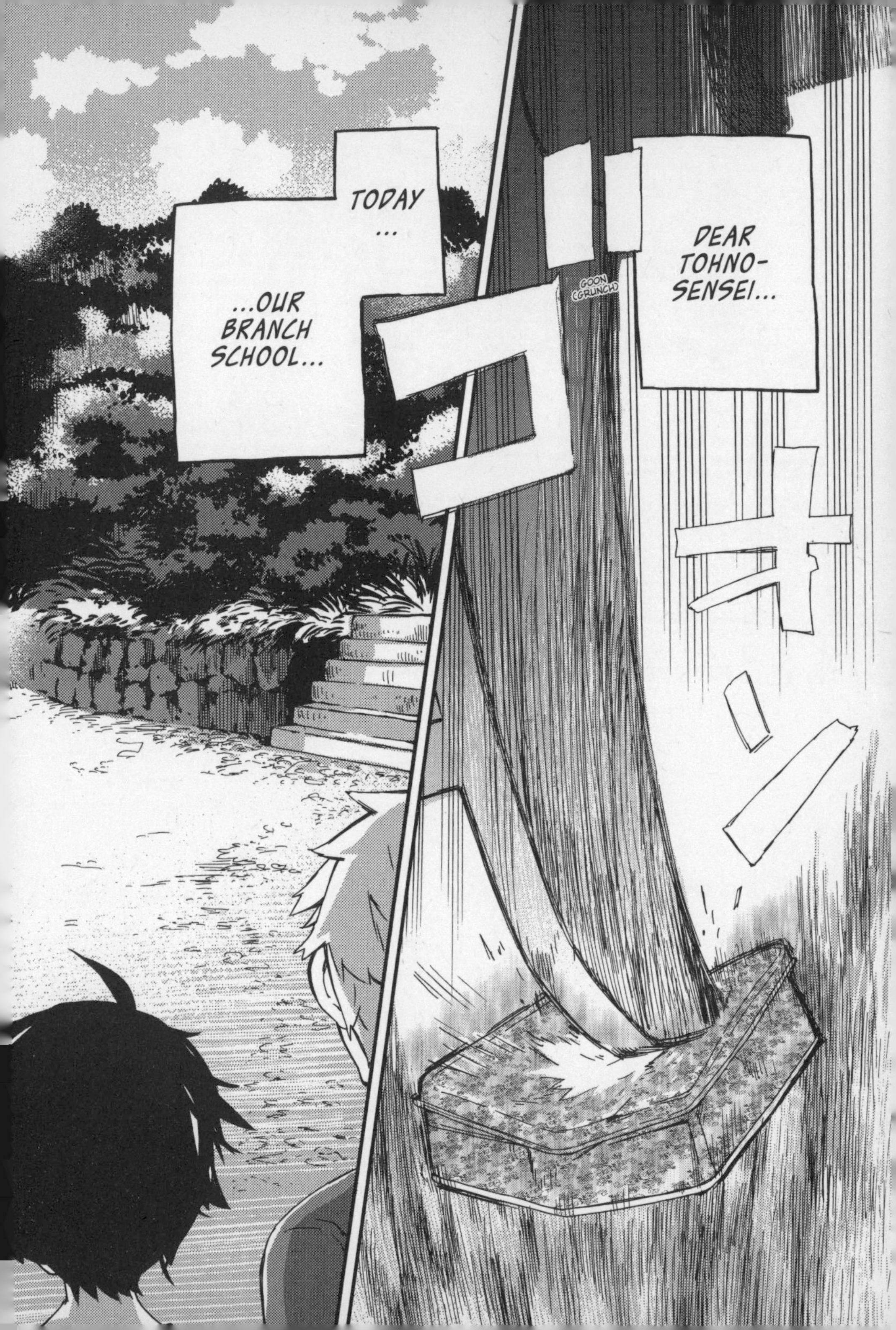
DEAR TOHNO-SENSEI...
GOON (GRUNCH)
TODAY ...
...OUR BRANCH SCHOOL...

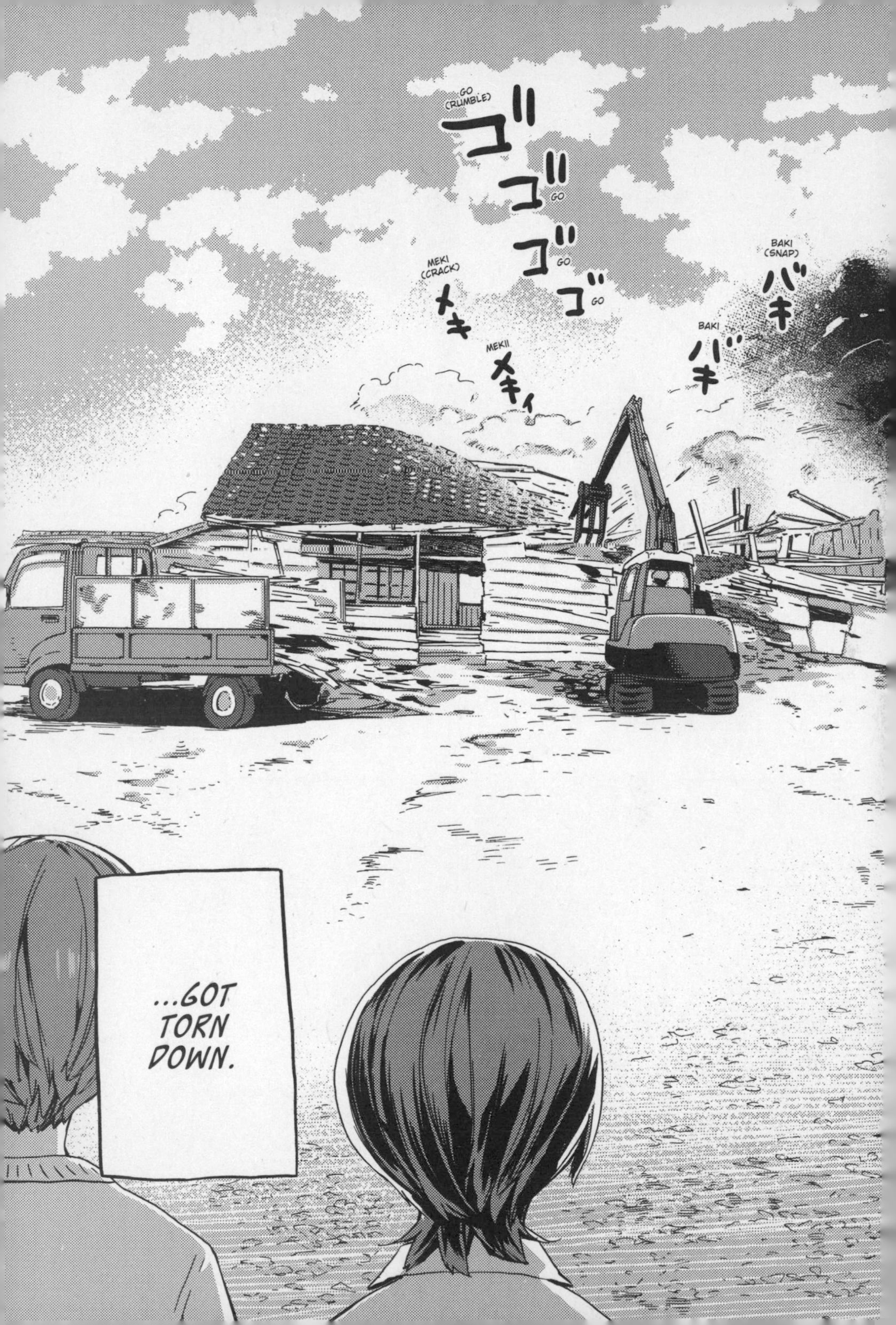
GO (RUMBLE)
GO
GO
GO
BAKI (SNAP)
BAKI
MEKI (CRACK)
MEKII
...GOT TORN DOWN.

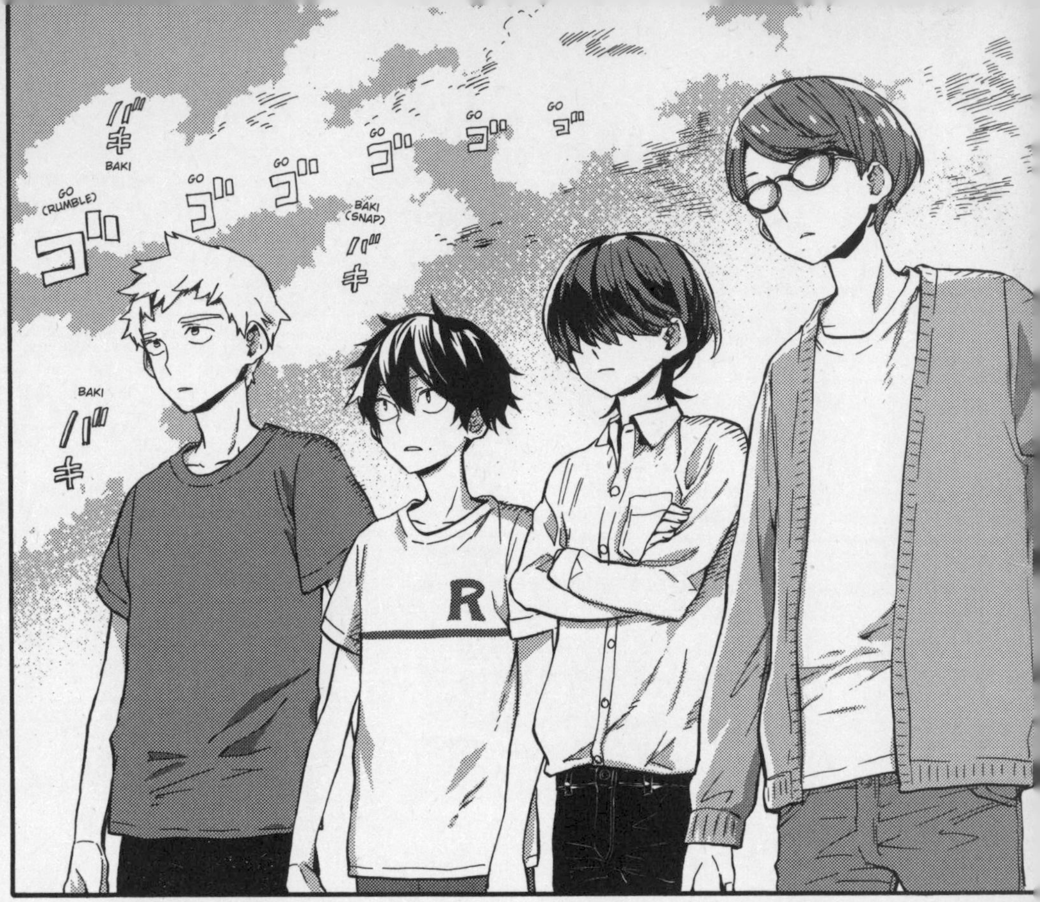
GO ゴ
GO ゴ
GO ゴ
BAKI (SNAP) バキ
GO ゴ
GO ゴ
BAKI バキ
GO (RUMBLE) ゴ
BAKI バキ

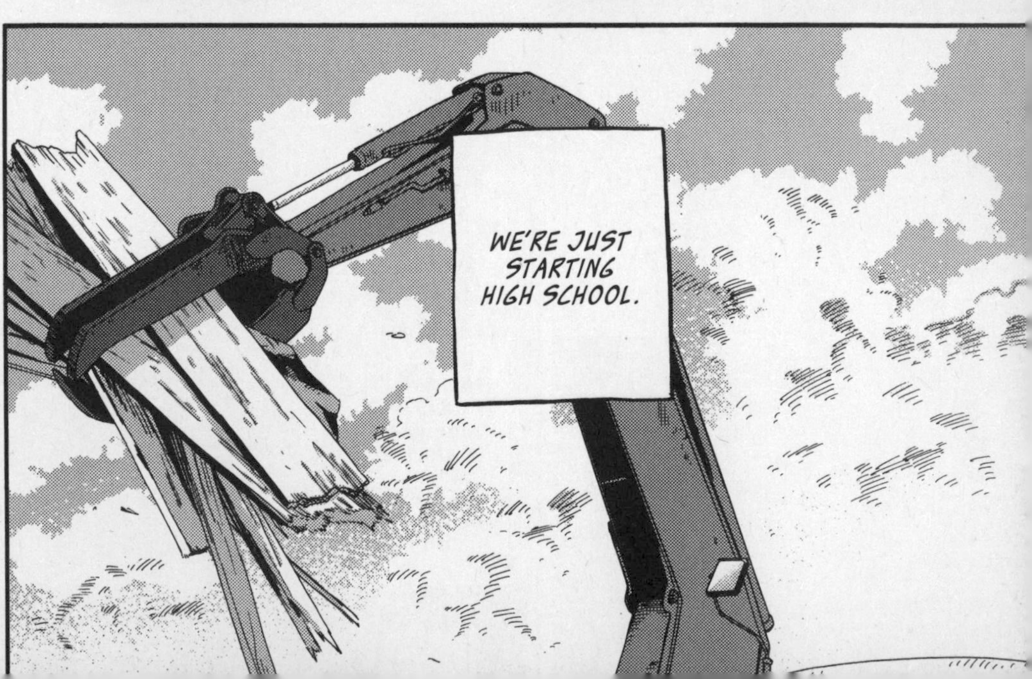
WE'RE JUST STARTING HIGH SCHOOL.

1. WAKKAMONDON

Translation → Youngsters

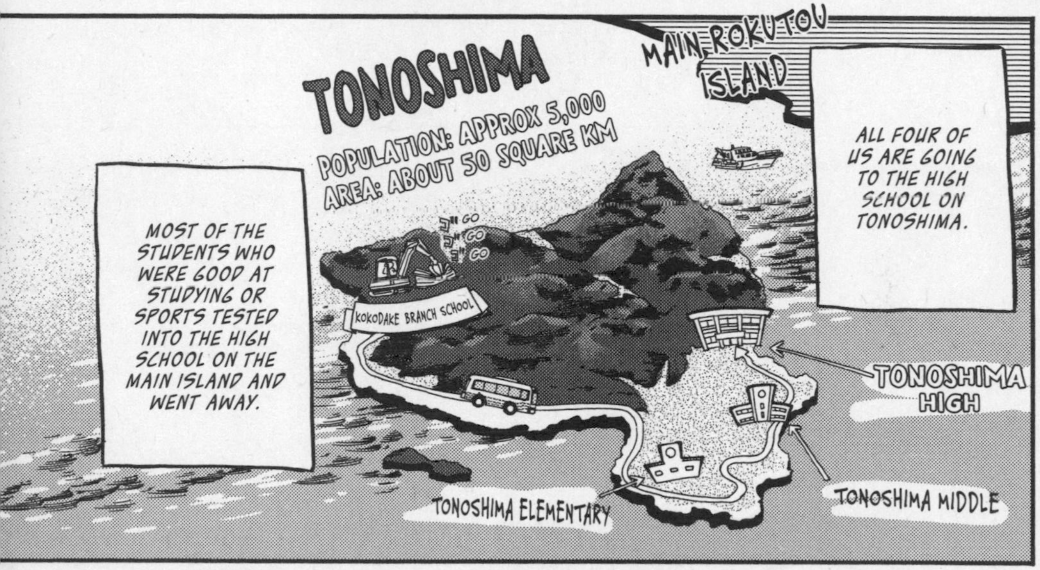
MAIN ROKUTOU ISLAND
ALL FOUR OF US ARE GOING TO THE HIGH SCHOOL ON TONOSHIMA.
TONOSHIMA
POPULATION: APPROX 5,000
AREA: ABOUT 50 SQUARE KM
GO GO GO
TONOSHIMA HIGH
KOKODAKE BRANCH SCHOOL
MOST OF THE STUDENTS WHO WERE GOOD AT STUDYING OR SPORTS TESTED INTO THE HIGH SCHOOL ON THE MAIN ISLAND AND WENT AWAY.
TONOSHIMA MIDDLE
TONOSHIMA ELEMENTARY

SIGN: TONOSHIMA HIGH ENTRANCE CEREMONY

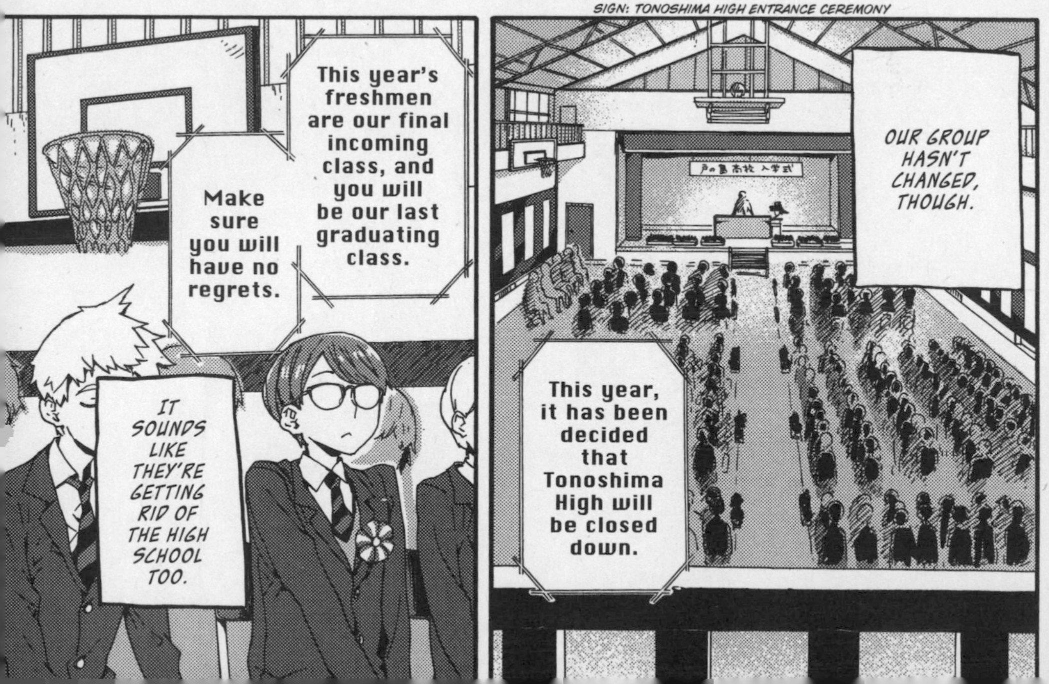
OUR GROUP HASN'T CHANGED, THOUGH.
This year, it has been decided that Tonoshima High will be closed down.
This year's freshmen are our final incoming class, and you will be our last graduating class.
Make sure you will have no regrets.
IT SOUNDS LIKE THEY'RE GETTING RID OF THE HIGH SCHOOL TOO.

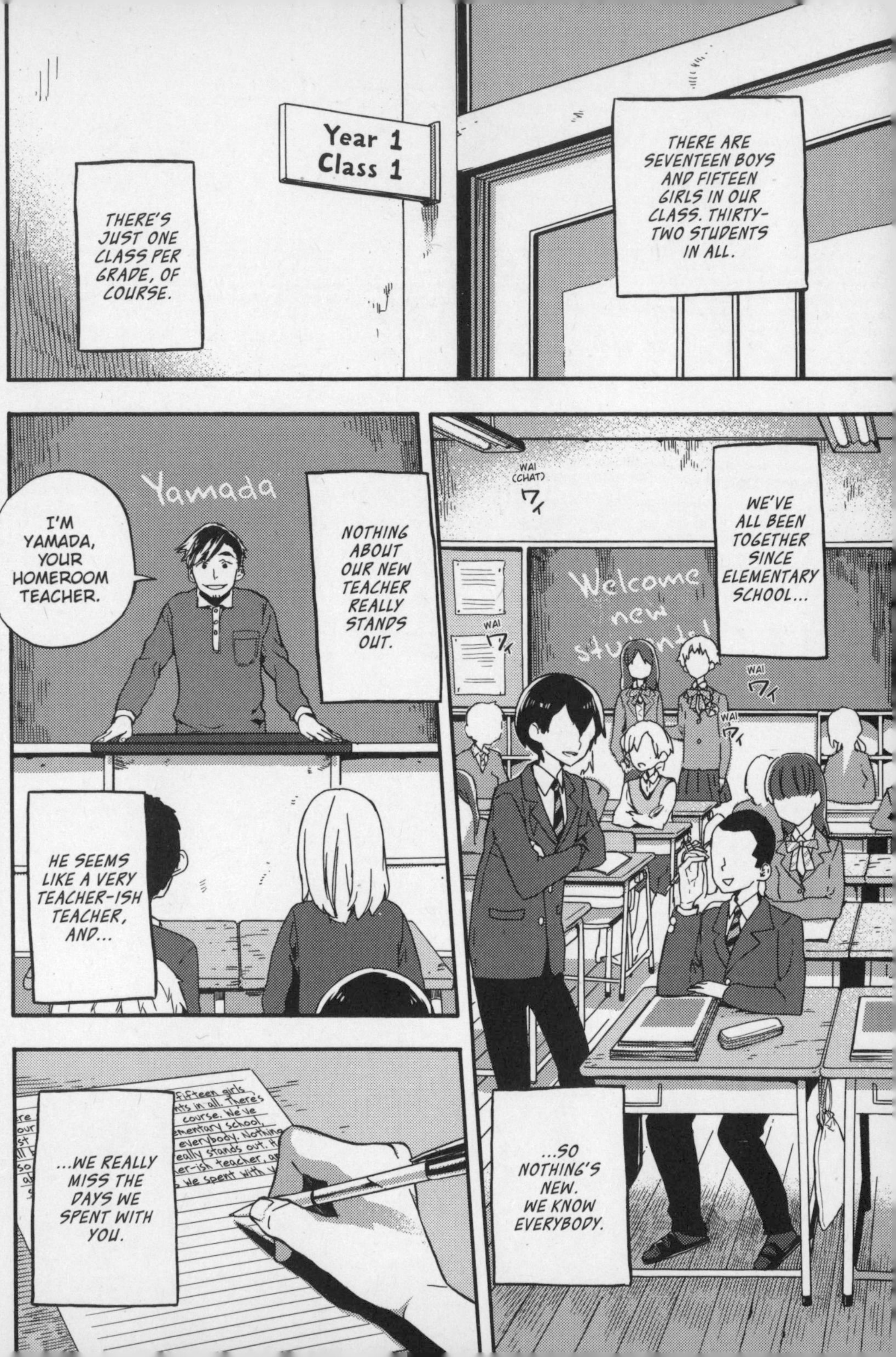
THERE ARE SEVENTEEN BOYS AND FIFTEEN GIRLS IN OUR CLASS. THIRTY-TWO STUDENTS IN ALL.
Year 1 Class 1
THERE'S JUST ONE CLASS PER GRADE, OF COURSE.
WE'VE ALL BEEN TOGETHER SINCE ELEMENTARY SCHOOL...
WAI (CHAT)
Welcome new students!
WAI
WAI
WAI
...SO NOTHING'S NEW. WE KNOW EVERYBODY.
Yamada
NOTHING ABOUT OUR NEW TEACHER REALLY STANDS OUT.
I'M YAMADA, YOUR HOMEROOM TEACHER.
HE SEEMS LIKE A VERY TEACHER-ISH TEACHER, AND...
...WE REALLY MISS THE DAYS WE SPENT WITH YOU.

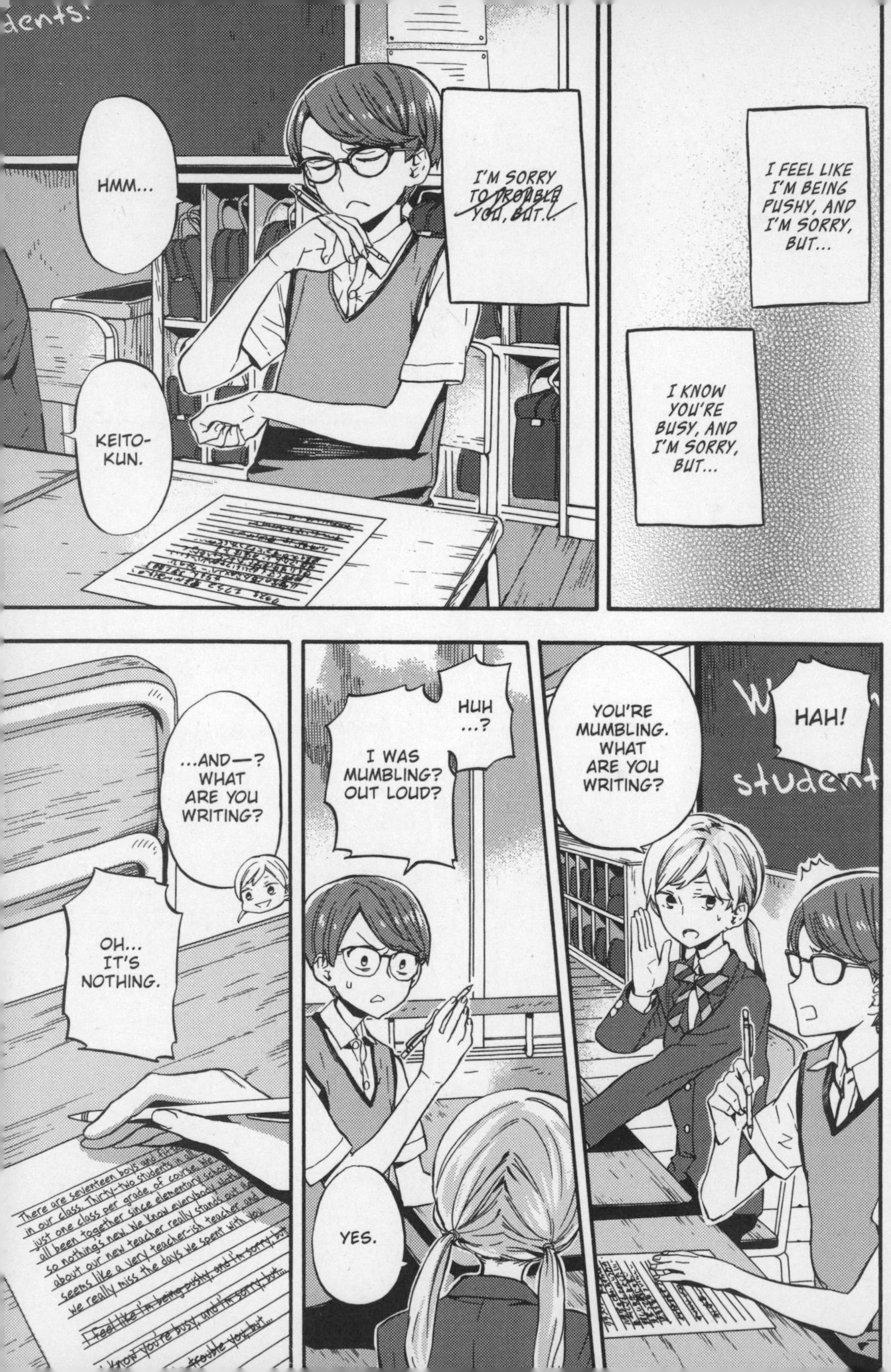
I FEEL LIKE I'M BEING PUSHY, AND I'M SORRY, BUT...
I KNOW YOU'RE BUSY, AND I'M SORRY, BUT...
I'M SORRY TO TROUBLE YOU, BUT...
HMM...
KEITO-KUN.
HAH!
YOU'RE MUMBLING. WHAT ARE YOU WRITING?
HUH ...?
I WAS MUMBLING? OUT LOUD?
YES.
...AND—? WHAT ARE YOU WRITING?
OH... IT'S NOTHING.
There are seventeen boys and
in our class. Thirty-two students
just one class per grade of course. We
all been together since elementary
so nothing's new. We know everybody
about our new teacher really stands out
seems like a very teacher-ish teacher and
we really miss the days we spent with you.
I feel like I'm being pushy, and I'm sorry, but...
I know you're busy, and I'm sorry, but...
trouble you, but...

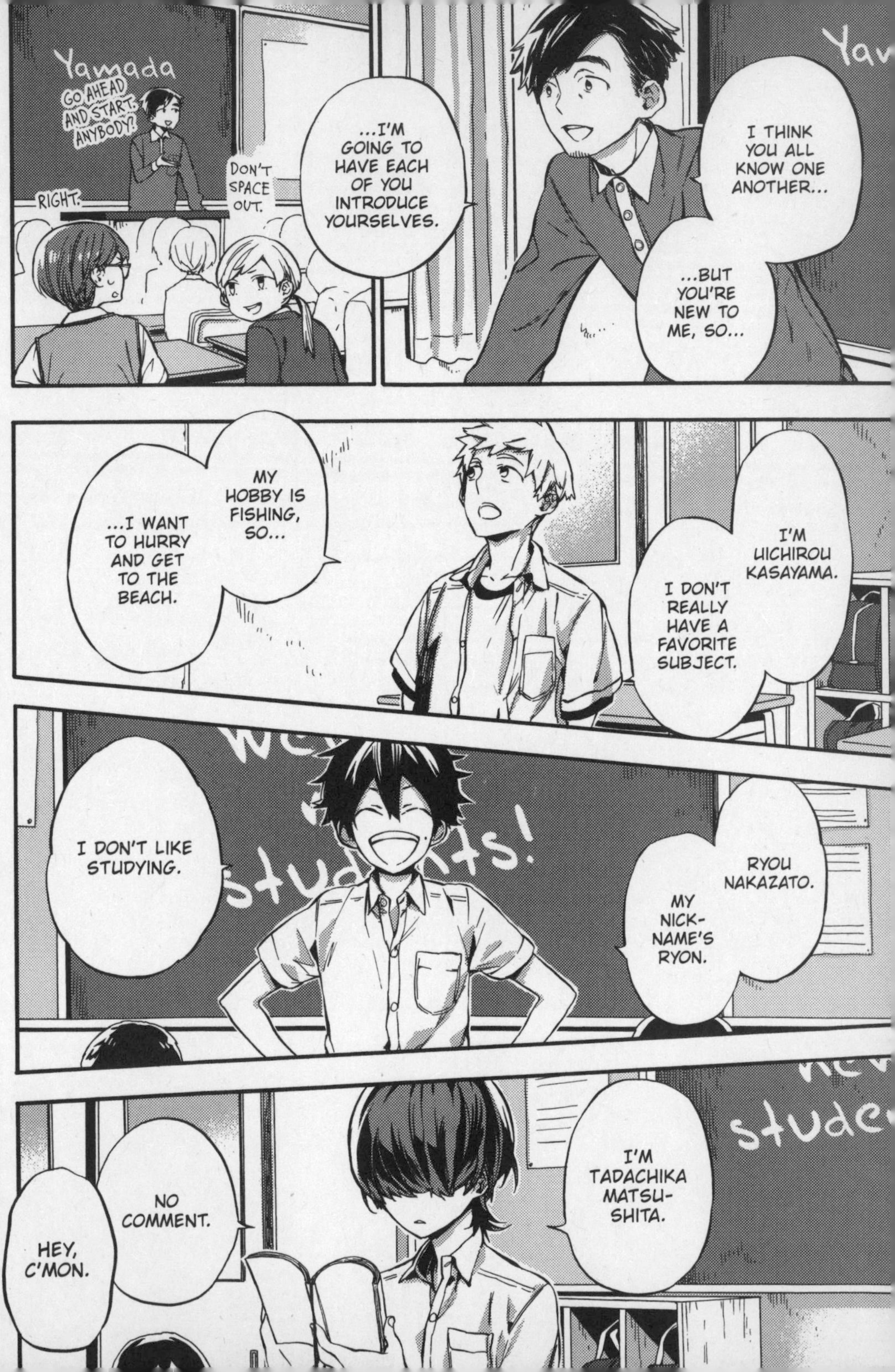
I THINK YOU ALL KNOW ONE ANOTHER...
...BUT YOU'RE NEW TO ME, SO...
...I'M GOING TO HAVE EACH OF YOU INTRODUCE YOURSELVES.
Yamada
GO AHEAD AND START, ANYBODY?
DON'T SPACE OUT.
RIGHT.
I'M UICHIROU KASAYAMA.
I DON'T REALLY HAVE A FAVORITE SUBJECT.
MY HOBBY IS FISHING, SO...
...I WANT TO HURRY AND GET TO THE BEACH.
RYOU NAKAZATO.
MY NICK-NAME'S RYON.
I DON'T LIKE STUDYING.
I'M TADACHIKA MATSU-SHITA.
NO COMMENT.
HEY, C'MON.

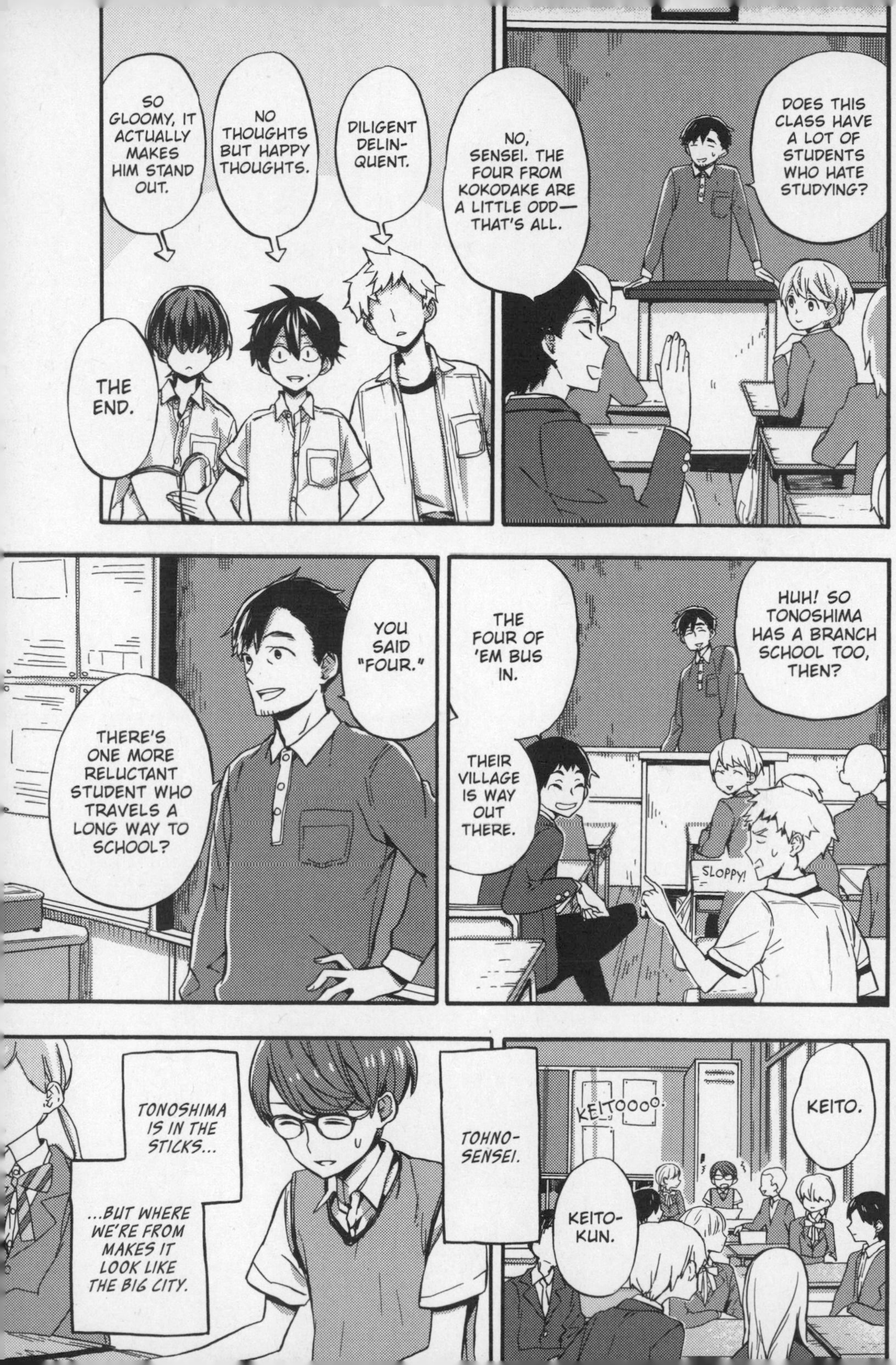
DOES THIS CLASS HAVE A LOT OF STUDENTS WHO HATE STUDYING?
NO, SENSEI. THE FOUR FROM KOKODAKE ARE A LITTLE ODD—THAT'S ALL.
DILIGENT DELINQUENT.
NO THOUGHTS BUT HAPPY THOUGHTS.
SO GLOOMY, IT ACTUALLY MAKES HIM STAND OUT.
THE END.
HUH! SO TONOSHIMA HAS A BRANCH SCHOOL TOO, THEN?
THE FOUR OF 'EM BUS IN.
THEIR VILLAGE IS WAY OUT THERE.
SLOPPY!
YOU SAID "FOUR."
THERE'S ONE MORE RELUCTANT STUDENT WHO TRAVELS A LONG WAY TO SCHOOL?
KEITO.
KEITOOOO.
KEITO-KUN.
TOHNO-SENSEI.
TONOSHIMA IS IN THE STICKS...
...BUT WHERE WE'RE FROM MAKES IT LOOK LIKE THE BIG CITY.

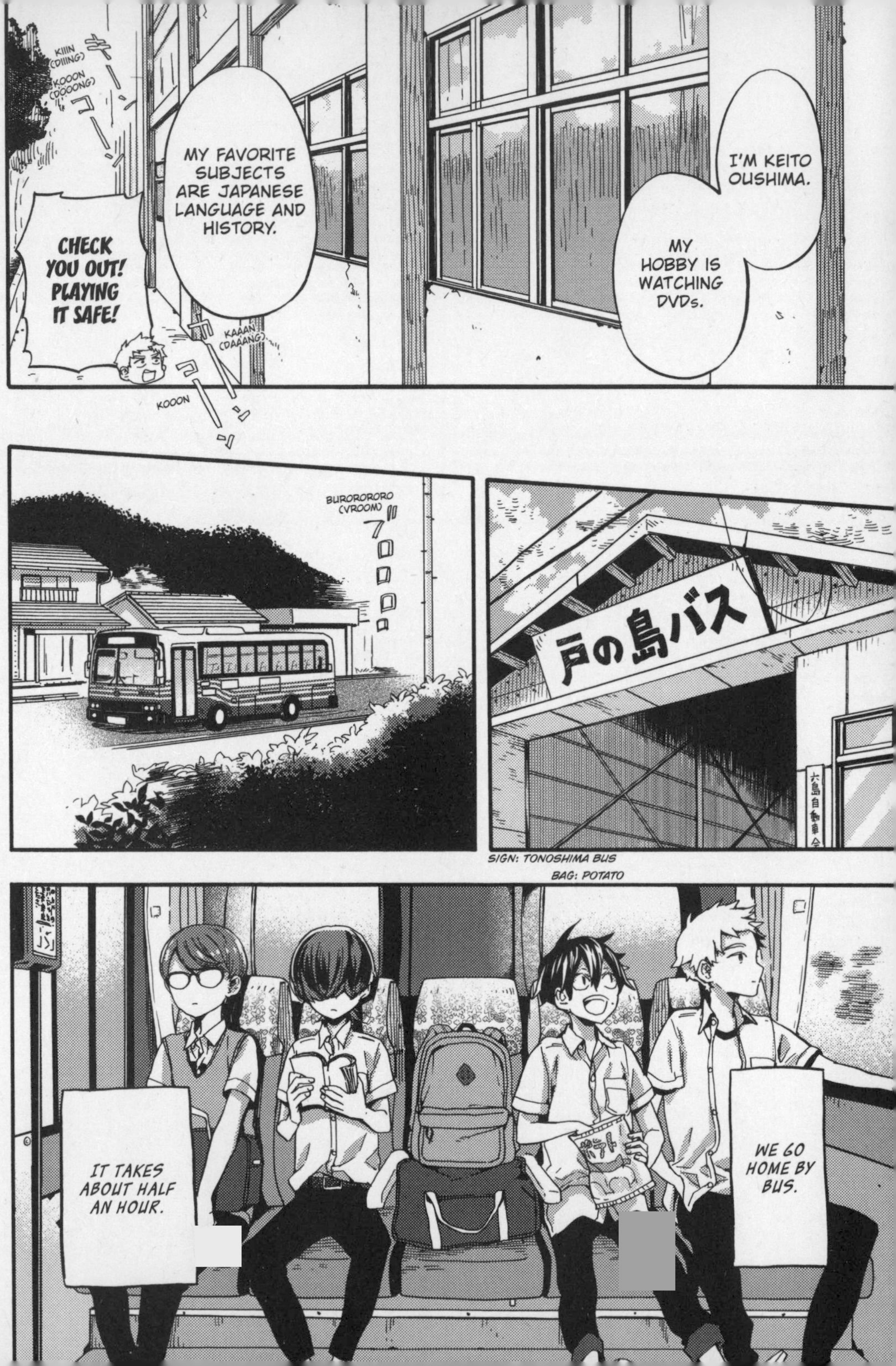
I'M KEITO OUSHIMA.
MY HOBBY IS WATCHING DVDs.
MY FAVORITE SUBJECTS ARE JAPANESE LANGUAGE AND HISTORY.
KIIN (PIIING)
KOOON (DOOONG)
CHECK YOU OUT! PLAYING IT SAFE!
KAAAN (DAAANG)
KOOON
戸の島バス
SIGN: TONOSHIMA BUS
BURORORORO (VROOM)
BAG: POTATO
WE GO HOME BY BUS.
IT TAKES ABOUT HALF AN HOUR.

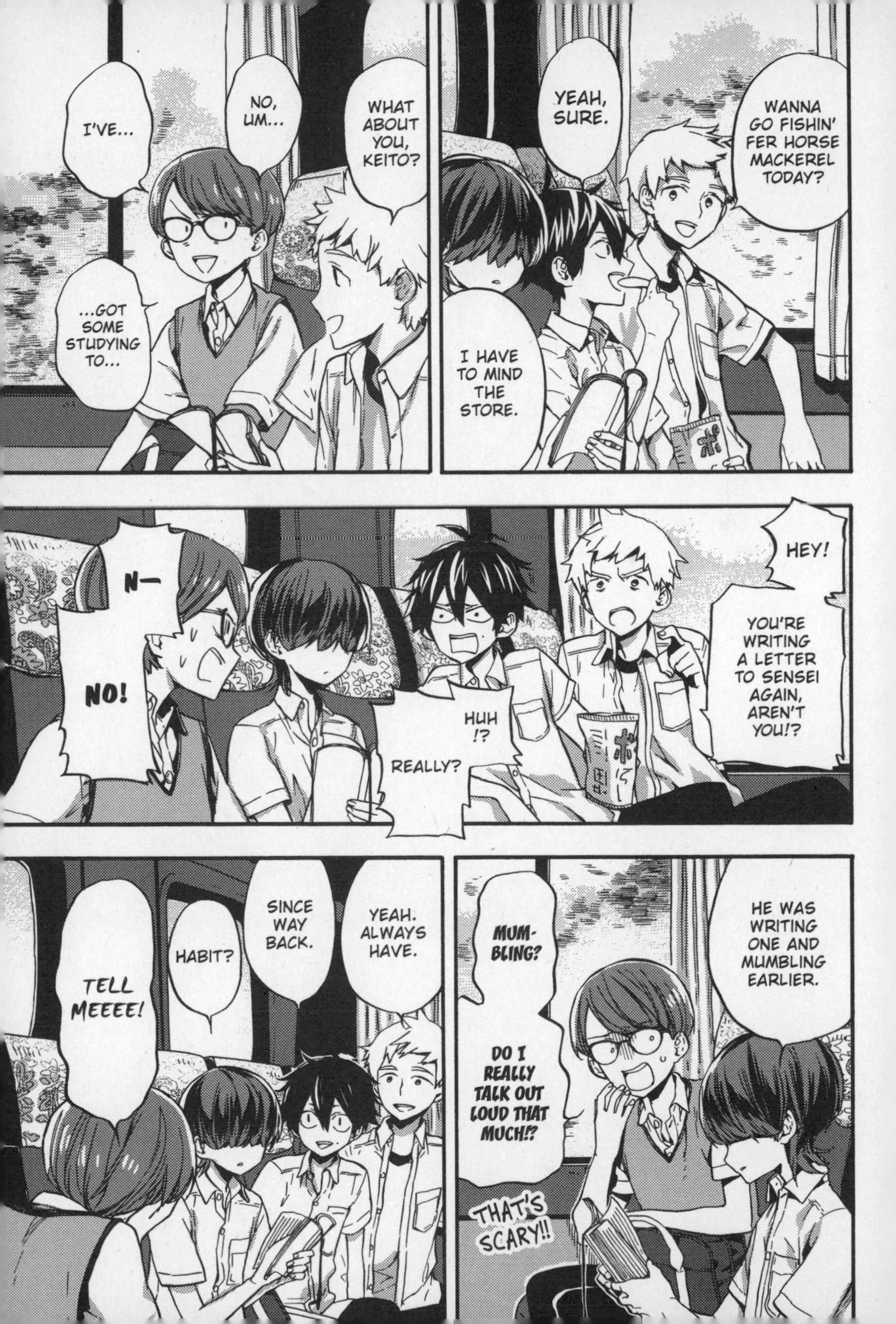

WANNA GO FISHIN' FER HORSE MACKEREL TODAY?
YEAH, SURE.
I HAVE TO MIND THE STORE.
WHAT ABOUT YOU, KEITO?
NO, UM...
I'VE...
...GOT SOME STUDYING TO...
HEY!
YOU'RE WRITING A LETTER TO SENSEI AGAIN, AREN'T YOU!?
HUH !?
REALLY?
N—
NO!
HE WAS WRITING ONE AND MUMBLING EARLIER.
MUM-BLING?
DO I REALLY TALK OUT LOUD THAT MUCH!?
THAT'S SCARY!!
YEAH. ALWAYS HAVE.
SINCE WAY BACK.
HABIT?
TELL MEEEE!

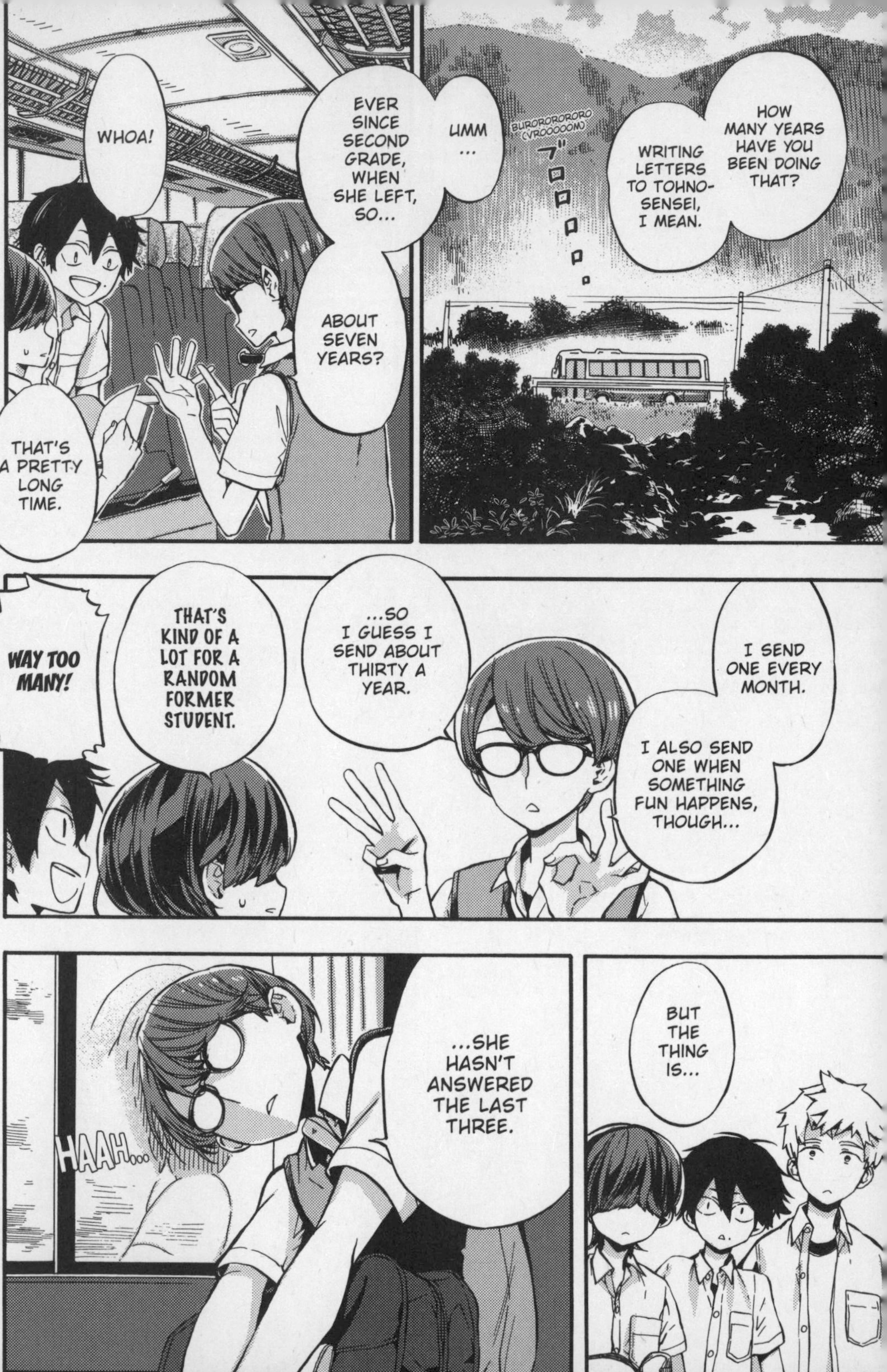
HOW MANY YEARS HAVE YOU BEEN DOING THAT?
WRITING LETTERS TO TOHNO-SENSEI, I MEAN.
BURORORORORO (VROOOOOM)
UMM ...
EVER SINCE SECOND GRADE, WHEN SHE LEFT, SO...
ABOUT SEVEN YEARS?
WHOA!
THAT'S A PRETTY LONG TIME.
I SEND ONE EVERY MONTH.
I ALSO SEND ONE WHEN SOMETHING FUN HAPPENS, THOUGH...
...SO I GUESS I SEND ABOUT THIRTY A YEAR.
THAT'S KIND OF A LOT FOR A RANDOM FORMER STUDENT.
WAY TOO MANY!
BUT THE THING IS...
...SHE HASN'T ANSWERED THE LAST THREE.
HAAAH...

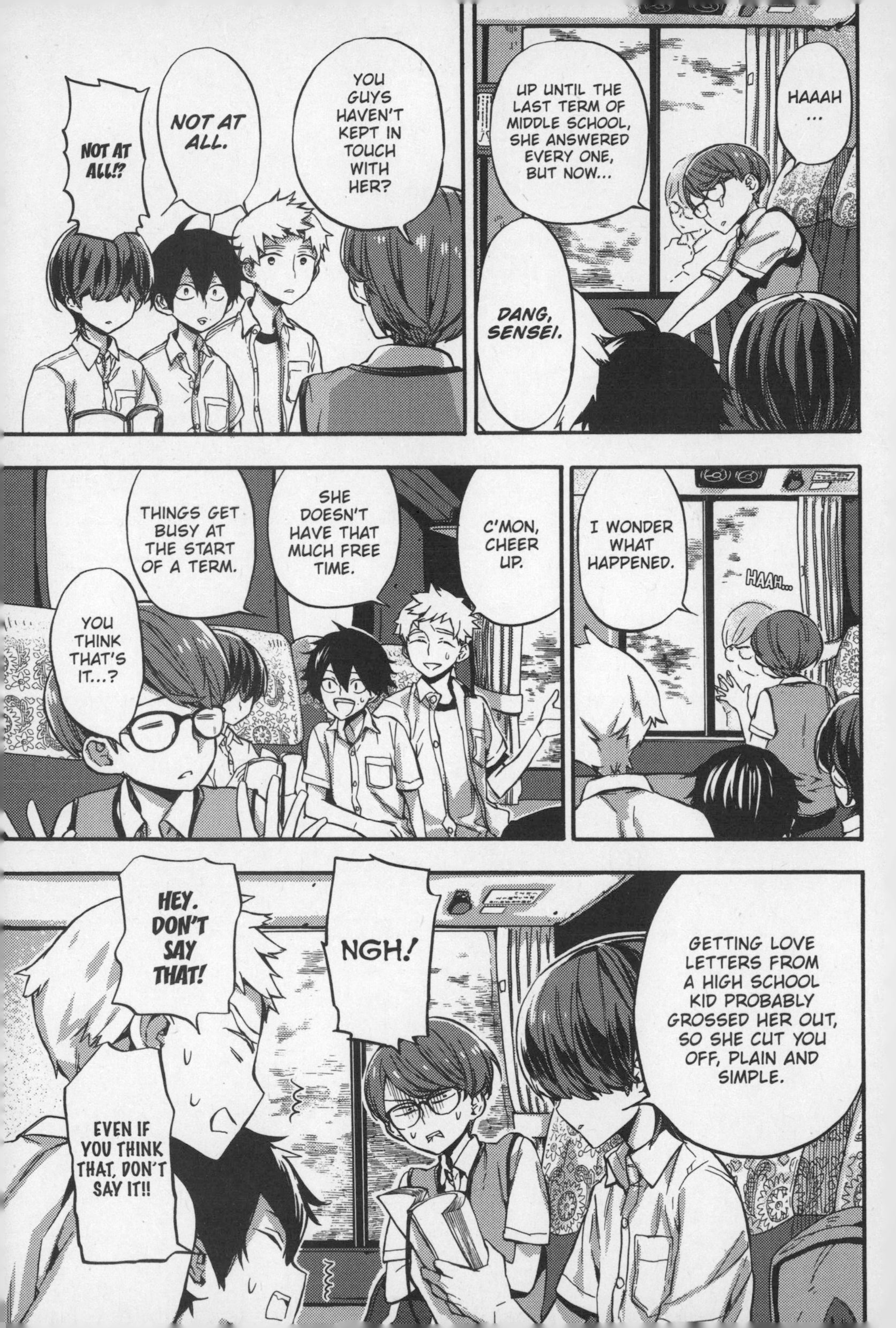
HAAAH ...
UP UNTIL THE LAST TERM OF MIDDLE SCHOOL, SHE ANSWERED EVERY ONE, BUT NOW...
DANG, SENSEI.
YOU GUYS HAVEN'T KEPT IN TOUCH WITH HER?
NOT AT ALL.
NOT AT ALL!?
I WONDER WHAT HAPPENED.
HAAH...
C'MON, CHEER UP.
SHE DOESN'T HAVE THAT MUCH FREE TIME.
THINGS GET BUSY AT THE START OF A TERM.
YOU THINK THAT'S IT...?
GETTING LOVE LETTERS FROM A HIGH SCHOOL KID PROBABLY GROSSED HER OUT, SO SHE CUT YOU OFF, PLAIN AND SIMPLE.
NGH!
HEY. DON'T SAY THAT!
EVEN IF YOU THINK THAT, DON'T SAY IT!!

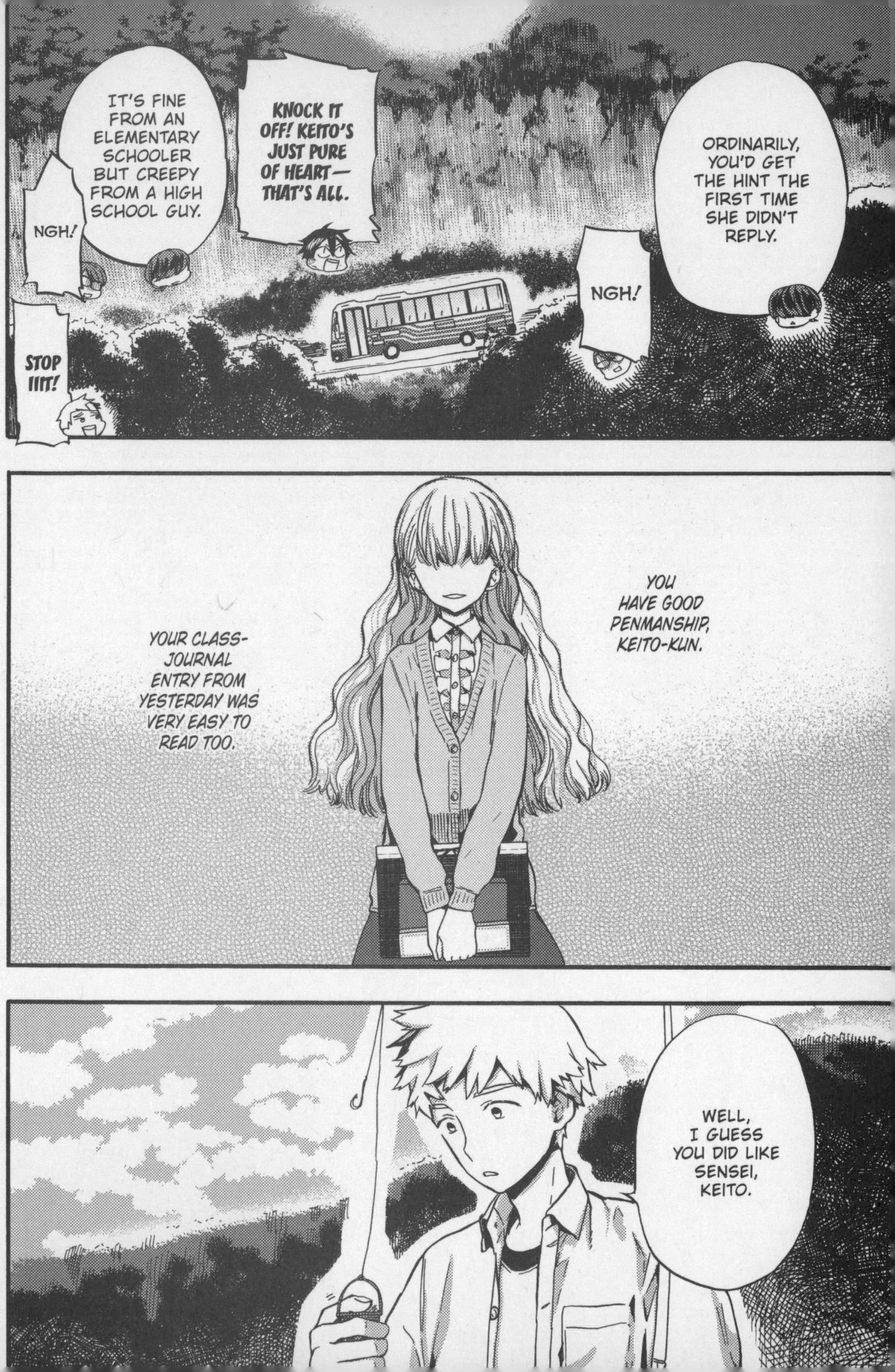
ORDINARILY, YOU'D GET THE HINT THE FIRST TIME SHE DIDN'T REPLY.
NGH!
KNOCK IT OFF! KEITO'S JUST PURE OF HEART—THAT'S ALL.
IT'S FINE FROM AN ELEMENTARY SCHOOLER BUT CREEPY FROM A HIGH SCHOOL GUY.
NGH!
STOP IIIT!
YOU HAVE GOOD PENMANSHIP, KEITO-KUN.
YOUR CLASS-JOURNAL ENTRY FROM YESTERDAY WAS VERY EASY TO READ TOO.
WELL, I GUESS YOU DID LIKE SENSEI, KEITO.

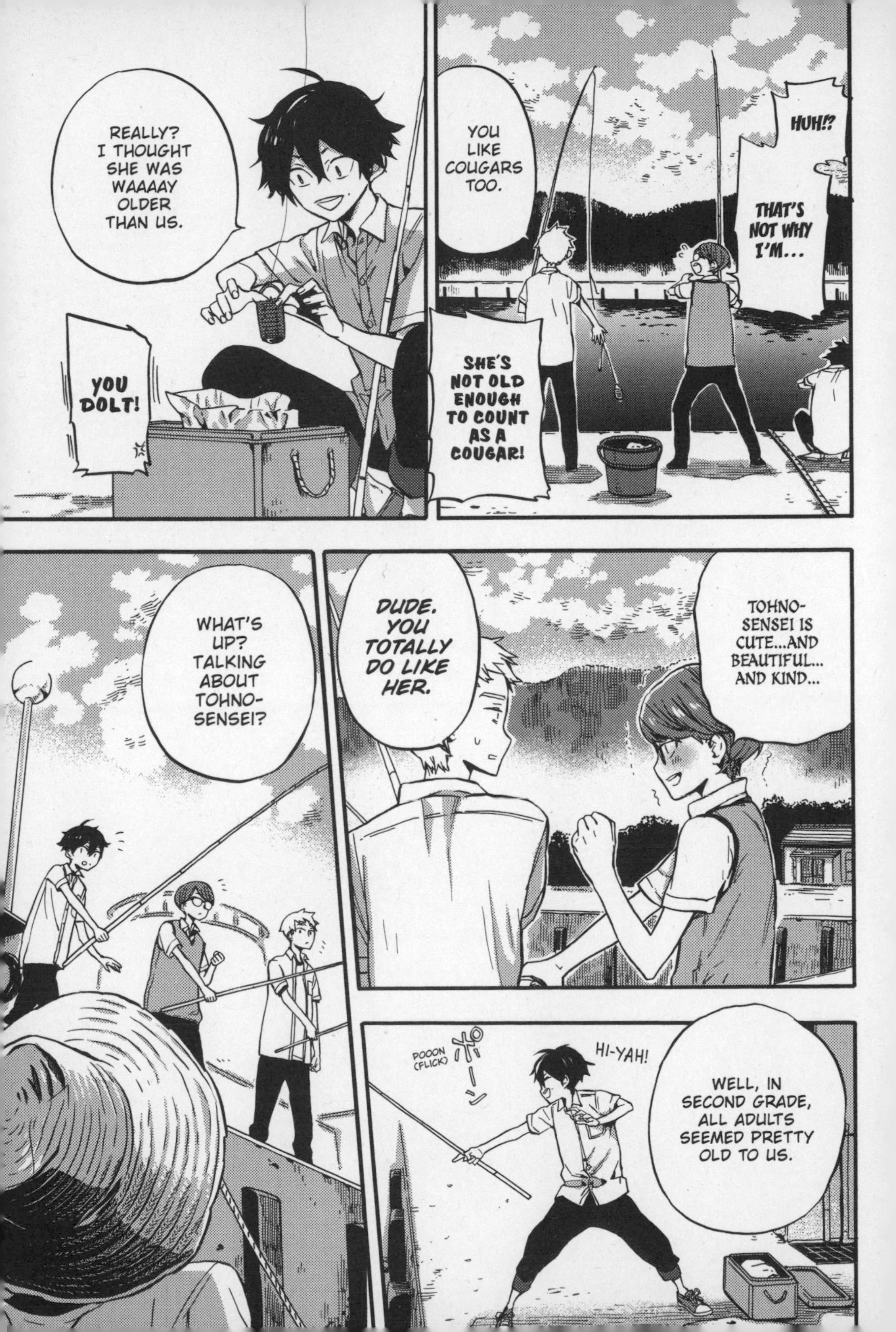

HUH!?
THAT'S NOT WHY I'M...
YOU LIKE COUGARS TOO.
SHE'S NOT OLD ENOUGH TO COUNT AS A COUGAR!
REALLY? I THOUGHT SHE WAS WAAAAY OLDER THAN US.
YOU DOLT!
TOHNO-SENSEI IS CUTE...AND BEAUTIFUL... AND KIND...
DUDE. YOU TOTALLY DO LIKE HER.
WELL, IN SECOND GRADE, ALL ADULTS SEEMED PRETTY OLD TO US.
HI-YAH!
POOON (FLICK)
WHAT'S UP? TALKING ABOUT TOHNO-SENSEI?

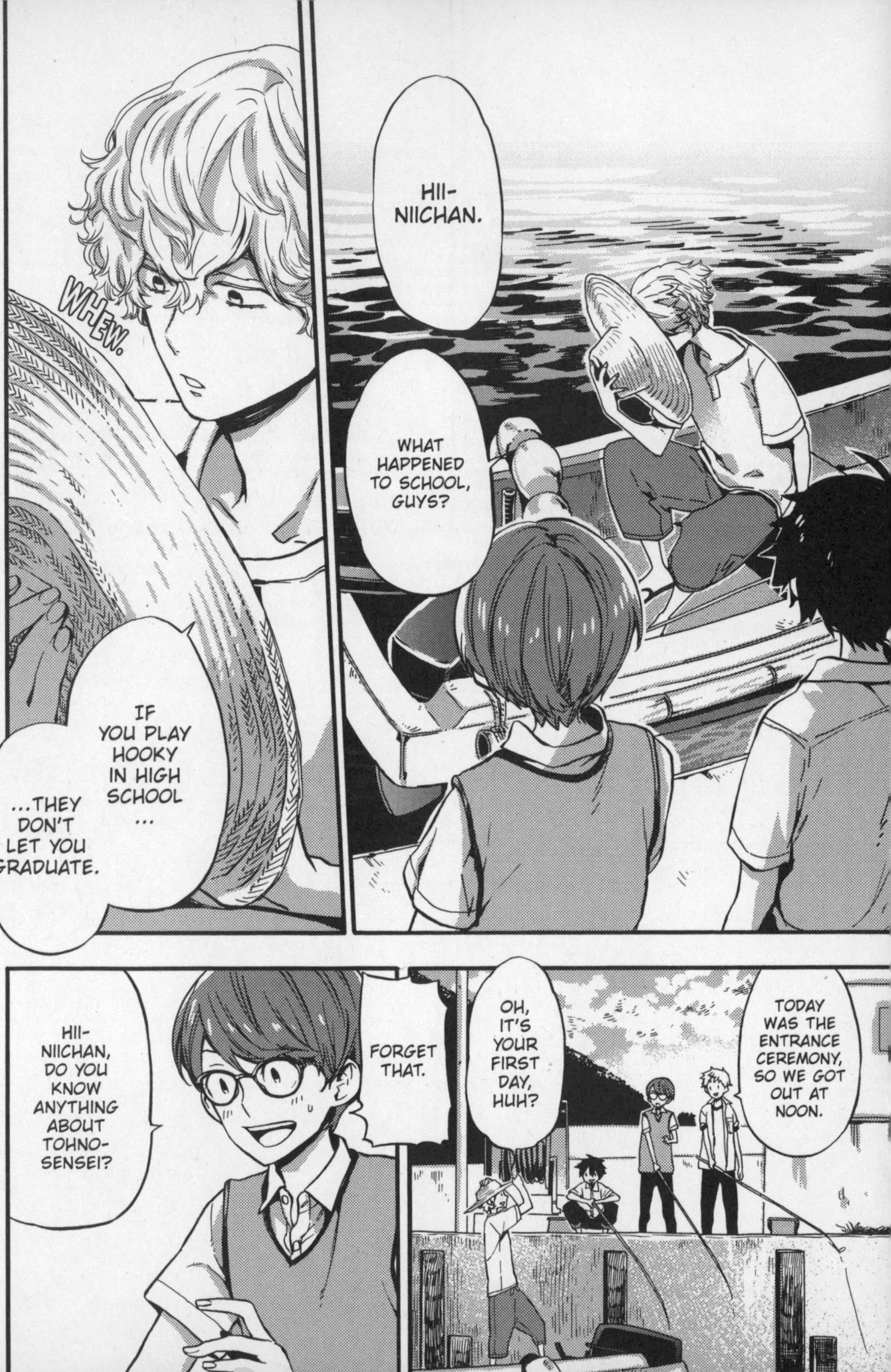
HII-NIICHAN.
WHAT HAPPENED TO SCHOOL, GUYS?
WHEW.
IF YOU PLAY HOOKY IN HIGH SCHOOL ...
...THEY DON'T LET YOU GRADUATE.
TODAY WAS THE ENTRANCE CEREMONY, SO WE GOT OUT AT NOON.
OH, IT'S YOUR FIRST DAY, HUH?
FORGET THAT.
HII-NIICHAN, DO YOU KNOW ANYTHING ABOUT TOHNO-SENSEI?

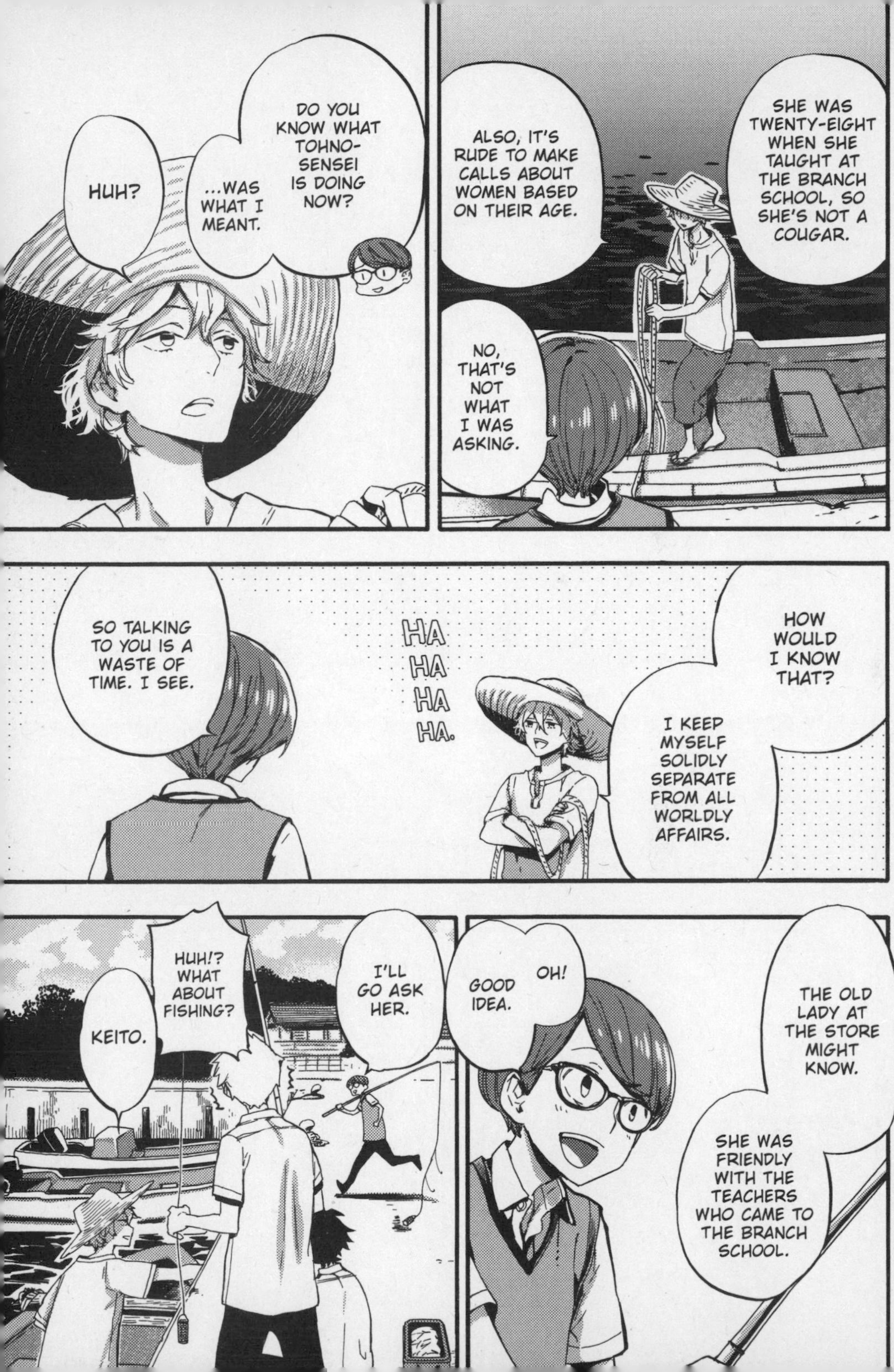
SHE WAS TWENTY-EIGHT WHEN SHE TAUGHT AT THE BRANCH SCHOOL, SO SHE'S NOT A COUGAR.
ALSO, IT'S RUDE TO MAKE CALLS ABOUT WOMEN BASED ON THEIR AGE.
NO, THAT'S NOT WHAT I WAS ASKING.
DO YOU KNOW WHAT TOHNO-SENSEI IS DOING NOW?
...WAS WHAT I MEANT.
HUH?
HOW WOULD I KNOW THAT?
I KEEP MYSELF SOLIDLY SEPARATE FROM ALL WORLDLY AFFAIRS.
HA HA HA HA.
SO TALKING TO YOU IS A WASTE OF TIME. I SEE.
THE OLD LADY AT THE STORE MIGHT KNOW.
SHE WAS FRIENDLY WITH THE TEACHERS WHO CAME TO THE BRANCH SCHOOL.
OH!
GOOD IDEA.
I'LL GO ASK HER.
HUH!? WHAT ABOUT FISHING?
KEITO.

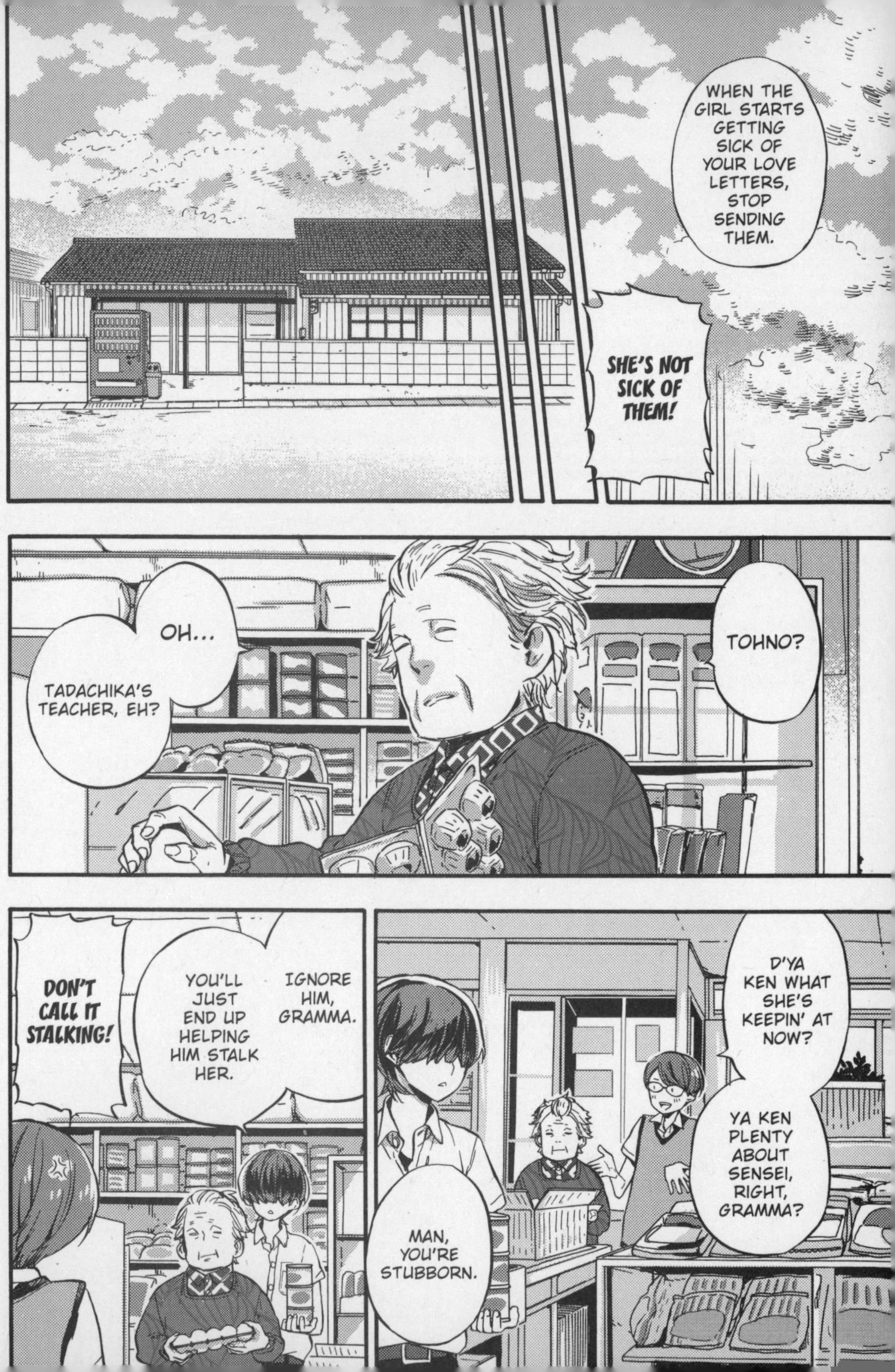
WHEN THE GIRL STARTS GETTING SICK OF YOUR LOVE LETTERS, STOP SENDING THEM.
SHE'S NOT SICK OF THEM!
TOHNO?
OH...
TADACHIKA'S TEACHER, EH?
D'YA KEN WHAT SHE'S KEEPIN' AT NOW?
YA KEN PLENTY ABOUT SENSEI, RIGHT, GRAMMA?
MAN, YOU'RE STUBBORN.
IGNORE HIM, GRAMMA.
YOU'LL JUST END UP HELPING HIM STALK HER.
DON'T CALL IT STALKING!

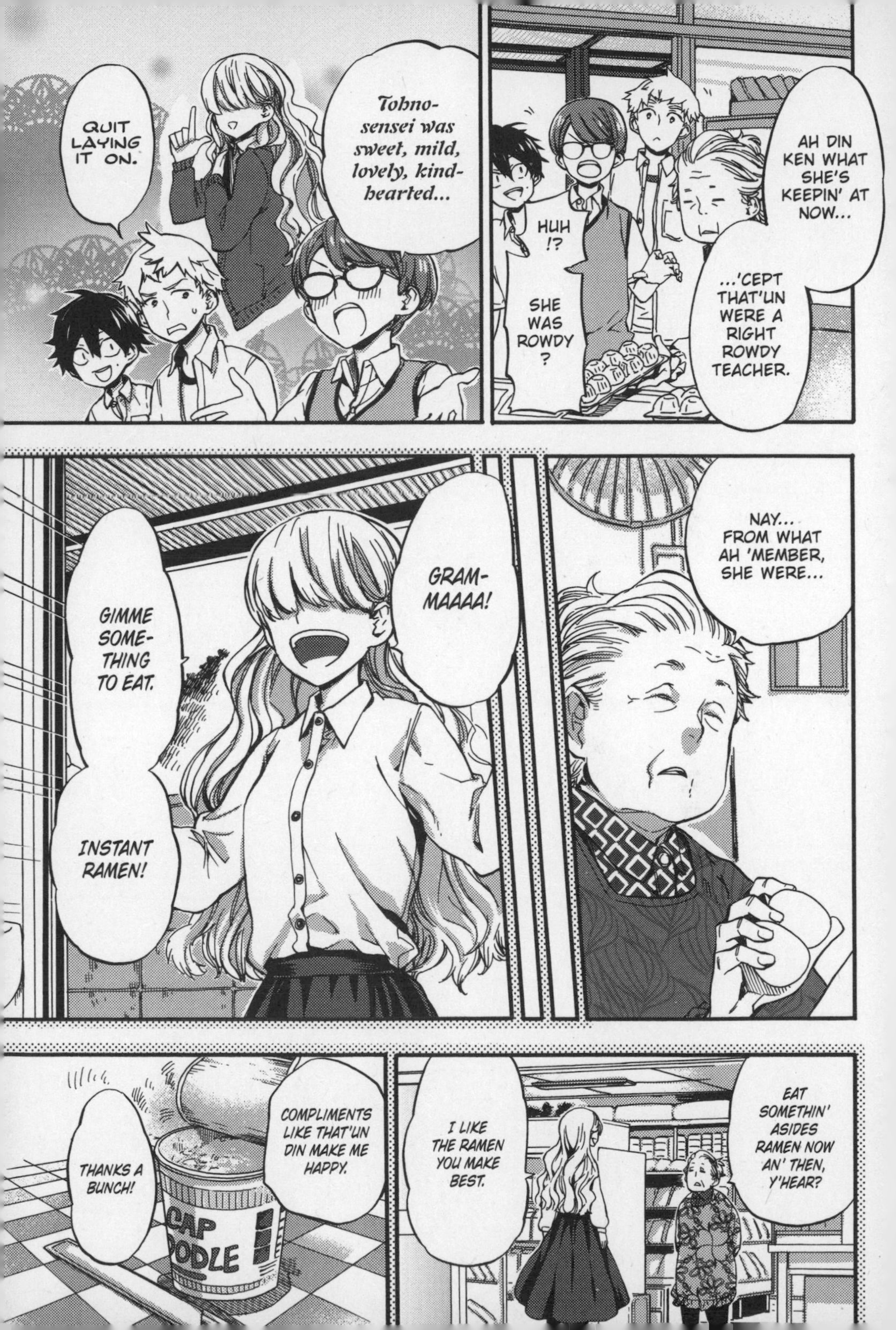
AH DIN KEN WHAT SHE'S KEEPIN' AT NOW...
...'CEPT THAT'UN WERE A RIGHT ROWDY TEACHER.
HUH!?
SHE WAS ROWDY?
Tohno-sensei was sweet, mild, lovely, kind-hearted...
QUIT LAYING IT ON.
NAY... FROM WHAT AH 'MEMBER, SHE WERE...
GRAM-MAAAA!
GIMME SOMETHING TO EAT.
INSTANT RAMEN!
EAT SOMETHIN' ASIDES RAMEN NOW AN' THEN, Y'HEAR?
I LIKE THE RAMEN YOU MAKE BEST.
COMPLIMENTS LIKE THAT'UN DIN MAKE ME HAPPY.
THANKS A BUNCH!
CAP OODLE

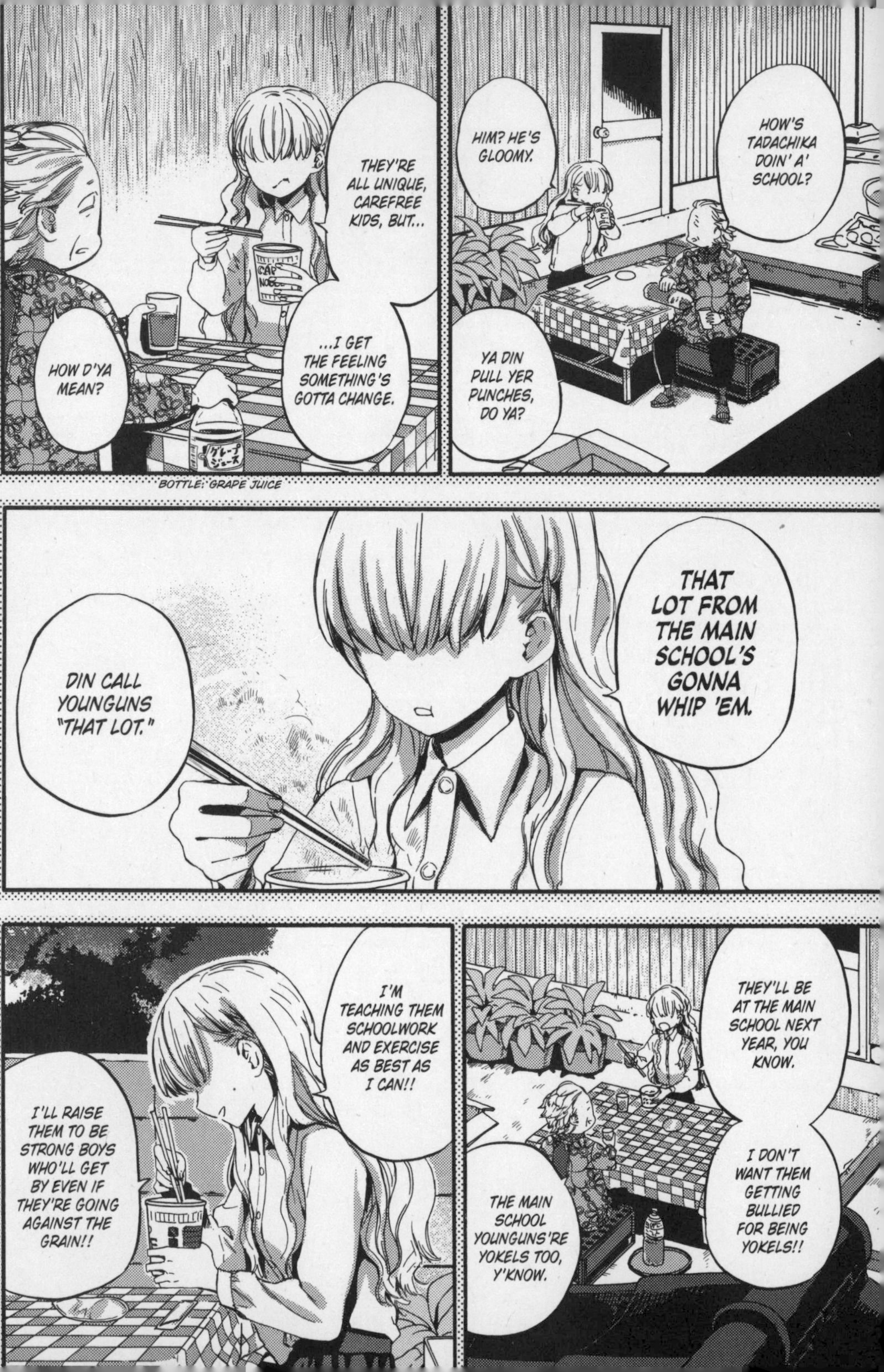
HOW'S TADACHIKA DOIN' A' SCHOOL?
HIM? HE'S GLOOMY.
YA DIN PULL YER PUNCHES, DO YA?
THEY'RE ALL UNIQUE, CAREFREE KIDS, BUT...
...I GET THE FEELING SOMETHING'S GOTTA CHANGE.
HOW D'YA MEAN?
グレープジュース
BOTTLE: GRAPE JUICE
THAT LOT FROM THE MAIN SCHOOL'S GONNA WHIP 'EM.
DIN CALL YOUNGUNS "THAT LOT."
THEY'LL BE AT THE MAIN SCHOOL NEXT YEAR, YOU KNOW.
I DON'T WANT THEM GETTING BULLIED FOR BEING YOKELS!!
THE MAIN SCHOOL YOUNGUNS'RE YOKELS TOO, Y'KNOW.
I'M TEACHING THEM SCHOOLWORK AND EXERCISE AS BEST AS I CAN!!
I'LL RAISE THEM TO BE STRONG BOYS WHO'LL GET BY EVEN IF THEY'RE GOING AGAINST THE GRAIN!!

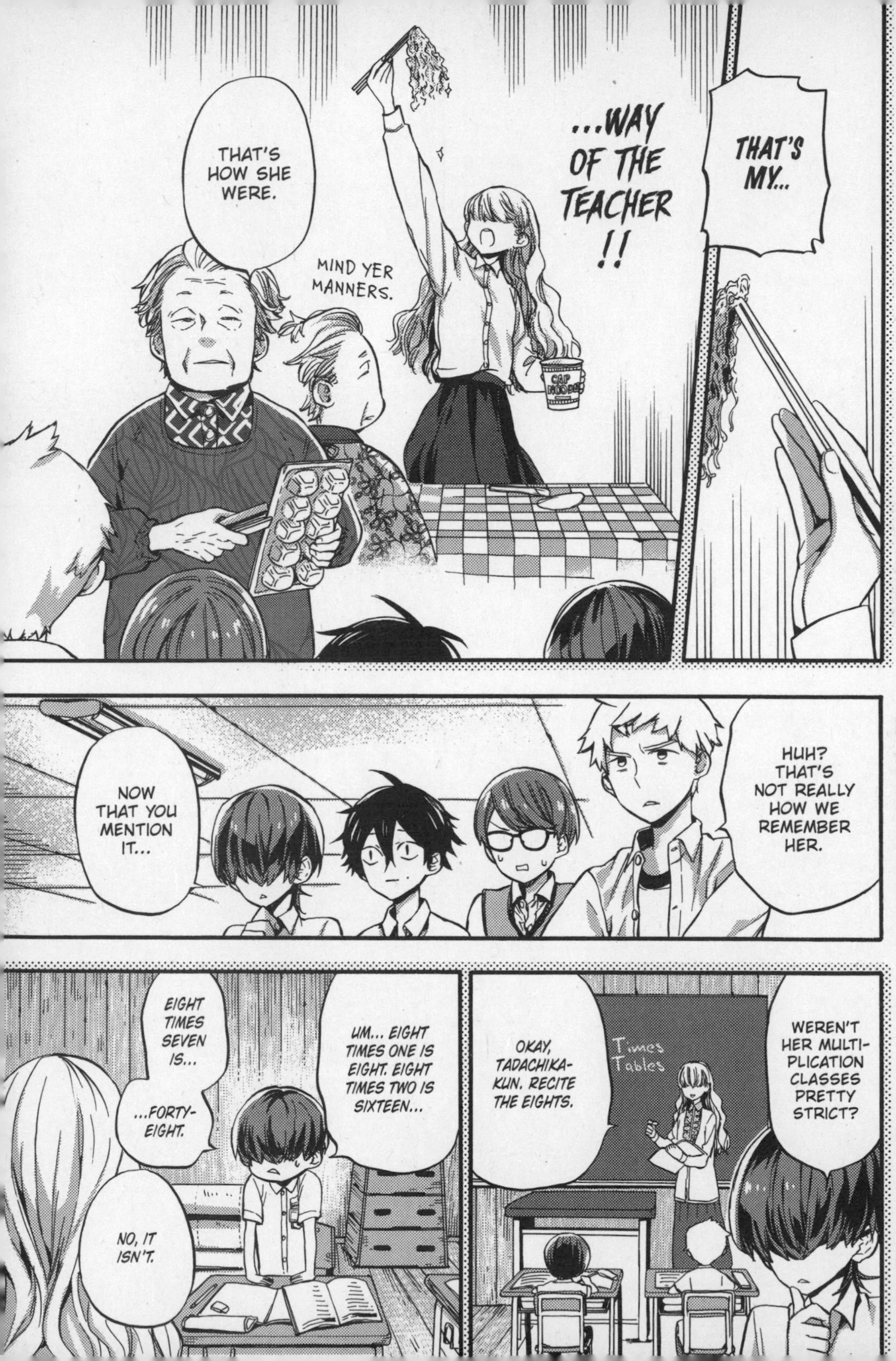
THAT'S MY...
...WAY OF THE TEACHER !!
THAT'S HOW SHE WERE.
MIND YER MANNERS.
CUP NOODLE
HUH? THAT'S NOT REALLY HOW WE REMEMBER HER.
NOW THAT YOU MENTION IT...
WEREN'T HER MULTI-PLICATION CLASSES PRETTY STRICT?
Times Tables
OKAY, TADACHIKA-KUN. RECITE THE EIGHTS.
UM... EIGHT TIMES ONE IS EIGHT. EIGHT TIMES TWO IS SIXTEEN...
EIGHT TIMES SEVEN IS...
...FORTY-EIGHT.
NO, IT ISN'T.

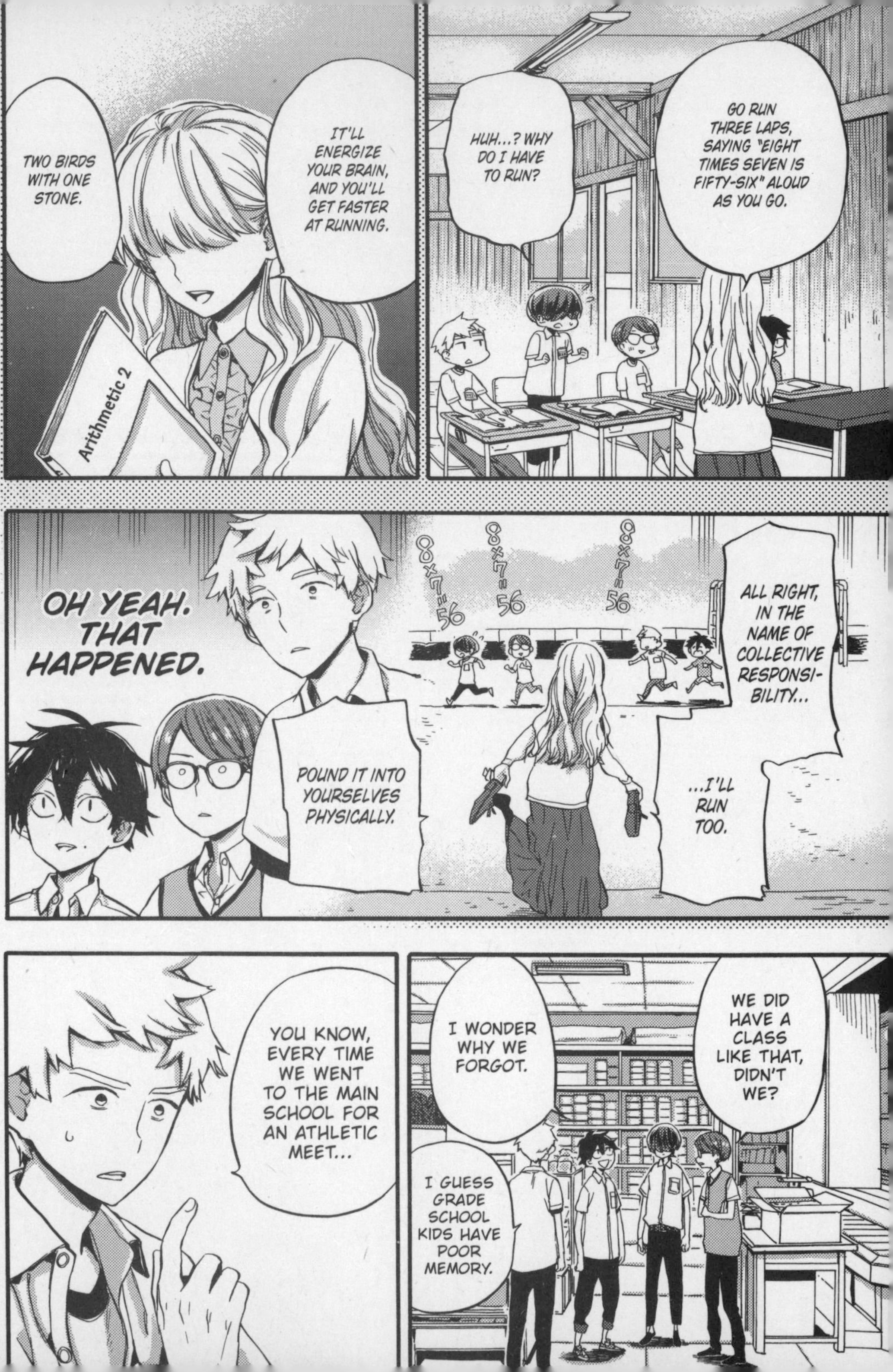
GO RUN THREE LAPS, SAYING "EIGHT TIMES SEVEN IS FIFTY-SIX" ALOUD AS YOU GO.
HUH...? WHY DO I HAVE TO RUN?
IT'LL ENERGIZE YOUR BRAIN, AND YOU'LL GET FASTER AT RUNNING.
TWO BIRDS WITH ONE STONE.
Arithmetic 2
ALL RIGHT, IN THE NAME OF COLLECTIVE RESPONSIBILITY...
...I'LL RUN TOO.
8×7=56 8×7=56 8×7=56
POUND IT INTO YOURSELVES PHYSICALLY.
OH YEAH. THAT HAPPENED.
WE DID HAVE A CLASS LIKE THAT, DIDN'T WE?
I WONDER WHY WE FORGOT.
I GUESS GRADE SCHOOL KIDS HAVE POOR MEMORY.
YOU KNOW, EVERY TIME WE WENT TO THE MAIN SCHOOL FOR AN ATHLETIC MEET...

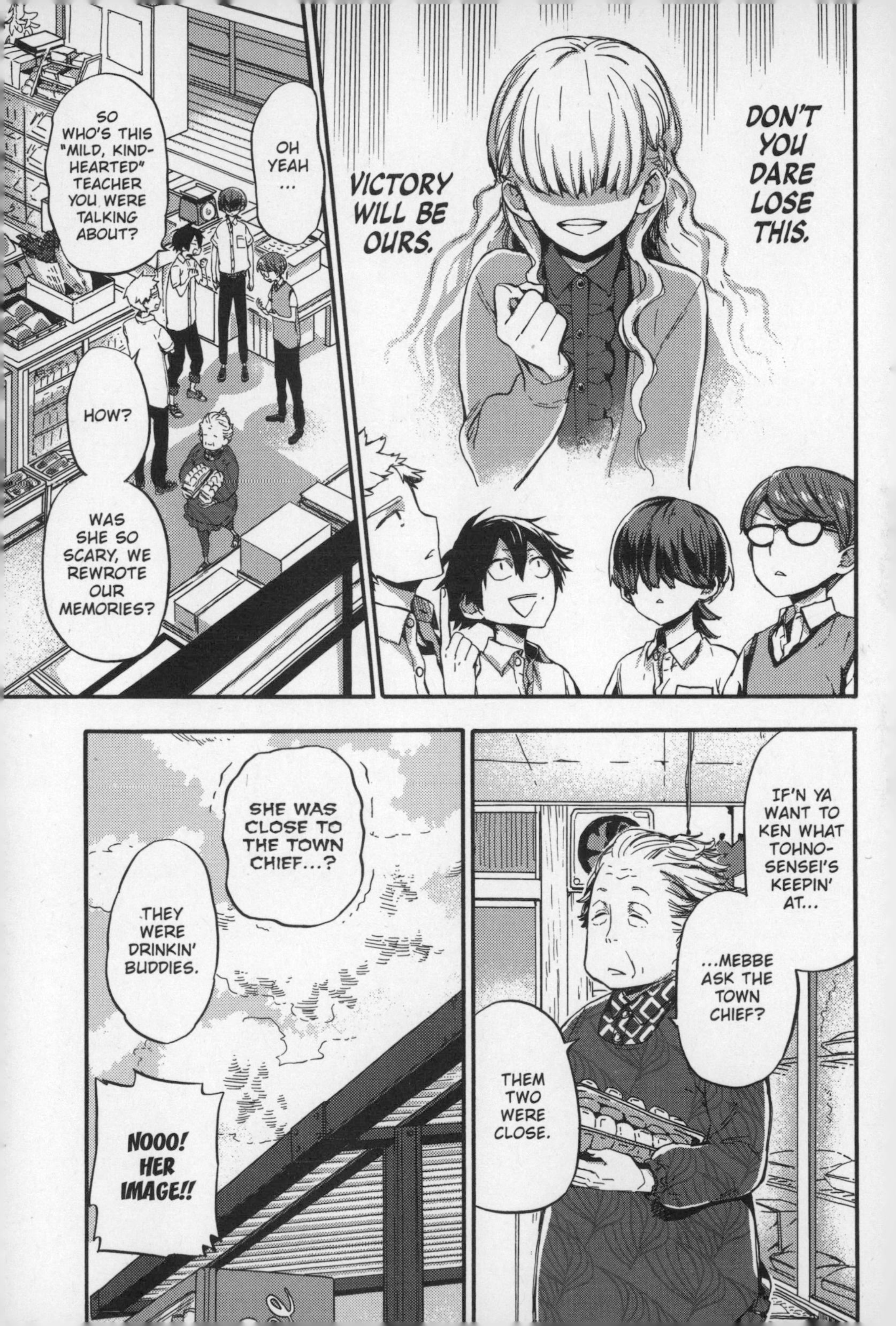
DON'T YOU DARE LOSE THIS.
VICTORY WILL BE OURS.
OH YEAH ...
SO WHO'S THIS "MILD, KIND-HEARTED" TEACHER YOU WERE TALKING ABOUT?
HOW?
WAS SHE SO SCARY, WE REWROTE OUR MEMORIES?
IF'N YA WANT TO KEN WHAT TOHNO-SENSEI'S KEEPIN' AT...
...MEBBE ASK THE TOWN CHIEF?
THEM TWO WERE CLOSE.
SHE WAS CLOSE TO THE TOWN CHIEF...?
THEY WERE DRINKIN' BUDDIES.
NOOO! HER IMAGE!!

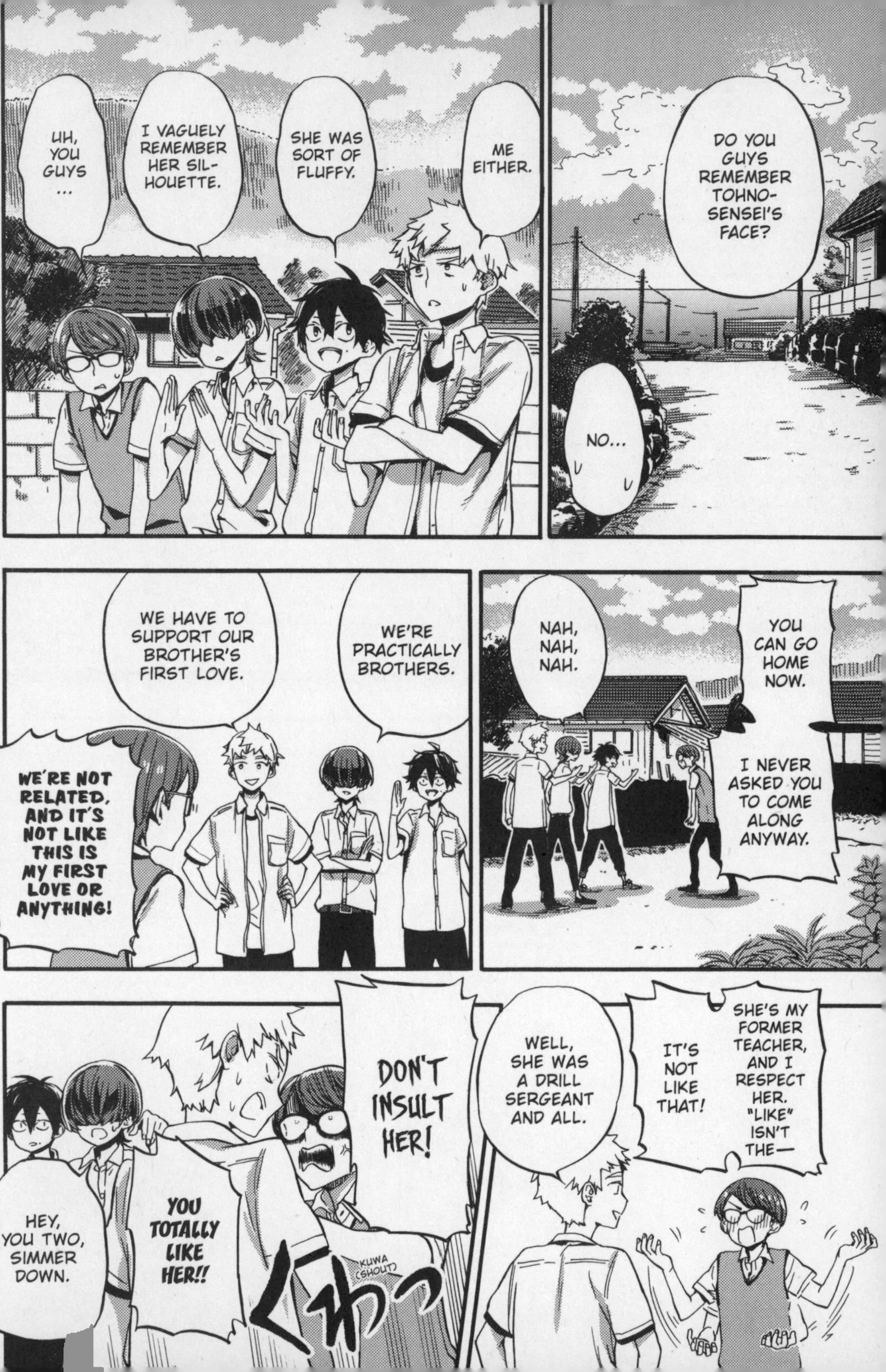
DO YOU GUYS REMEMBER TOHNO-SENSEI'S FACE?
NO...
ME EITHER.
SHE WAS SORT OF FLUFFY.
I VAGUELY REMEMBER HER SIL-HOUETTE.
UH, YOU GUYS...
YOU CAN GO HOME NOW.
I NEVER ASKED YOU TO COME ALONG ANYWAY.
NAH, NAH, NAH.
WE'RE PRACTICALLY BROTHERS.
WE HAVE TO SUPPORT OUR BROTHER'S FIRST LOVE.
WE'RE NOT RELATED, AND IT'S NOT LIKE THIS IS MY FIRST LOVE OR ANYTHING!
SHE'S MY FORMER TEACHER, AND I RESPECT HER. "LIKE" ISN'T THE—
IT'S NOT LIKE THAT!
WELL, SHE WAS A DRILL SERGEANT AND ALL.
DON'T INSULT HER!
KUWA (SHOUT)
YOU TOTALLY LIKE HER!!
HEY, YOU TWO, SIMMER DOWN.

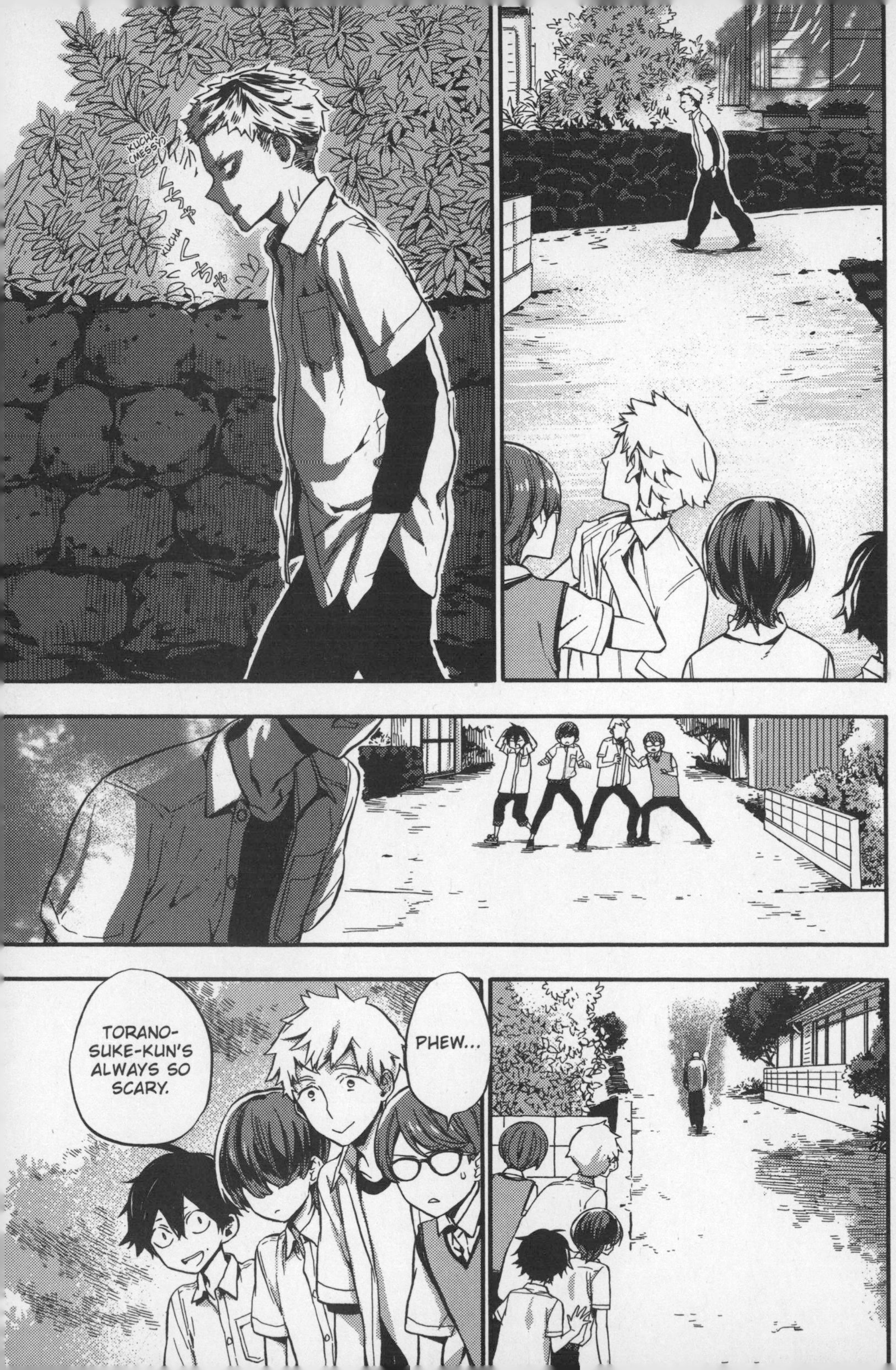
KUCHA (MESS)
KUCHA
PHEW...
TORANO-SUKE-KUN'S ALWAYS SO SCARY.

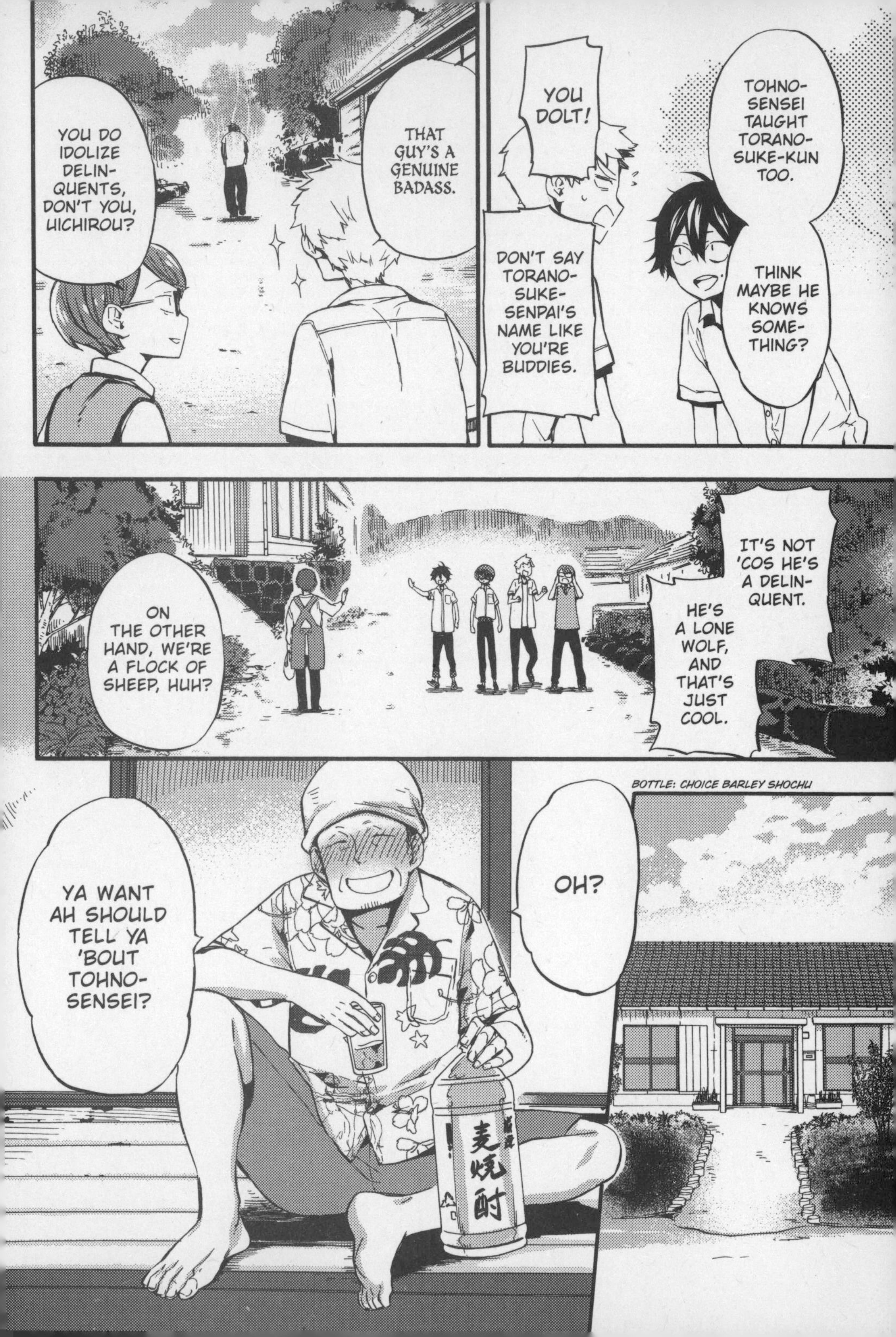
TOHNO-SENSEI TAUGHT TORANO-SUKE-KUN TOO.
THINK MAYBE HE KNOWS SOME-THING?
YOU DOLT!
DON'T SAY TORANO-SUKE-SENPAI'S NAME LIKE YOU'RE BUDDIES.
THAT GUY'S A GENUINE BADASS.
YOU DO IDOLIZE DELIN-QUENTS, DON'T YOU, UICHIROU?
IT'S NOT 'COS HE'S A DELIN-QUENT.
HE'S A LONE WOLF, AND THAT'S JUST COOL.
ON THE OTHER HAND, WE'RE A FLOCK OF SHEEP, HUH?
BOTTLE: CHOICE BARLEY SHOCHU
OH?
YA WANT AH SHOULD TELL YA 'BOUT TOHNO-SENSEI?
麦焼酎

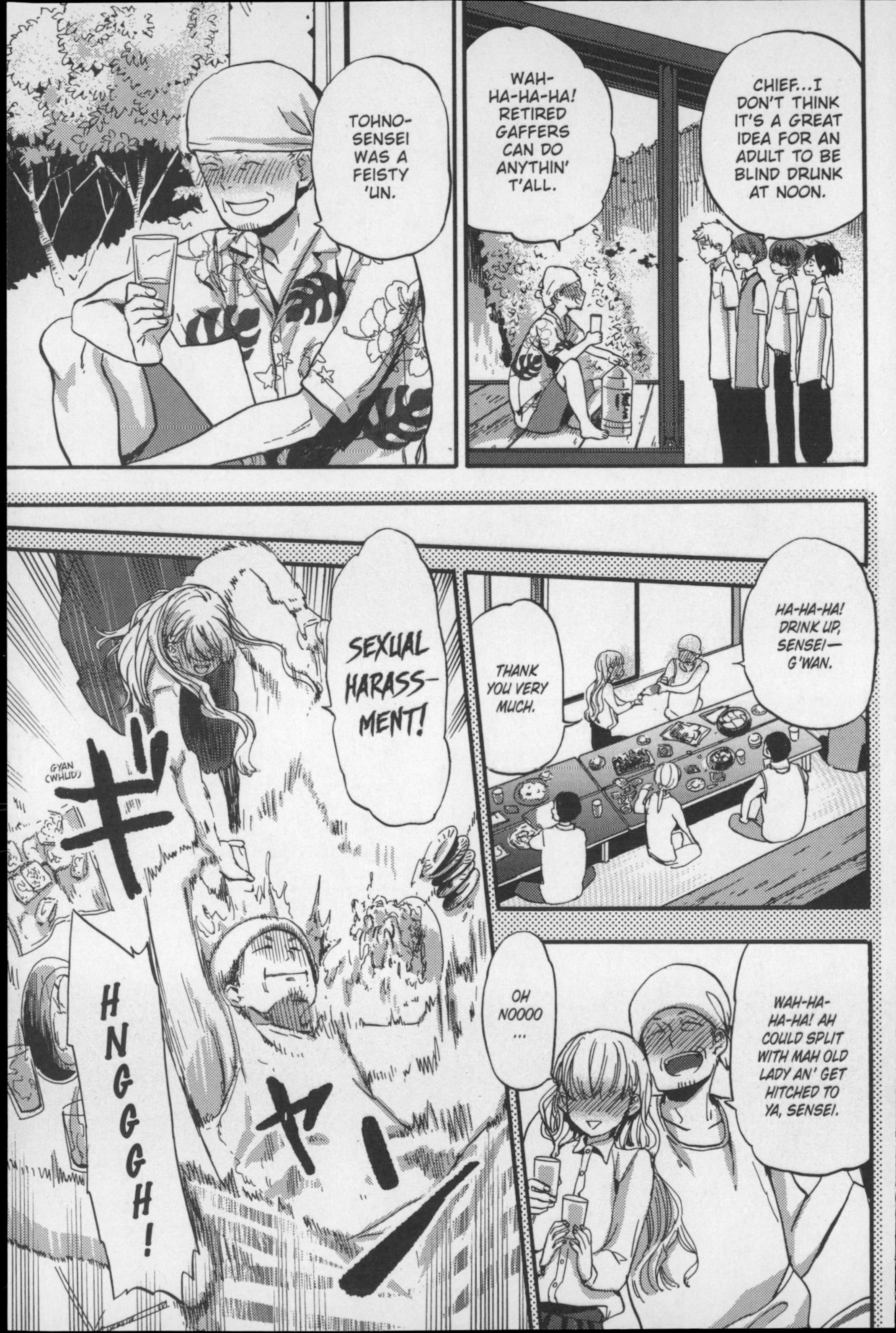
CHIEF...I DON'T THINK IT'S A GREAT IDEA FOR AN ADULT TO BE BLIND DRUNK AT NOON.
WAH-HA-HA-HA! RETIRED GAFFERS CAN DO ANYTHIN' T'ALL.
TOHNO-SENSEI WAS A FEISTY 'UN.
HA-HA-HA! DRINK UP, SENSEI—G'WAN.
THANK YOU VERY MUCH.
WAH-HA-HA! AH COULD SPLIT WITH MAH OLD LADY AN' GET HITCHED TO YA, SENSEI.
OH NOOOO ...
SEXUAL HARASS-MENT!
GYAN (WHUD)
HNGGGGH!

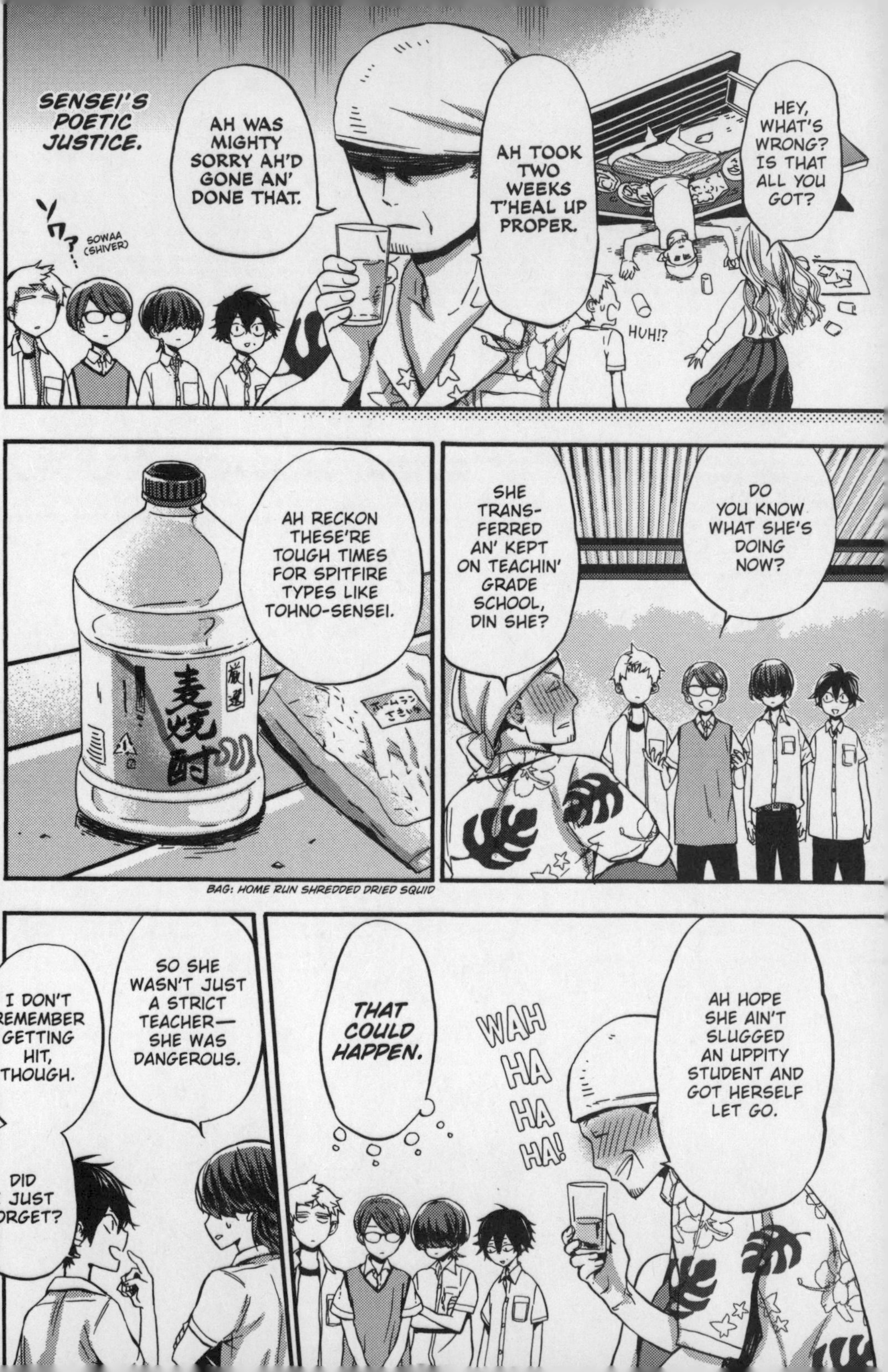
HEY, WHAT'S WRONG? IS THAT ALL YOU GOT?
HUH!?
AH TOOK TWO WEEKS T'HEAL UP PROPER.
AH WAS MIGHTY SORRY AH'D GONE AN' DONE THAT.
SENSEI'S POETIC JUSTICE.
ソワァ
SOWAA (SHIVER)
DO YOU KNOW WHAT SHE'S DOING NOW?
SHE TRANSFERRED AN' KEPT ON TEACHIN' GRADE SCHOOL, DIN SHE?
AH RECKON THESE'RE TOUGH TIMES FOR SPITFIRE TYPES LIKE TOHNO-SENSEI.
厳選
麦焼酎
ホームラン さきいか
BAG: HOME RUN SHREDDED DRIED SQUID
AH HOPE SHE AIN'T SLUGGED AN UPPITY STUDENT AND GOT HERSELF LET GO.
WAH HA HA HA!
THAT COULD HAPPEN.
SO SHE WASN'T JUST A STRICT TEACHER—SHE WAS DANGEROUS.
I DON'T REMEMBER GETTING HIT, THOUGH.
DID I JUST FORGET?

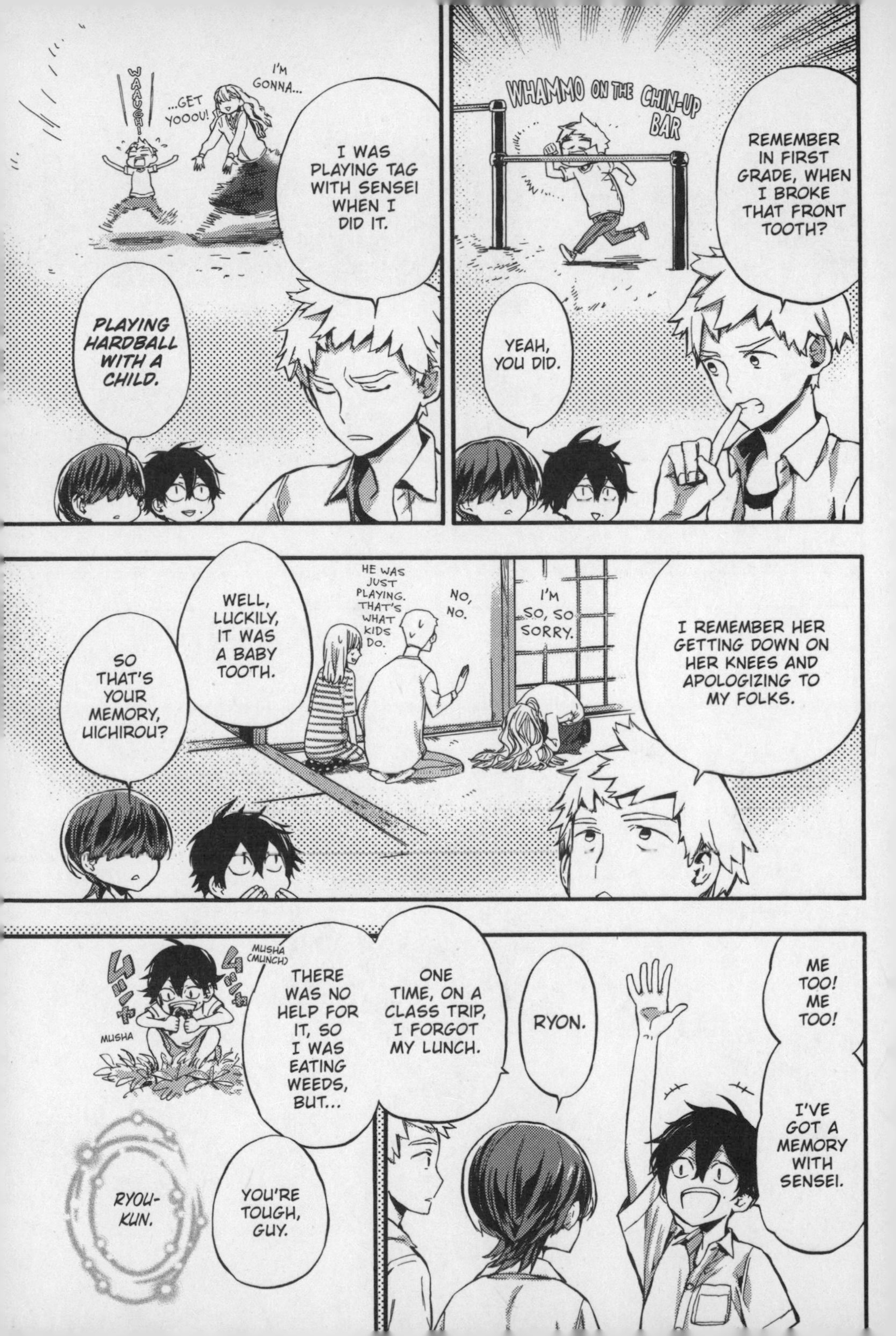
WHAMMO ON THE CHIN-UP BAR
REMEMBER IN FIRST GRADE, WHEN I BROKE THAT FRONT TOOTH?
YEAH, YOU DID.
I WAS PLAYING TAG WITH SENSEI WHEN I DID IT.
I'M GONNA...
...GET YOOOU!
WAAAUGH!
PLAYING HARDBALL WITH A CHILD.
I REMEMBER HER GETTING DOWN ON HER KNEES AND APOLOGIZING TO MY FOLKS.
I'M SO, SO SORRY.
NO, NO.
HE WAS JUST PLAYING. THAT'S WHAT KIDS DO.
WELL, LUCKILY, IT WAS A BABY TOOTH.
SO THAT'S YOUR MEMORY, UICHIROU?
ME TOO! ME TOO!
I'VE GOT A MEMORY WITH SENSEI.
RYON.
ONE TIME, ON A CLASS TRIP, I FORGOT MY LUNCH.
THERE WAS NO HELP FOR IT, SO I WAS EATING WEEDS, BUT...
MUSHA (MUNCH)
MUSHA
RYOU-KUN.
YOU'RE TOUGH, GUY.

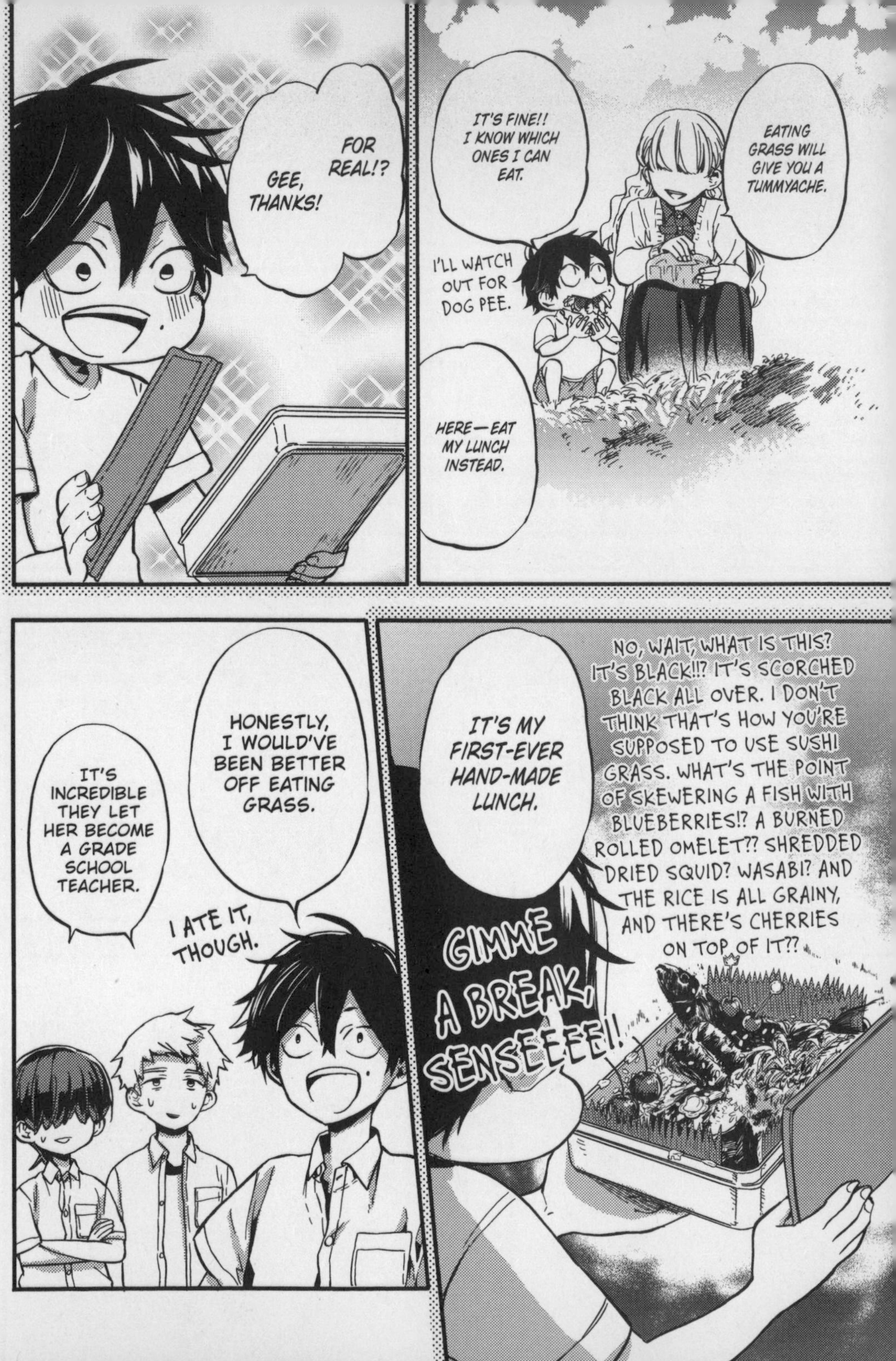

EATING GRASS WILL GIVE YOU A TUMMYACHE.
IT'S FINE!! I KNOW WHICH ONES I CAN EAT.
I'LL WATCH OUT FOR DOG PEE.
HERE—EAT MY LUNCH INSTEAD.
FOR REAL!?
GEE, THANKS!
IT'S MY FIRST-EVER HAND-MADE LUNCH.
NO, WAIT, WHAT IS THIS? IT'S BLACK!!? IT'S SCORCHED BLACK ALL OVER. I DON'T THINK THAT'S HOW YOU'RE SUPPOSED TO USE SUSHI GRASS. WHAT'S THE POINT OF SKEWERING A FISH WITH BLUEBERRIES!? A BURNED ROLLED OMELET?? SHREDDED DRIED SQUID? WASABI? AND THE RICE IS ALL GRAINY, AND THERE'S CHERRIES ON TOP OF IT??
GIMME A BREAK, SENSEEEE!!
HONESTLY, I WOULD'VE BEEN BETTER OFF EATING GRASS.
IT'S INCREDIBLE THEY LET HER BECOME A GRADE SCHOOL TEACHER.
I ATE IT, THOUGH.

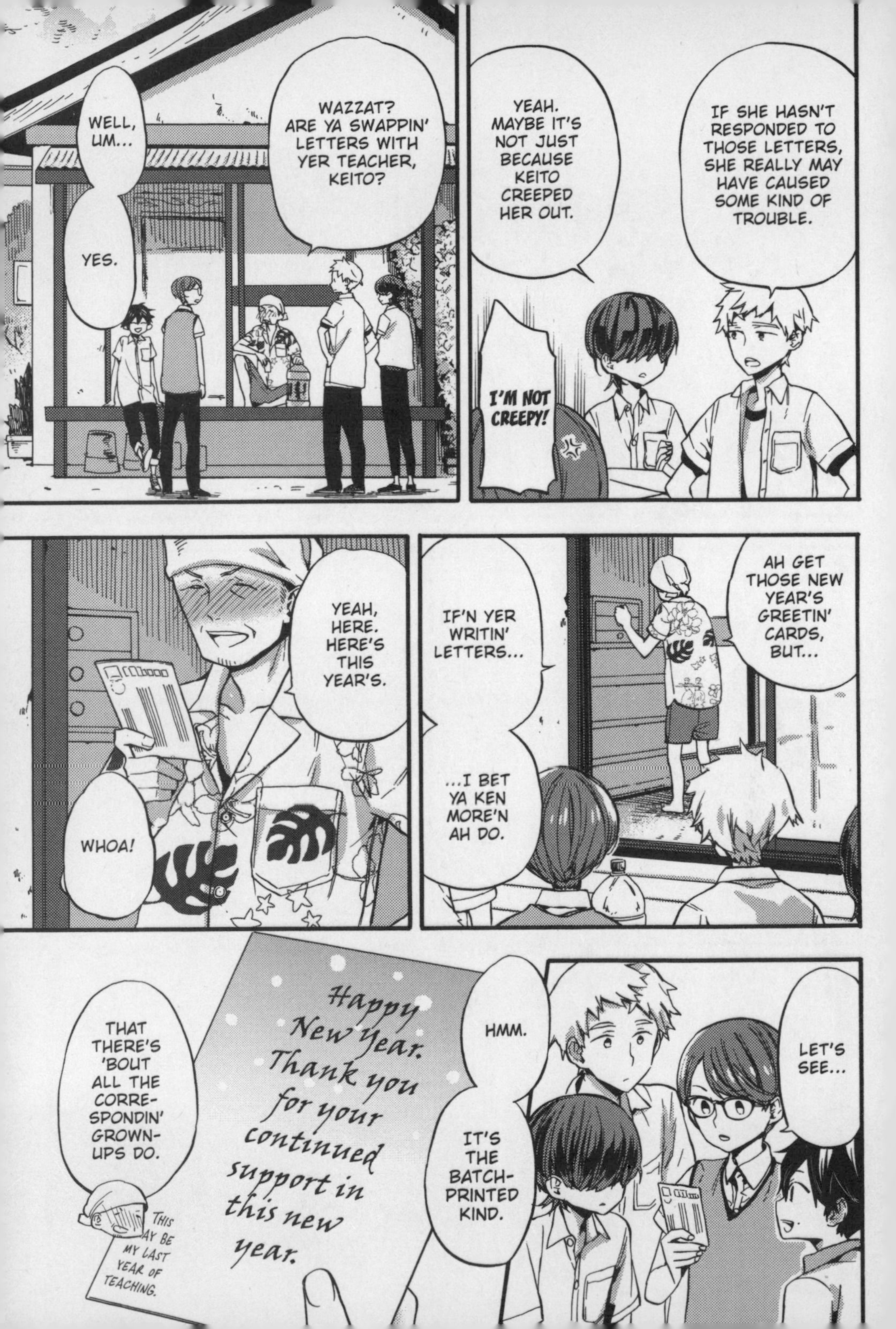
IF SHE HASN'T RESPONDED TO THOSE LETTERS, SHE REALLY MAY HAVE CAUSED SOME KIND OF TROUBLE.
YEAH. MAYBE IT'S NOT JUST BECAUSE KEITO CREEPED HER OUT.
I'M NOT CREEPY!
WAZZAT? ARE YA SWAPPIN' LETTERS WITH YER TEACHER, KEITO?
WELL, UM...
YES.
AH GET THOSE NEW YEAR'S GREETIN' CARDS, BUT...
IF'N YER WRITIN' LETTERS...
...I BET YA KEN MORE'N AH DO.
YEAH, HERE. HERE'S THIS YEAR'S.
WHOA!
LET'S SEE...
HMM.
IT'S THE BATCH-PRINTED KIND.
Happy New Year. Thank you for your continued support in this new year.
THAT THERE'S 'BOUT ALL THE CORRE-SPONDIN' GROWN-UPS DO.
THIS AY BE MY LAST YEAR OF TEACHING.

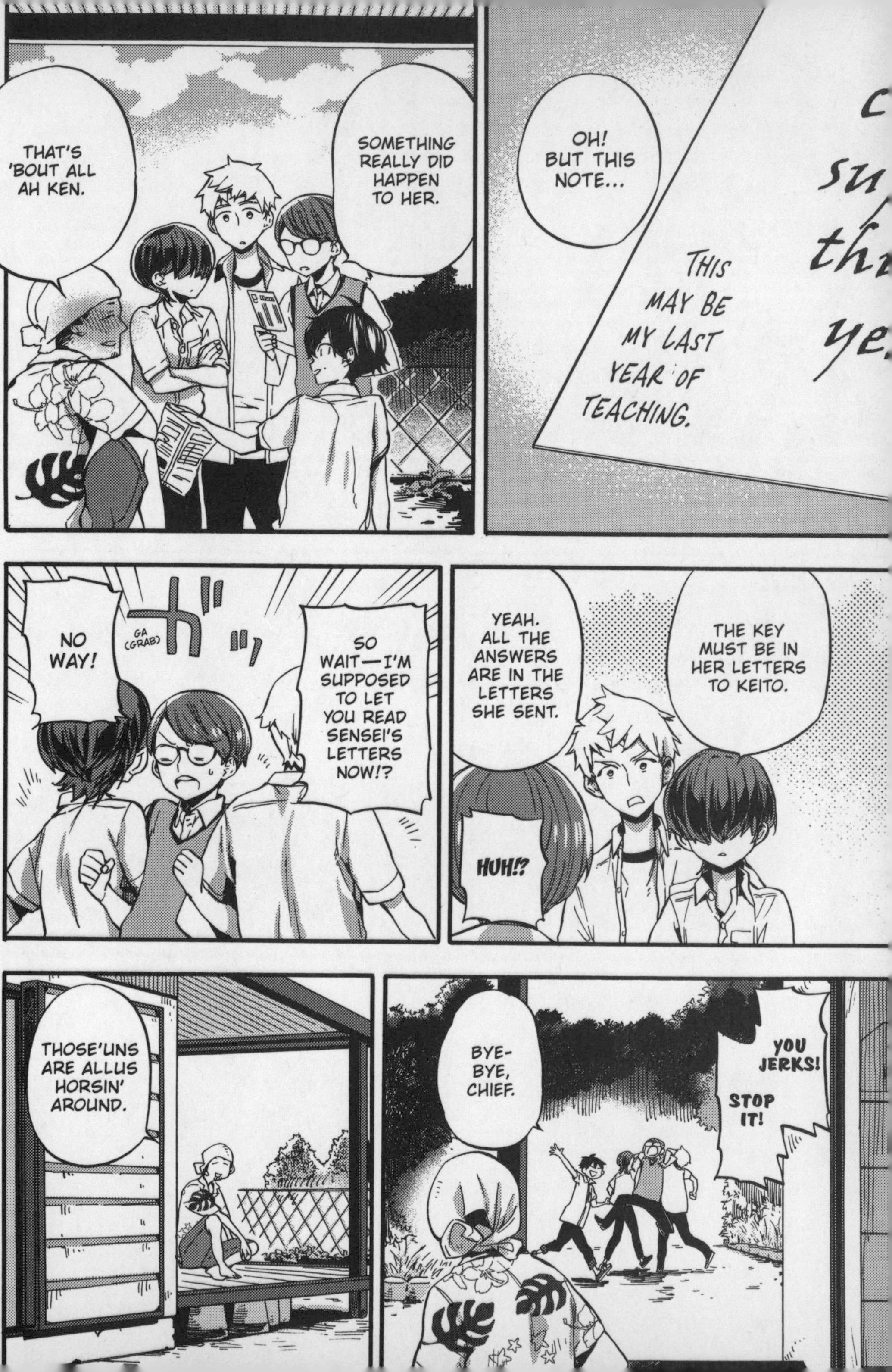
OH! BUT THIS NOTE...
THIS MAY BE MY LAST YEAR OF TEACHING.
SOMETHING REALLY DID HAPPEN TO HER.
THAT'S 'BOUT ALL AH KEN.
THE KEY MUST BE IN HER LETTERS TO KEITO.
YEAH. ALL THE ANSWERS ARE IN THE LETTERS SHE SENT.
HUH!?
SO WAIT—I'M SUPPOSED TO LET YOU READ SENSEI'S LETTERS NOW!?
GA (GRAB)
NO WAY!
YOU JERKS!
STOP IT!
BYE-BYE, CHIEF.
THOSE'UNS ARE ALLUS HORSIN' AROUND.

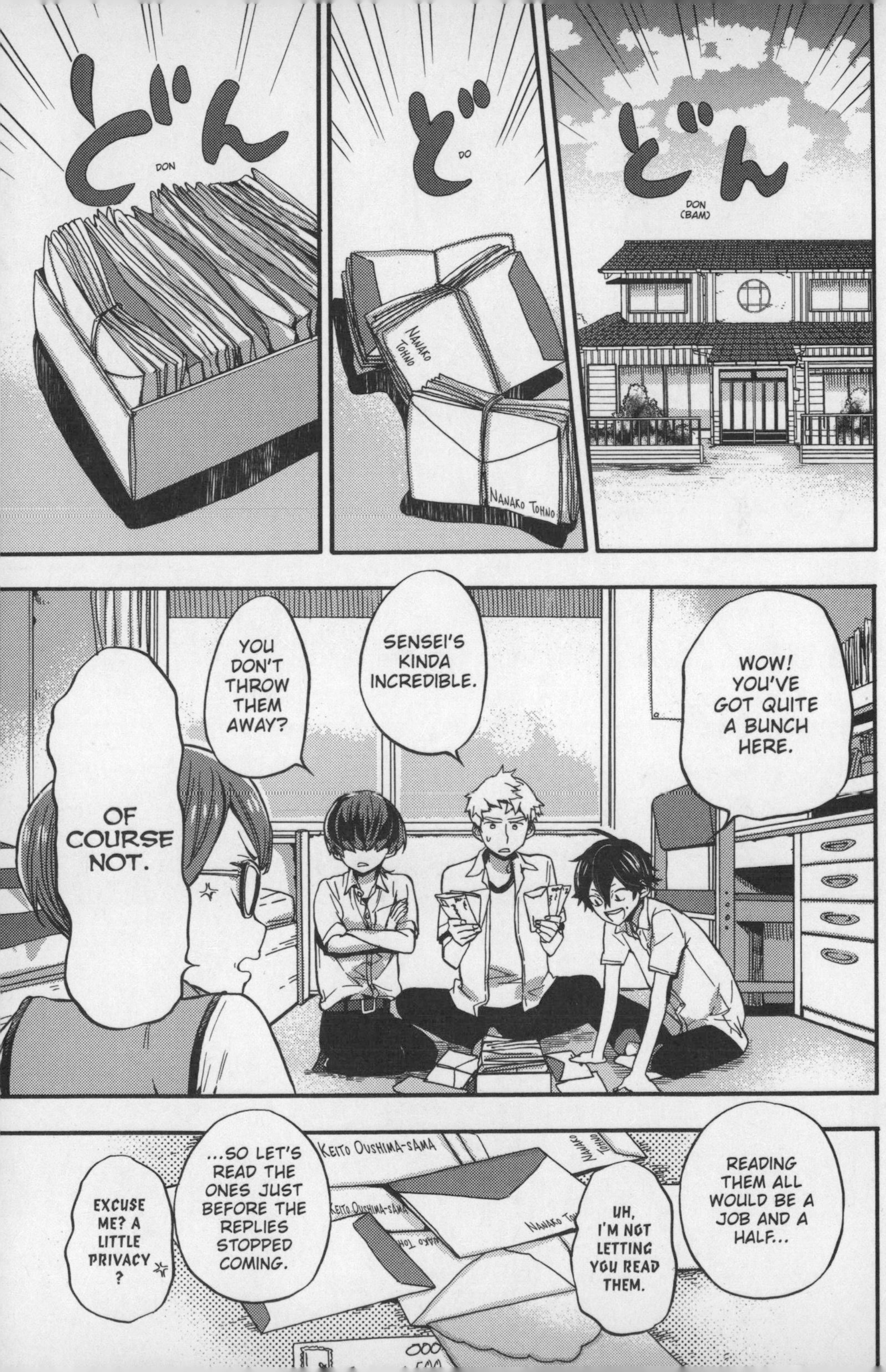
どん
DON
(BAM)
ど
DO
NANAKO TOHNO
NANAKO TOHNO
どん
DON
WOW! YOU'VE GOT QUITE A BUNCH HERE.
SENSEI'S KINDA INCREDIBLE.
YOU DON'T THROW THEM AWAY?
OF COURSE NOT.
NANAKO TOHNO
KEITO OUSHIMA-SAMA
KEITO OUSHIMA-SAMA
NANAKO TOHNO
READING THEM ALL WOULD BE A JOB AND A HALF...
UH, I'M NOT LETTING YOU READ THEM.
...SO LET'S READ THE ONES JUST BEFORE THE REPLIES STOPPED COMING.
EXCUSE ME? A LITTLE PRIVACY?

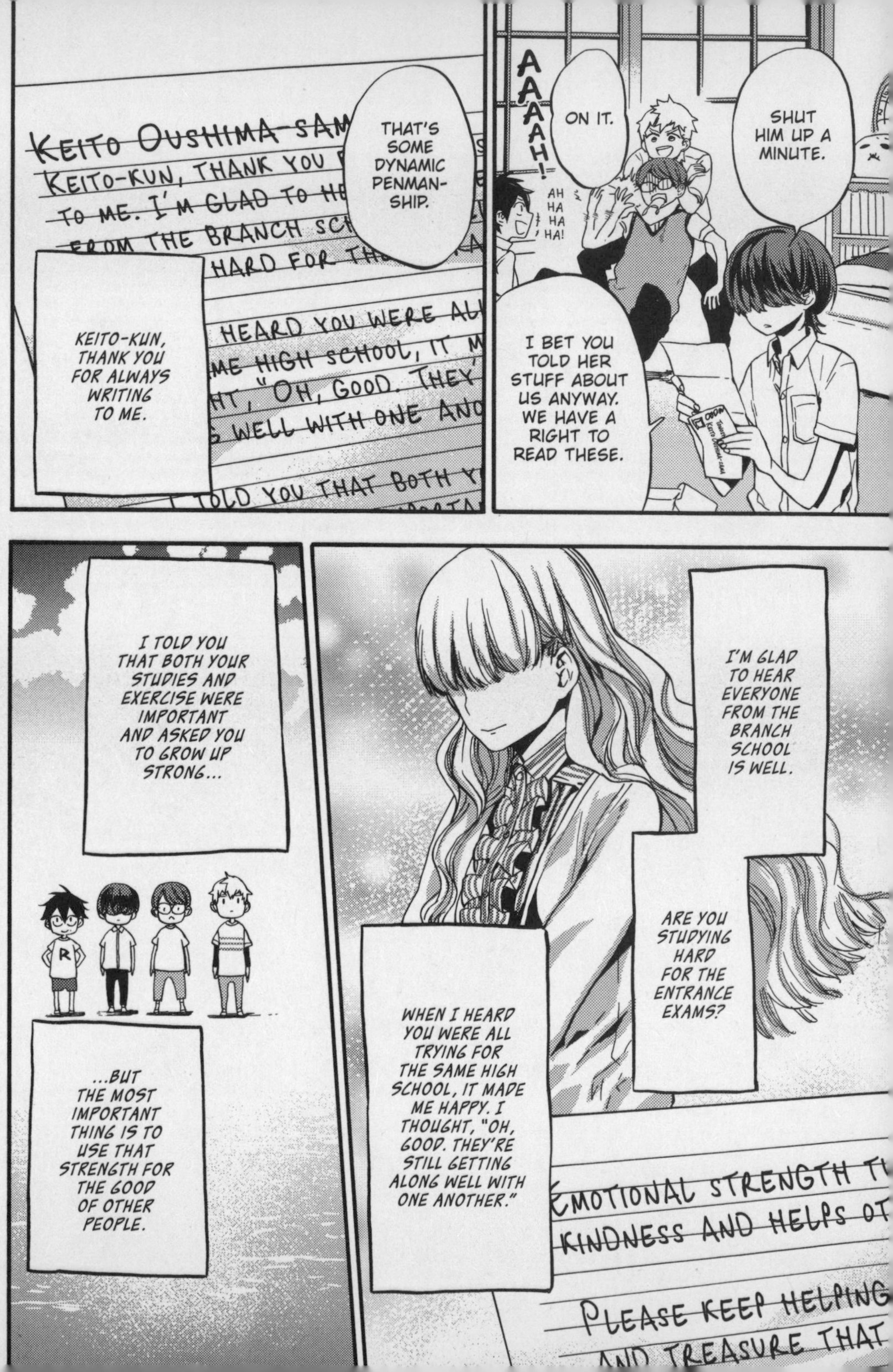
SHUT HIM UP A MINUTE.
ON IT.
AAAAAH!
AH HA HA HA!
I BET YOU TOLD HER STUFF ABOUT US ANYWAY. WE HAVE A RIGHT TO READ THESE.
KEITO OUSHIMA-SAM
KEITO-KUN, THANK YOU
TO ME. I'M GLAD TO HE
FROM THE BRANCH SC
HARD FOR TH
HEARD YOU WERE AL
ME HIGH SCHOOL, IT M
HT, "OH, GOOD. THEY
S WELL WITH ONE ANO
TOLD YOU THAT BOTH Y
THAT'S SOME DYNAMIC PENMANSHIP.
KEITO-KUN, THANK YOU FOR ALWAYS WRITING TO ME.
I'M GLAD TO HEAR EVERYONE FROM THE BRANCH SCHOOL IS WELL.
ARE YOU STUDYING HARD FOR THE ENTRANCE EXAMS?
WHEN I HEARD YOU WERE ALL TRYING FOR THE SAME HIGH SCHOOL, IT MADE ME HAPPY. I THOUGHT, "OH, GOOD. THEY'RE STILL GETTING ALONG WELL WITH ONE ANOTHER."
EMOTIONAL STRENGTH T
KINDNESS AND HELPS OT
PLEASE KEEP HELPING
AND TREASURE THAT
I TOLD YOU THAT BOTH YOUR STUDIES AND EXERCISE WERE IMPORTANT AND ASKED YOU TO GROW UP STRONG...
R
...BUT THE MOST IMPORTANT THING IS TO USE THAT STRENGTH FOR THE GOOD OF OTHER PEOPLE.

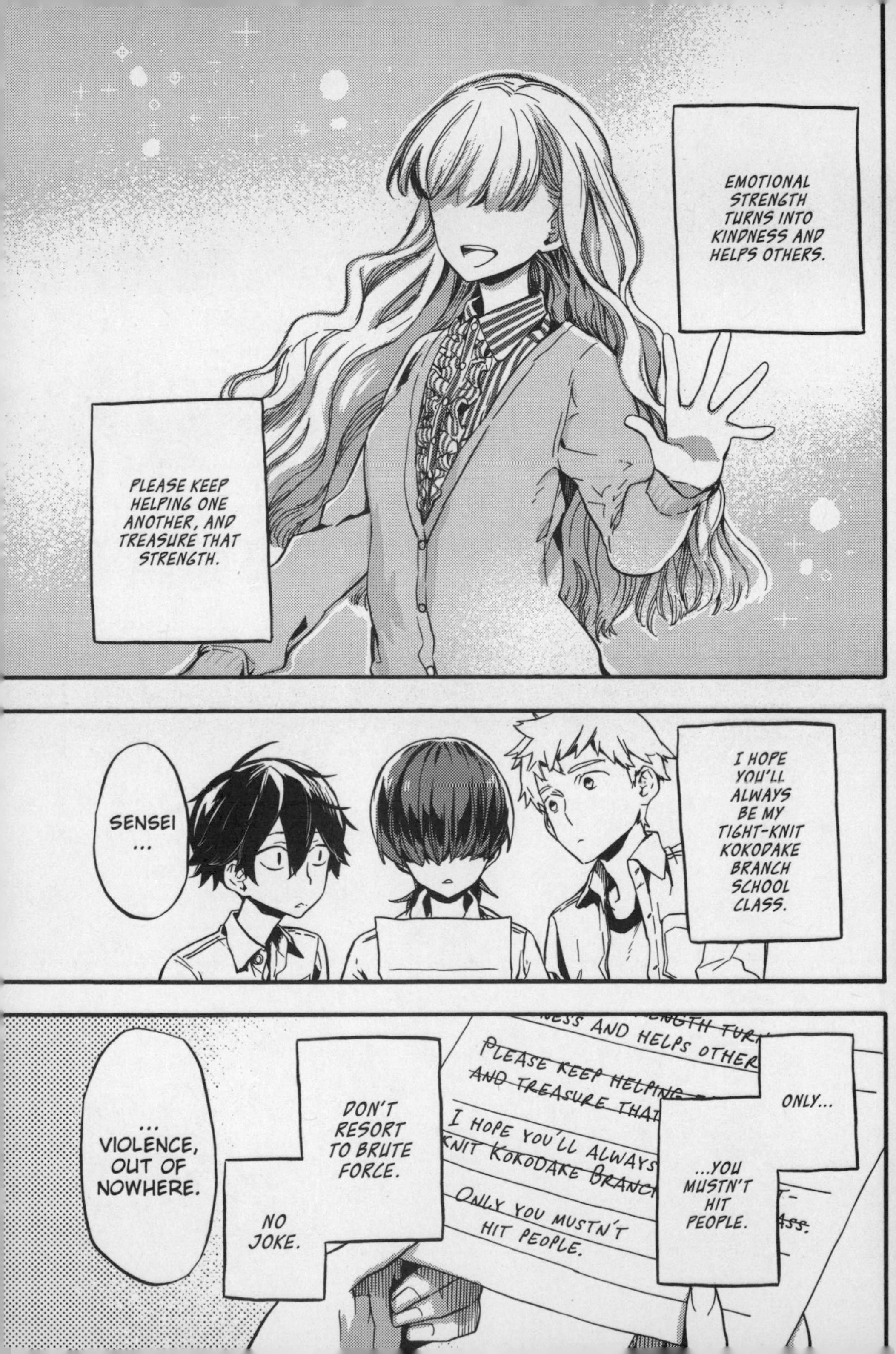
EMOTIONAL STRENGTH TURNS INTO KINDNESS AND HELPS OTHERS.
PLEASE KEEP HELPING ONE ANOTHER, AND TREASURE THAT STRENGTH.
I HOPE YOU'LL ALWAYS BE MY TIGHT-KNIT KOKODAKE BRANCH SCHOOL CLASS.
SENSEI ...
AND HELPS
PLEASE KEEP
AND TREASURE
I HOPE YOU'LL ALWAYS
KOKODAKE
ONLY YOU MUSTN'T HIT PEOPLE.
ONLY...
...YOU MUSTN'T HIT PEOPLE.
DON'T RESORT TO BRUTE FORCE.
NO JOKE.
... VIOLENCE, OUT OF NOWHERE.

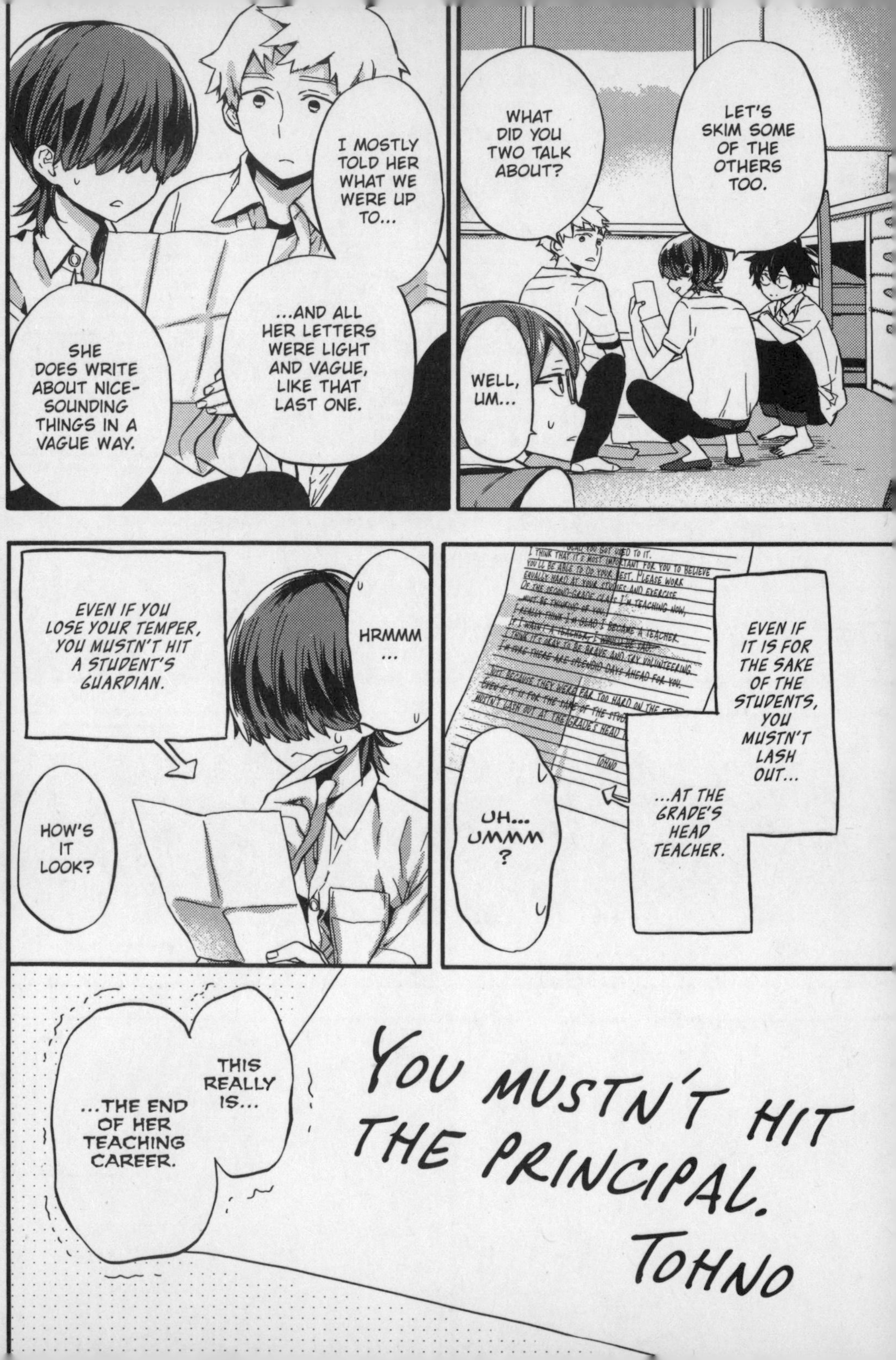
LET'S SKIM SOME OF THE OTHERS TOO.
WHAT DID YOU TWO TALK ABOUT?
WELL, UM...
I MOSTLY TOLD HER WHAT WE WERE UP TO...
...AND ALL HER LETTERS WERE LIGHT AND VAGUE, LIKE THAT LAST ONE.
SHE DOES WRITE ABOUT NICE-SOUNDING THINGS IN A VAGUE WAY.
I THINK THAT IT'S MOST IMPORTANT FOR YOU TO BELIEVE
YOU'LL BE ABLE TO DO YOUR BEST. PLEASE WORK
EQUALLY HARD AT YOUR STUDIES AND EXERCISE.
I REALLY THINK I'M GLAD I BECAME A TEACHER.
TOHNO
EVEN IF IT IS FOR THE SAKE OF THE STUDENTS, YOU MUSTN'T LASH OUT...
...AT THE GRADE'S HEAD TEACHER.
UH... UMMM ?
HRMMM ...
EVEN IF YOU LOSE YOUR TEMPER, YOU MUSTN'T HIT A STUDENT'S GUARDIAN.
HOW'S IT LOOK?
YOU MUSTN'T HIT THE PRINCIPAL. TOHNO
THIS REALLY IS...
...THE END OF HER TEACHING CAREER.

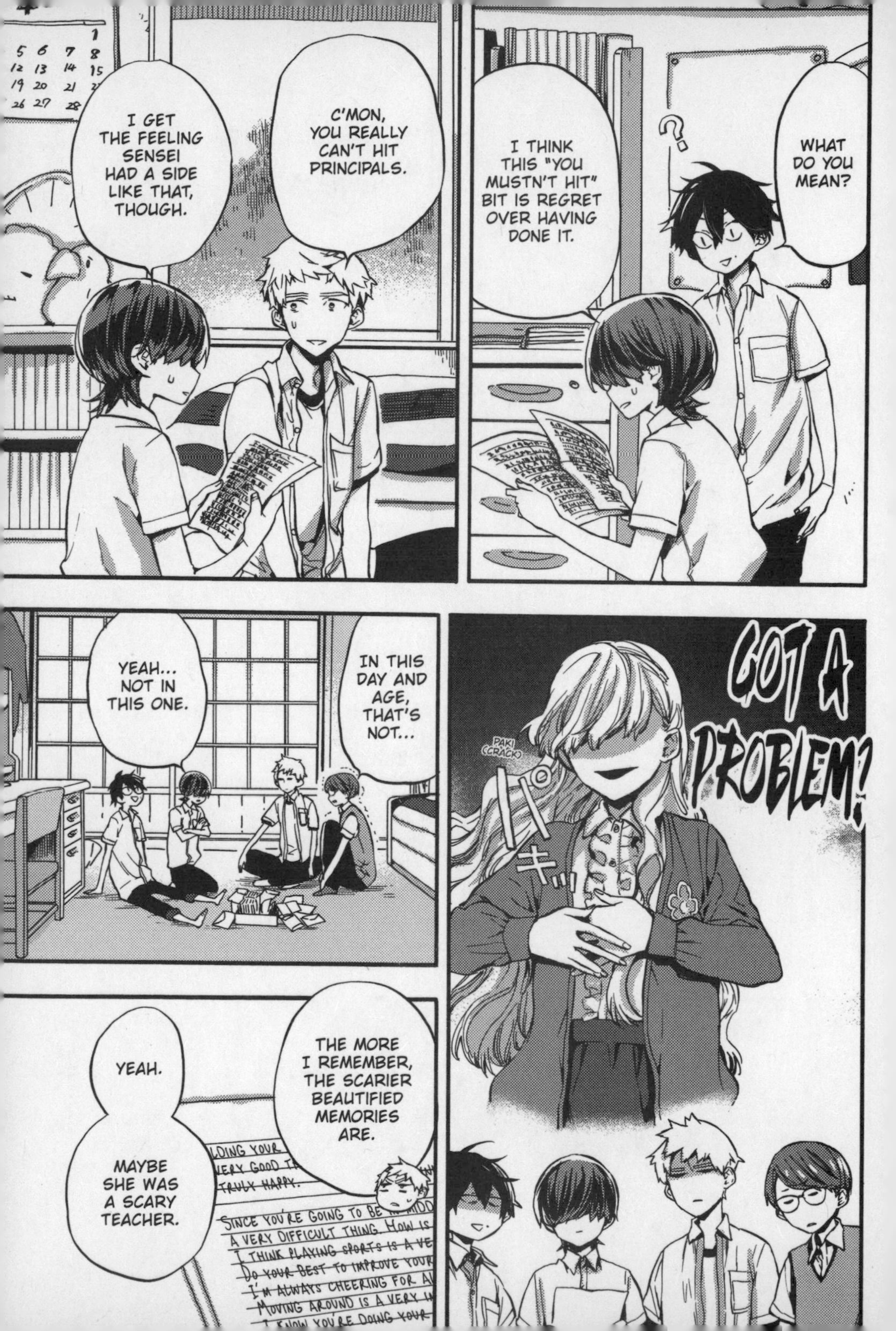
WHAT DO YOU MEAN?
I THINK THIS "YOU MUSTN'T HIT" BIT IS REGRET OVER HAVING DONE IT.
C'MON, YOU REALLY CAN'T HIT PRINCIPALS.
I GET THE FEELING SENSEI HAD A SIDE LIKE THAT, THOUGH.
GOT A PROBLEM?
PAKI (CRACK)
IN THIS DAY AND AGE, THAT'S NOT...
YEAH... NOT IN THIS ONE.
THE MORE I REMEMBER, THE SCARIER BEAUTIFIED MEMORIES ARE.
YEAH.
MAYBE SHE WAS A SCARY TEACHER.
LDING YOUR
VERY GOOD T
TRULY HAPPY.
SINCE YOU'RE GOING TO BE IN MIDD
A VERY DIFFICULT THING. HOW IS
I THINK PLAYING SPORTS IS A VE
DO YOUR BEST TO IMPROVE YOUR
I'M ALWAYS CHEERING FOR A
MOVING AROUND IS A VERY I
I KNOW YOU'RE DOING YOUR

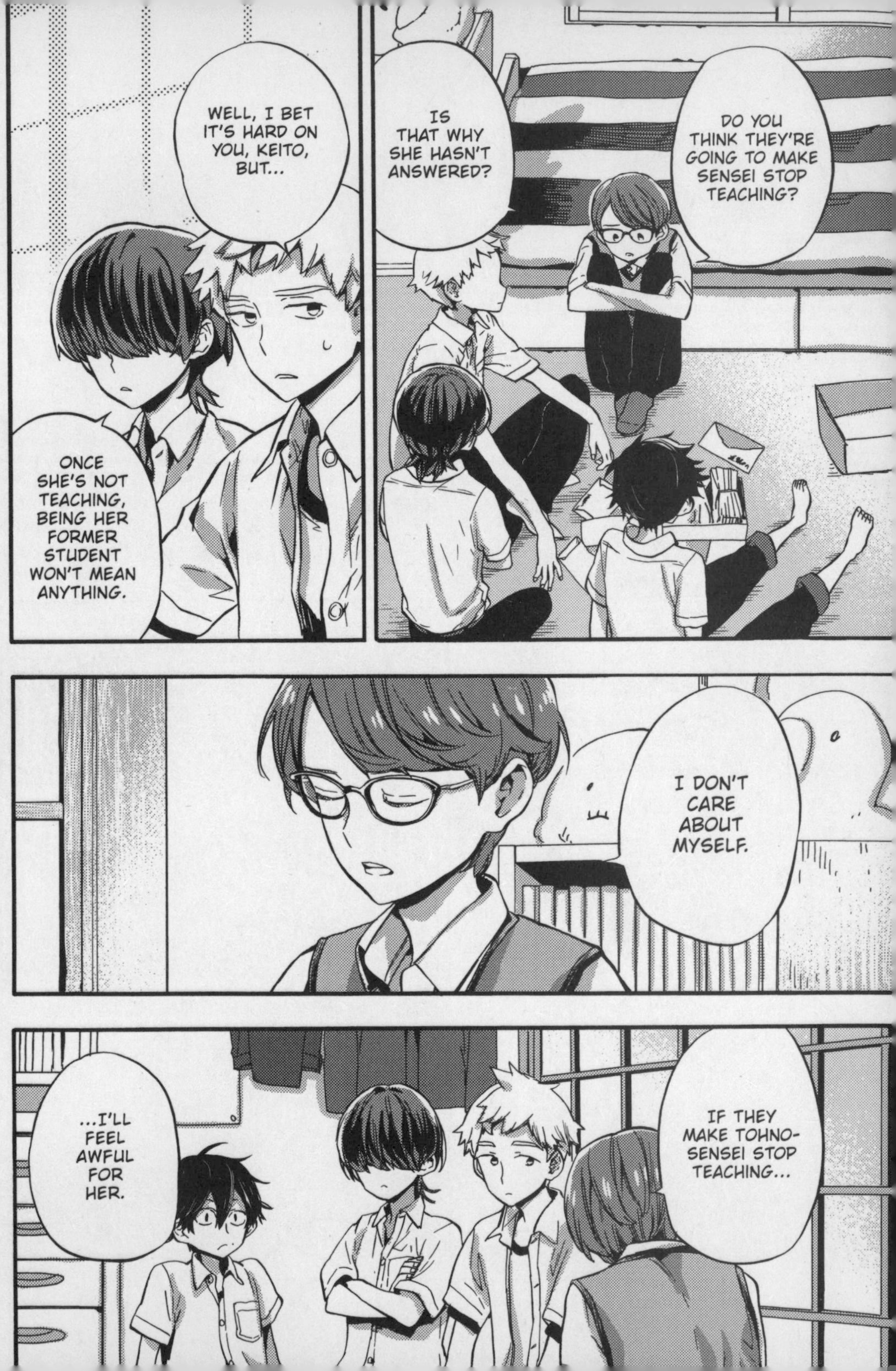
DO YOU THINK THEY'RE GOING TO MAKE SENSEI STOP TEACHING?
IS THAT WHY SHE HASN'T ANSWERED?
WELL, I BET IT'S HARD ON YOU, KEITO, BUT...
ONCE SHE'S NOT TEACHING, BEING HER FORMER STUDENT WON'T MEAN ANYTHING.
I DON'T CARE ABOUT MYSELF.
IF THEY MAKE TOHNO-SENSEI STOP TEACHING...
...I'LL FEEL AWFUL FOR HER.

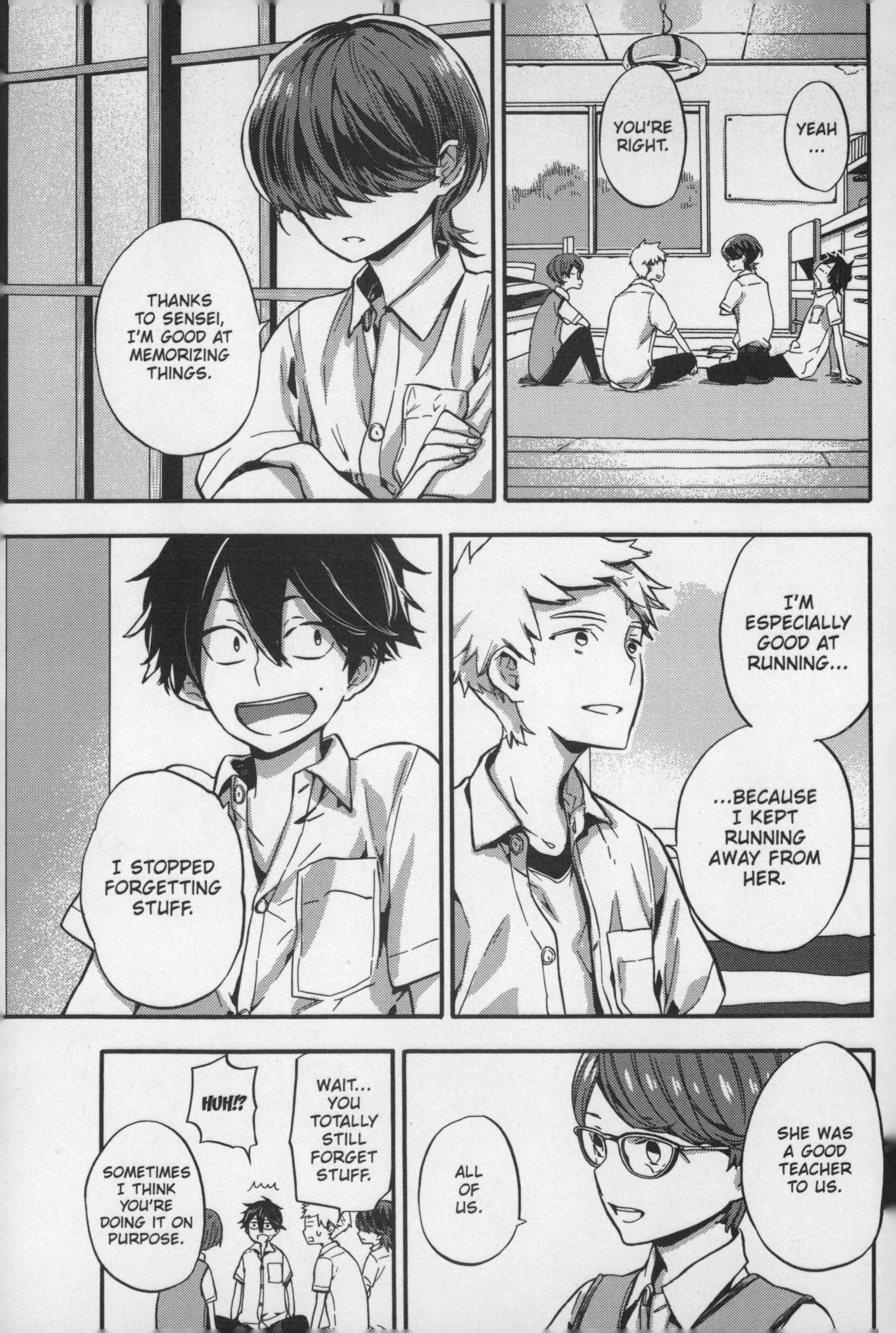
YEAH...
YOU'RE RIGHT.
THANKS TO SENSEI, I'M GOOD AT MEMORIZING THINGS.
I'M ESPECIALLY GOOD AT RUNNING...
...BECAUSE I KEPT RUNNING AWAY FROM HER.
I STOPPED FORGETTING STUFF.
SHE WAS A GOOD TEACHER TO US.
ALL OF US.
WAIT... YOU TOTALLY STILL FORGET STUFF.
HUH!?
SOMETIMES I THINK YOU'RE DOING IT ON PURPOSE.

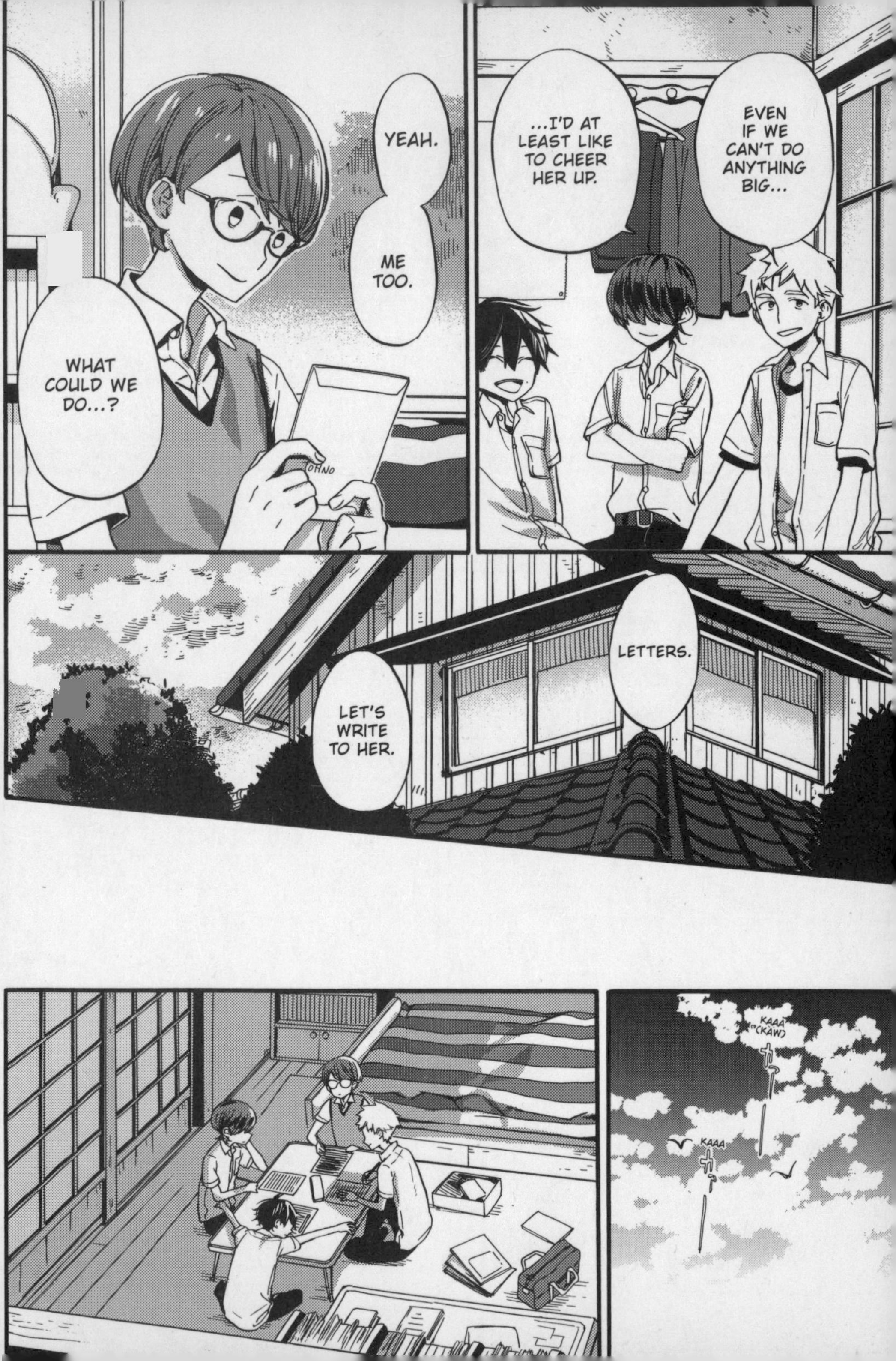
EVEN IF WE CAN'T DO ANYTHING BIG...
...I'D AT LEAST LIKE TO CHEER HER UP.
YEAH.
ME TOO.
OHNO
WHAT COULD WE DO...?
LETTERS.
LET'S WRITE TO HER.
KAAA (KAW)
KAAA

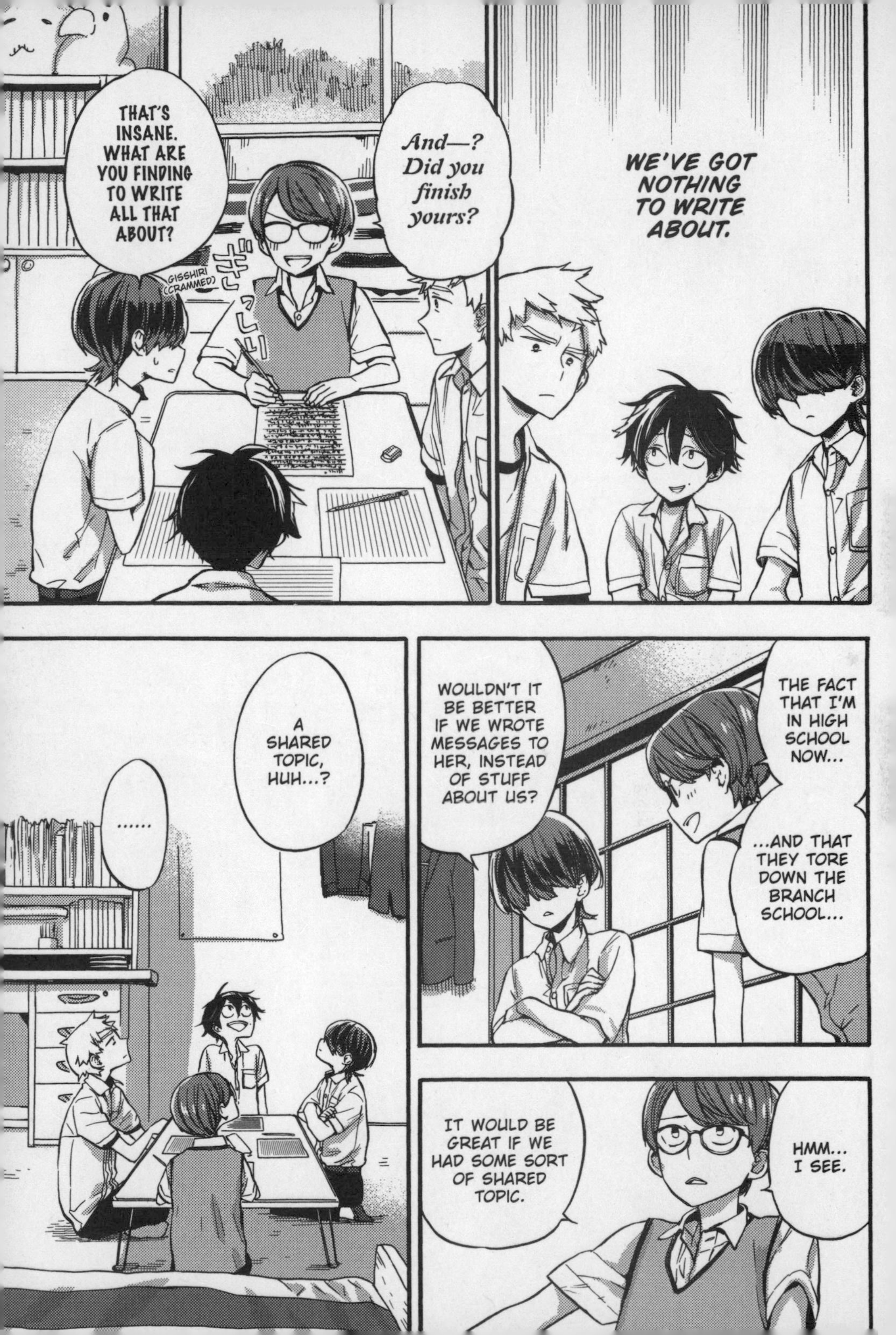
WE'VE GOT NOTHING TO WRITE ABOUT.
And—? Did you finish yours?
GISSHIRI (CRAMMED)
THAT'S INSANE. WHAT ARE YOU FINDING TO WRITE ALL THAT ABOUT?
THE FACT THAT I'M IN HIGH SCHOOL NOW...
...AND THAT THEY TORE DOWN THE BRANCH SCHOOL...
WOULDN'T IT BE BETTER IF WE WROTE MESSAGES TO HER, INSTEAD OF STUFF ABOUT US?
HMM... I SEE.
IT WOULD BE GREAT IF WE HAD SOME SORT OF SHARED TOPIC.
A SHARED TOPIC, HUH...?
......

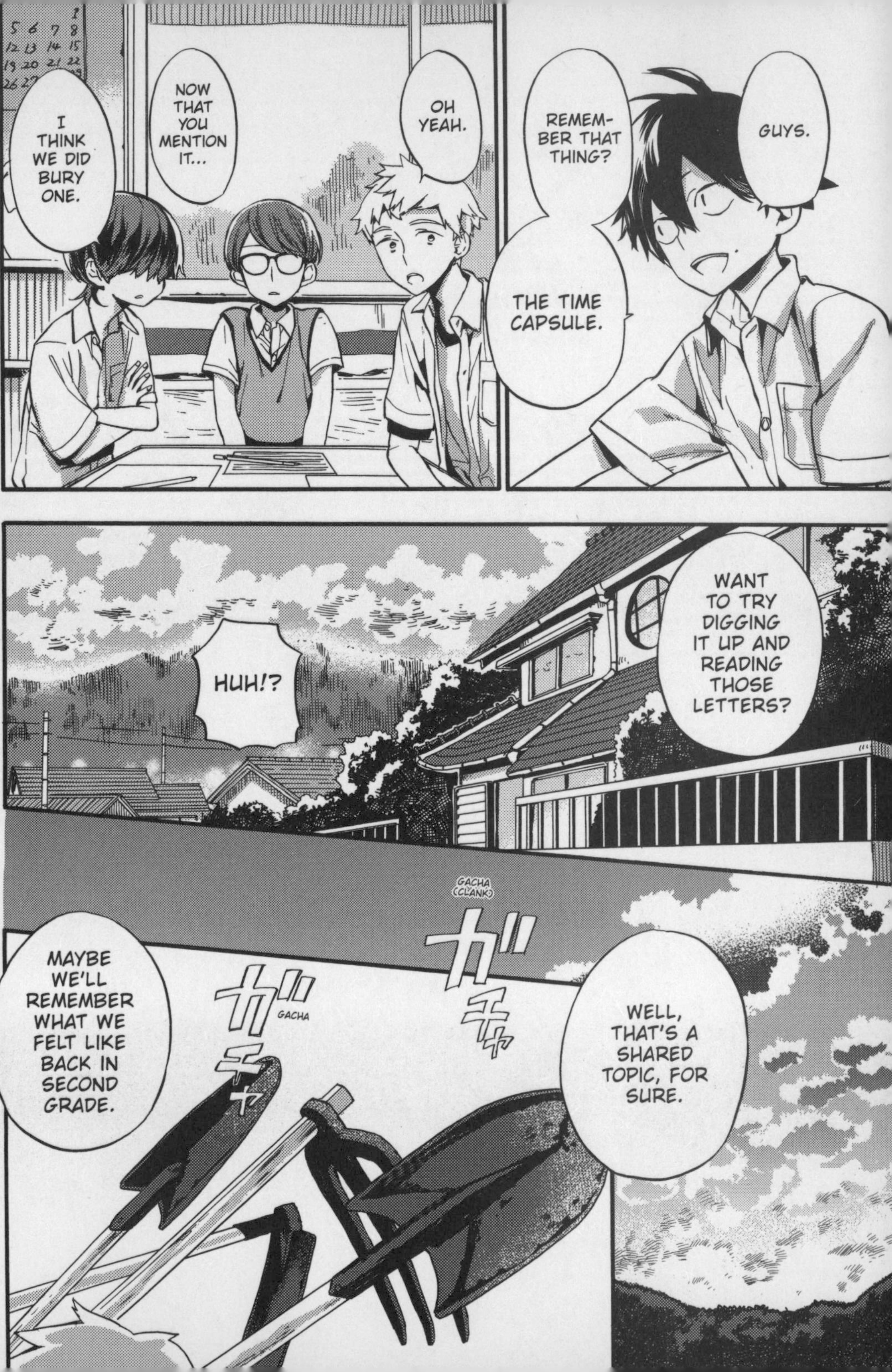
GUYS.
REMEM-BER THAT THING?
THE TIME CAPSULE.
OH YEAH.
NOW THAT YOU MENTION IT...
I THINK WE DID BURY ONE.
WANT TO TRY DIGGING IT UP AND READING THOSE LETTERS?
HUH!?
GACHA (CLANK)
WELL, THAT'S A SHARED TOPIC, FOR SURE.
GACHA
MAYBE WE'LL REMEMBER WHAT WE FELT LIKE BACK IN SECOND GRADE.

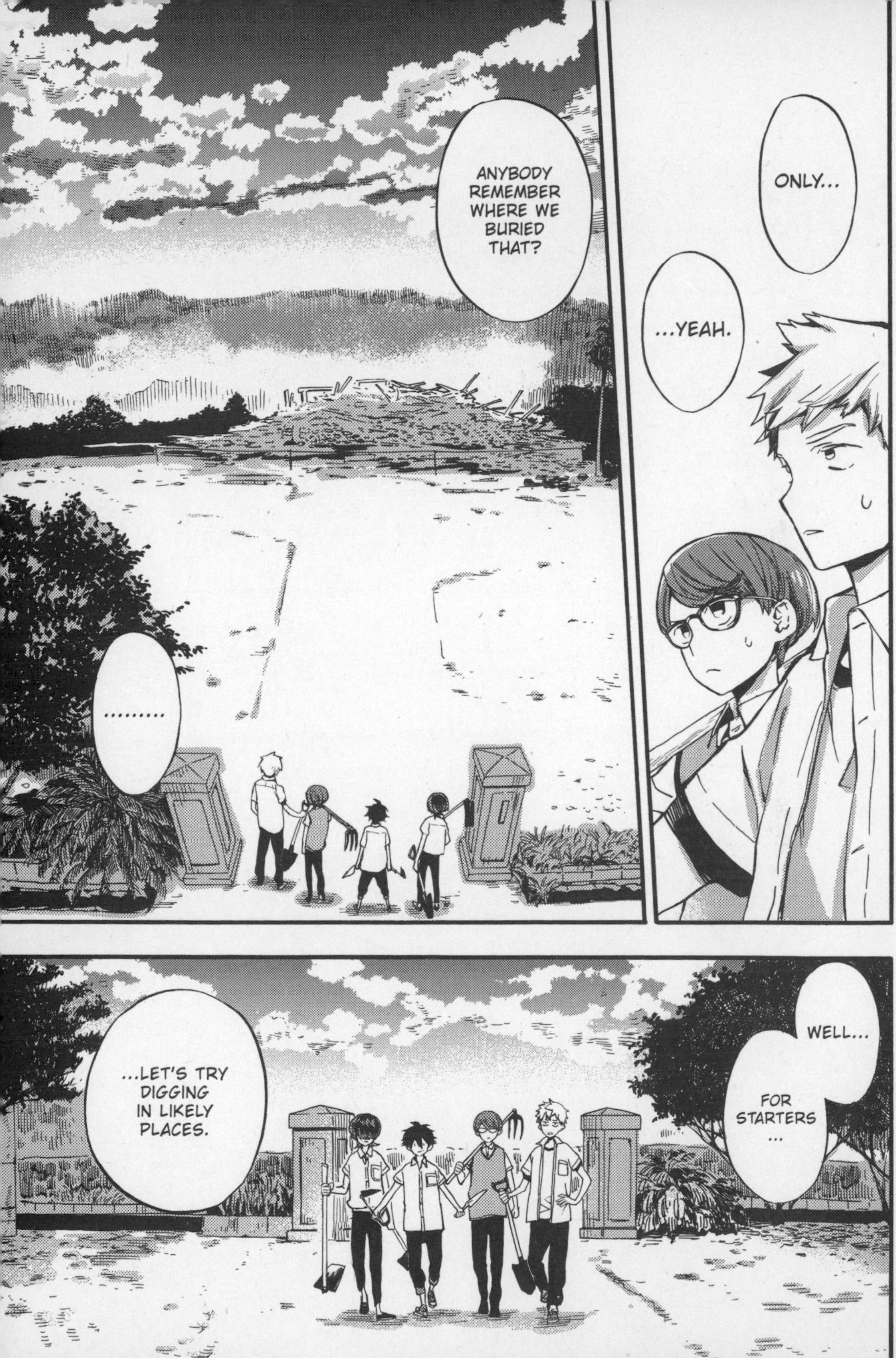
ONLY...
...YEAH.
ANYBODY REMEMBER WHERE WE BURIED THAT?
....
WELL...
FOR STARTERS ...
...LET'S TRY DIGGING IN LIKELY PLACES.

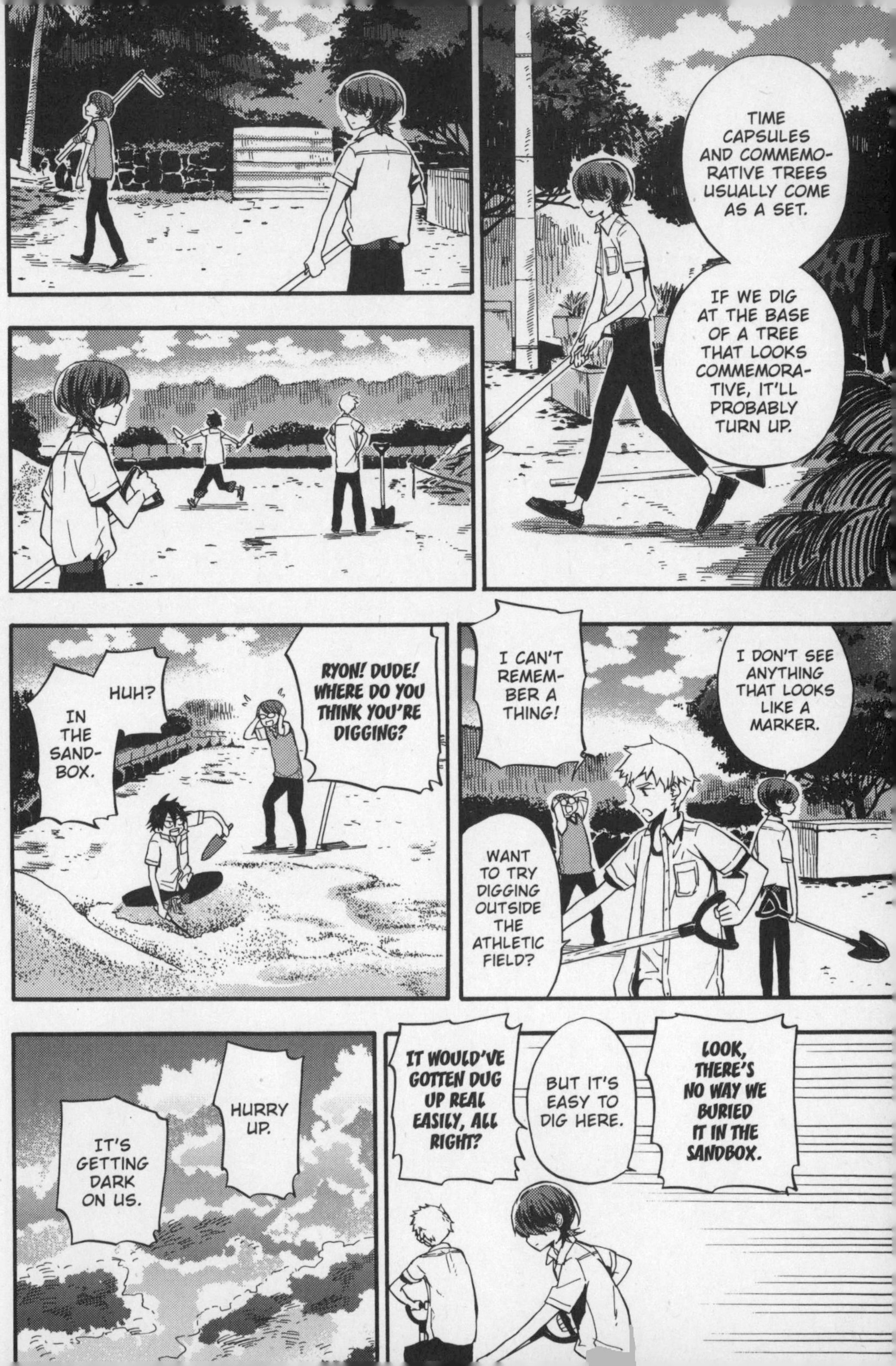
TIME CAPSULES AND COMMEMORATIVE TREES USUALLY COME AS A SET.
IF WE DIG AT THE BASE OF A TREE THAT LOOKS COMMEMORATIVE, IT'LL PROBABLY TURN UP.
I DON'T SEE ANYTHING THAT LOOKS LIKE A MARKER.
I CAN'T REMEMBER A THING!
WANT TO TRY DIGGING OUTSIDE THE ATHLETIC FIELD?
RYON! DUDE! WHERE DO YOU THINK YOU'RE DIGGING?
HUH?
IN THE SANDBOX.
LOOK, THERE'S NO WAY WE BURIED IT IN THE SANDBOX.
BUT IT'S EASY TO DIG HERE.
IT WOULD'VE GOTTEN DUG UP REAL EASILY, ALL RIGHT?
HURRY UP.
IT'S GETTING DARK ON US.

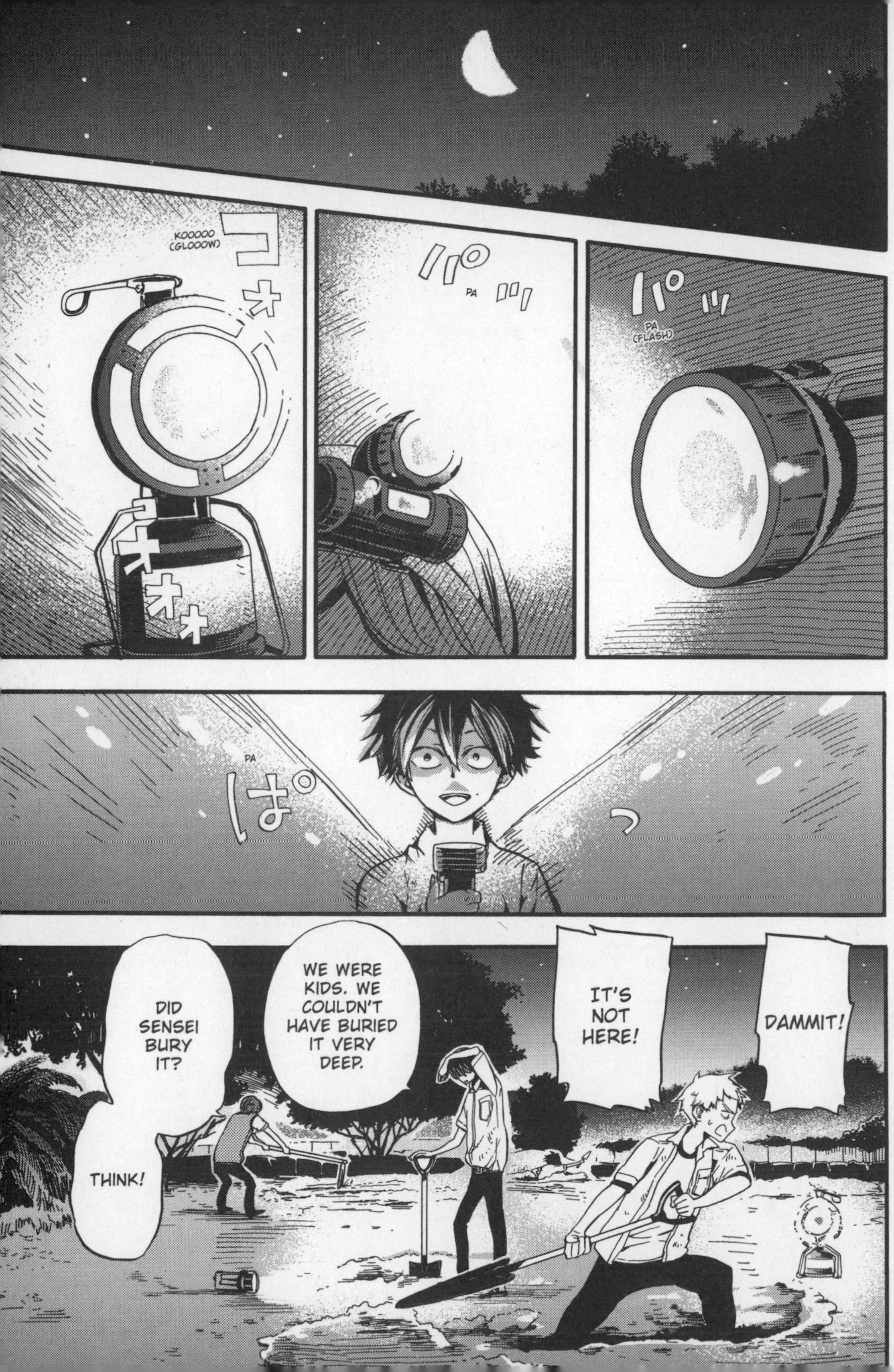
パッ
PA
(FLASH)
パッ
PA
KOOOOO
(GLOOOW)
ぱっ
PA
DAMMIT!
IT'S NOT HERE!
WE WERE KIDS. WE COULDN'T HAVE BURIED IT VERY DEEP.
DID SENSEI BURY IT?
THINK!

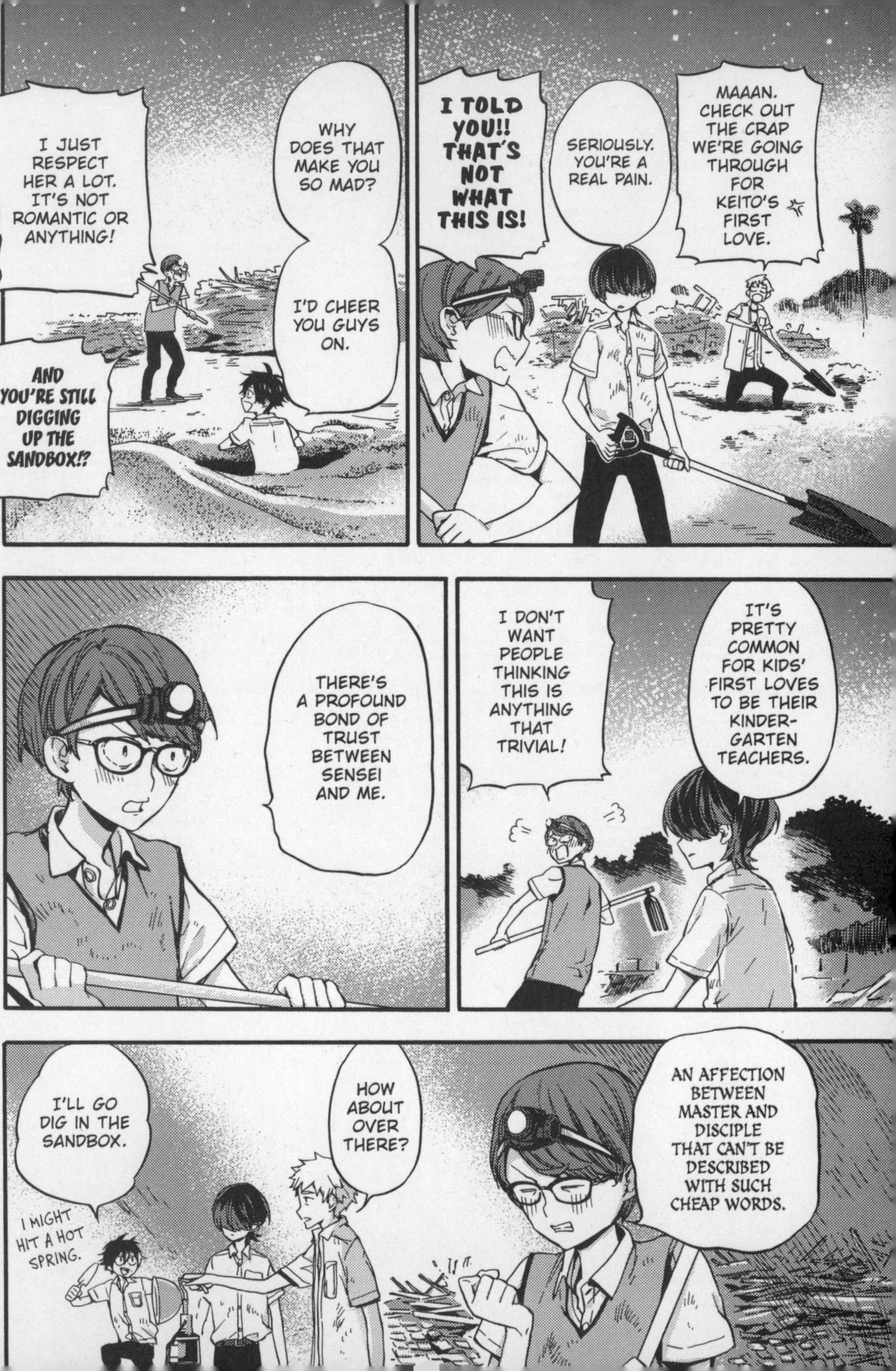
MAAAN. CHECK OUT THE CRAP WE'RE GOING THROUGH FOR KEITO'S FIRST LOVE.
SERIOUSLY. YOU'RE A REAL PAIN.
I TOLD YOU!! THAT'S NOT WHAT THIS IS!
WHY DOES THAT MAKE YOU SO MAD?
I'D CHEER YOU GUYS ON.
I JUST RESPECT HER A LOT. IT'S NOT ROMANTIC OR ANYTHING!
AND YOU'RE STILL DIGGING UP THE SANDBOX!?
IT'S PRETTY COMMON FOR KIDS' FIRST LOVES TO BE THEIR KINDER-GARTEN TEACHERS.
I DON'T WANT PEOPLE THINKING THIS IS ANYTHING THAT TRIVIAL!
THERE'S A PROFOUND BOND OF TRUST BETWEEN SENSEI AND ME.
AN AFFECTION BETWEEN MASTER AND DISCIPLE THAT CAN'T BE DESCRIBED WITH SUCH CHEAP WORDS.
HOW ABOUT OVER THERE?
I'LL GO DIG IN THE SANDBOX.
I MIGHT HIT A HOT SPRING.

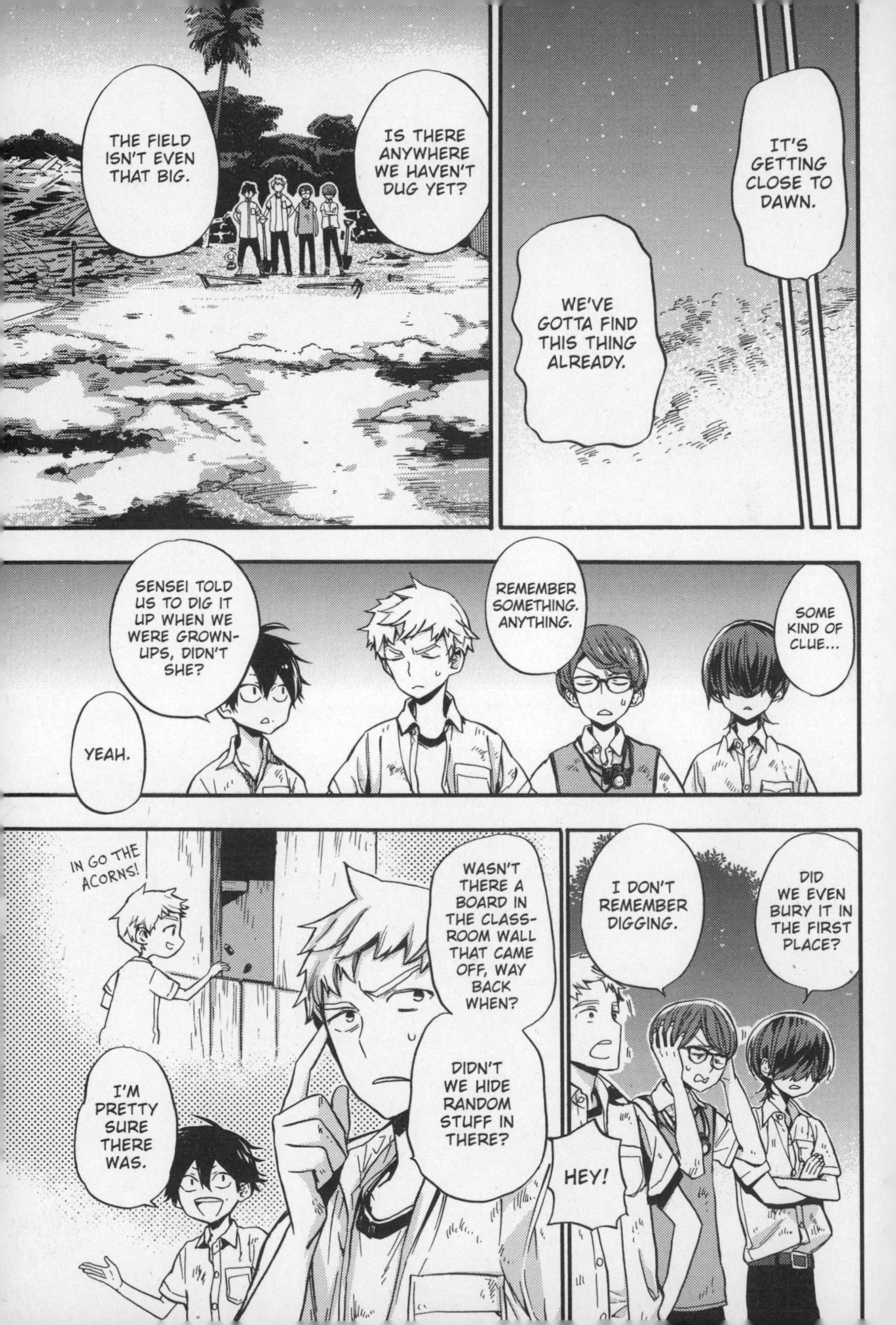
IT'S GETTING CLOSE TO DAWN.
WE'VE GOTTA FIND THIS THING ALREADY.
IS THERE ANYWHERE WE HAVEN'T DUG YET?
THE FIELD ISN'T EVEN THAT BIG.
SOME KIND OF CLUE...
REMEMBER SOMETHING. ANYTHING.
SENSEI TOLD US TO DIG IT UP WHEN WE WERE GROWN-UPS, DIDN'T SHE?
YEAH.
DID WE EVEN BURY IT IN THE FIRST PLACE?
I DON'T REMEMBER DIGGING.
HEY!
WASN'T THERE A BOARD IN THE CLASSROOM WALL THAT CAME OFF, WAY BACK WHEN?
DIDN'T WE HIDE RANDOM STUFF IN THERE?
IN GO THE ACORNS!
I'M PRETTY SURE THERE WAS.

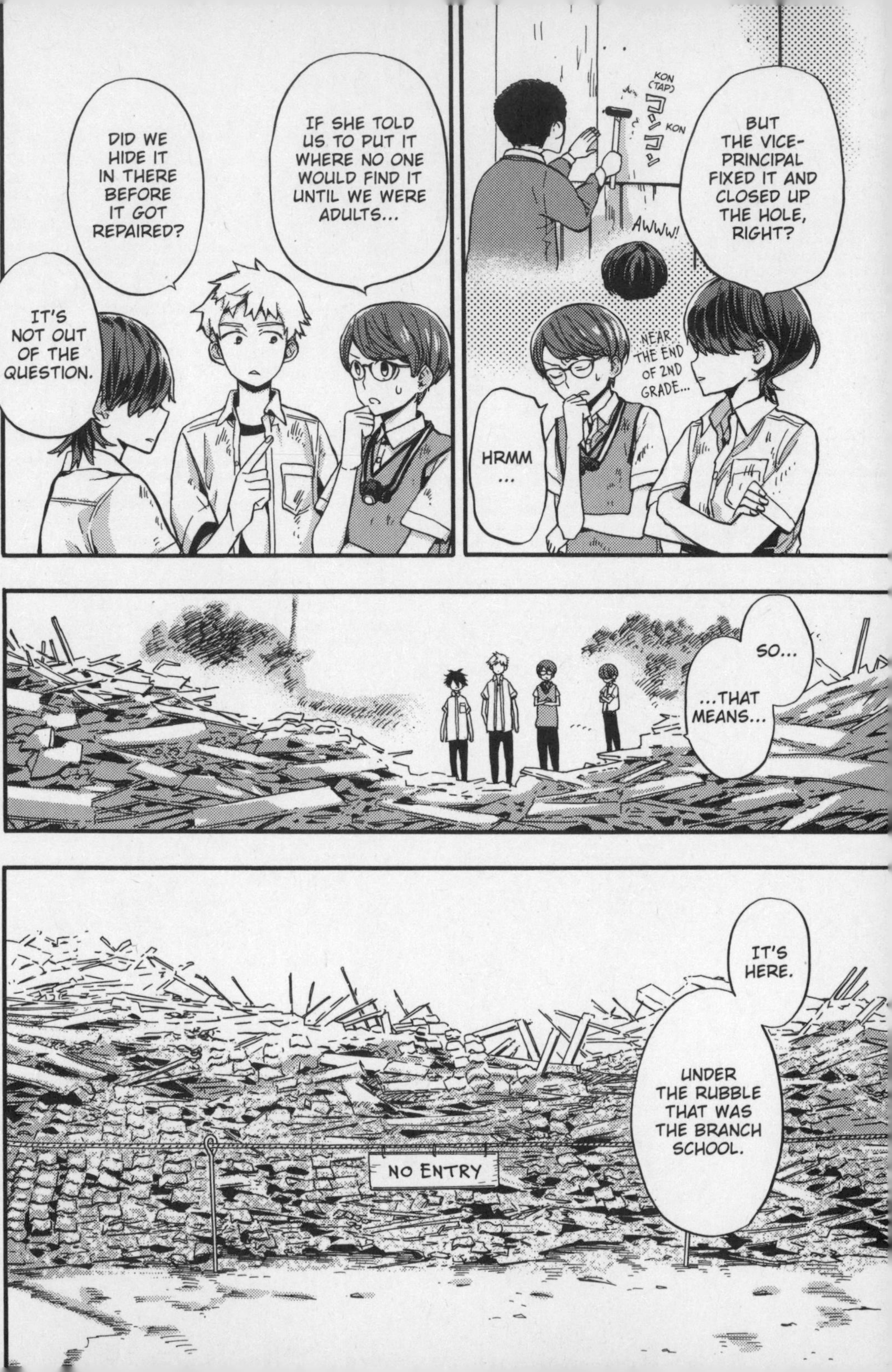
BUT THE VICE-PRINCIPAL FIXED IT AND CLOSED UP THE HOLE, RIGHT?
KON (TAP) KON
AWWW!
NEAR THE END OF 2ND GRADE...
HRMM...
IF SHE TOLD US TO PUT IT WHERE NO ONE WOULD FIND IT UNTIL WE WERE ADULTS...
DID WE HIDE IT IN THERE BEFORE IT GOT REPAIRED?
IT'S NOT OUT OF THE QUESTION.
SO...
...THAT MEANS...
IT'S HERE.
UNDER THE RUBBLE THAT WAS THE BRANCH SCHOOL.
NO ENTRY

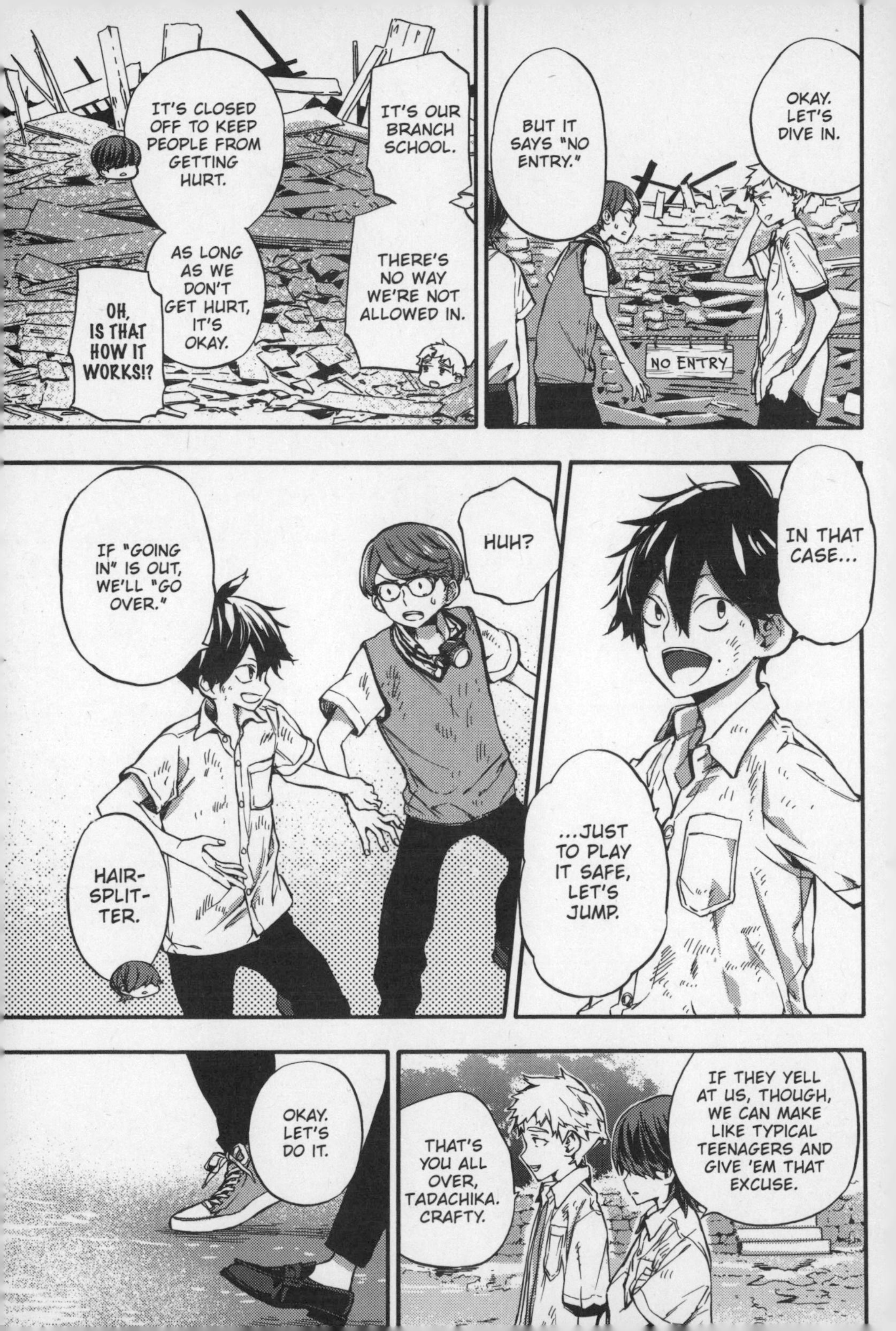
OKAY. LET'S DIVE IN.
BUT IT SAYS "NO ENTRY."
NO ENTRY
IT'S OUR BRANCH SCHOOL.
THERE'S NO WAY WE'RE NOT ALLOWED IN.
IT'S CLOSED OFF TO KEEP PEOPLE FROM GETTING HURT.
AS LONG AS WE DON'T GET HURT, IT'S OKAY.
OH, IS THAT HOW IT WORKS!?
IN THAT CASE...
...JUST TO PLAY IT SAFE, LET'S JUMP.
HUH?
IF "GOING IN" IS OUT, WE'LL "GO OVER."
HAIR-SPLITTER.
IF THEY YELL AT US, THOUGH, WE CAN MAKE LIKE TYPICAL TEENAGERS AND GIVE 'EM THAT EXCUSE.
THAT'S YOU ALL OVER, TADACHIKA. CRAFTY.
OKAY. LET'S DO IT.

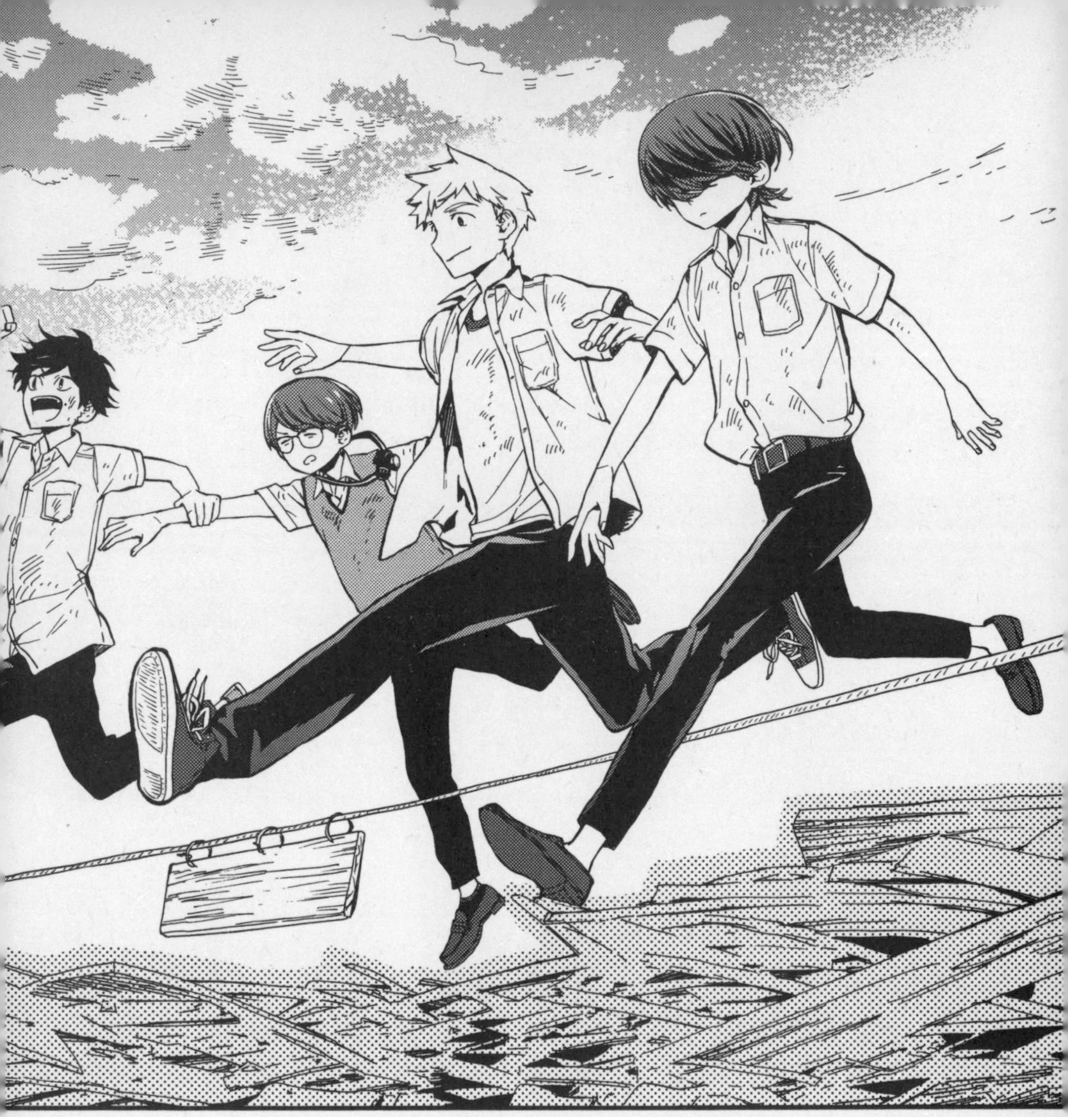

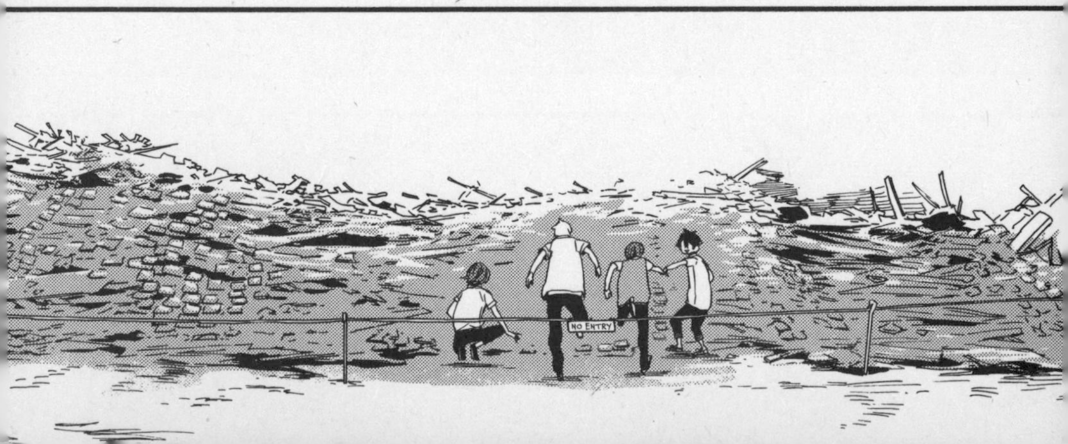
NO ENTRY

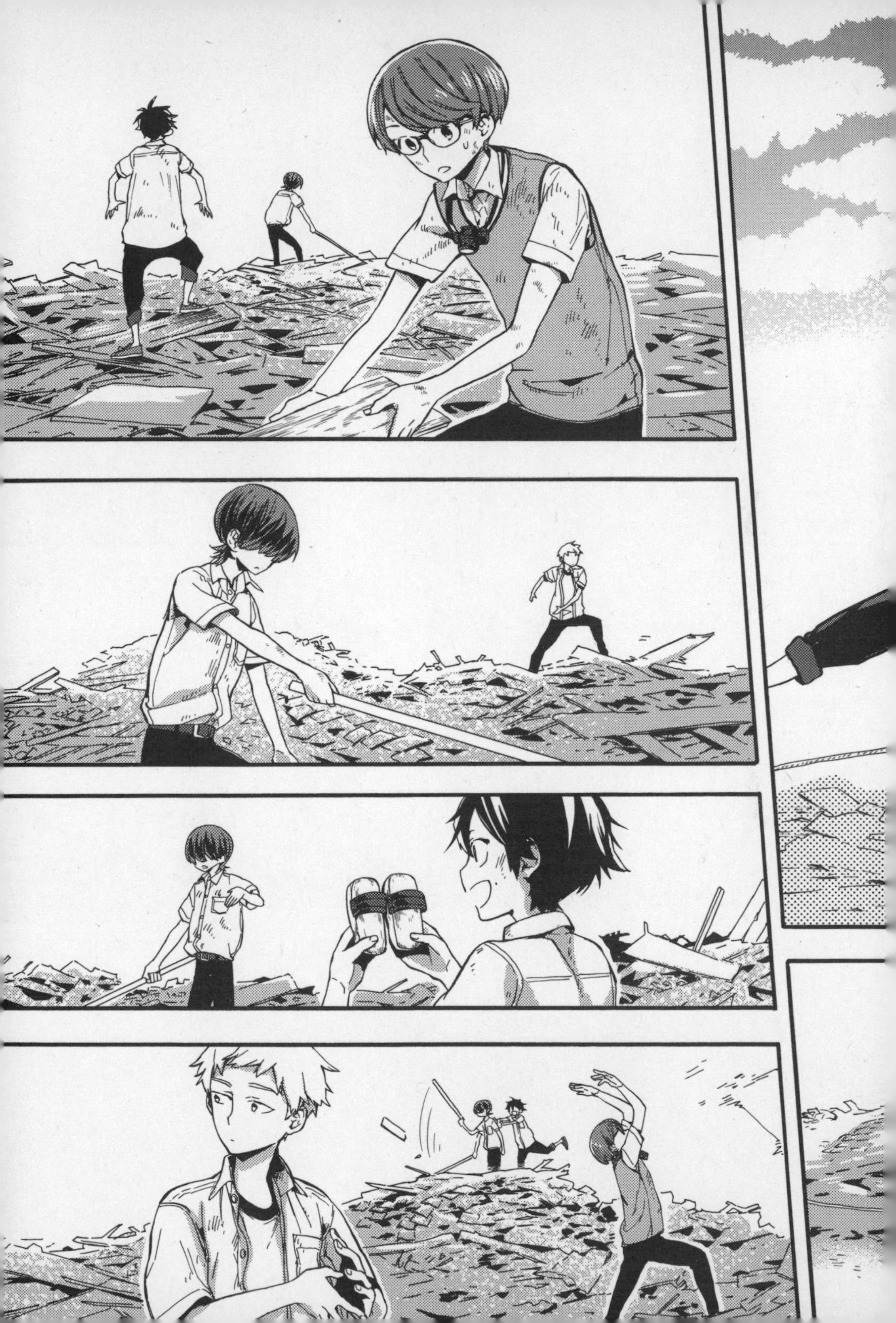

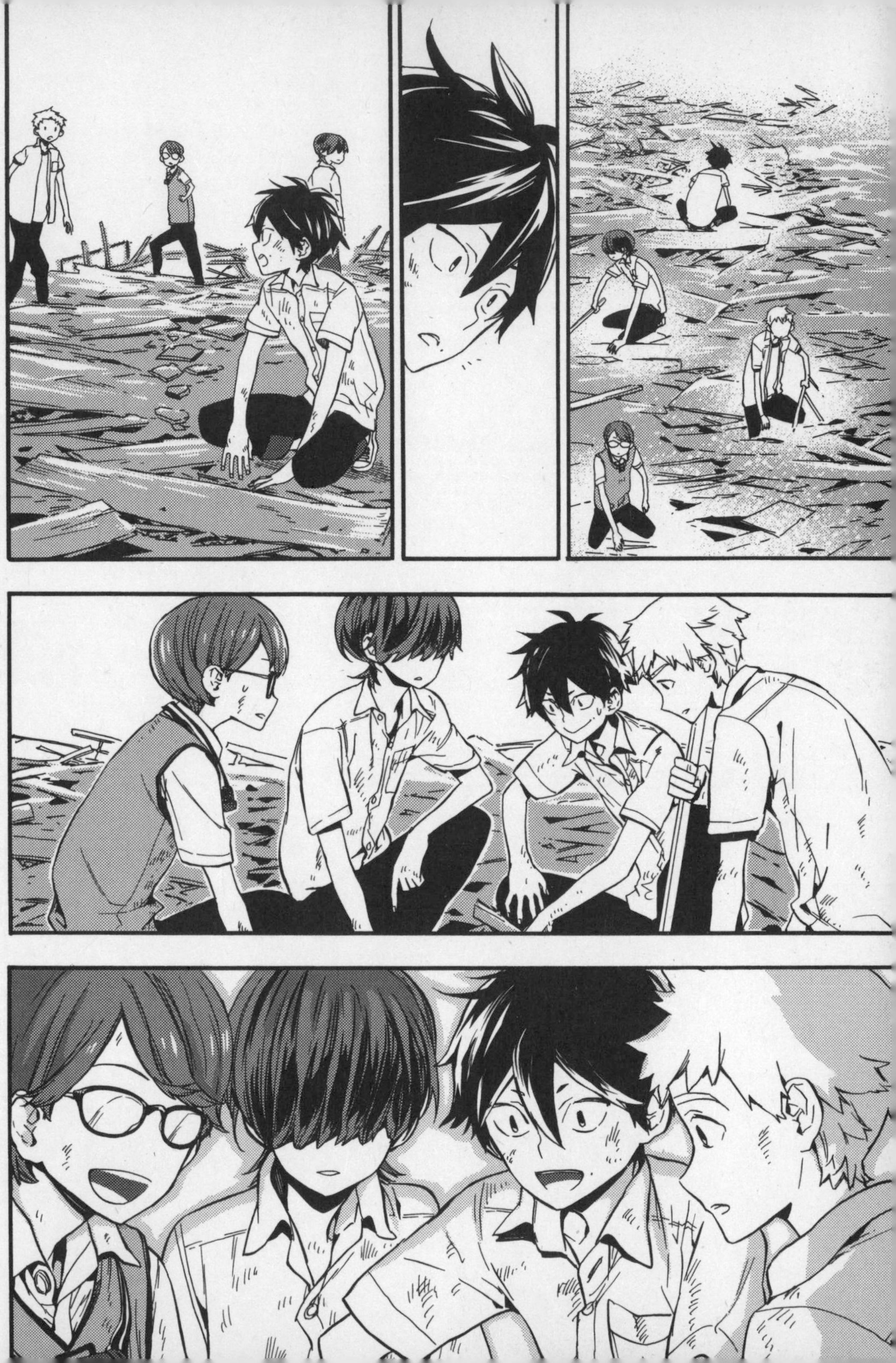

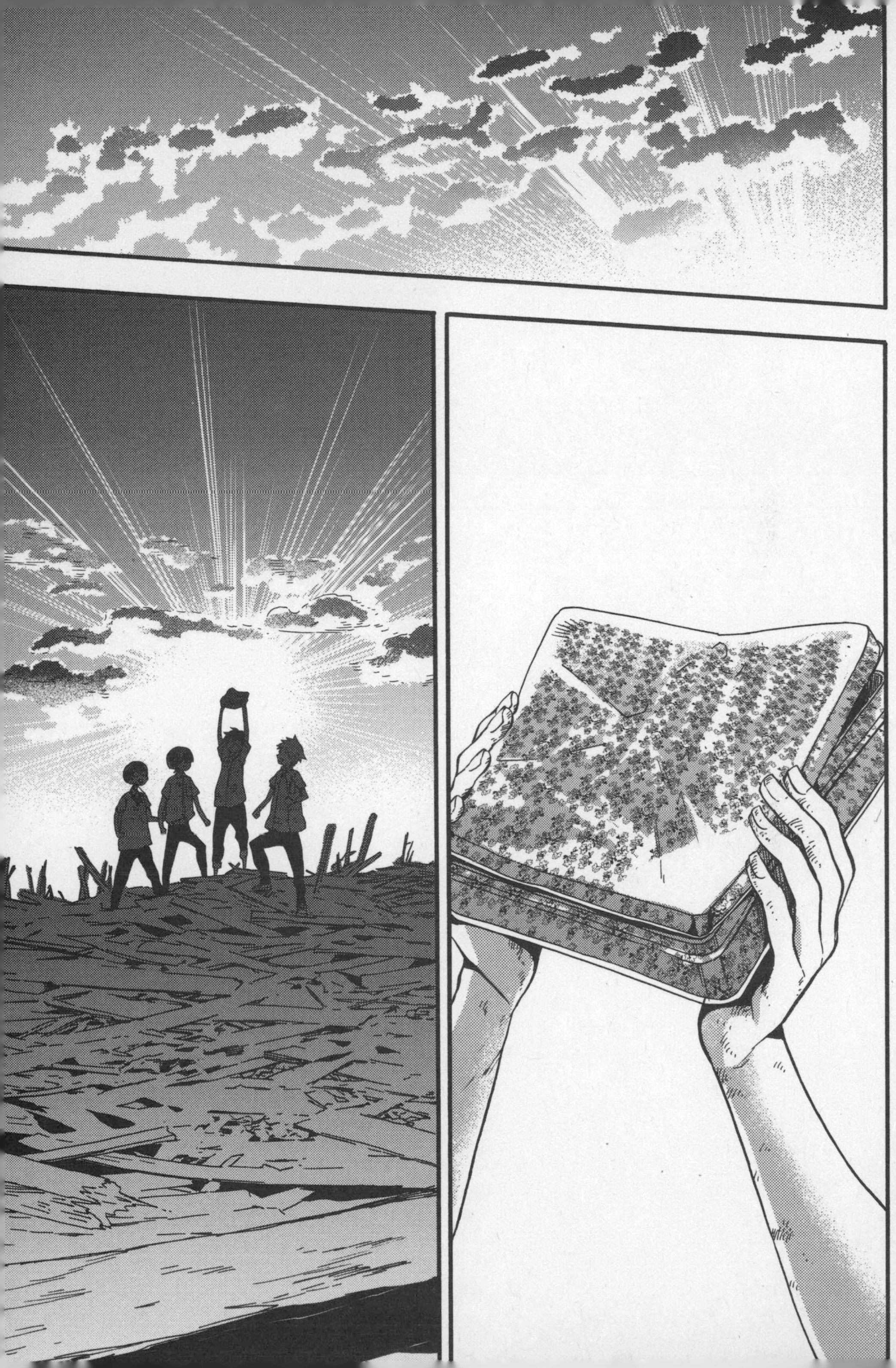

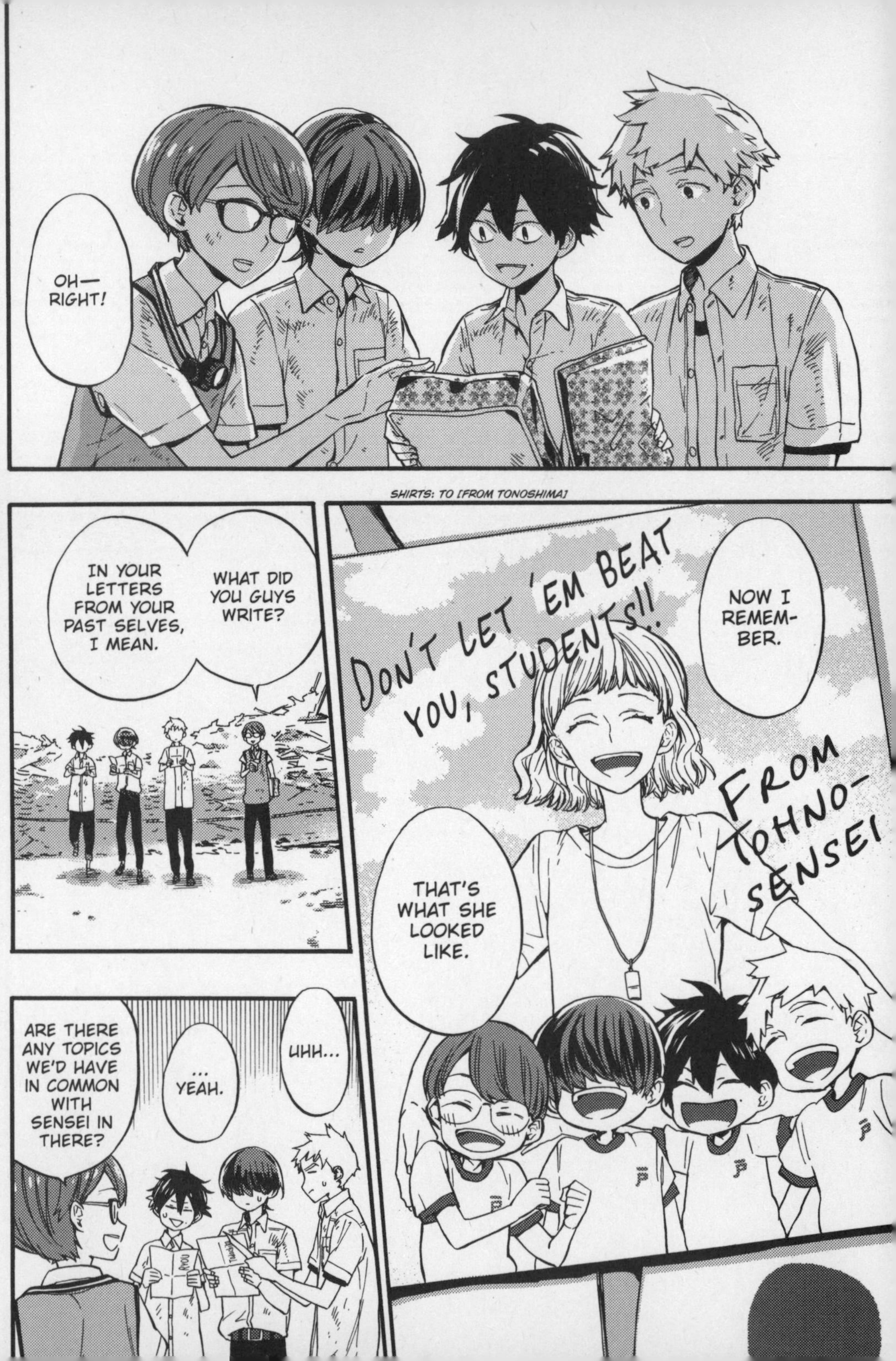
OH— RIGHT!
SHIRTS: TO [FROM TONOSHIMA]
NOW I REMEM-BER.
DON'T LET 'EM BEAT YOU, STUDENTS!!
FROM TOHNO-SENSEI
THAT'S WHAT SHE LOOKED LIKE.
WHAT DID YOU GUYS WRITE?
IN YOUR LETTERS FROM YOUR PAST SELVES, I MEAN.
UHH...
... YEAH.
ARE THERE ANY TOPICS WE'D HAVE IN COMMON WITH SENSEI IN THERE?

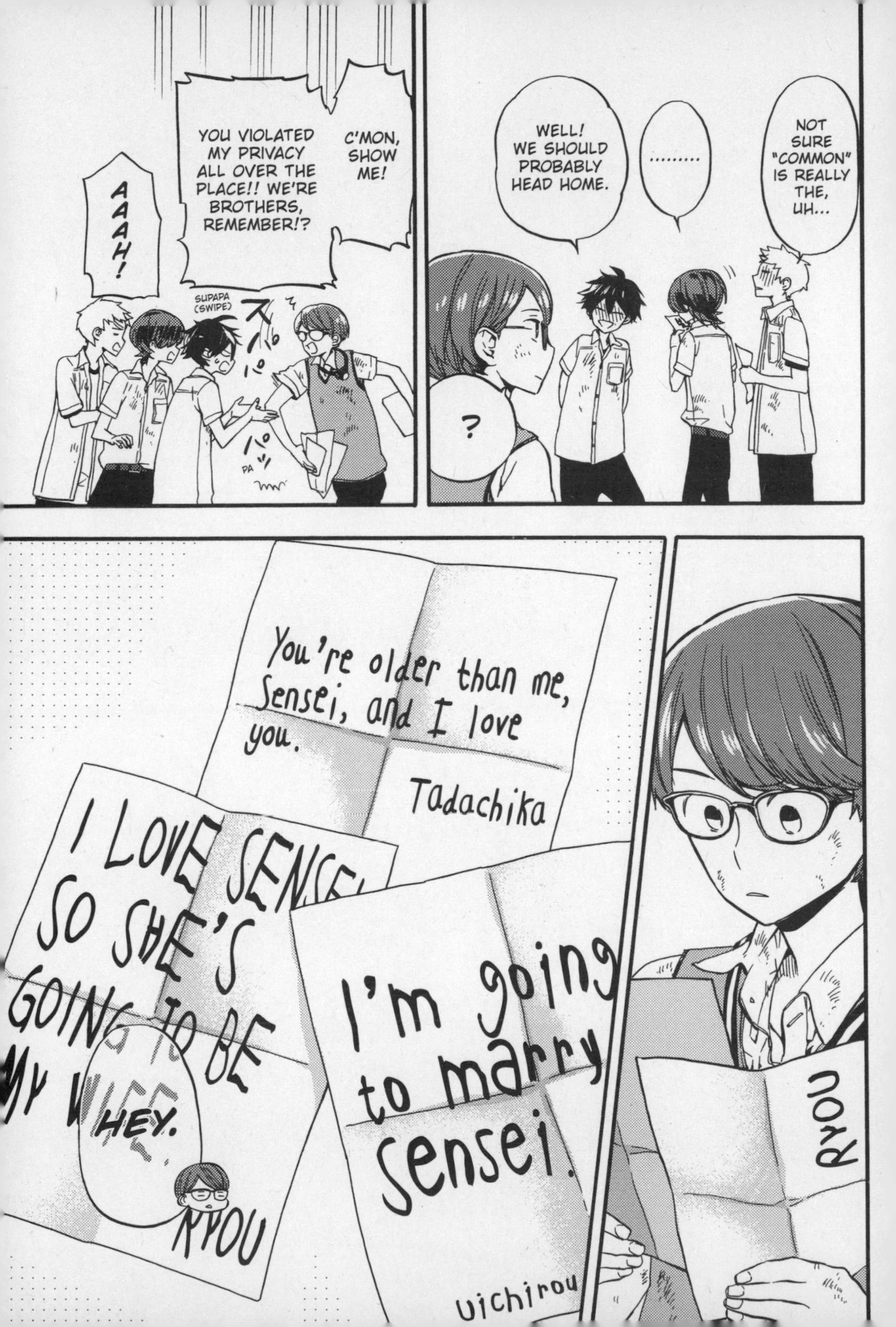
NOT SURE "COMMON" IS REALLY THE, UH...
....
WELL! WE SHOULD PROBABLY HEAD HOME.
?
C'MON, SHOW ME!
YOU VIOLATED MY PRIVACY ALL OVER THE PLACE!! WE'RE BROTHERS, REMEMBER!?
AAAH!
SUPAPA (SWIPE)
PA
RYOU
You're older than me, Sensei, and I love you.
Tadachika
I LOVE SENSE
SO SHE'S GOING TO BE MY W
RYOU
I'm going to marry Sensei.
Uichirou
HEY.

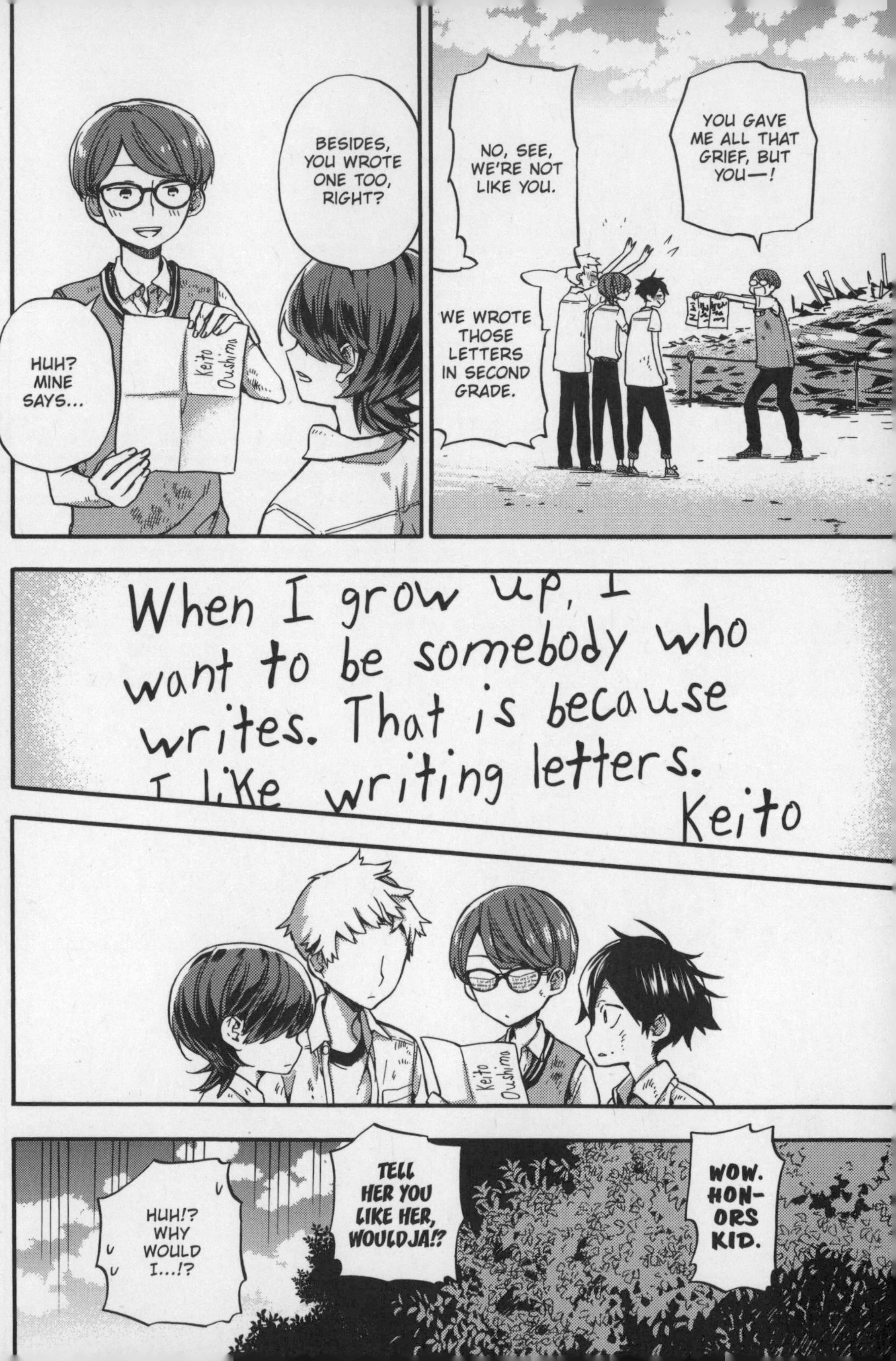
YOU GAVE ME ALL THAT GRIEF, BUT YOU—!
NO, SEE, WE'RE NOT LIKE YOU.
WE WROTE THOSE LETTERS IN SECOND GRADE.
BESIDES, YOU WROTE ONE TOO, RIGHT?
HUH? MINE SAYS...
Keito Oushima
When I grow up, I want to be somebody who writes. That is because I like writing letters.
Keito
Keito Oushima
WOW. HON-ORS KID.
TELL HER YOU LIKE HER, WOULDJA!?
HUH!? WHY WOULD I...!?

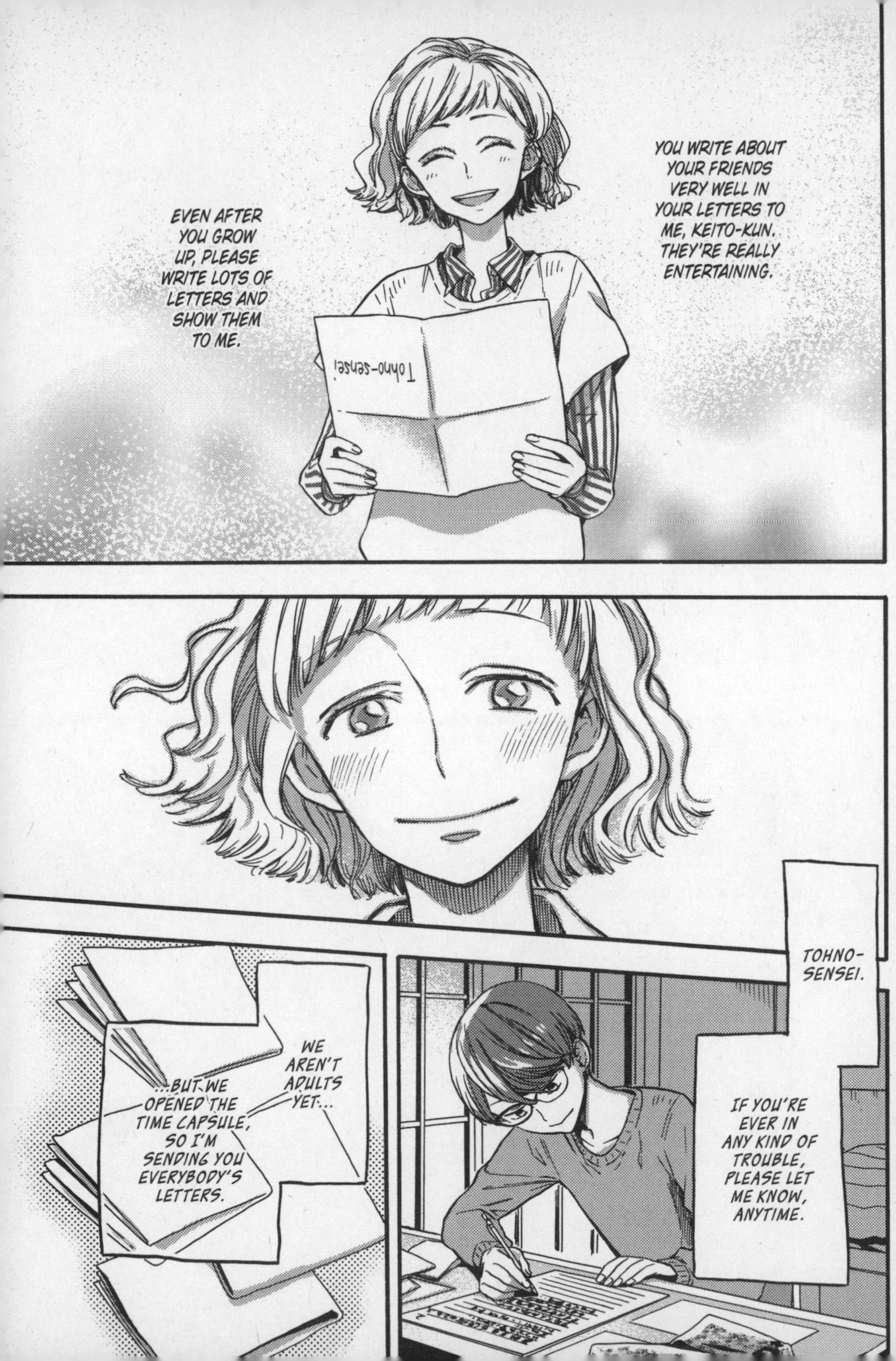
YOU WRITE ABOUT YOUR FRIENDS VERY WELL IN YOUR LETTERS TO ME, KEITO-KUN. THEY'RE REALLY ENTERTAINING.
EVEN AFTER YOU GROW UP, PLEASE WRITE LOTS OF LETTERS AND SHOW THEM TO ME.
Tohno-sensei!
TOHNO-SENSEI.
IF YOU'RE EVER IN ANY KIND OF TROUBLE, PLEASE LET ME KNOW, ANYTIME.
WE AREN'T ADULTS YET...
...BUT WE OPENED THE TIME CAPSULE, SO I'M SENDING YOU EVERYBODY'S LETTERS.

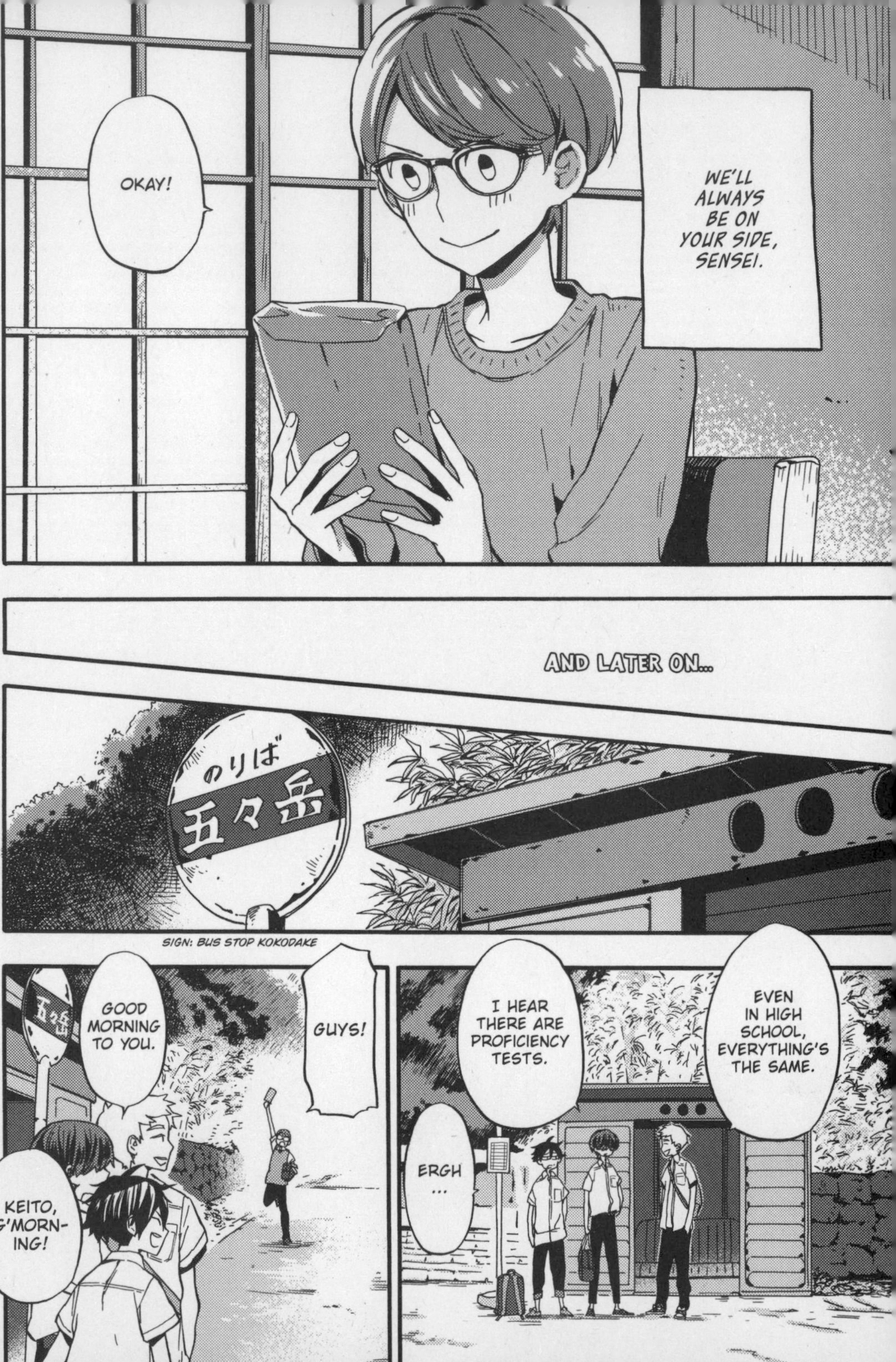
WE'LL ALWAYS BE ON YOUR SIDE, SENSEI.
OKAY!
AND LATER ON...
のりば
五々岳
SIGN: BUS STOP KOKODAKE
EVEN IN HIGH SCHOOL, EVERYTHING'S THE SAME.
I HEAR THERE ARE PROFICIENCY TESTS.
ERGH ...
GUYS!
GOOD MORNING TO YOU.
KEITO, G'MORNING!

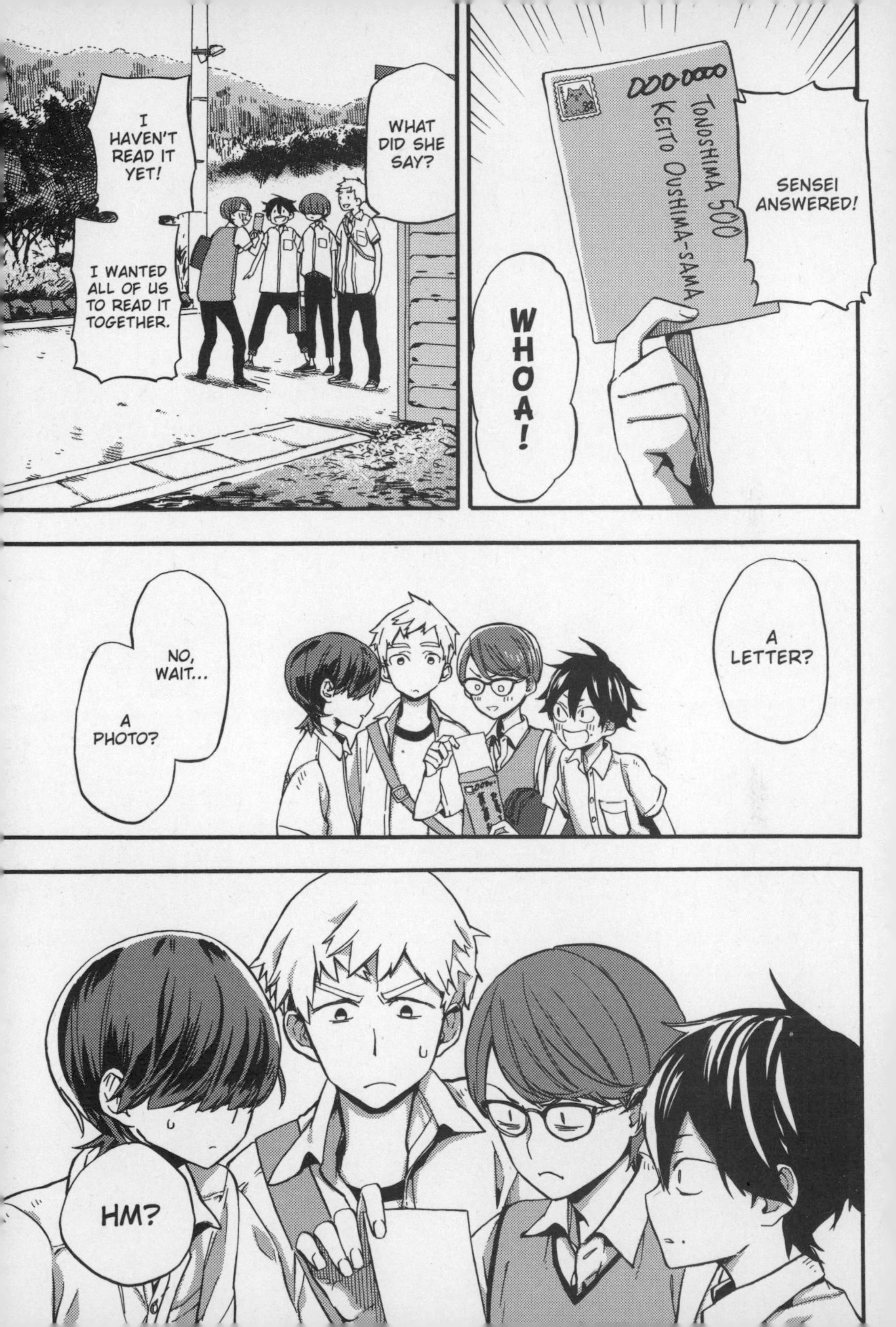
SENSEI ANSWERED!
000-0000
TONOSHIMA 500
KEITO OUSHIMA-SAMA
WHOA!
WHAT DID SHE SAY?
I HAVEN'T READ IT YET!
I WANTED ALL OF US TO READ IT TOGETHER.
A LETTER?
NO, WAIT...
A PHOTO?
HM?

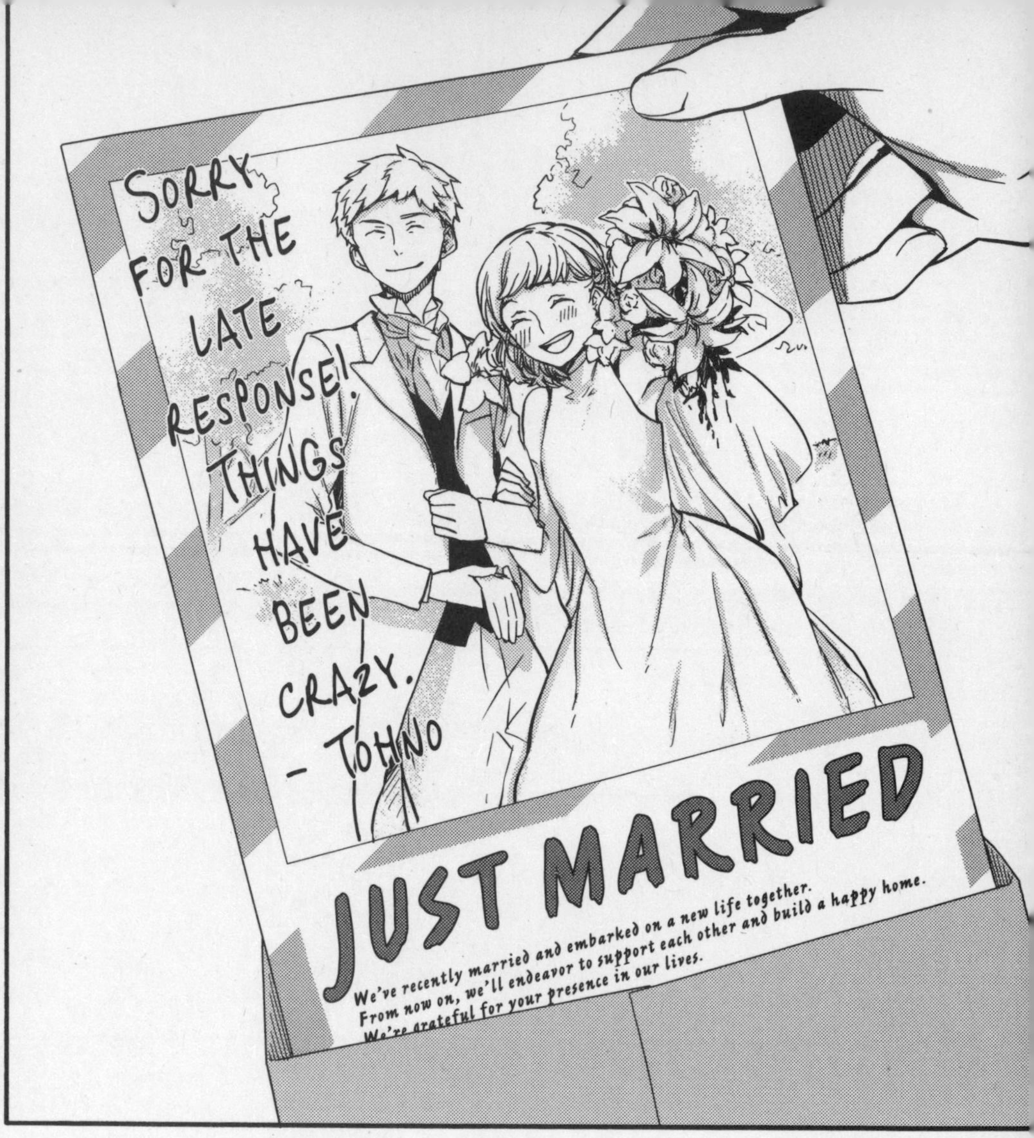
SORRY FOR THE LATE RESPONSE! THINGS HAVE BEEN CRAZY. - TOHNO
JUST MARRIED
We've recently married and embarked on a new life together.
From now on, we'll endeavor to support each other and build a happy home.
We're grateful for your presence in our lives.
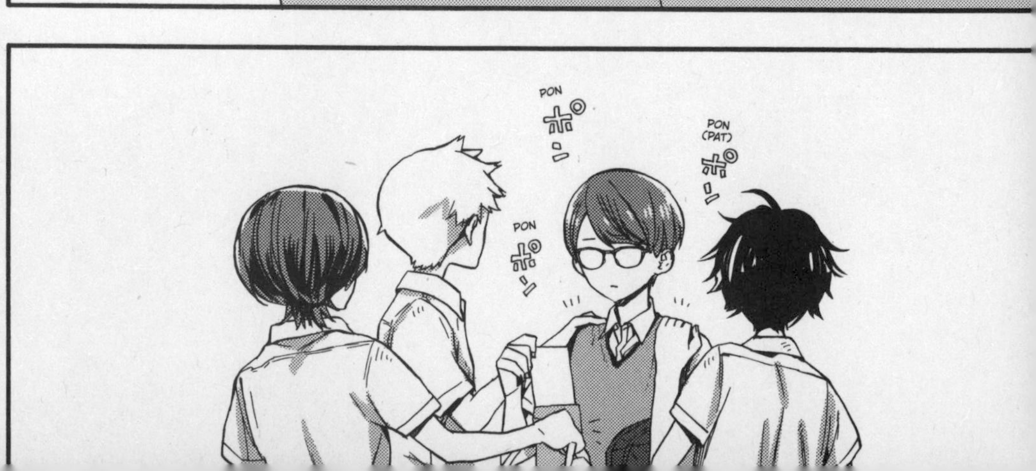
PON (PAT)
PON
PON

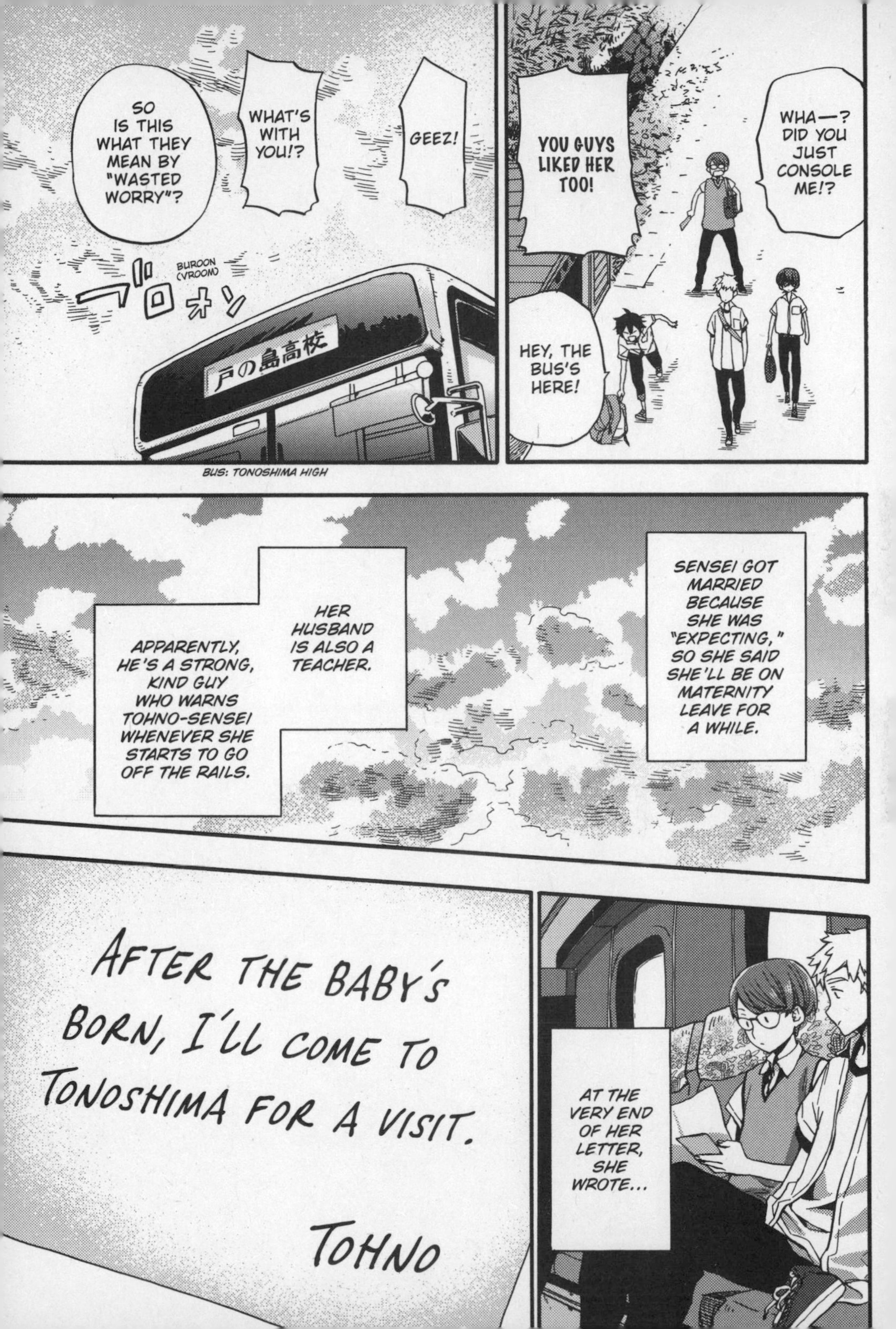
WHA—? DID YOU JUST CONSOLE ME!?
YOU GUYS LIKED HER TOO!
HEY, THE BUS'S HERE!
GEEZ!
WHAT'S WITH YOU!?
SO IS THIS WHAT THEY MEAN BY "WASTED WORRY"?
ブロオン
BUROON (VROOM)
戸の島高校
BUS: TONOSHIMA HIGH
SENSEI GOT MARRIED BECAUSE SHE WAS "EXPECTING," SO SHE SAID SHE'LL BE ON MATERNITY LEAVE FOR A WHILE.
HER HUSBAND IS ALSO A TEACHER.
APPARENTLY, HE'S A STRONG, KIND GUY WHO WARNS TOHNO-SENSEI WHENEVER SHE STARTS TO GO OFF THE RAILS.
AT THE VERY END OF HER LETTER, SHE WROTE...
AFTER THE BABY'S BORN, I'LL COME TO TONOSHIMA FOR A VISIT.
TOHNO

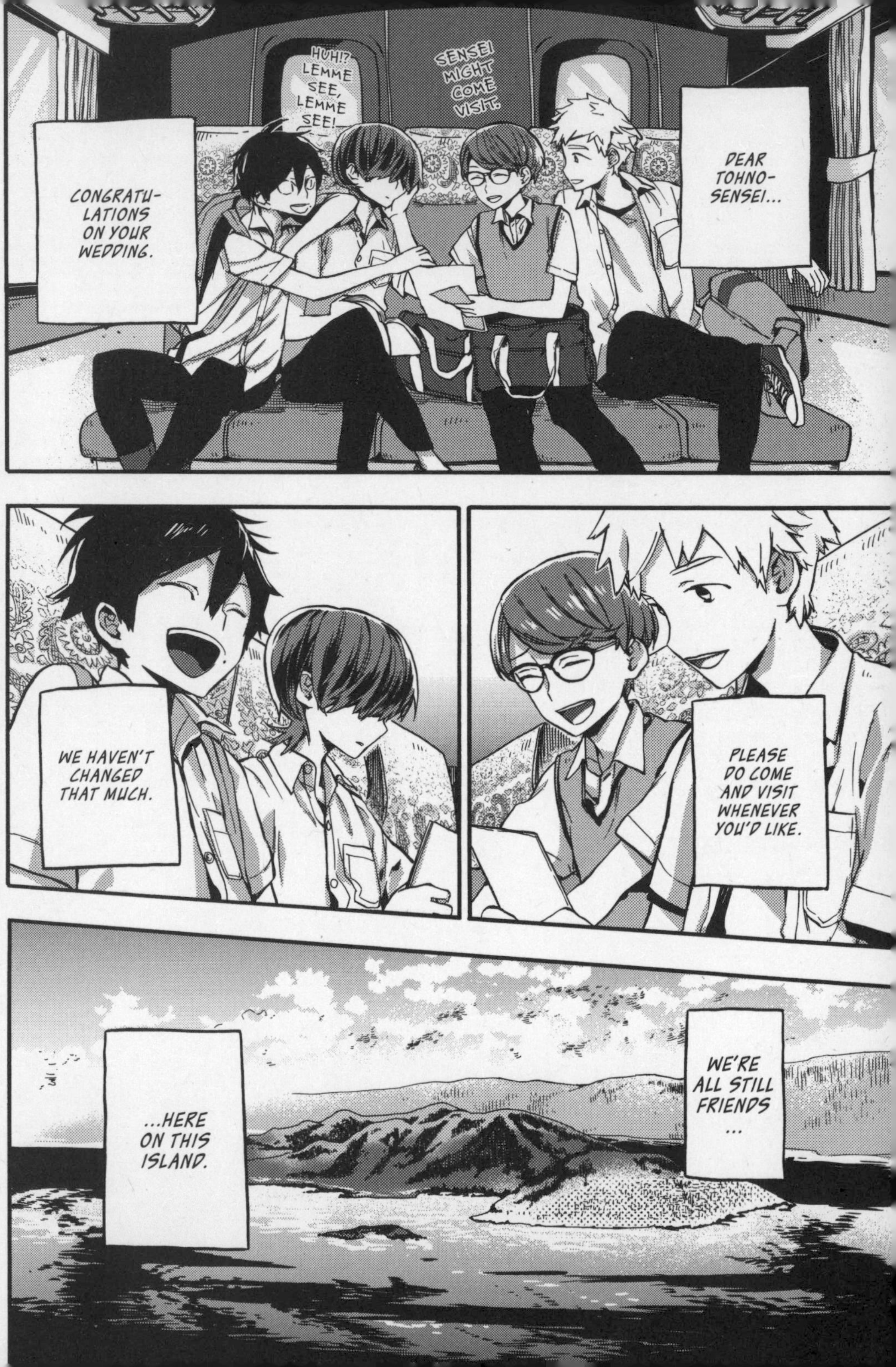
DEAR TOHNO-SENSEI...
SENSEI MIGHT COME VISIT.
HUH!? LEMME SEE, LEMME SEE!
CONGRATULATIONS ON YOUR WEDDING.
PLEASE DO COME AND VISIT WHENEVER YOU'D LIKE.
WE HAVEN'T CHANGED THAT MUCH.
WE'RE ALL STILL FRIENDS...
...HERE ON THIS ISLAND.

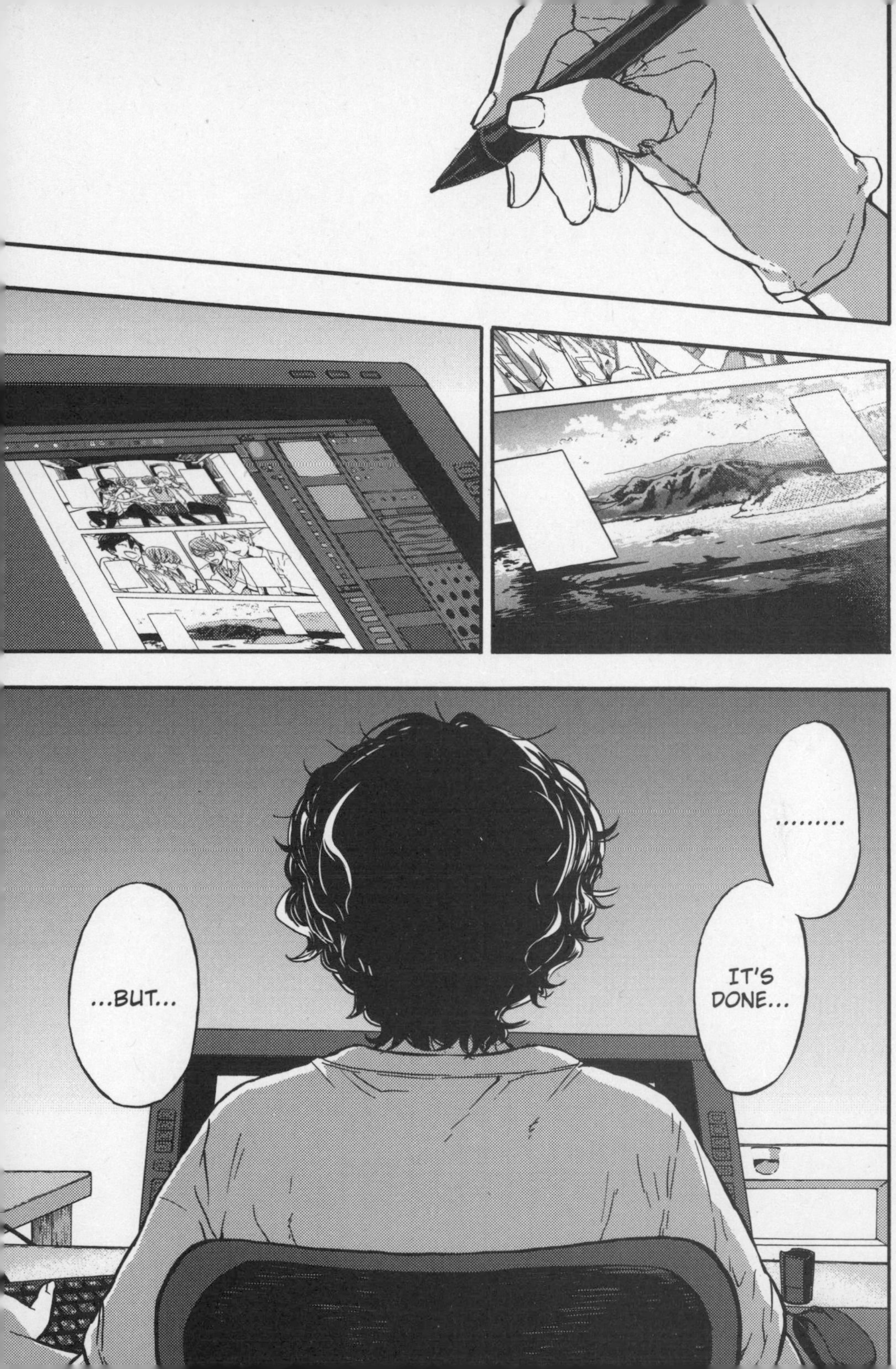
....
IT'S DONE...
...BUT...

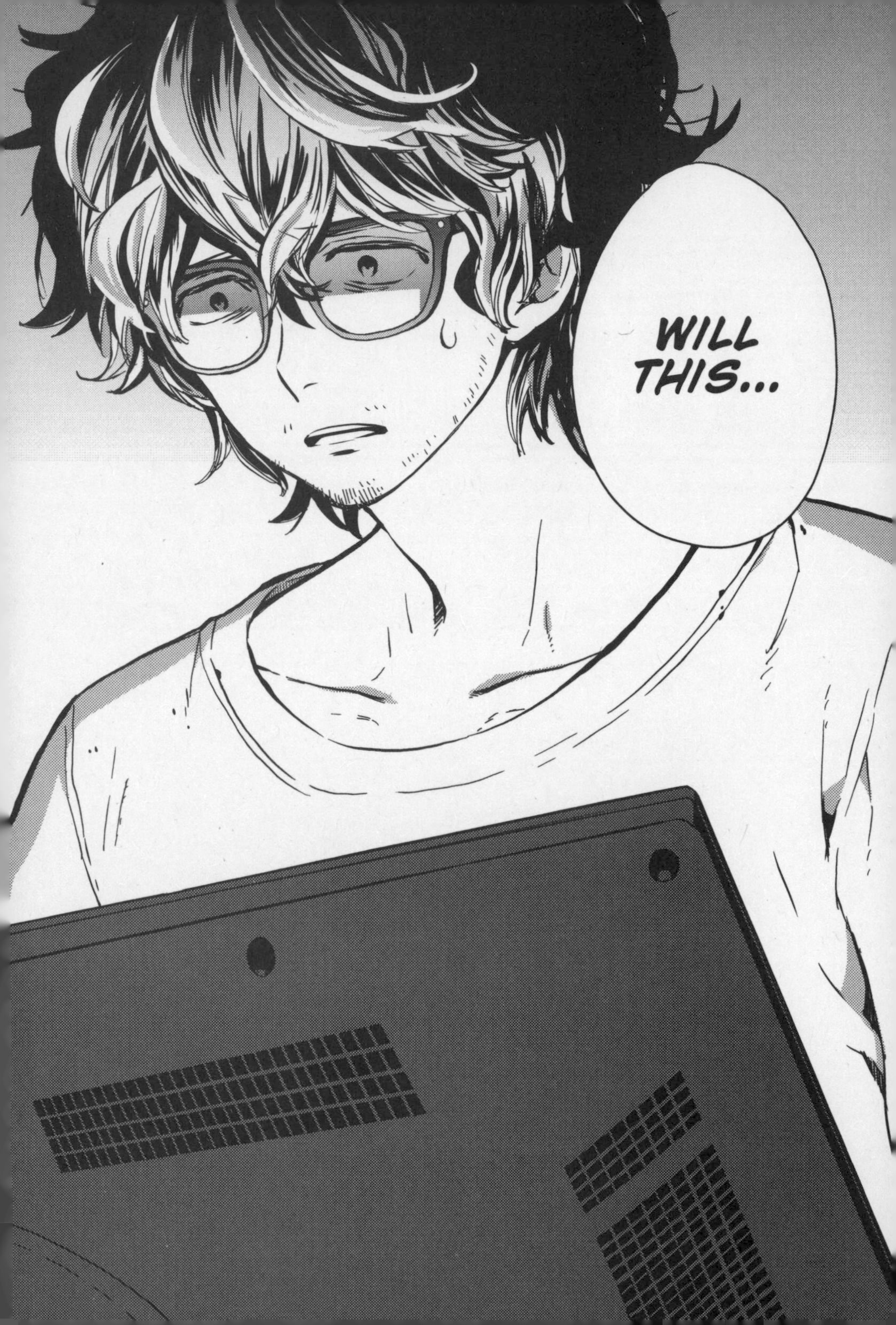
WILL THIS...

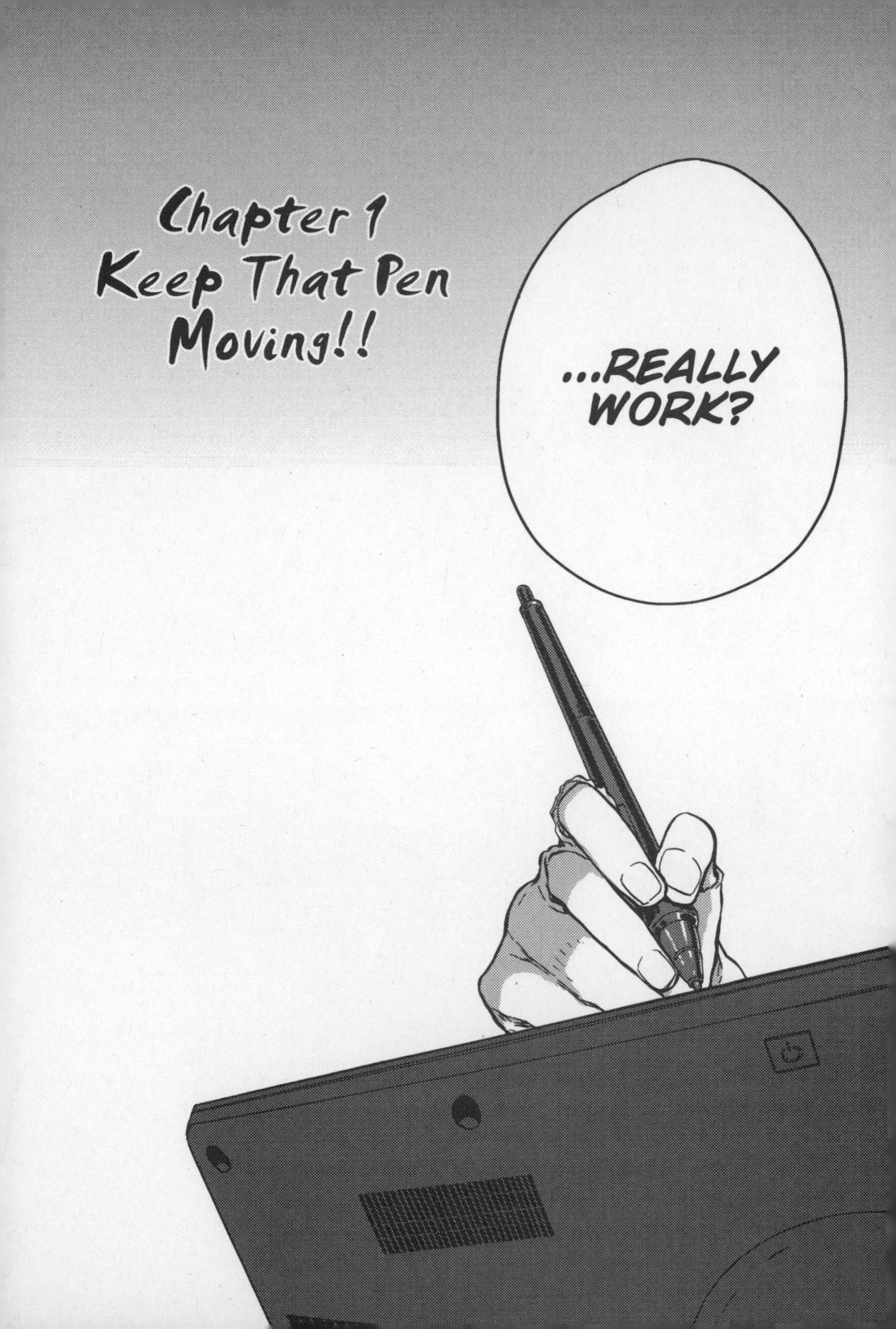
Chapter 1
Keep That Pen Moving!!
...REALLY WORK?

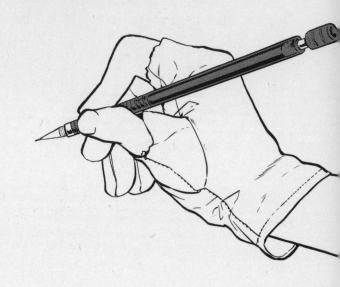

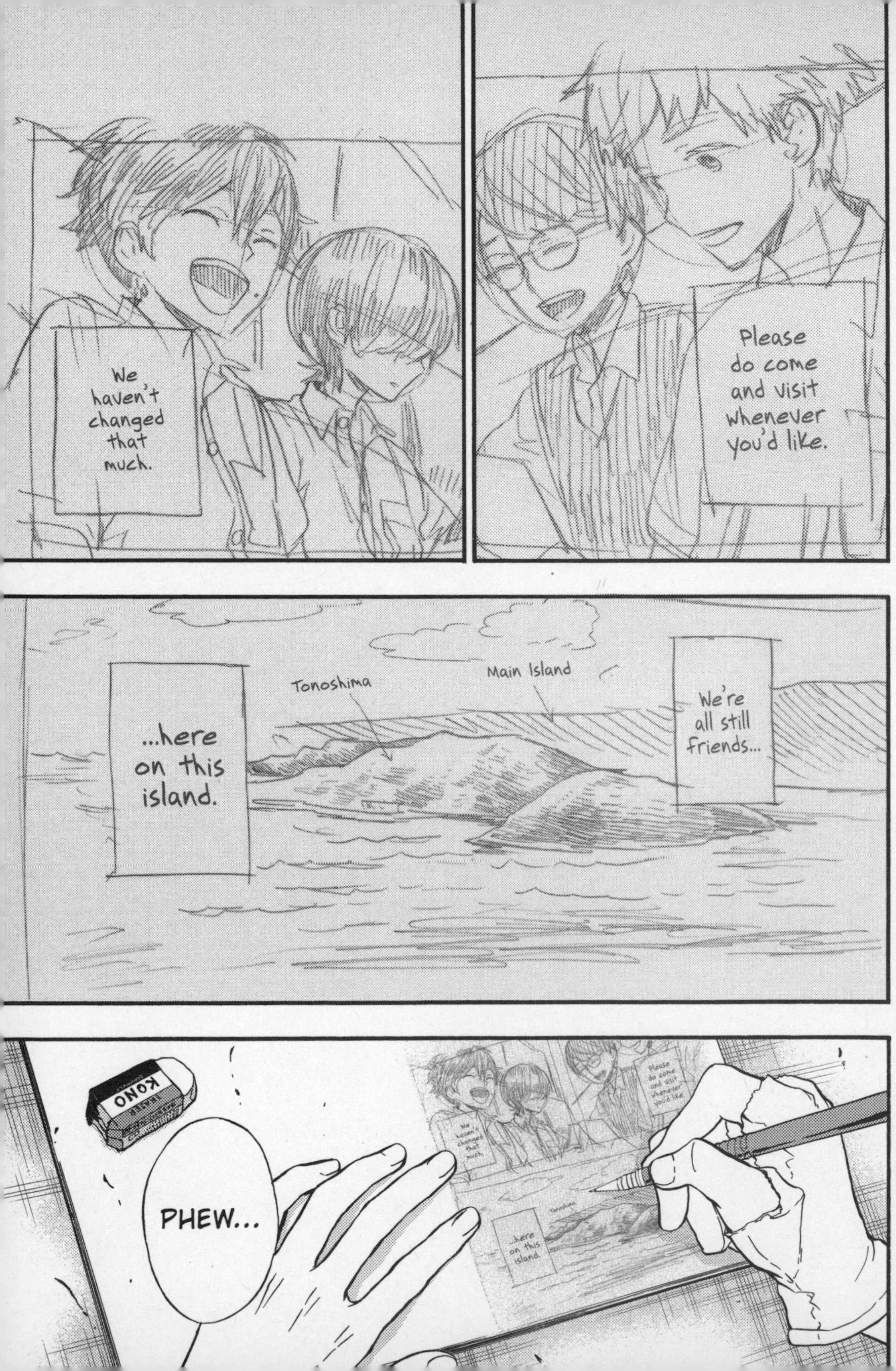
Please do come and visit whenever you'd like.
We haven't changed that much.
We're all still friends...
Main Island
Tonoshima
...here on this island.
KONO
PHEW...

Chapter 2 The Agony and Chaos Until Chapter 1 Is Done

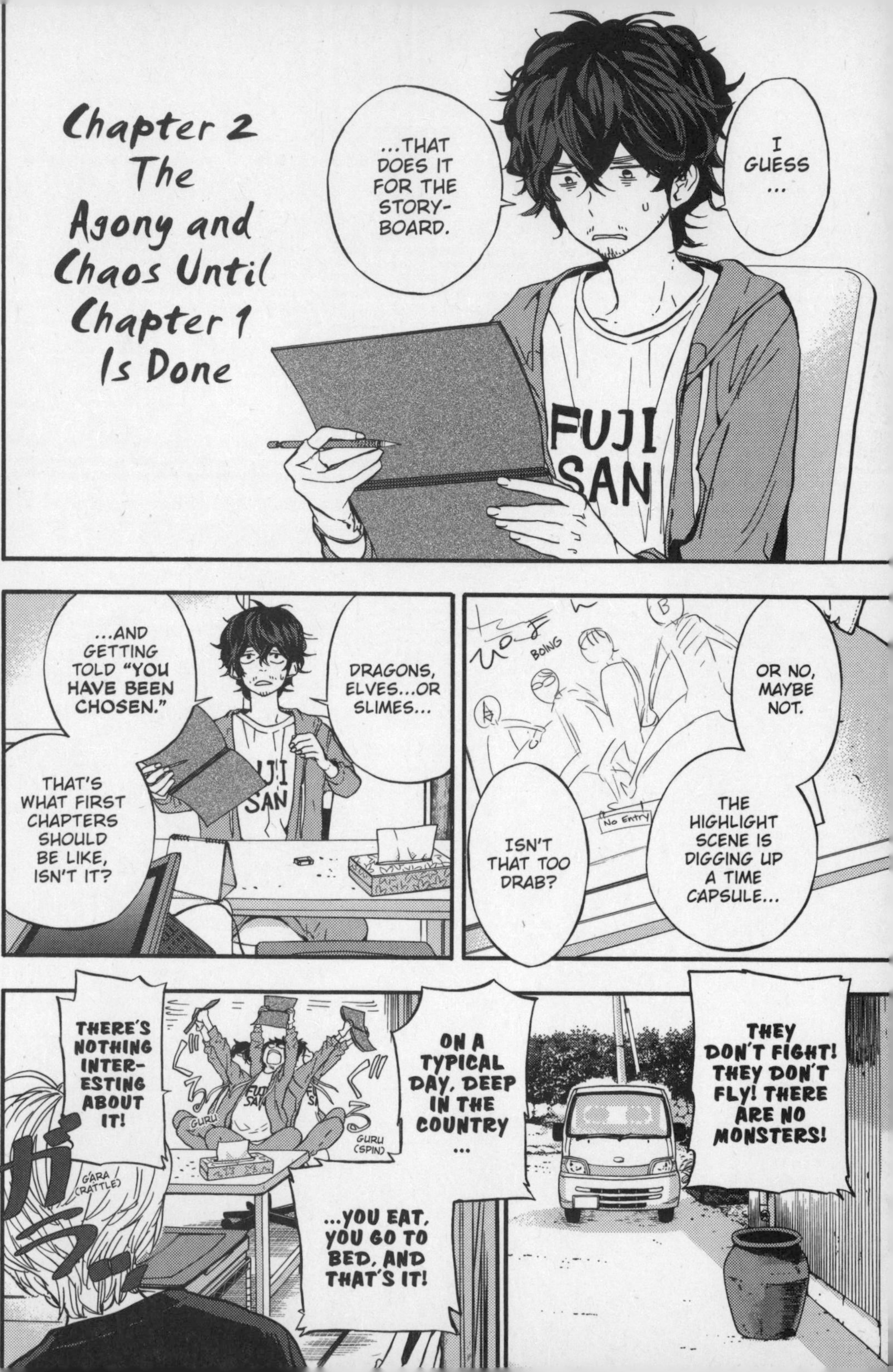
I GUESS...
...THAT DOES IT FOR THE STORY-BOARD.
FUJI SAN
OR NO, MAYBE NOT.
BOING
THE HIGHLIGHT SCENE IS DIGGING UP A TIME CAPSULE...
ISN'T THAT TOO DRAB?
No Entry
DRAGONS, ELVES...OR SLIMES...
...AND GETTING TOLD "YOU HAVE BEEN CHOSEN."
THAT'S WHAT FIRST CHAPTERS SHOULD BE LIKE, ISN'T IT?
THEY DON'T FIGHT! THEY DON'T FLY! THERE ARE NO MONSTERS!
ON A TYPICAL DAY, DEEP IN THE COUNTRY...
...YOU EAT, YOU GO TO BED, AND THAT'S IT!
THERE'S NOTHING INTER-ESTING ABOUT IT!
GURU
GURU (SPIN)
GARA (RATTLE)

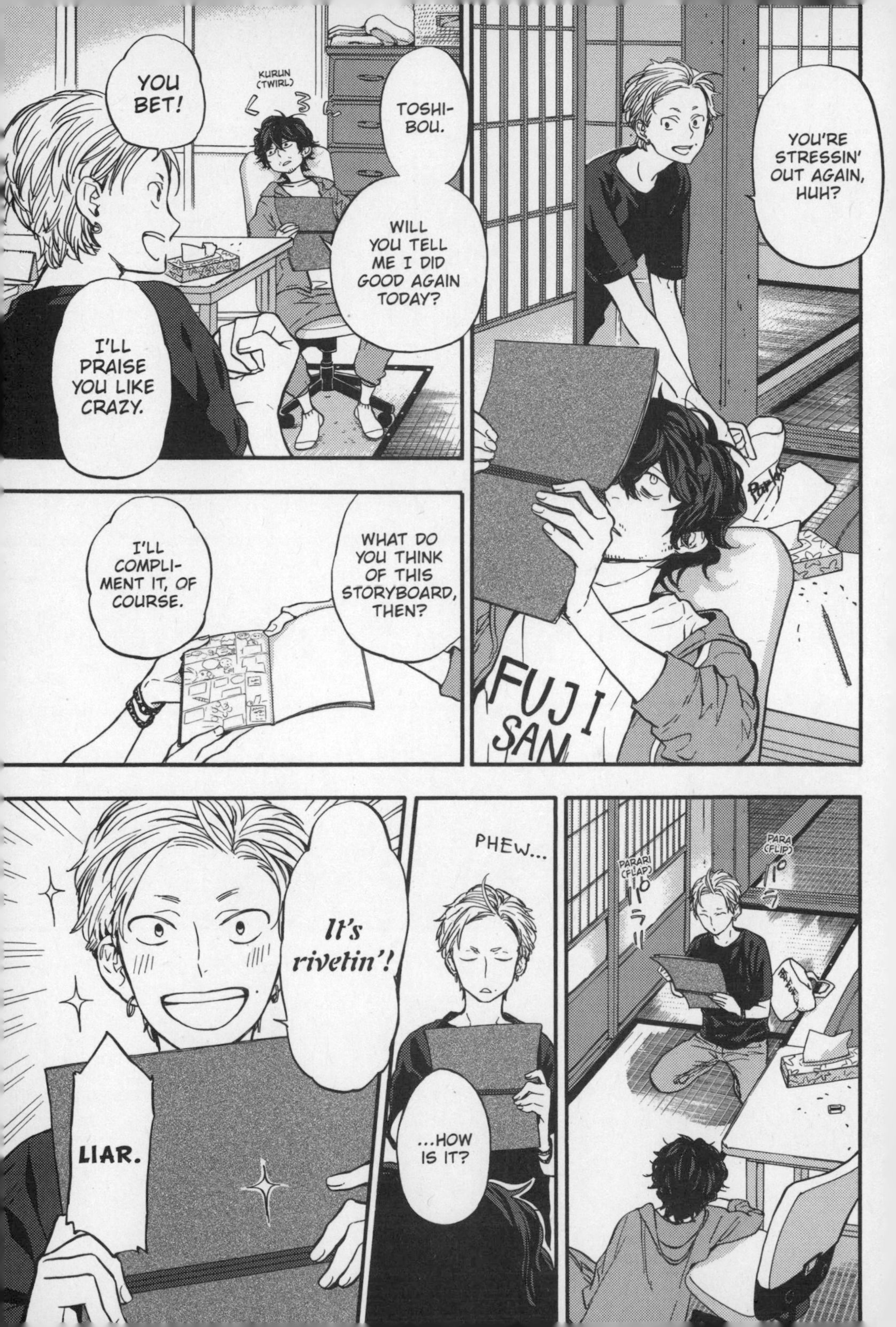
YOU'RE STRESSIN' OUT AGAIN, HUH?
FUJI SAN
TOSHI-BOU.
WILL YOU TELL ME I DID GOOD AGAIN TODAY?
KURUN (TWIRL)
YOU BET!
I'LL PRAISE YOU LIKE CRAZY.
WHAT DO YOU THINK OF THIS STORYBOARD, THEN?
I'LL COMPLIMENT IT, OF COURSE.
PARA (FLIP)
PARARI (FLAP)
PHEW...
...HOW IS IT?
It's rivetin'!
LIAR.

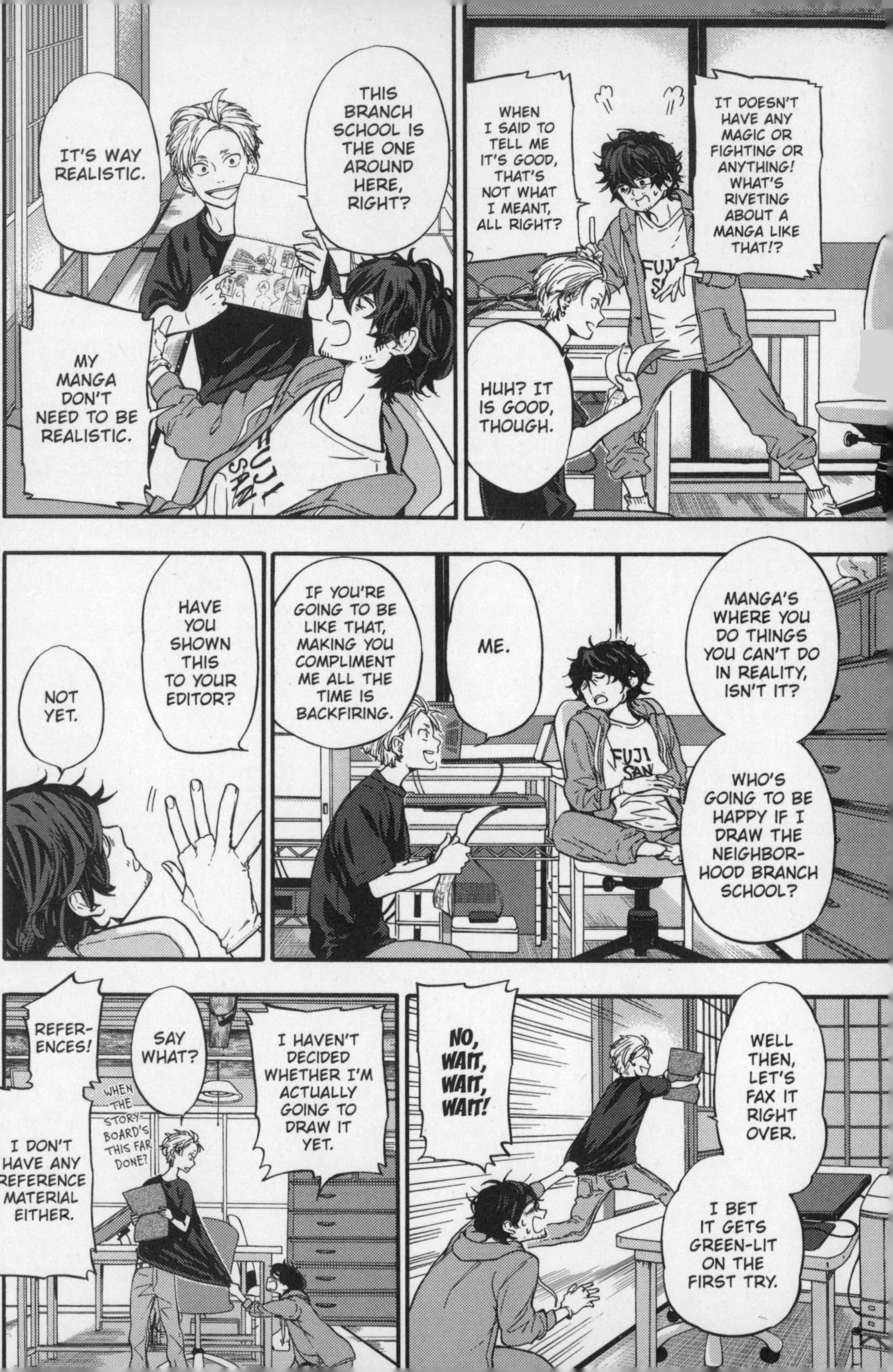
IT DOESN'T HAVE ANY MAGIC OR FIGHTING OR ANYTHING! WHAT'S RIVETING ABOUT A MANGA LIKE THAT!?
WHEN I SAID TO TELL ME IT'S GOOD, THAT'S NOT WHAT I MEANT, ALL RIGHT?
HUH? IT IS GOOD, THOUGH.
THIS BRANCH SCHOOL IS THE ONE AROUND HERE, RIGHT?
IT'S WAY REALISTIC.
MY MANGA DON'T NEED TO BE REALISTIC.
MANGA'S WHERE YOU DO THINGS YOU CAN'T DO IN REALITY, ISN'T IT?
WHO'S GOING TO BE HAPPY IF I DRAW THE NEIGHBOR-HOOD BRANCH SCHOOL?
ME.
IF YOU'RE GOING TO BE LIKE THAT, MAKING YOU COMPLIMENT ME ALL THE TIME IS BACKFIRING.
HAVE YOU SHOWN THIS TO YOUR EDITOR?
NOT YET.
WELL THEN, LET'S FAX IT RIGHT OVER.
I BET IT GETS GREEN-LIT ON THE FIRST TRY.
NO, WAIT, WAIT, WAIT!
I HAVEN'T DECIDED WHETHER I'M ACTUALLY GOING TO DRAW IT YET.
SAY WHAT?
REFER-ENCES!
WHEN THE STORY-BOARD'S THIS FAR DONE?
I DON'T HAVE ANY REFERENCE MATERIAL EITHER.

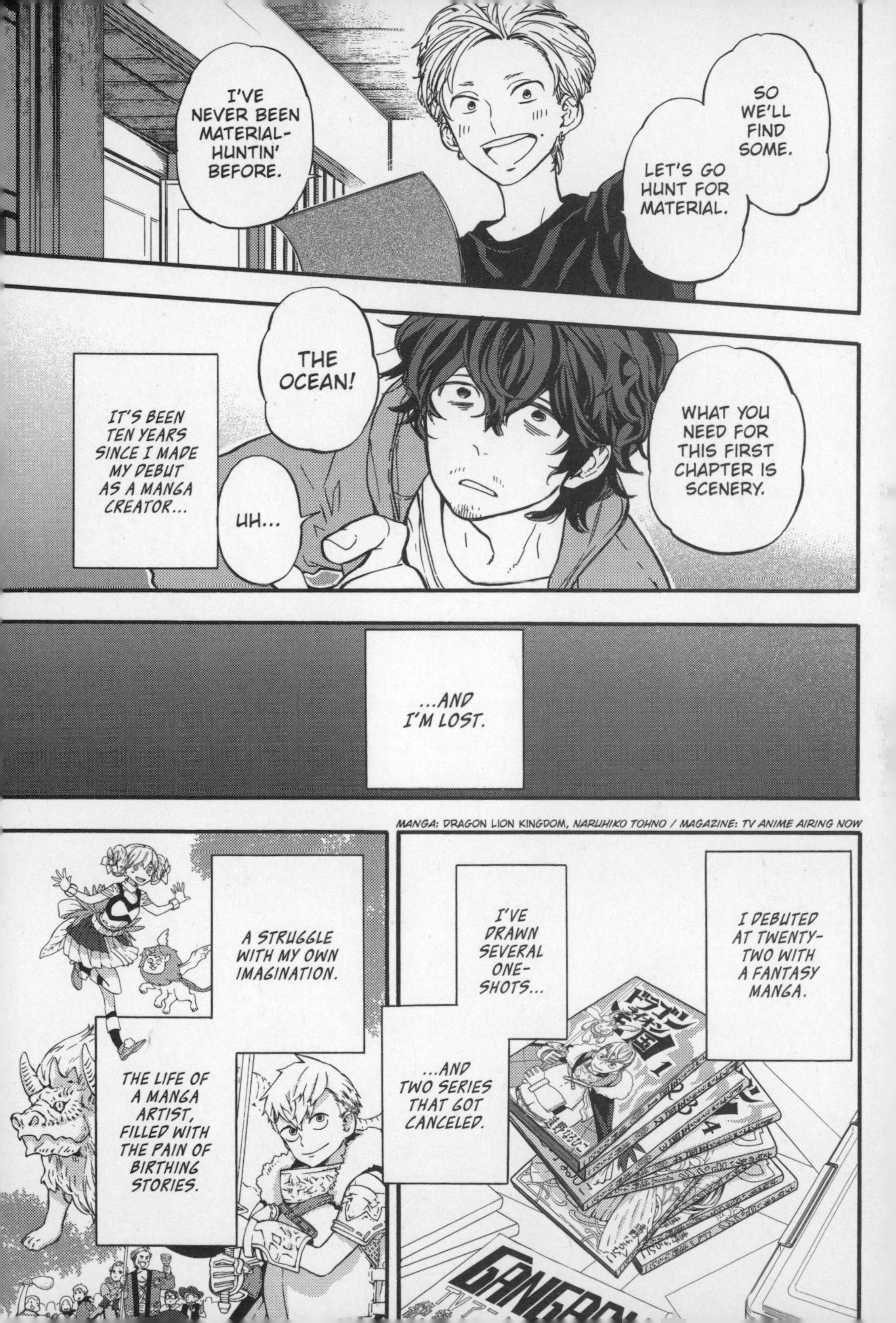
SO WE'LL FIND SOME.
LET'S GO HUNT FOR MATERIAL.
I'VE NEVER BEEN MATERIAL-HUNTIN' BEFORE.
WHAT YOU NEED FOR THIS FIRST CHAPTER IS SCENERY.
THE OCEAN!
UH...
IT'S BEEN TEN YEARS SINCE I MADE MY DEBUT AS A MANGA CREATOR...
...AND I'M LOST.
MANGA: DRAGON LION KINGDOM, NARUHIKO TOHNO / MAGAZINE: TV ANIME AIRING NOW
I DEBUTED AT TWENTY-TWO WITH A FANTASY MANGA.
I'VE DRAWN SEVERAL ONE-SHOTS...
...AND TWO SERIES THAT GOT CANCELED.
A STRUGGLE WITH MY OWN IMAGINATION.
THE LIFE OF A MANGA ARTIST, FILLED WITH THE PAIN OF BIRTHING STORIES.

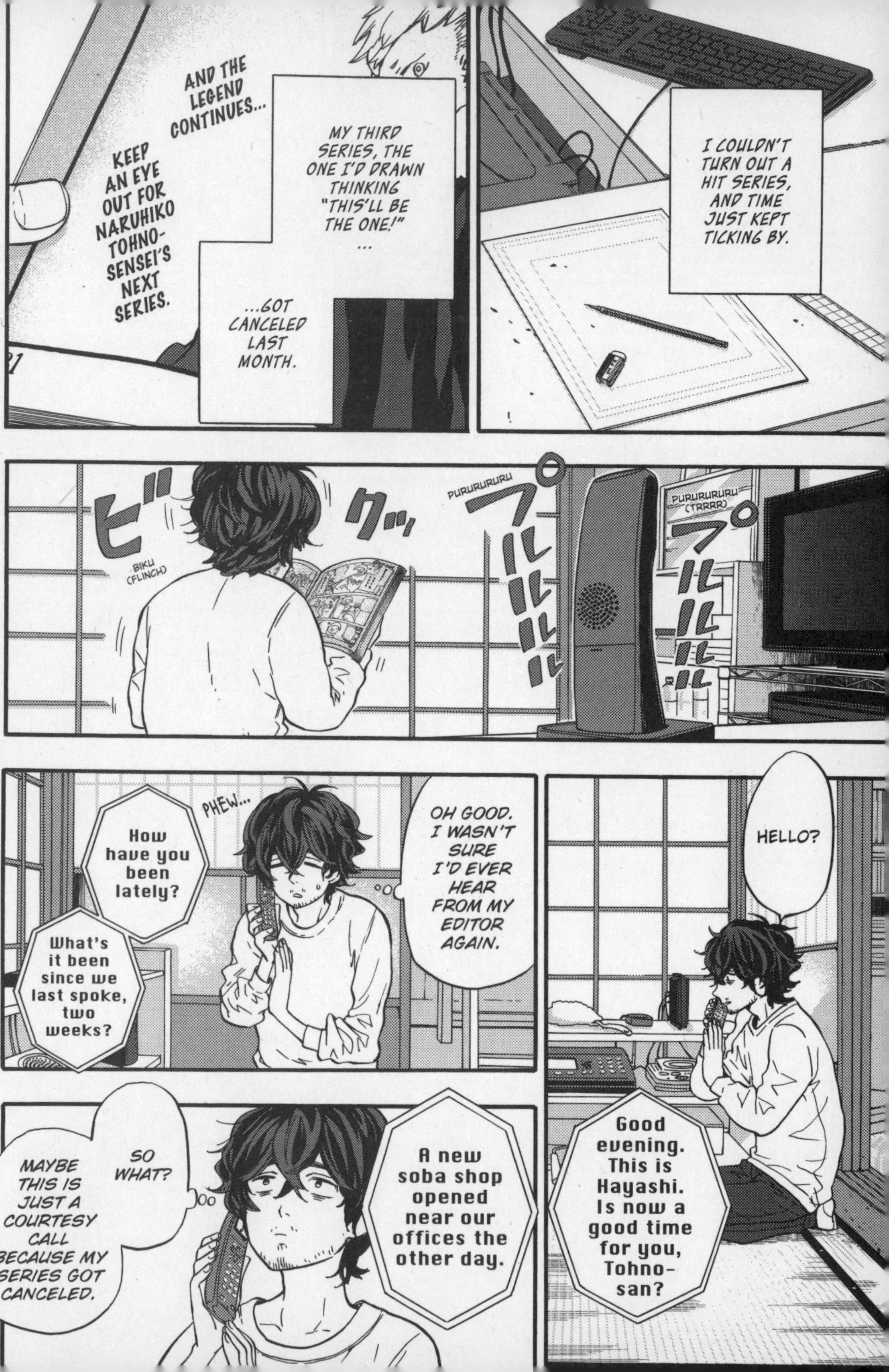
I COULDN'T TURN OUT A HIT SERIES, AND TIME JUST KEPT TICKING BY.
MY THIRD SERIES, THE ONE I'D DRAWN THINKING "THIS'LL BE THE ONE!" ...
...GOT CANCELED LAST MONTH.
AND THE LEGEND CONTINUES...
KEEP AN EYE OUT FOR NARUHIKO TOHNO-SENSEI'S NEXT SERIES.
プルルルル
PURURURURU (TRRRR)
プルルルル
PURURURURU
グッ
ビ
BIKU (FLINCH)
HELLO?
Good evening. This is Hayashi. Is now a good time for you, Tohno-san?
OH GOOD. I WASN'T SURE I'D EVER HEAR FROM MY EDITOR AGAIN.
PHEW...
How have you been lately?
What's it been since we last spoke, two weeks?
A new soba shop opened near our offices the other day.
SO WHAT?
MAYBE THIS IS JUST A COURTESY CALL BECAUSE MY SERIES GOT CANCELED.

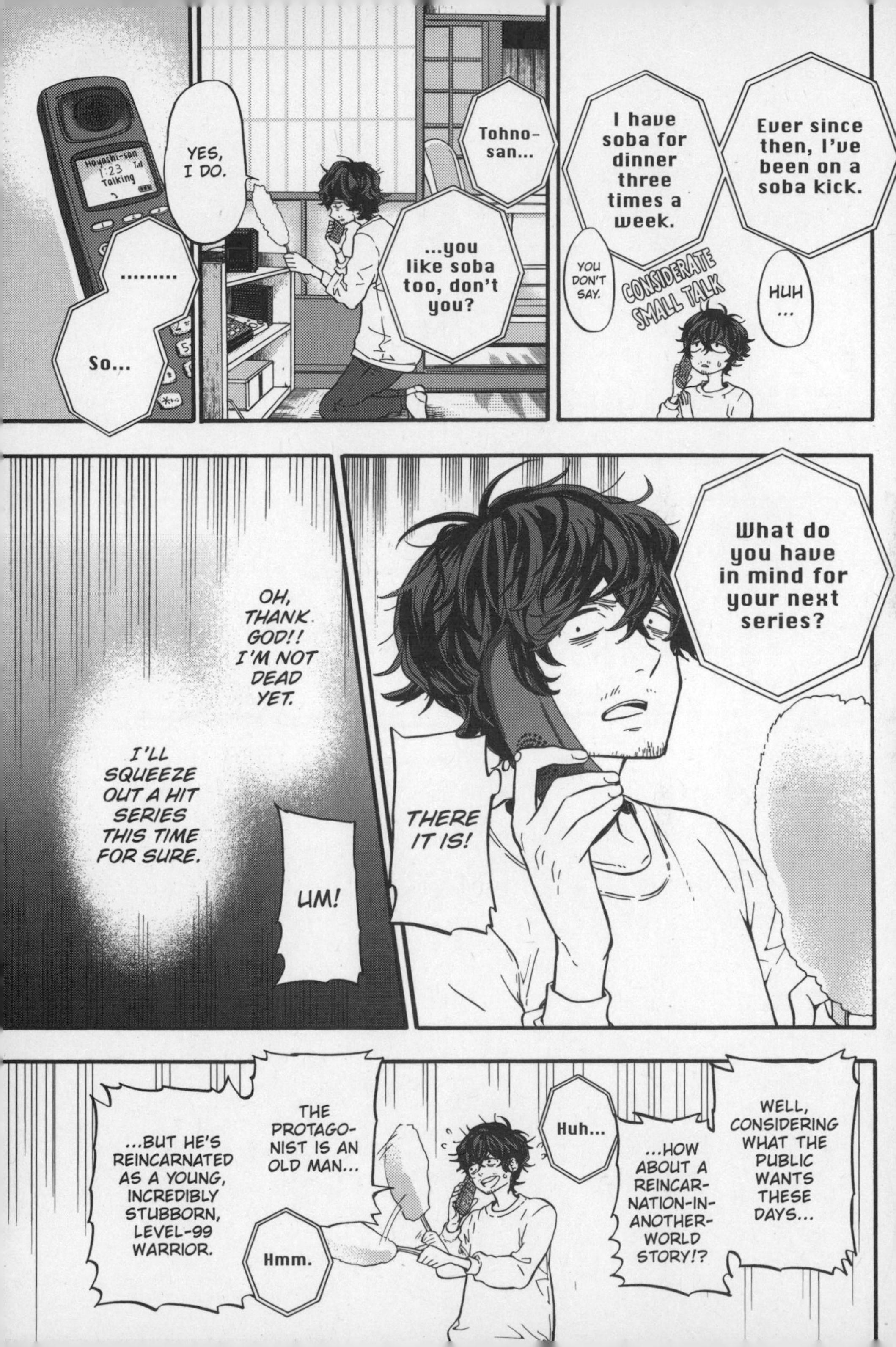
Ever since then, I've been on a soba kick.
I have soba for dinner three times a week.
HUH...
CONSIDERATE SMALL TALK
YOU DON'T SAY.
Tohno-san...
...you like soba too, don't you?
YES, I DO.
Hayashi-san 1:23 Talking
....
So...
What do you have in mind for your next series?
THERE IT IS!
UM!
OH, THANK GOD!! I'M NOT DEAD YET.
I'LL SQUEEZE OUT A HIT SERIES THIS TIME FOR SURE.
WELL, CONSIDERING WHAT THE PUBLIC WANTS THESE DAYS...
Huh...
...HOW ABOUT A REINCARNATION-IN-ANOTHER-WORLD STORY!?
THE PROTAGONIST IS AN OLD MAN...
Hmm.
...BUT HE'S REINCARNATED AS A YOUNG, INCREDIBLY STUBBORN, LEVEL-99 WARRIOR.

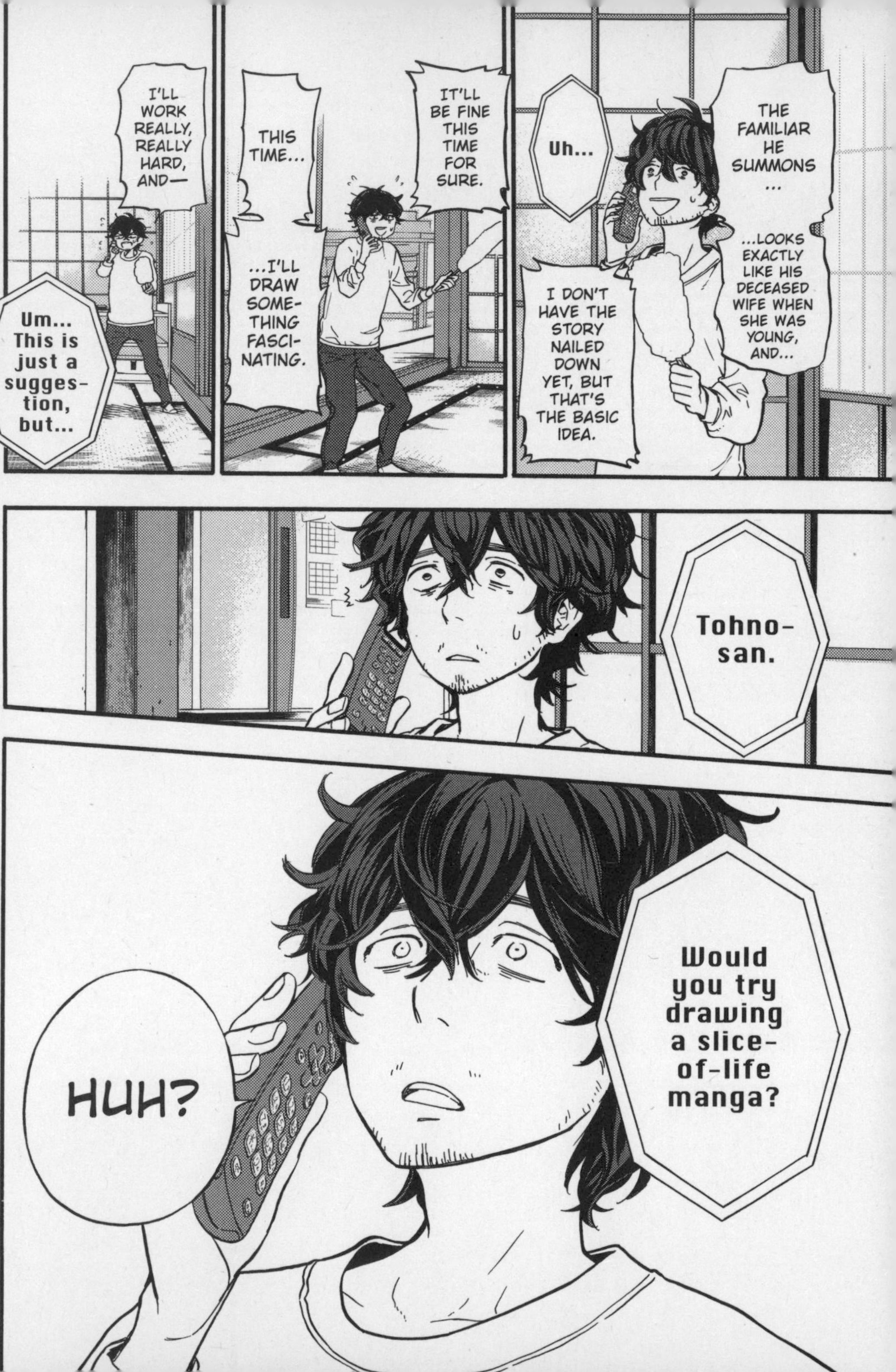
THE FAMILIAR HE SUMMONS ...
...LOOKS EXACTLY LIKE HIS DECEASED WIFE WHEN SHE WAS YOUNG, AND...
Uh...
I DON'T HAVE THE STORY NAILED DOWN YET, BUT THAT'S THE BASIC IDEA.
IT'LL BE FINE THIS TIME FOR SURE.
THIS TIME...
...I'LL DRAW SOMETHING FASCINATING.
I'LL WORK REALLY, REALLY HARD, AND—
Um... This is just a suggestion, but...
Tohno-san.
Would you try drawing a slice-of-life manga?
HUH?

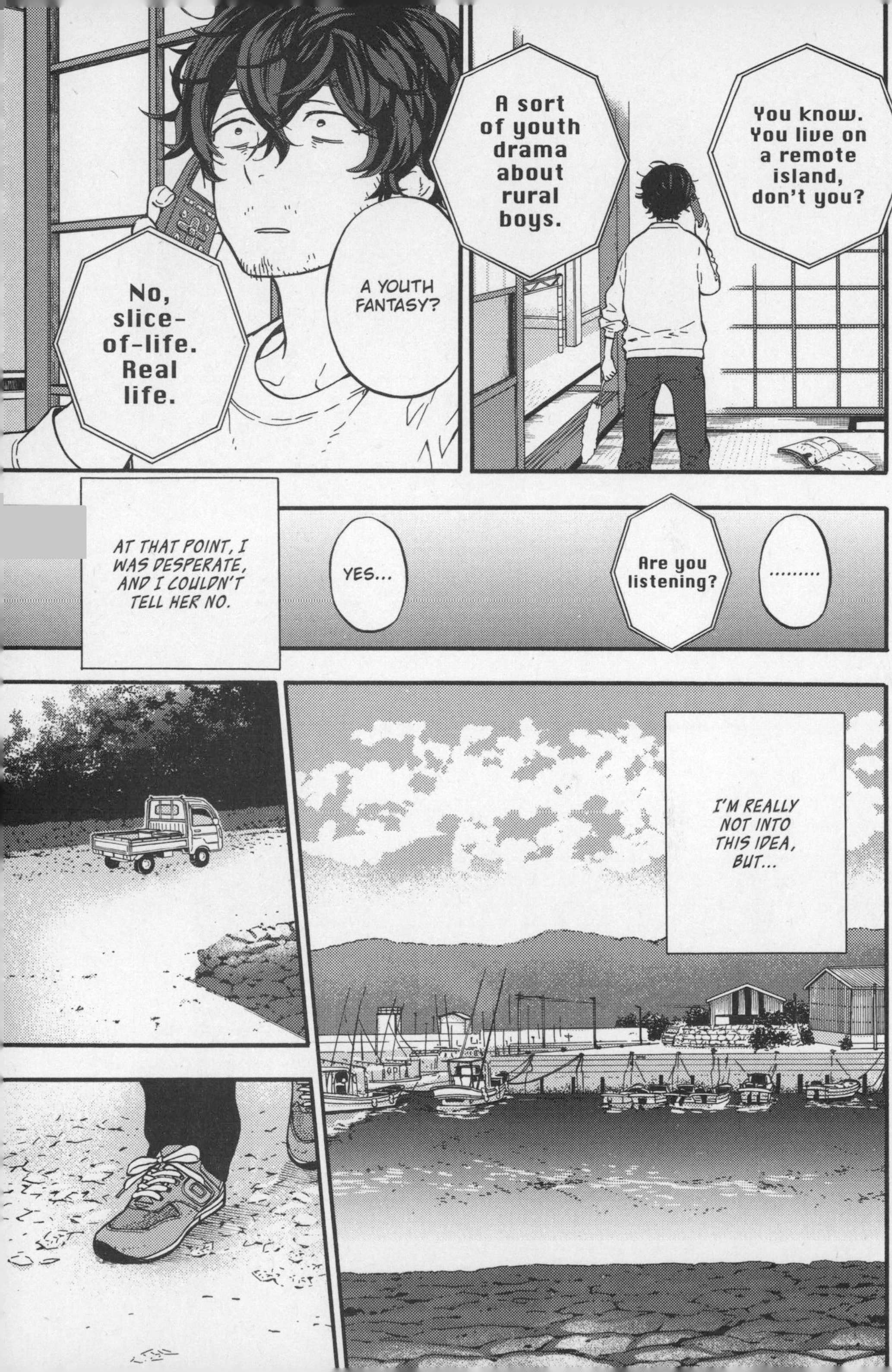
You know. You live on a remote island, don't you?
A sort of youth drama about rural boys.
A YOUTH FANTASY?
No, slice-of-life. Real life.
....
Are you listening?
YES...
AT THAT POINT, I WAS DESPERATE, AND I COULDN'T TELL HER NO.
I'M REALLY NOT INTO THIS IDEA, BUT...

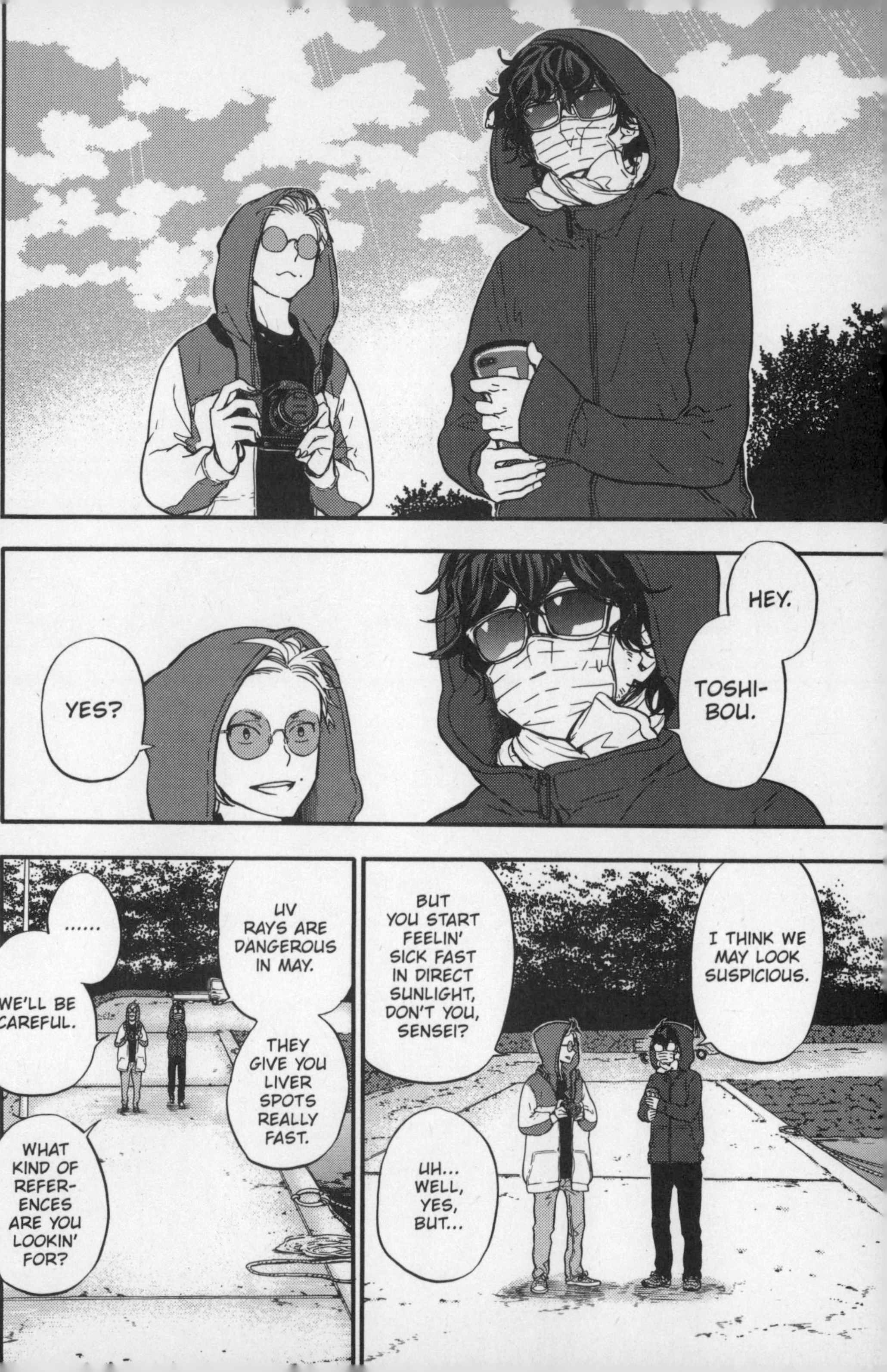
HEY.
TOSHI-BOU.
YES?
I THINK WE MAY LOOK SUSPICIOUS.
BUT YOU START FEELIN' SICK FAST IN DIRECT SUNLIGHT, DON'T YOU, SENSEI?
UH... WELL, YES, BUT...
UV RAYS ARE DANGEROUS IN MAY.
THEY GIVE YOU LIVER SPOTS REALLY FAST.
......
WE'LL BE CAREFUL.
WHAT KIND OF REFERENCES ARE YOU LOOKIN' FOR?

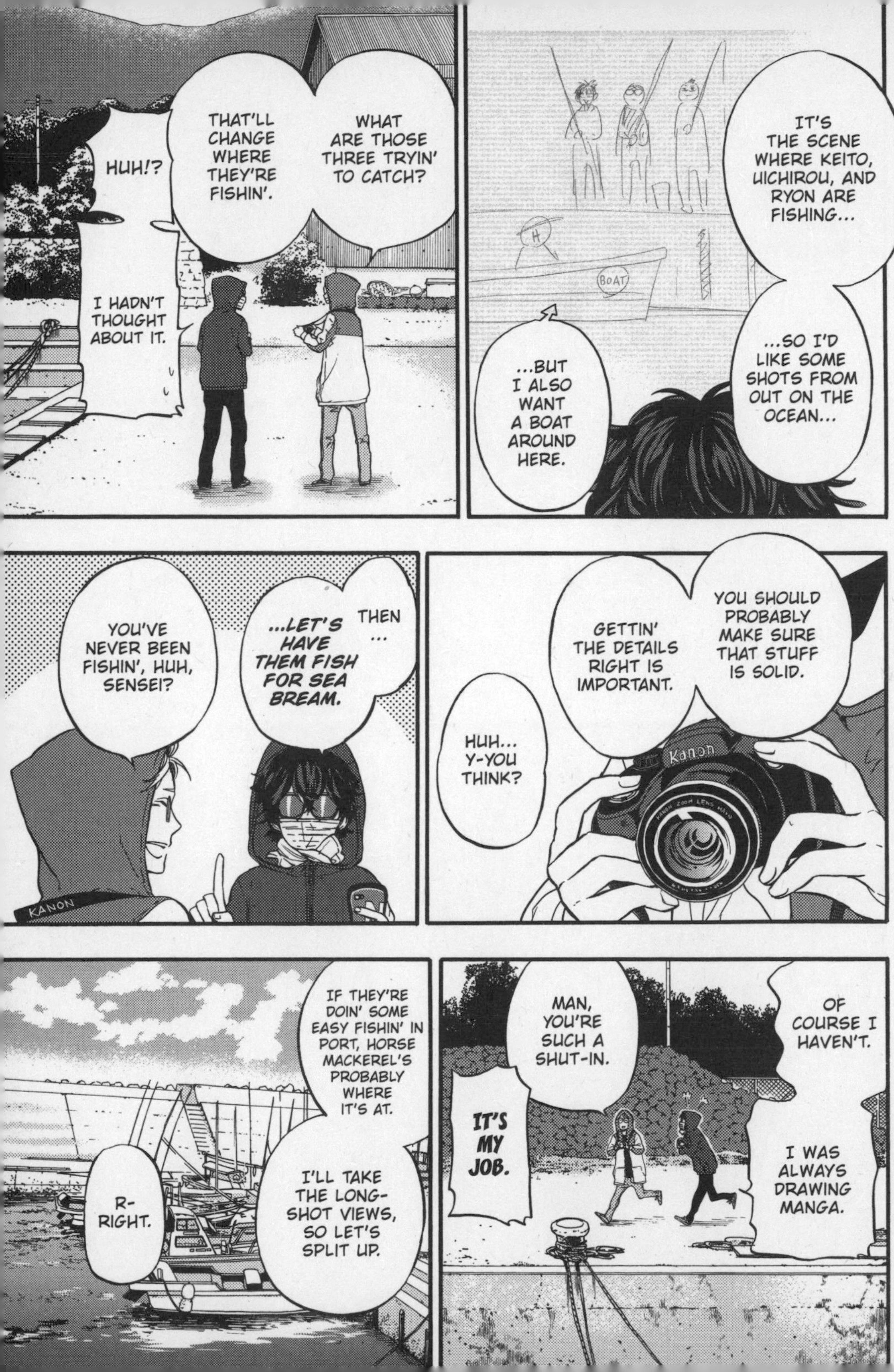
IT'S THE SCENE WHERE KEITO, UICHIROU, AND RYON ARE FISHING...
...SO I'D LIKE SOME SHOTS FROM OUT ON THE OCEAN...
...BUT I ALSO WANT A BOAT AROUND HERE.
BOAT
WHAT ARE THOSE THREE TRYIN' TO CATCH?
THAT'LL CHANGE WHERE THEY'RE FISHIN'.
HUH!?
I HADN'T THOUGHT ABOUT IT.
YOU SHOULD PROBABLY MAKE SURE THAT STUFF IS SOLID.
GETTIN' THE DETAILS RIGHT IS IMPORTANT.
HUH... Y-YOU THINK?
Kanon
THEN ...
...LET'S HAVE THEM FISH FOR SEA BREAM.
YOU'VE NEVER BEEN FISHIN', HUH, SENSEI?
KANON
OF COURSE I HAVEN'T.
I WAS ALWAYS DRAWING MANGA.
MAN, YOU'RE SUCH A SHUT-IN.
IT'S MY JOB.
IF THEY'RE DOIN' SOME EASY FISHIN' IN PORT, HORSE MACKEREL'S PROBABLY WHERE IT'S AT.
I'LL TAKE THE LONG-SHOT VIEWS, SO LET'S SPLIT UP.
R-RIGHT.

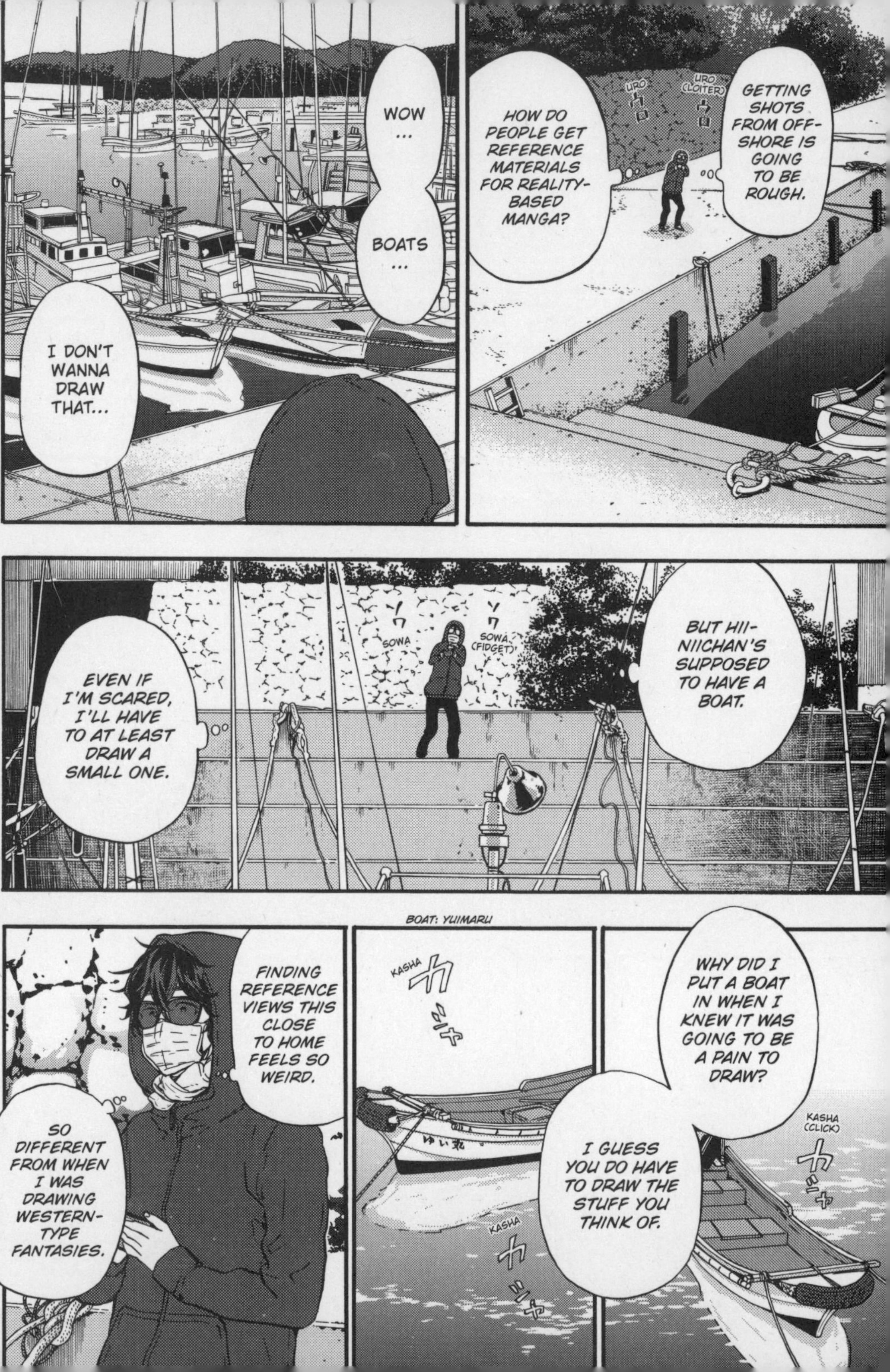

GETTING SHOTS FROM OFF-SHORE IS GOING TO BE ROUGH.
URO (LOITER)
URO
HOW DO PEOPLE GET REFERENCE MATERIALS FOR REALITY-BASED MANGA?
WOW ... BOATS ...
I DON'T WANNA DRAW THAT...
BUT HII-NIICHAN'S SUPPOSED TO HAVE A BOAT.
SOWA (FIDGET)
SOWA
EVEN IF I'M SCARED, I'LL HAVE TO AT LEAST DRAW A SMALL ONE.
WHY DID I PUT A BOAT IN WHEN I KNEW IT WAS GOING TO BE A PAIN TO DRAW?
KASHA (CLICK)
I GUESS YOU DO HAVE TO DRAW THE STUFF YOU THINK OF.
BOAT: YUIMARU
KASHA
KASHA
FINDING REFERENCE VIEWS THIS CLOSE TO HOME FEELS SO WEIRD.
SO DIFFERENT FROM WHEN I WAS DRAWING WESTERN-TYPE FANTASIES.

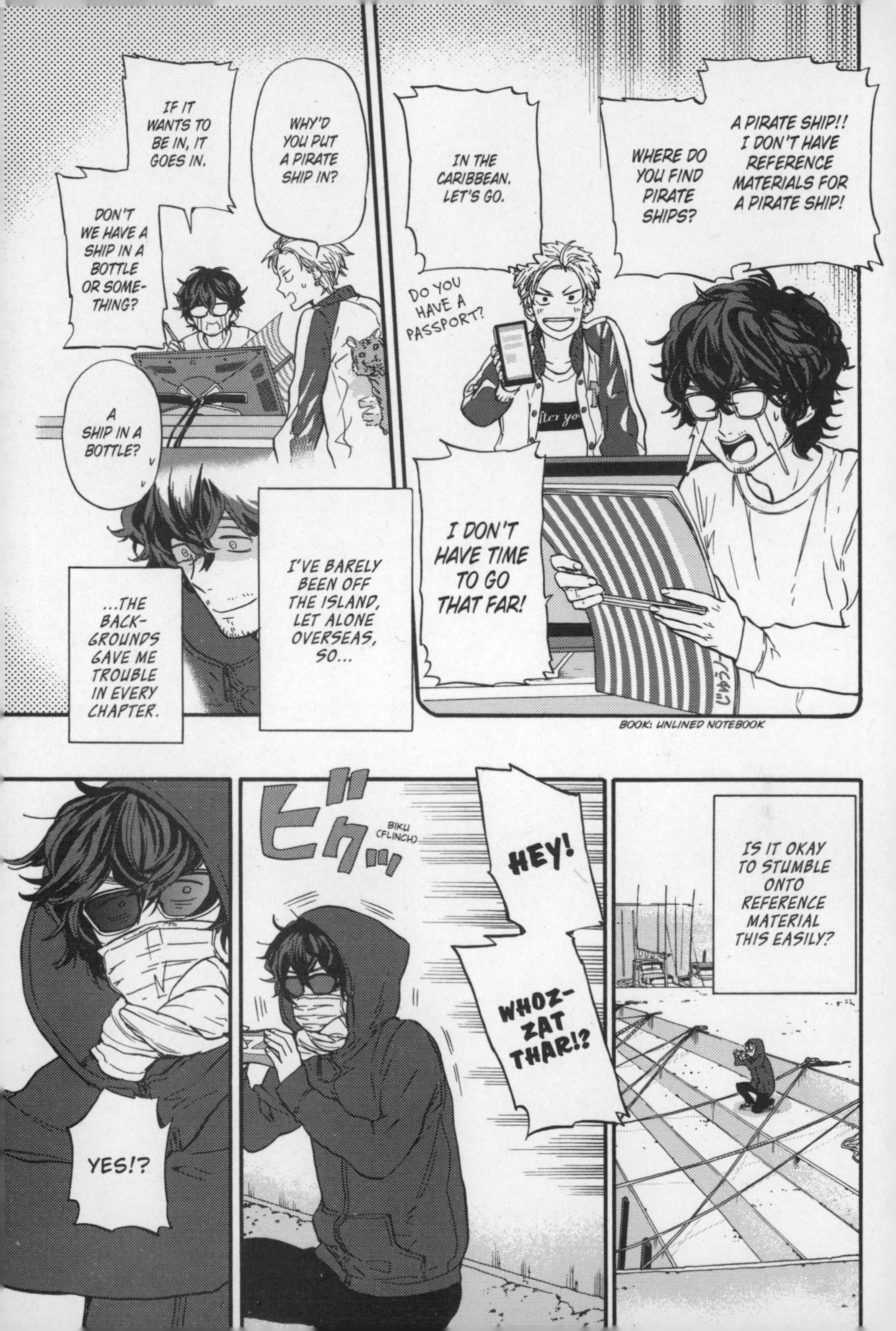
A PIRATE SHIP!! I DON'T HAVE REFERENCE MATERIALS FOR A PIRATE SHIP!
WHERE DO YOU FIND PIRATE SHIPS?
IN THE CARIBBEAN. LET'S GO.
DO YOU HAVE A PASSPORT?
I DON'T HAVE TIME TO GO THAT FAR!
BOOK: UNLINED NOTEBOOK
WHY'D YOU PUT A PIRATE SHIP IN?
IF IT WANTS TO BE IN, IT GOES IN.
DON'T WE HAVE A SHIP IN A BOTTLE OR SOME-THING?
A SHIP IN A BOTTLE?
I'VE BARELY BEEN OFF THE ISLAND, LET ALONE OVERSEAS, SO...
...THE BACK-GROUNDS GAVE ME TROUBLE IN EVERY CHAPTER.
IS IT OKAY TO STUMBLE ONTO REFERENCE MATERIAL THIS EASILY?
HEY!
WHOZ-ZAT THAR!?
ビクッ
BIKU (FLINCH)
YES!?

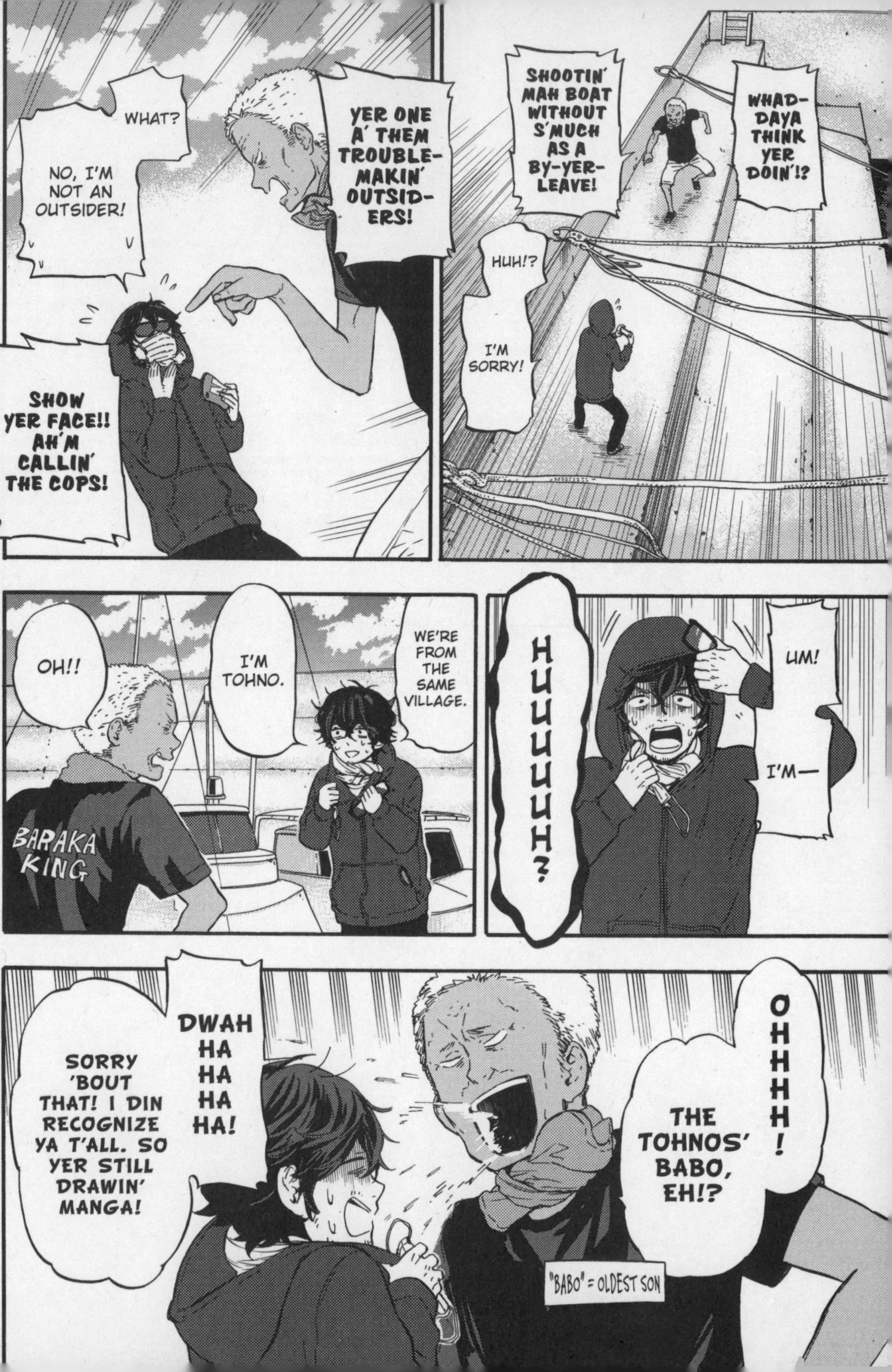
WHAD-DAYA THINK YER DOIN'!?
SHOOTIN' MAH BOAT WITHOUT S'MUCH AS A BY-YER-LEAVE!
HUH!?
I'M SORRY!
YER ONE A' THEM TROUBLE-MAKIN' OUTSID-ERS!
WHAT?
NO, I'M NOT AN OUTSIDER!
SHOW YER FACE!! AH'M CALLIN' THE COPS!
UM!
I'M—
HUUUUUUH?
WE'RE FROM THE SAME VILLAGE.
I'M TOHNO.
OH!!
BARAKA KING
OHHHH!
THE TOHNOS' BABO, EH!?
DWAH HA HA HA HA!
SORRY 'BOUT THAT! I DIN RECOGNIZE YA T'ALL. SO YER STILL DRAWIN' MANGA!
"BABO" = OLDEST SON

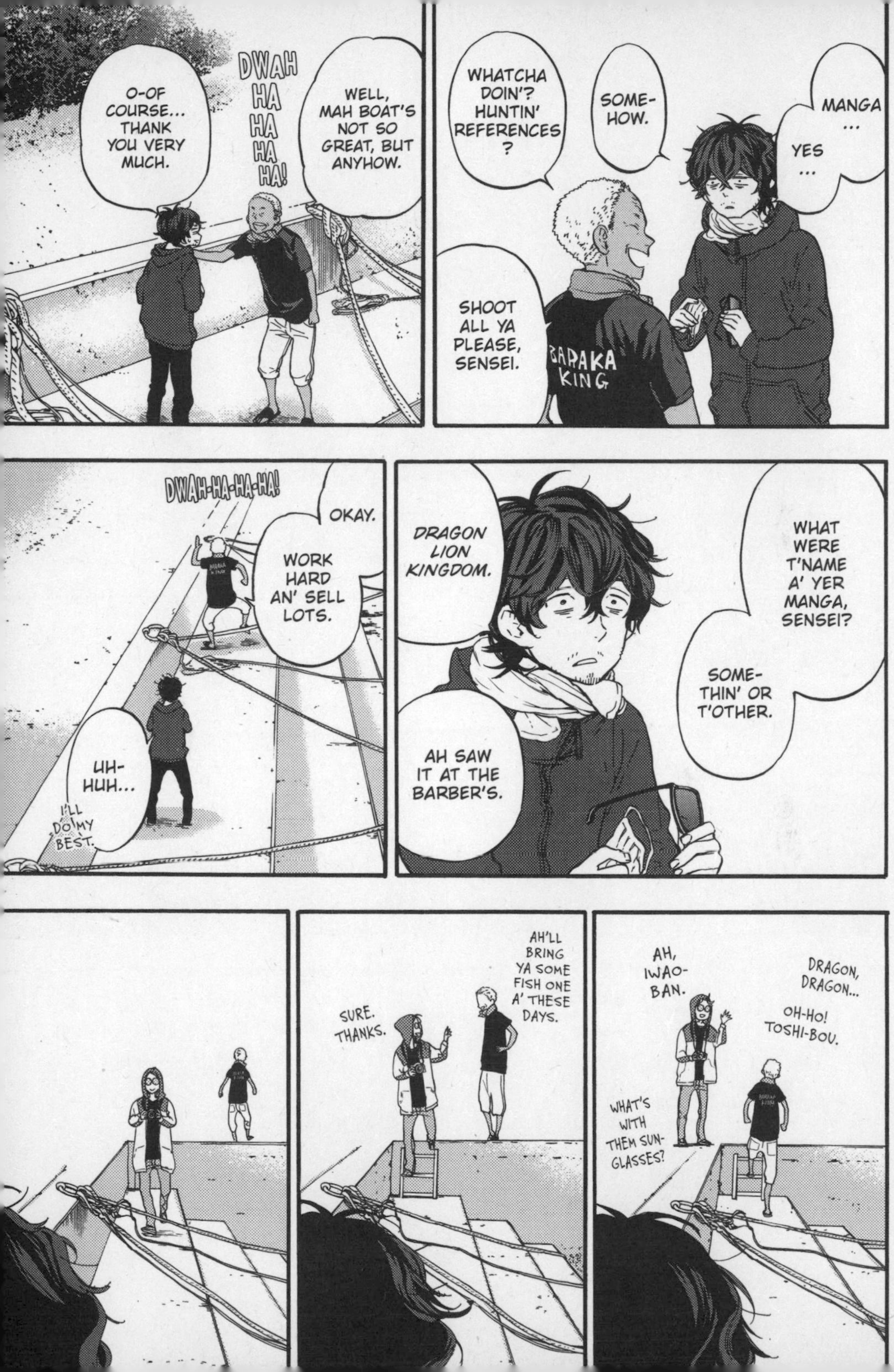
MANGA ... YES ...
SOME-HOW.
WHATCHA DOIN'? HUNTIN' REFERENCES?
SHOOT ALL YA PLEASE, SENSEI.
BARAKA KING
WELL, MAH BOAT'S NOT SO GREAT, BUT ANYHOW.
DWAH HA HA HA HA!
O-OF COURSE... THANK YOU VERY MUCH.
WHAT WERE T'NAME A' YER MANGA, SENSEI?
SOME-THIN' OR T'OTHER.
DRAGON LION KINGDOM.
AH SAW IT AT THE BARBER'S.
OKAY.
WORK HARD AN' SELL LOTS.
DWAH-HA-HA-HA!
UH-HUH...
I'LL DO MY BEST.
DRAGON, DRAGON...
OH-HO! TOSHI-BOU.
AH, IWAO-BAN.
WHAT'S WITH THEM SUN-GLASSES?
AH'LL BRING YA SOME FISH ONE A' THESE DAYS.
SURE. THANKS.

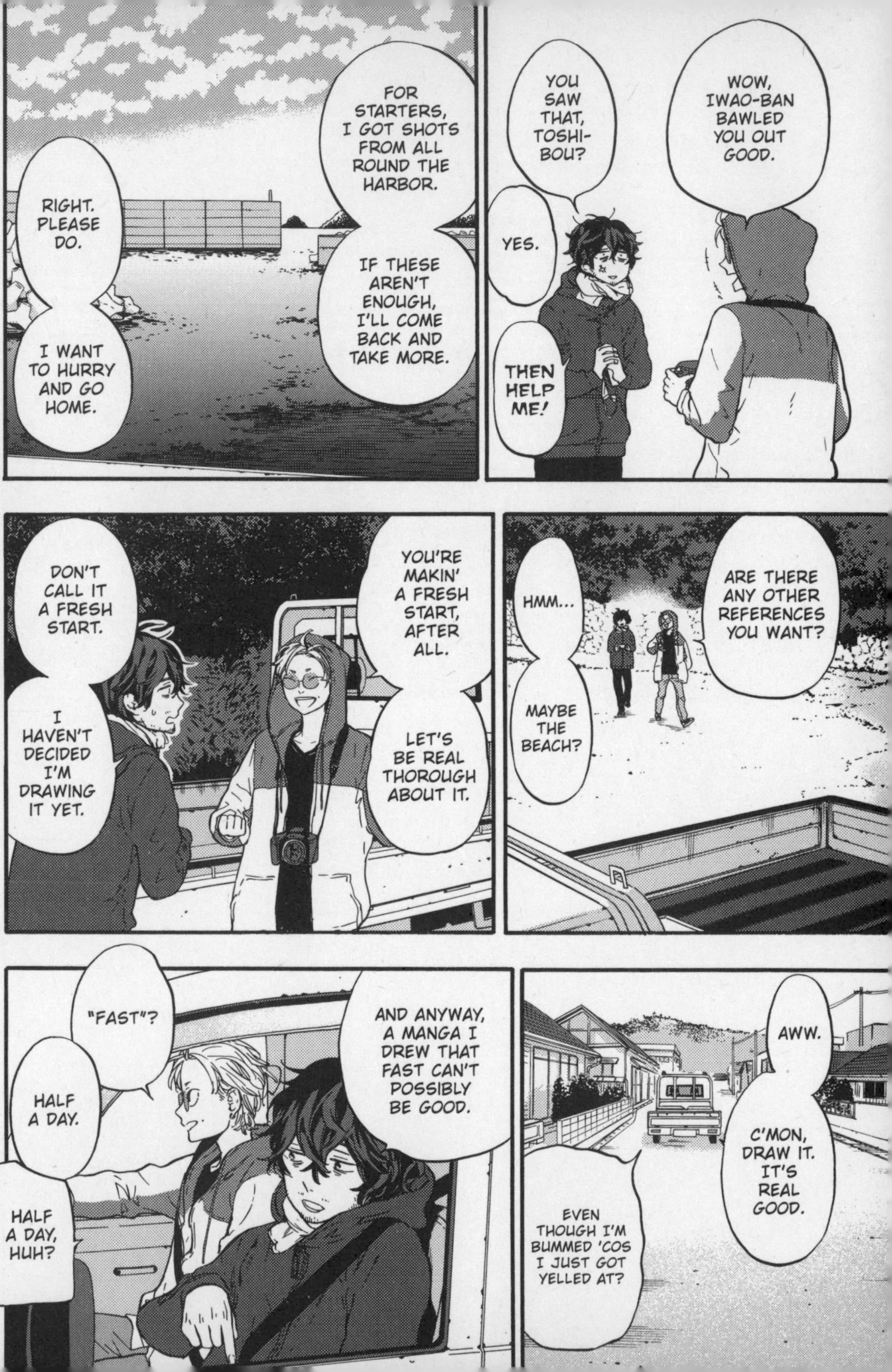
WOW, IWAO-BAN BAWLED YOU OUT GOOD.
YOU SAW THAT, TOSHI-BOU?
YES.
THEN HELP ME!
FOR STARTERS, I GOT SHOTS FROM ALL ROUND THE HARBOR.
IF THESE AREN'T ENOUGH, I'LL COME BACK AND TAKE MORE.
RIGHT. PLEASE DO.
I WANT TO HURRY AND GO HOME.
ARE THERE ANY OTHER REFERENCES YOU WANT?
HMM...
MAYBE THE BEACH?
YOU'RE MAKIN' A FRESH START, AFTER ALL.
LET'S BE REAL THOROUGH ABOUT IT.
DON'T CALL IT A FRESH START.
I HAVEN'T DECIDED I'M DRAWING IT YET.
AWW.
C'MON, DRAW IT. IT'S REAL GOOD.
EVEN THOUGH I'M BUMMED 'COS I JUST GOT YELLED AT?
AND ANYWAY, A MANGA I DREW THAT FAST CAN'T POSSIBLY BE GOOD.
"FAST"?
HALF A DAY.
HALF A DAY, HUH?

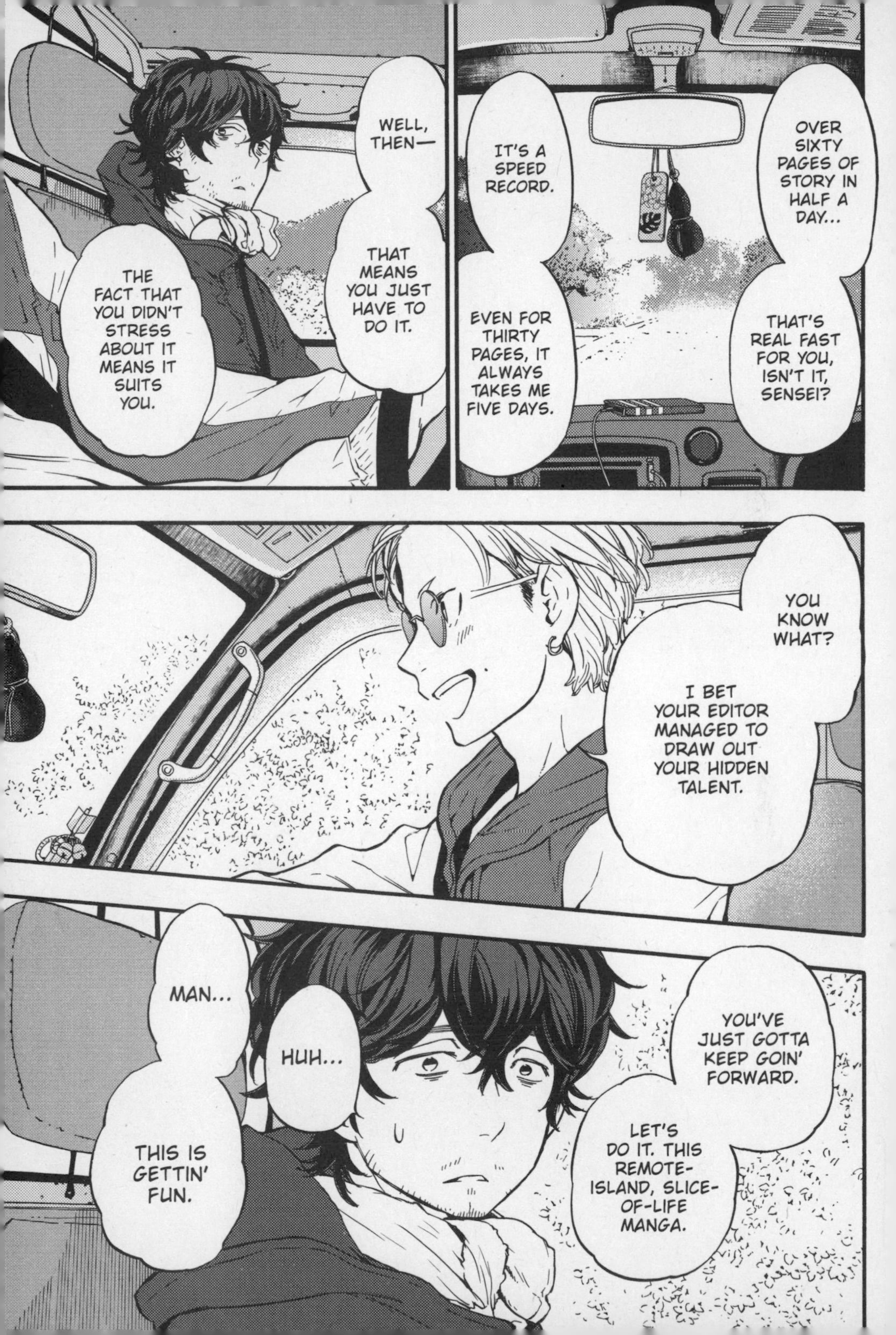
OVER SIXTY PAGES OF STORY IN HALF A DAY...
THAT'S REAL FAST FOR YOU, ISN'T IT, SENSEI?
IT'S A SPEED RECORD.
EVEN FOR THIRTY PAGES, IT ALWAYS TAKES ME FIVE DAYS.
WELL, THEN—
THAT MEANS YOU JUST HAVE TO DO IT.
THE FACT THAT YOU DIDN'T STRESS ABOUT IT MEANS IT SUITS YOU.
YOU KNOW WHAT?
I BET YOUR EDITOR MANAGED TO DRAW OUT YOUR HIDDEN TALENT.
YOU'VE JUST GOTTA KEEP GOIN' FORWARD.
LET'S DO IT. THIS REMOTE-ISLAND, SLICE-OF-LIFE MANGA.
HUH...
MAN...
THIS IS GETTIN' FUN.

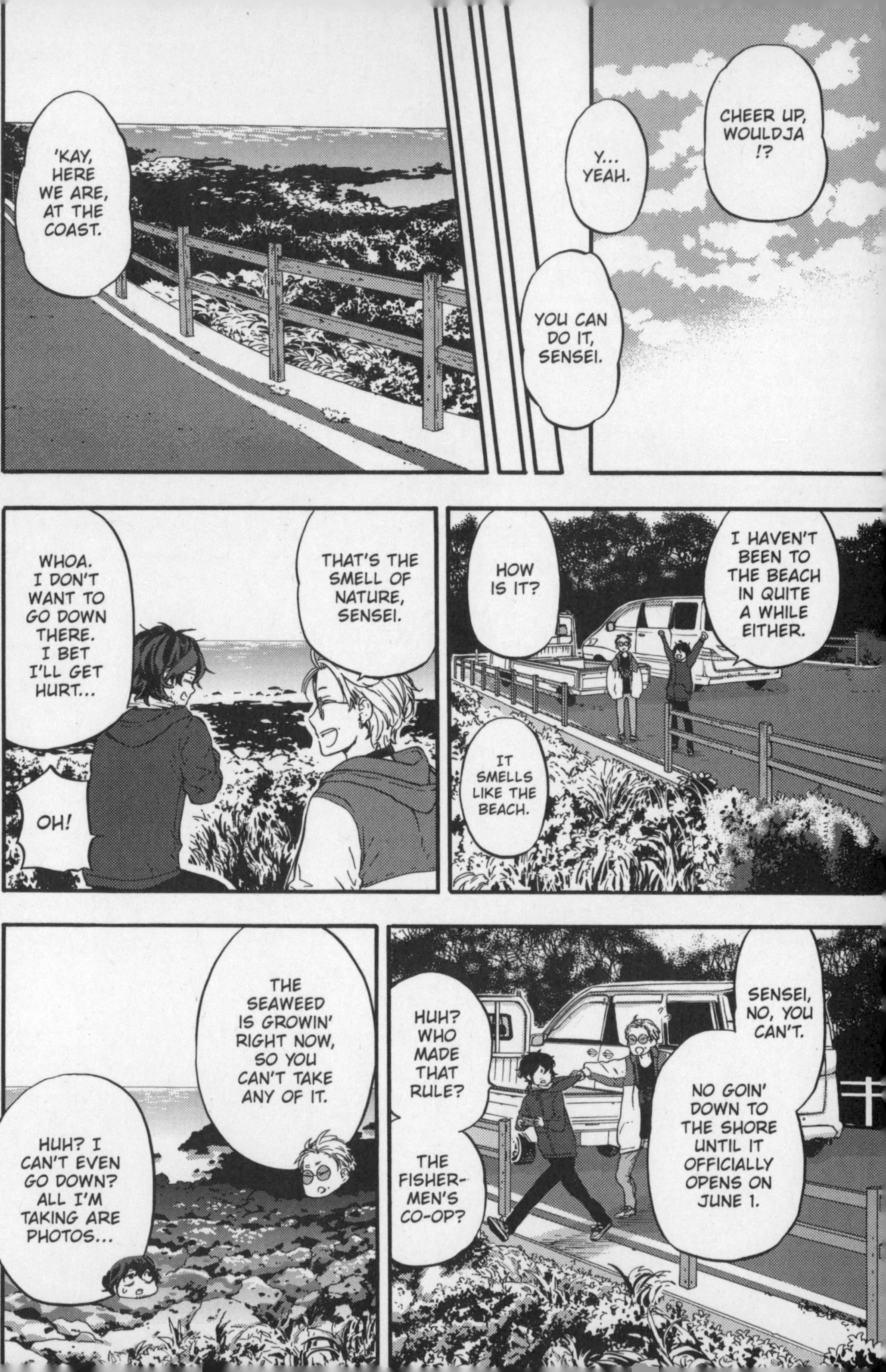
CHEER UP, WOULDJA!?
Y... YEAH.
YOU CAN DO IT, SENSEI.
'KAY, HERE WE ARE, AT THE COAST.
I HAVEN'T BEEN TO THE BEACH IN QUITE A WHILE EITHER.
HOW IS IT?
IT SMELLS LIKE THE BEACH.
THAT'S THE SMELL OF NATURE, SENSEI.
WHOA. I DON'T WANT TO GO DOWN THERE. I BET I'LL GET HURT...
OH!
SENSEI, NO, YOU CAN'T.
NO GOIN' DOWN TO THE SHORE UNTIL IT OFFICIALLY OPENS ON JUNE 1.
HUH? WHO MADE THAT RULE?
THE FISHERMEN'S CO-OP?
THE SEAWEED IS GROWIN' RIGHT NOW, SO YOU CAN'T TAKE ANY OF IT.
HUH? I CAN'T EVEN GO DOWN? ALL I'M TAKING ARE PHOTOS...

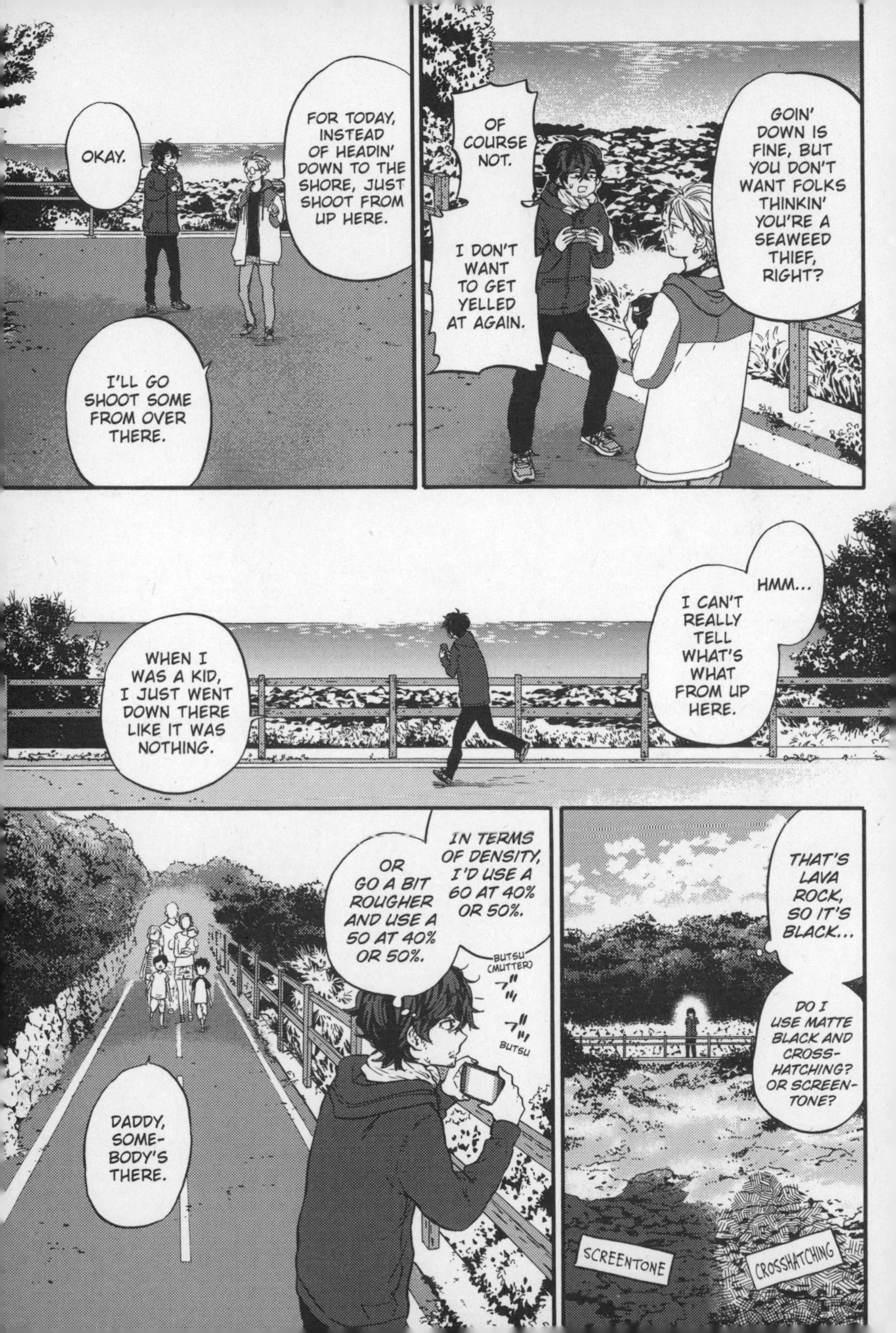
GOIN' DOWN IS FINE, BUT YOU DON'T WANT FOLKS THINKIN' YOU'RE A SEAWEED THIEF, RIGHT?
OF COURSE NOT.
I DON'T WANT TO GET YELLED AT AGAIN.
FOR TODAY, INSTEAD OF HEADIN' DOWN TO THE SHORE, JUST SHOOT FROM UP HERE.
OKAY.
I'LL GO SHOOT SOME FROM OVER THERE.
HMM... I CAN'T REALLY TELL WHAT'S WHAT FROM UP HERE.
WHEN I WAS A KID, I JUST WENT DOWN THERE LIKE IT WAS NOTHING.
THAT'S LAVA ROCK, SO IT'S BLACK...
DO I USE MATTE BLACK AND CROSS-HATCHING? OR SCREEN-TONE?
CROSSHATCHING
SCREENTONE
IN TERMS OF DENSITY, I'D USE A 60 AT 40% OR 50%.
OR GO A BIT ROUGHER AND USE A 50 AT 40% OR 50%.
BUTSU (MUTTER)
BUTSU
DADDY, SOMEBODY'S THERE.

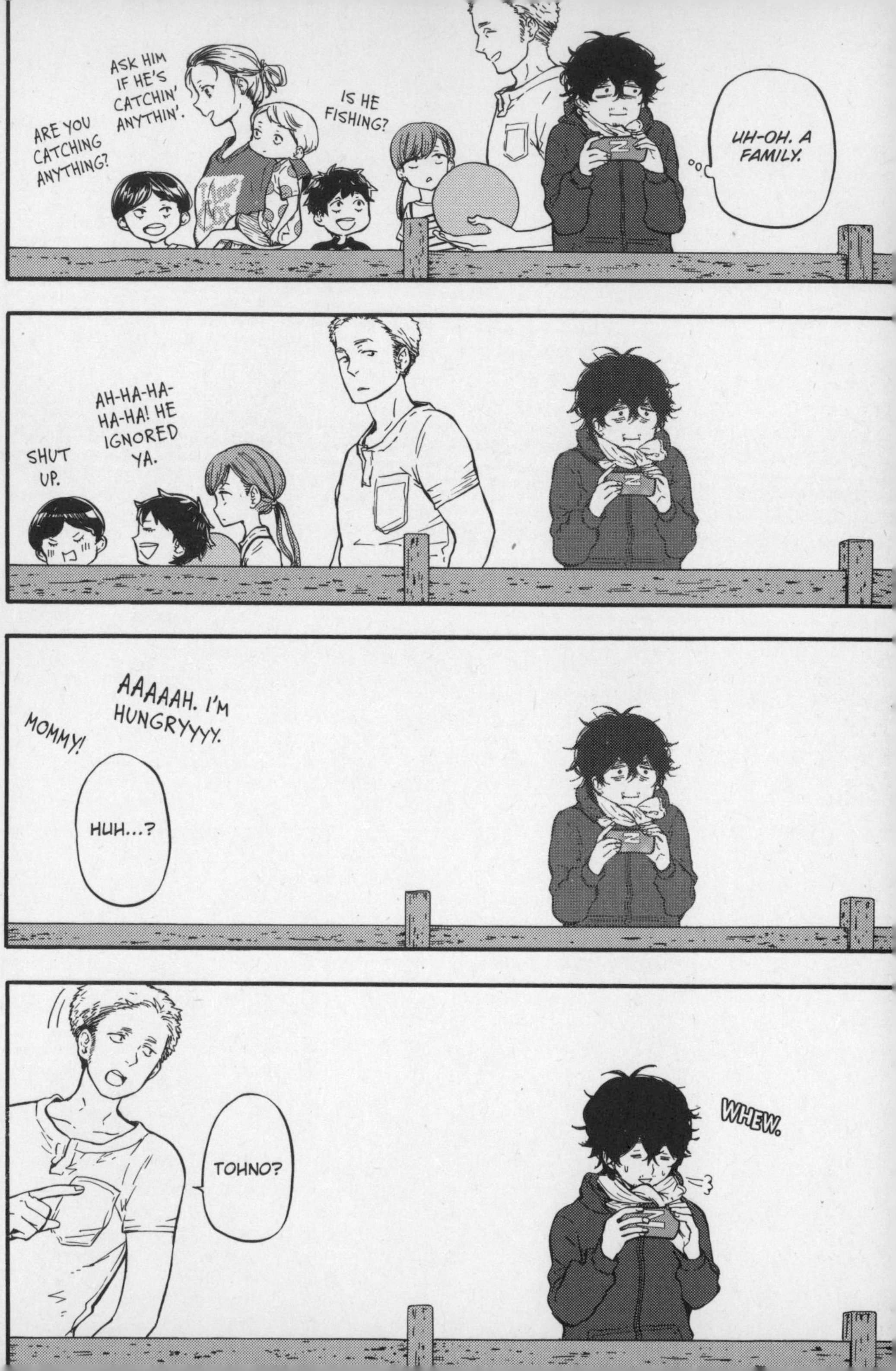
UH-OH. A FAMILY.
IS HE FISHING?
ASK HIM IF HE'S CATCHIN' ANYTHIN'.
ARE YOU CATCHING ANYTHING?
AH-HA-HA-HA-HA! HE IGNORED YA.
SHUT UP.
AAAAAH. I'M HUNGRYYYY.
MOMMY!
HUH...?
WHEW.
TOHNO?

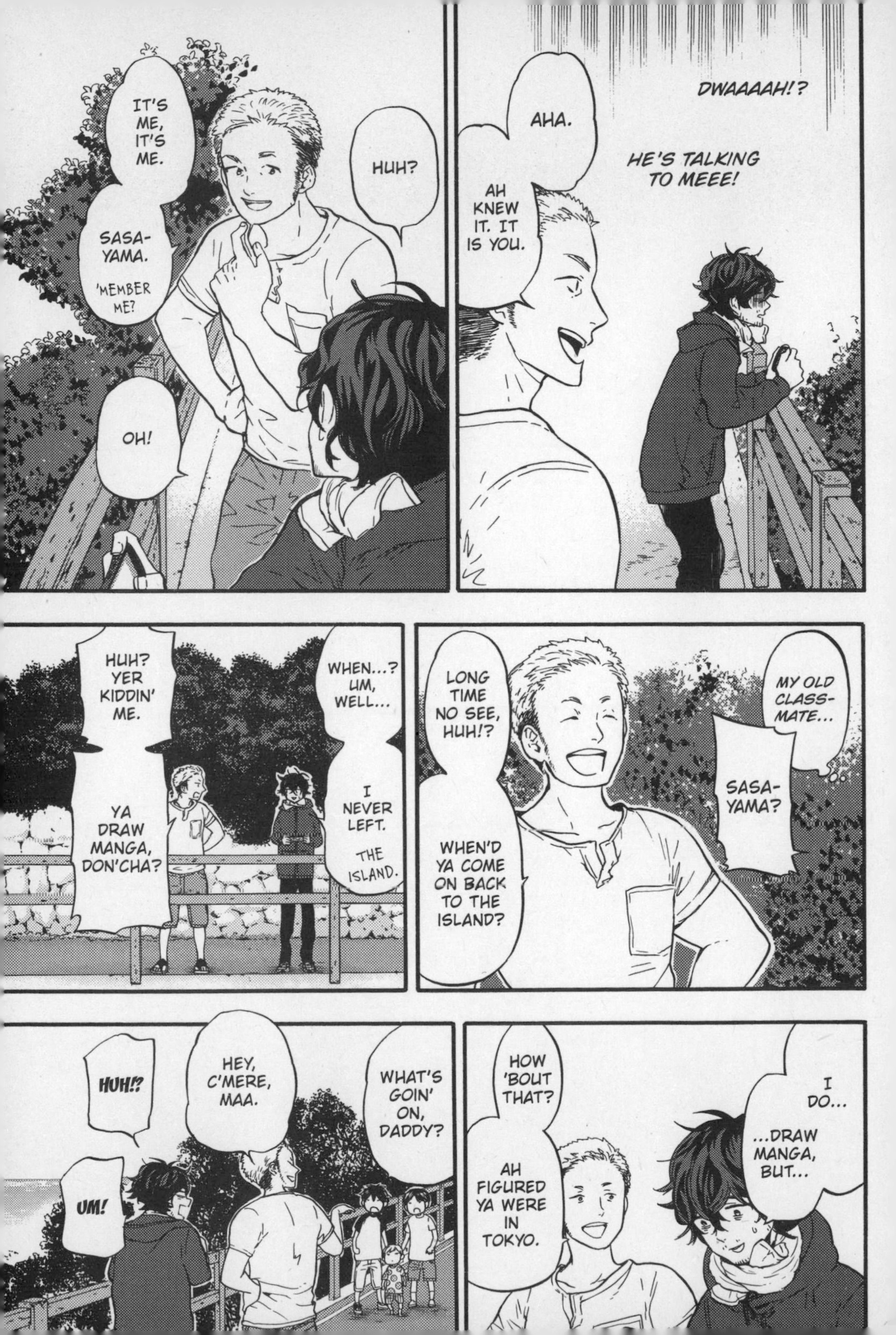
DWAAAAH!?
HE'S TALKING TO MEEE!
AHA.
AH KNEW IT. IT IS YOU.
HUH?
IT'S ME, IT'S ME.
SASA-YAMA.
'MEMBER ME?
OH!
MY OLD CLASS-MATE...
SASA-YAMA?
LONG TIME NO SEE, HUH!?
WHEN'D YA COME ON BACK TO THE ISLAND?
WHEN...? UM, WELL...
I NEVER LEFT.
THE ISLAND.
HUH? YER KIDDIN' ME.
YA DRAW MANGA, DON'CHA?
I DO...
...DRAW MANGA, BUT...
HOW 'BOUT THAT?
AH FIGURED YA WERE IN TOKYO.
WHAT'S GOIN' ON, DADDY?
HEY, C'MERE, MAA.
HUH!?
UM!

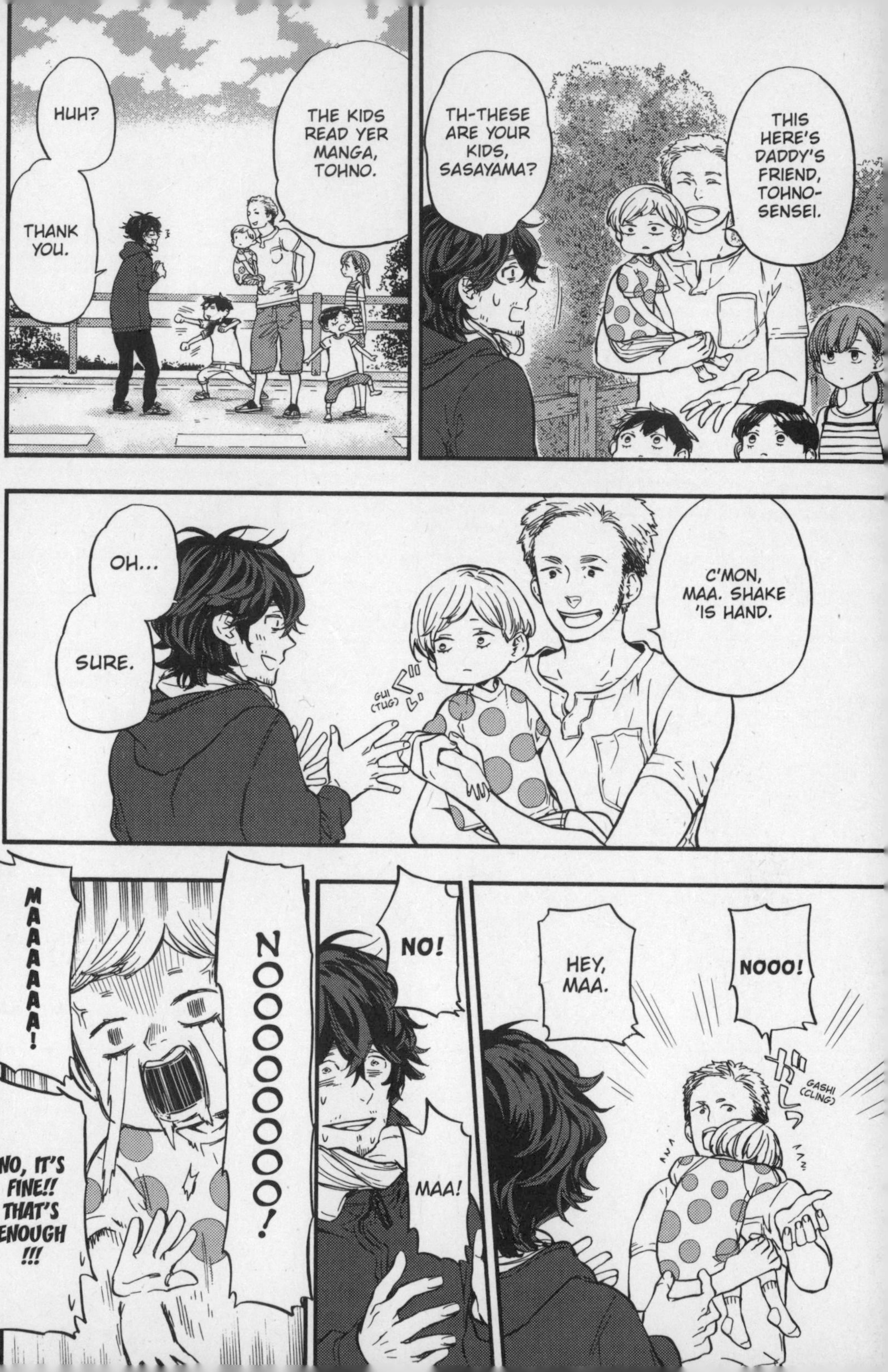
THIS HERE'S DADDY'S FRIEND, TOHNO-SENSEI.
TH-THESE ARE YOUR KIDS, SASAYAMA?
THE KIDS READ YER MANGA, TOHNO.
HUH?
THANK YOU.
C'MON, MAA. SHAKE 'IS HAND.
GUI (TUG)
OH...
SURE.
NOOO!
HEY, MAA.
GASHI (CLING)
NO!
MAA!
NOOOOOOOOO!
MAAAAAAA!
NO, IT'S FINE!! THAT'S ENOUGH!!!

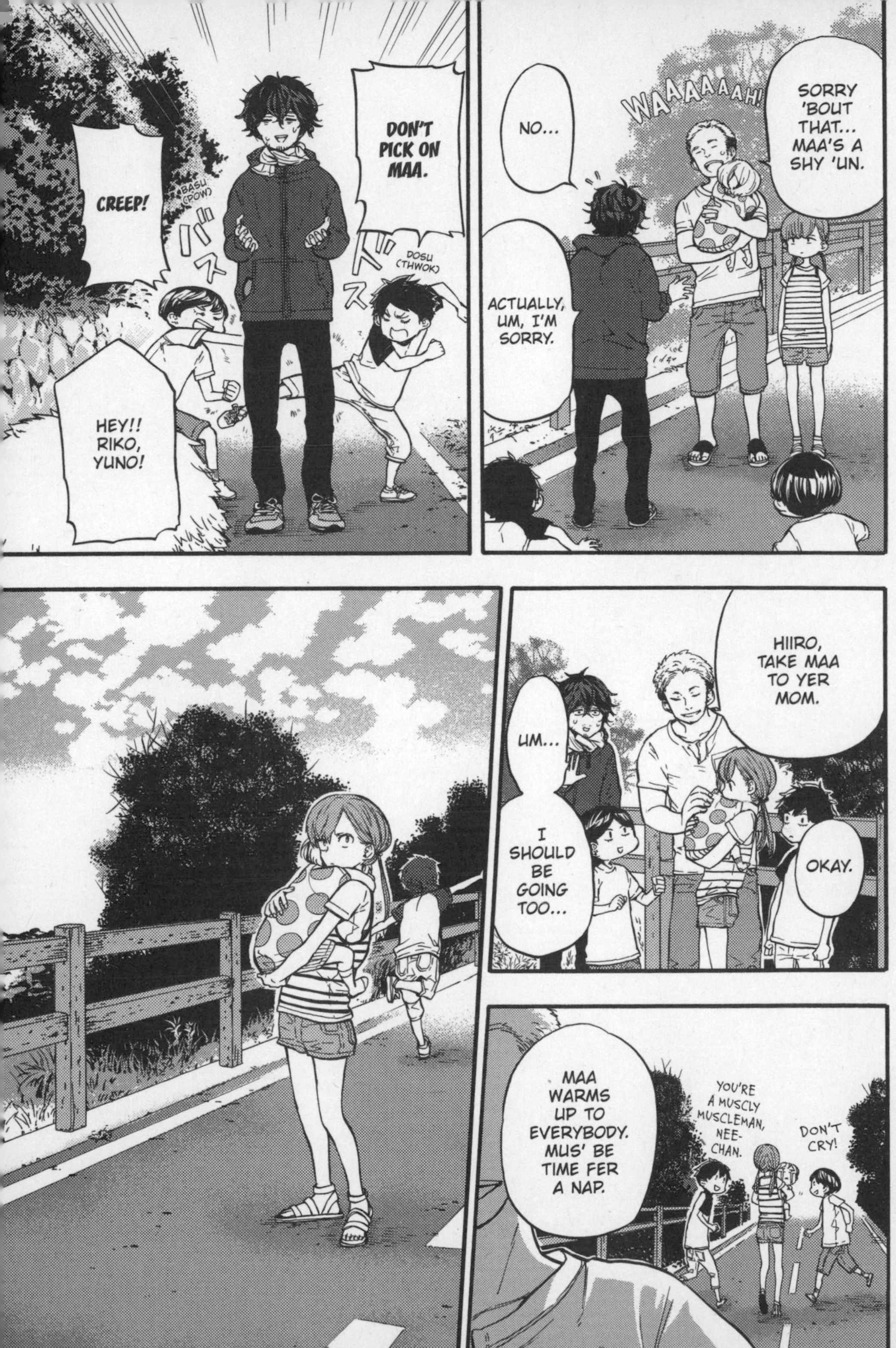
SORRY 'BOUT THAT... MAA'S A SHY 'UN.
WAAAAAAH!
NO...
ACTUALLY, UM, I'M SORRY.
DON'T PICK ON MAA.
ドス
DOSU (THWOK)
BASU (POW)
バス
CREEP!
HEY!! RIKO, YUNO!
HIIRO, TAKE MAA TO YER MOM.
OKAY.
UM...
I SHOULD BE GOING TOO...
DON'T CRY!
YOU'RE A MUSCLY MUSCLEMAN, NEE-CHAN.
MAA WARMS UP TO EVERYBODY. MUS' BE TIME FER A NAP.

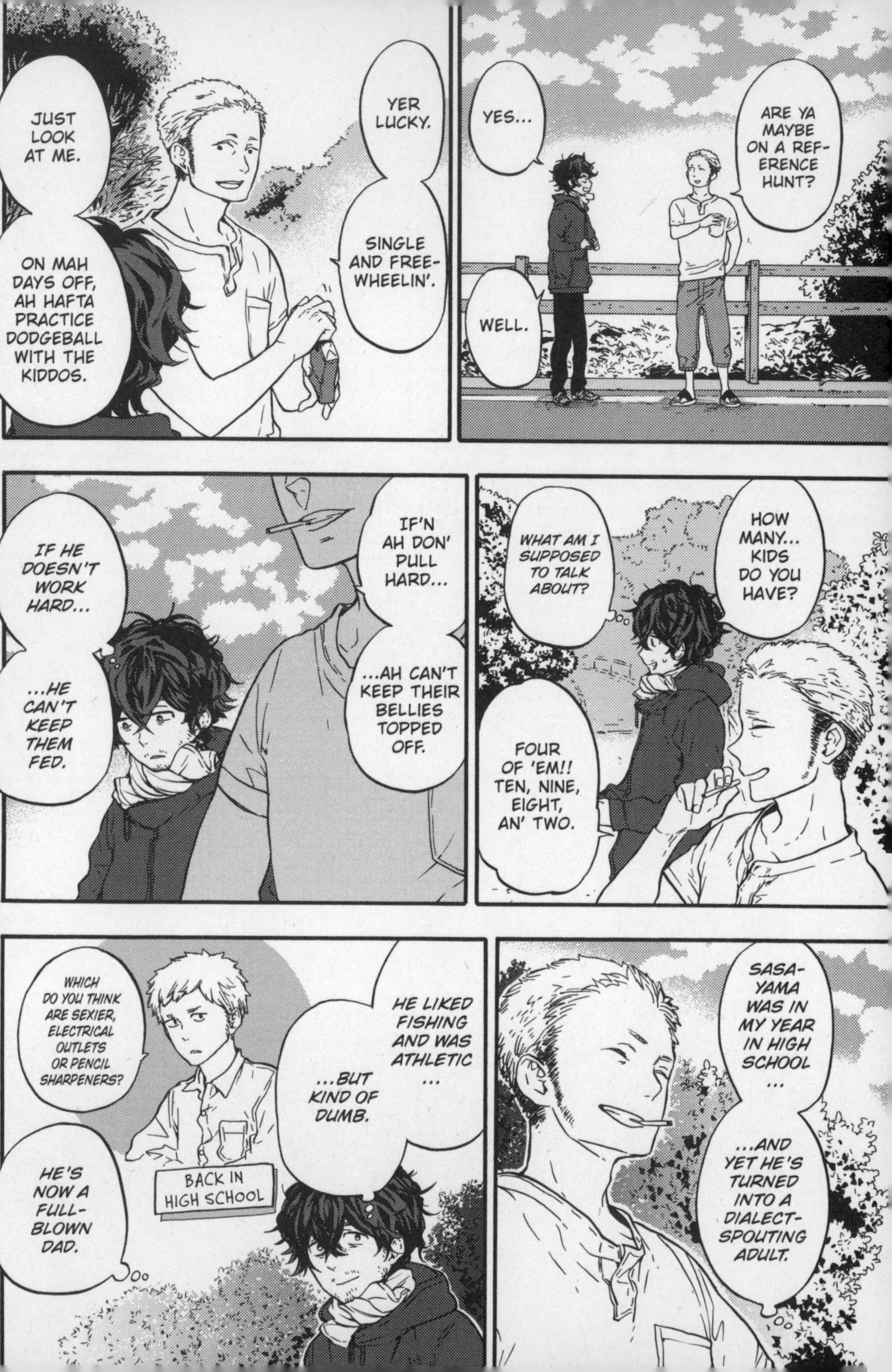
ARE YA MAYBE ON A REFERENCE HUNT?
YES...
WELL.
YER LUCKY.
SINGLE AND FREEWHEELIN'.
JUST LOOK AT ME.
ON MAH DAYS OFF, AH HAFTA PRACTICE DODGEBALL WITH THE KIDDOS.
HOW MANY... KIDS DO YOU HAVE?
WHAT AM I SUPPOSED TO TALK ABOUT?
FOUR OF 'EM!! TEN, NINE, EIGHT, AN' TWO.
IF'N AH DON' PULL HARD...
...AH CAN'T KEEP THEIR BELLIES TOPPED OFF.
IF HE DOESN'T WORK HARD...
...HE CAN'T KEEP THEM FED.
SASAYAMA WAS IN MY YEAR IN HIGH SCHOOL...
...AND YET HE'S TURNED INTO A DIALECT-SPOUTING ADULT.
HE LIKED FISHING AND WAS ATHLETIC...
...BUT KIND OF DUMB.
WHICH DO YOU THINK ARE SEXIER, ELECTRICAL OUTLETS OR PENCIL SHARPENERS?
BACK IN HIGH SCHOOL
HE'S NOW A FULL-BLOWN DAD.

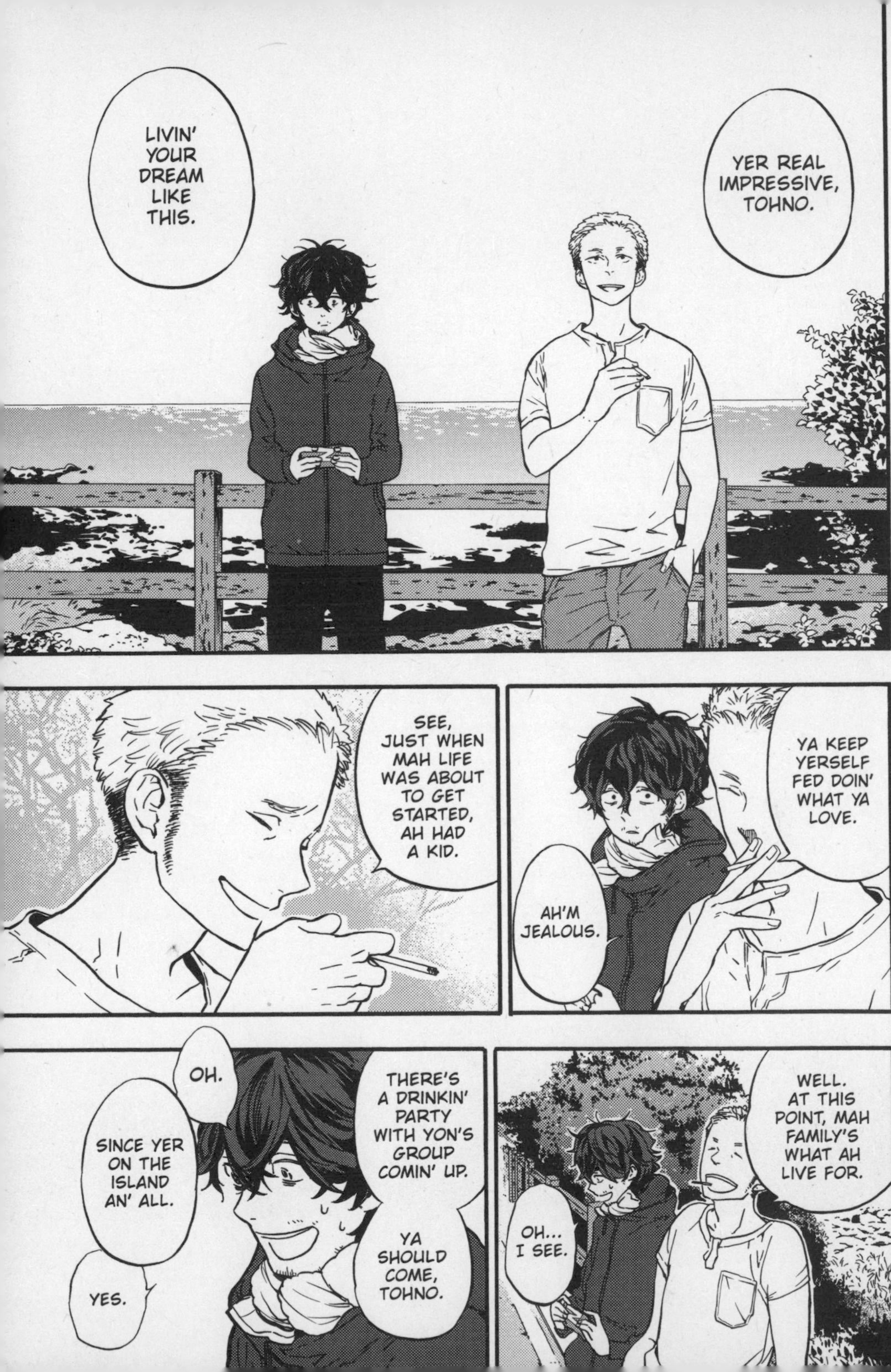

YER REAL IMPRESSIVE, TOHNO.
LIVIN' YOUR DREAM LIKE THIS.
YA KEEP YERSELF FED DOIN' WHAT YA LOVE.
AH'M JEALOUS.
SEE, JUST WHEN MAH LIFE WAS ABOUT TO GET STARTED, AH HAD A KID.
WELL. AT THIS POINT, MAH FAMILY'S WHAT AH LIVE FOR.
OH... I SEE.
OH.
SINCE YER ON THE ISLAND AN' ALL.
THERE'S A DRINKIN' PARTY WITH YON'S GROUP COMIN' UP.
YA SHOULD COME, TOHNO.
YES.

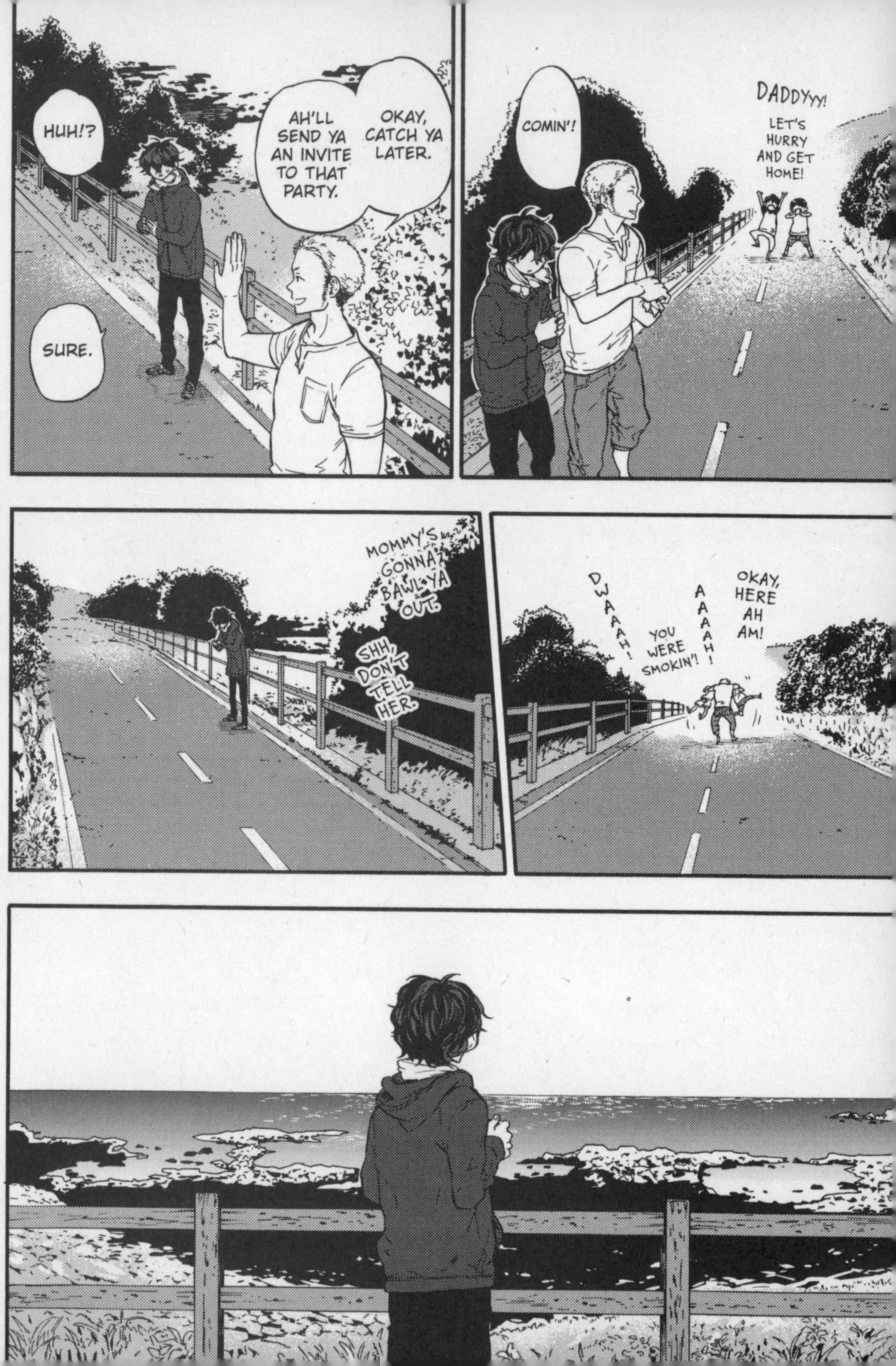
DADDYyy!
LET'S HURRY AND GET HOME!
COMIN'!
OKAY, CATCH YA LATER.
AH'LL SEND YA AN INVITE TO THAT PARTY.
HUH!?
SURE.
OKAY, HERE AH AM!
AAAAAH!
YOU WERE SMOKIN'!
DWAAAAH!
MOMMY'S GONNA BAWL YA OUT.
SHH, DON'T TELL HER.

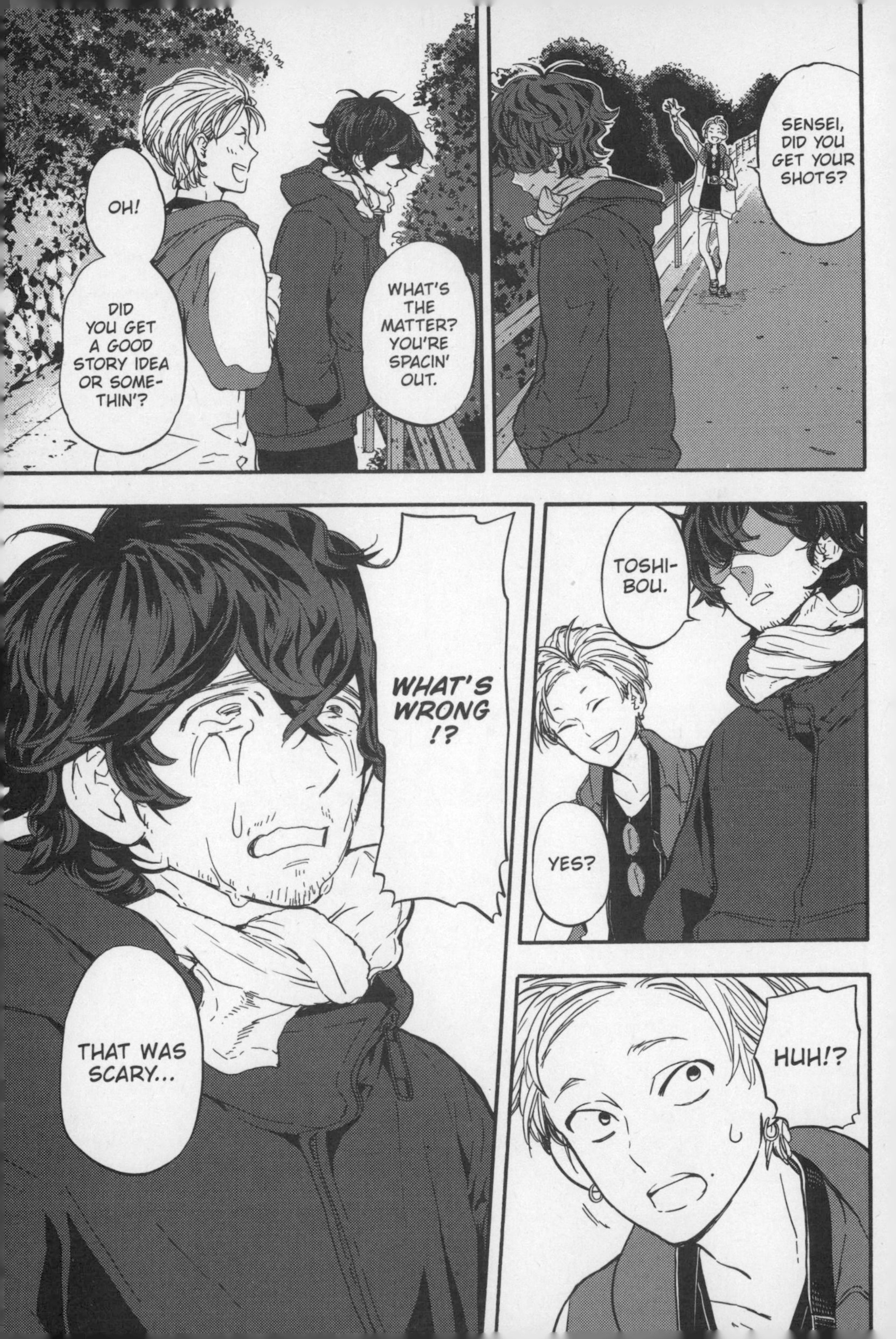

SENSEI, DID YOU GET YOUR SHOTS?
OH!
DID YOU GET A GOOD STORY IDEA OR SOME-THIN'?
WHAT'S THE MATTER? YOU'RE SPACIN' OUT.
TOSHI-BOU.
YES?
HUH!?
WHAT'S WRONG !?
THAT WAS SCARY...

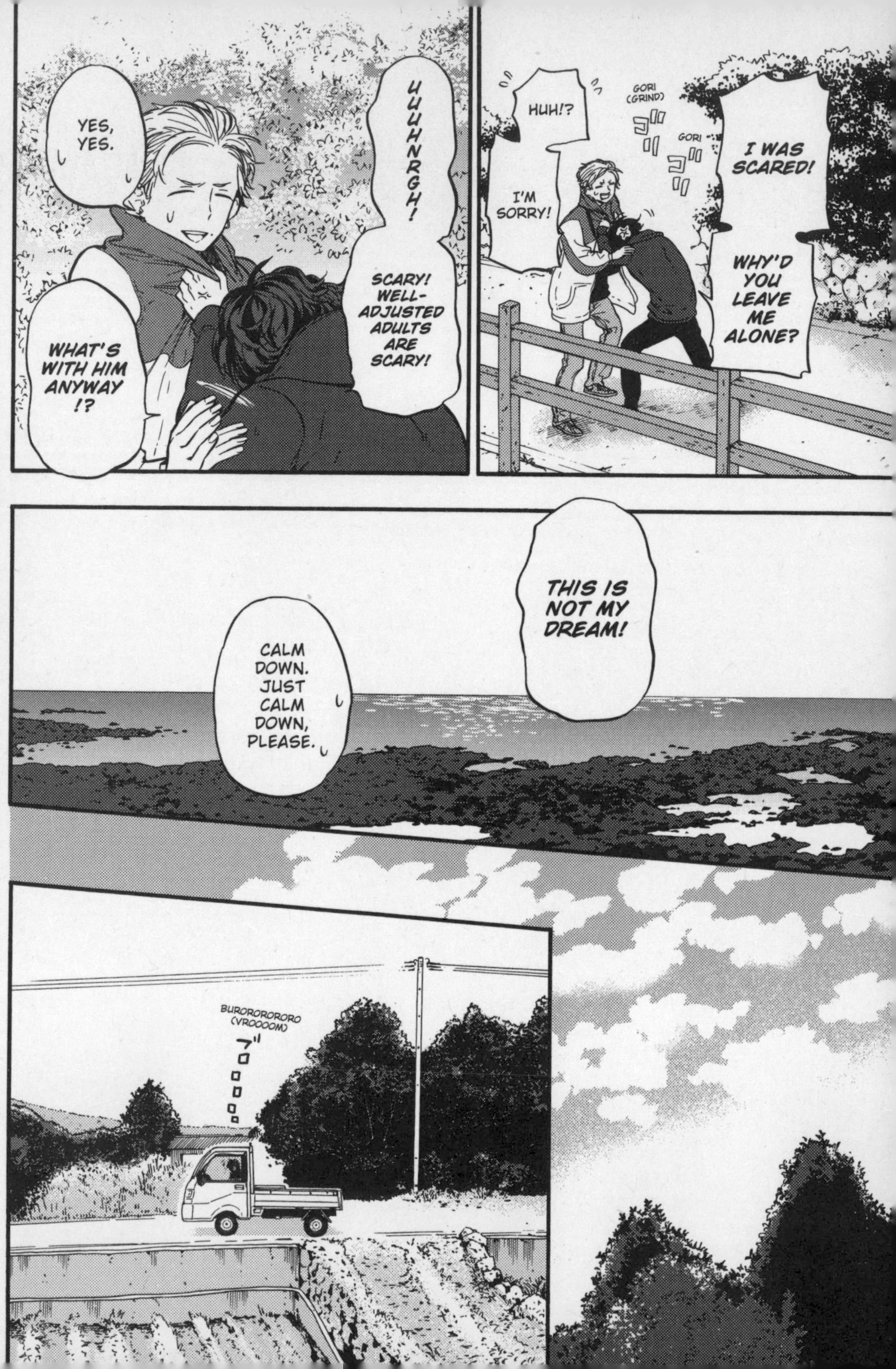
I WAS SCARED!
WHY'D YOU LEAVE ME ALONE?
HUH!?
GORI (GRIND)
GORI
I'M SORRY!
UUUHNRGH!
SCARY! WELL-ADJUSTED ADULTS ARE SCARY!
YES, YES.
WHAT'S WITH HIM ANYWAY !?
THIS IS NOT MY DREAM!
CALM DOWN. JUST CALM DOWN, PLEASE.
BURORORORORO (VROOOOM)

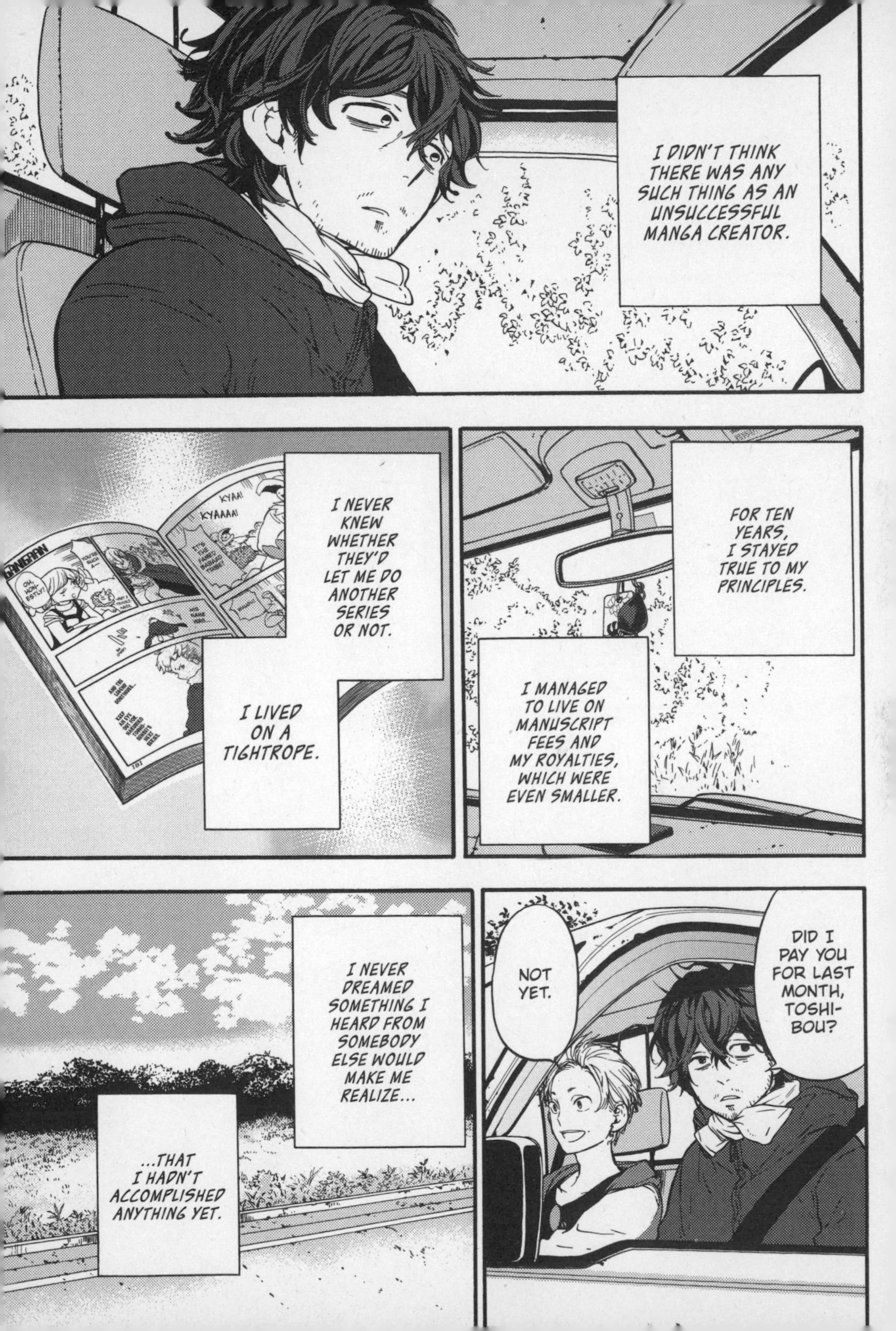
I DIDN'T THINK THERE WAS ANY SUCH THING AS AN UNSUCCESSFUL MANGA CREATOR.
FOR TEN YEARS, I STAYED TRUE TO MY PRINCIPLES.
I MANAGED TO LIVE ON MANUSCRIPT FEES AND MY ROYALTIES, WHICH WERE EVEN SMALLER.
I NEVER KNEW WHETHER THEY'D LET ME DO ANOTHER SERIES OR NOT.
KYAA!
KYAAAA!
I LIVED ON A TIGHTROPE.
DID I PAY YOU FOR LAST MONTH, TOSHI-BOU?
NOT YET.
I NEVER DREAMED SOMETHING I HEARD FROM SOMEBODY ELSE WOULD MAKE ME REALIZE...
...THAT I HADN'T ACCOMPLISHED ANYTHING YET.

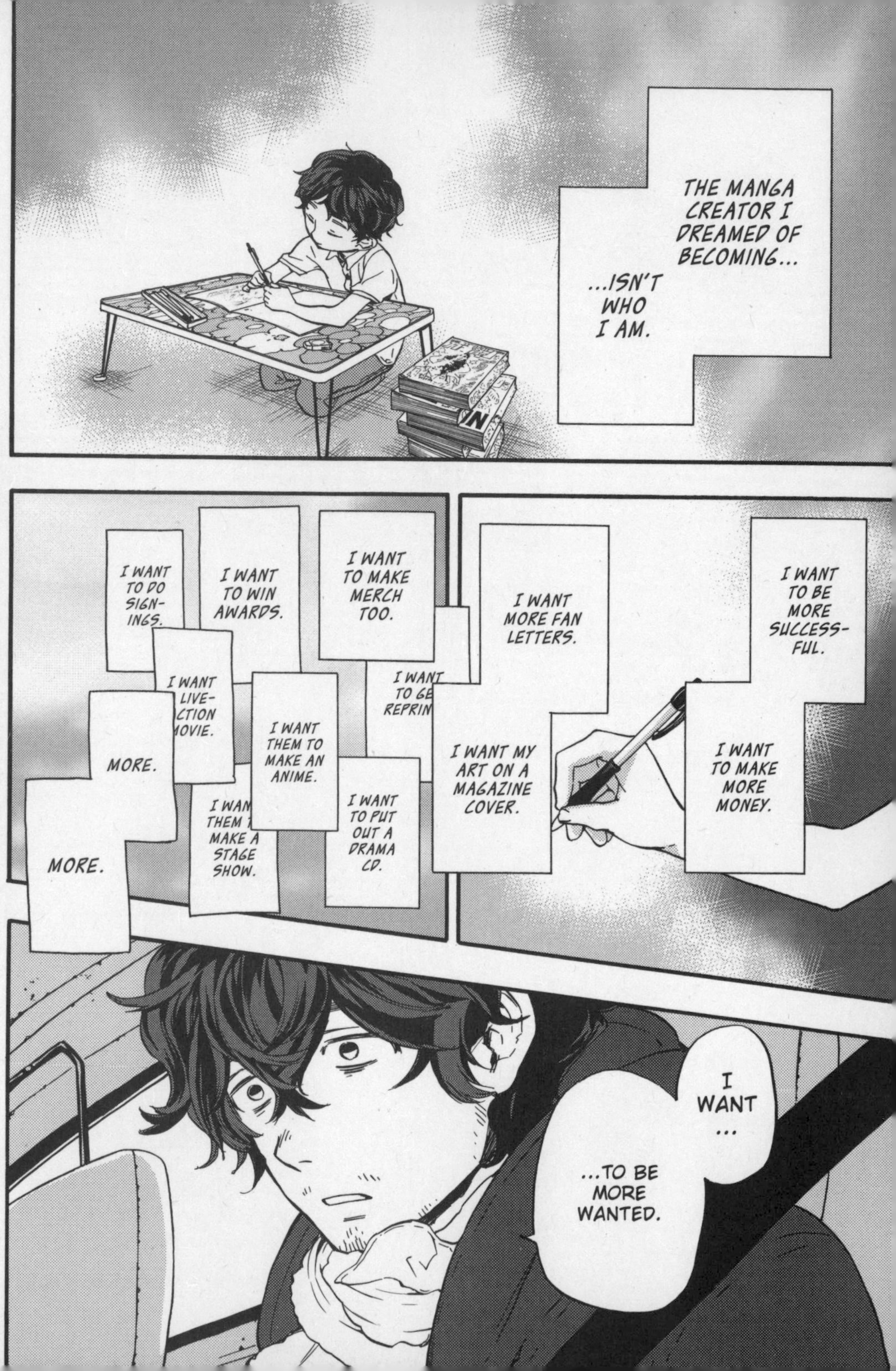
THE MANGA CREATOR I DREAMED OF BECOMING...
...ISN'T WHO I AM.
I WANT TO BE MORE SUCCESS-FUL.
I WANT MORE FAN LETTERS.
I WANT TO MAKE MORE MONEY.
I WANT MY ART ON A MAGAZINE COVER.
I WANT TO MAKE MERCH TOO.
I WANT TO GE REPRIN
I WANT TO WIN AWARDS.
I WANT TO DO SIGNINGS.
I WANT LIVE- CTION MOVIE.
I WANT TO PUT OUT A DRAMA CD.
I WANT THEM TO MAKE AN ANIME.
I WAN THEM T MAKE A STAGE SHOW.
MORE.
MORE.
I WANT...
...TO BE MORE WANTED.

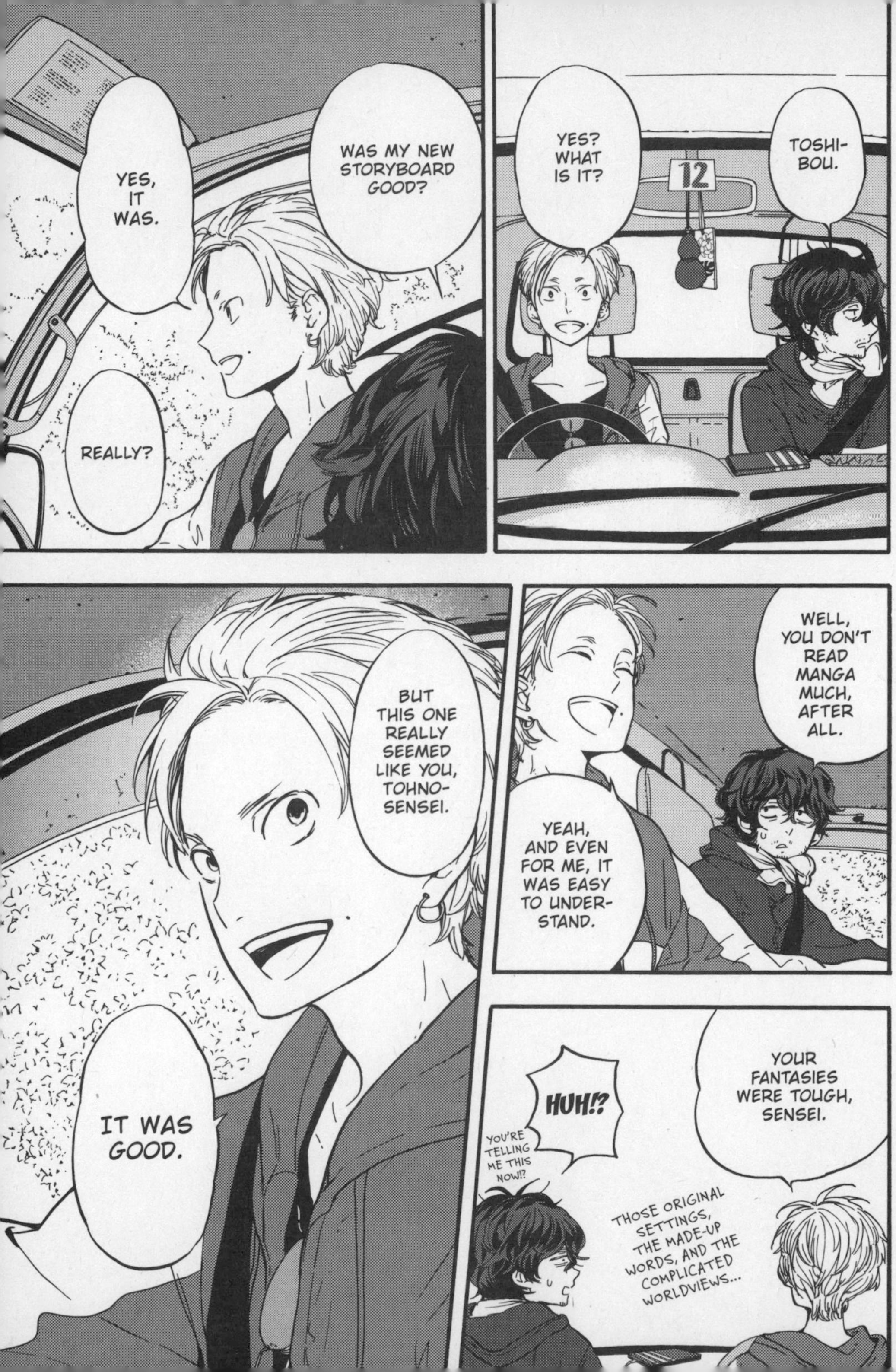
TOSHI-BOU.
YES? WHAT IS IT?
12
WAS MY NEW STORYBOARD GOOD?
YES, IT WAS.
REALLY?
WELL, YOU DON'T READ MANGA MUCH, AFTER ALL.
YEAH, AND EVEN FOR ME, IT WAS EASY TO UNDER-STAND.
YOUR FANTASIES WERE TOUGH, SENSEI.
THOSE ORIGINAL SETTINGS, THE MADE-UP WORDS, AND THE COMPLICATED WORLDVIEWS...
HUH!?
YOU'RE TELLING ME THIS NOW!?
BUT THIS ONE REALLY SEEMED LIKE YOU, TOHNO-SENSEI.
IT WAS GOOD.

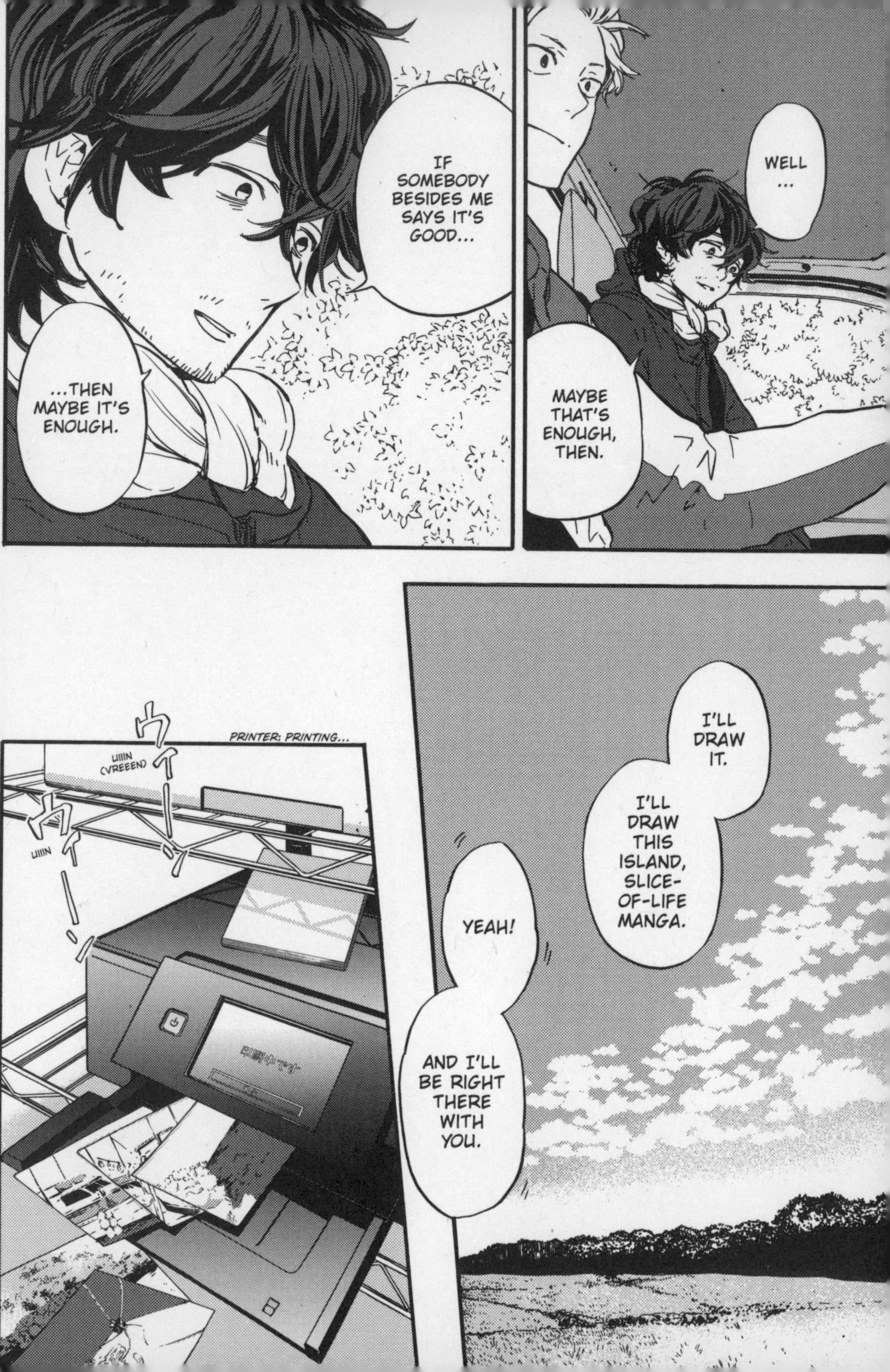
WELL...
MAYBE THAT'S ENOUGH, THEN.
IF SOMEBODY BESIDES ME SAYS IT'S GOOD...
...THEN MAYBE IT'S ENOUGH.
I'LL DRAW IT.
I'LL DRAW THIS ISLAND, SLICE-OF-LIFE MANGA.
YEAH!
AND I'LL BE RIGHT THERE WITH YOU.
PRINTER: PRINTING...
UIIIN (VREEEN)
UIIIN

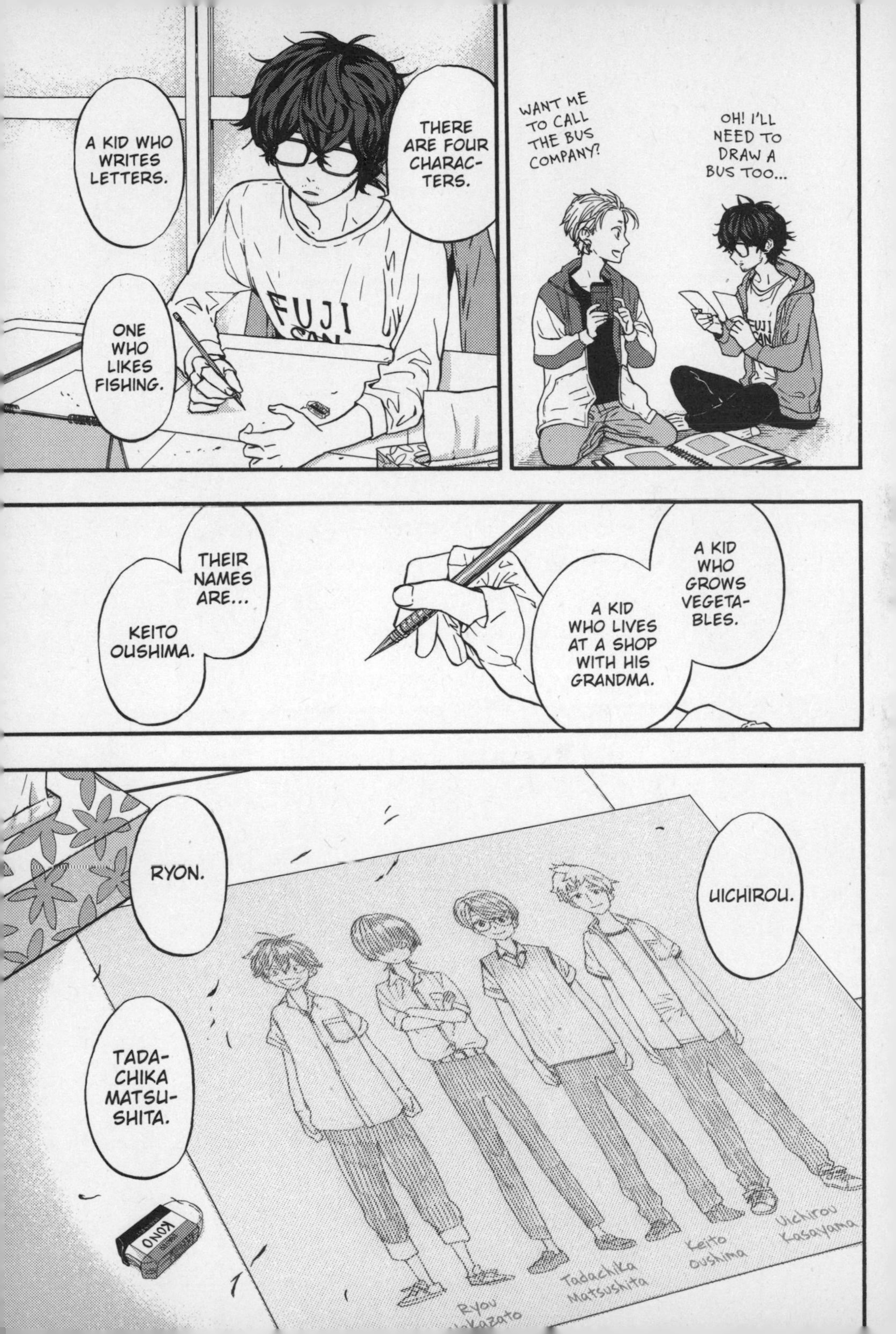
OH! I'LL NEED TO DRAW A BUS TOO...
WANT ME TO CALL THE BUS COMPANY?
THERE ARE FOUR CHARAC-TERS.
A KID WHO WRITES LETTERS.
FUJI
ONE WHO LIKES FISHING.
A KID WHO GROWS VEGETA-BLES.
A KID WHO LIVES AT A SHOP WITH HIS GRANDMA.
THEIR NAMES ARE...
KEITO OUSHIMA.
UICHIROU.
RYON.
TADA-CHIKA MATSU-SHITA.
Uichirou Kasayama
Keito Oushima
Tadachika Matsushita
Ryou
KONO

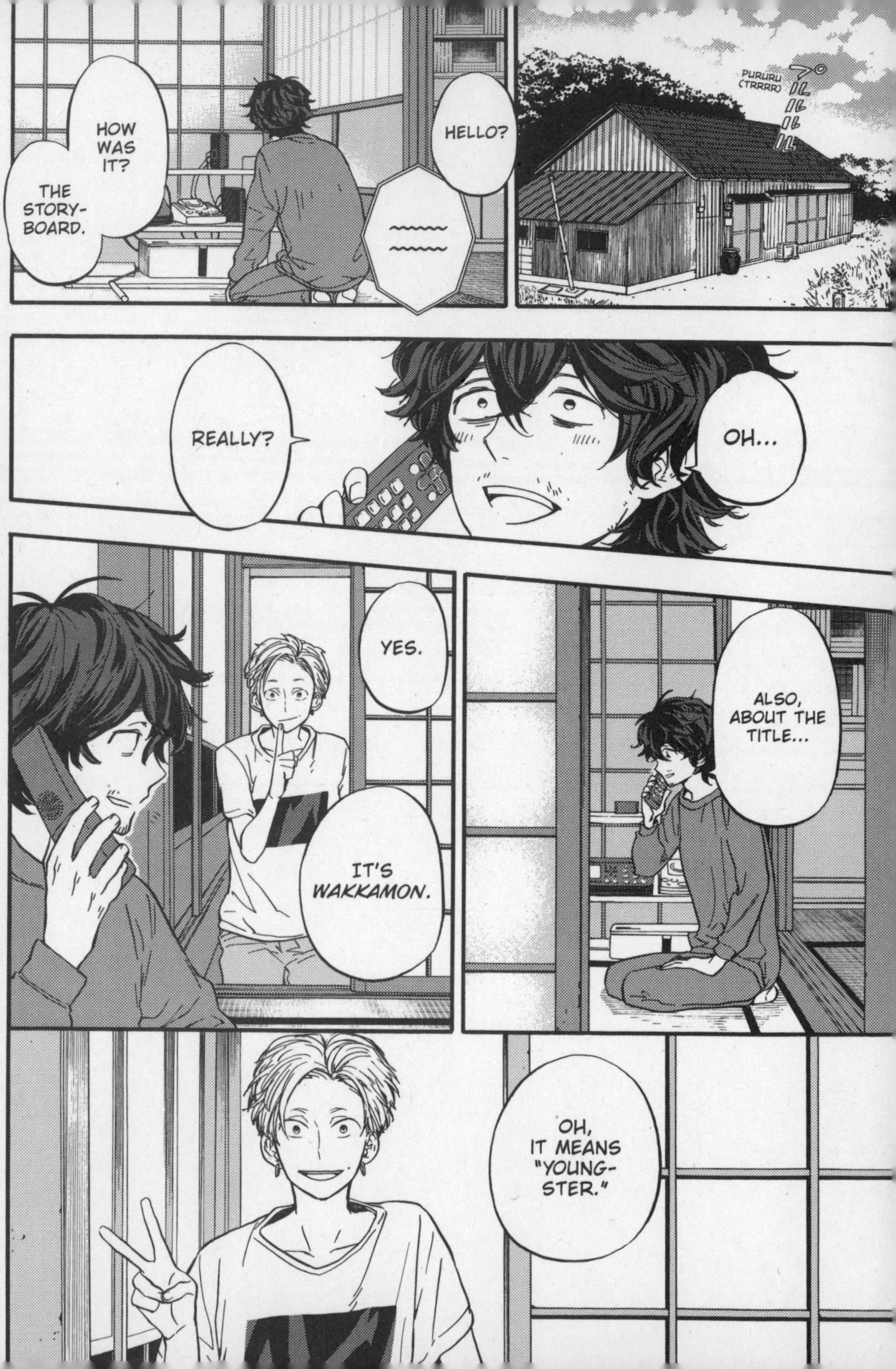
PURURU (TRRRR)
プルルル
HELLO?
HOW WAS IT?
THE STORYBOARD.
OH...
REALLY?
ALSO, ABOUT THE TITLE...
YES.
IT'S WAKKAMON.
OH, IT MEANS "YOUNGSTER."

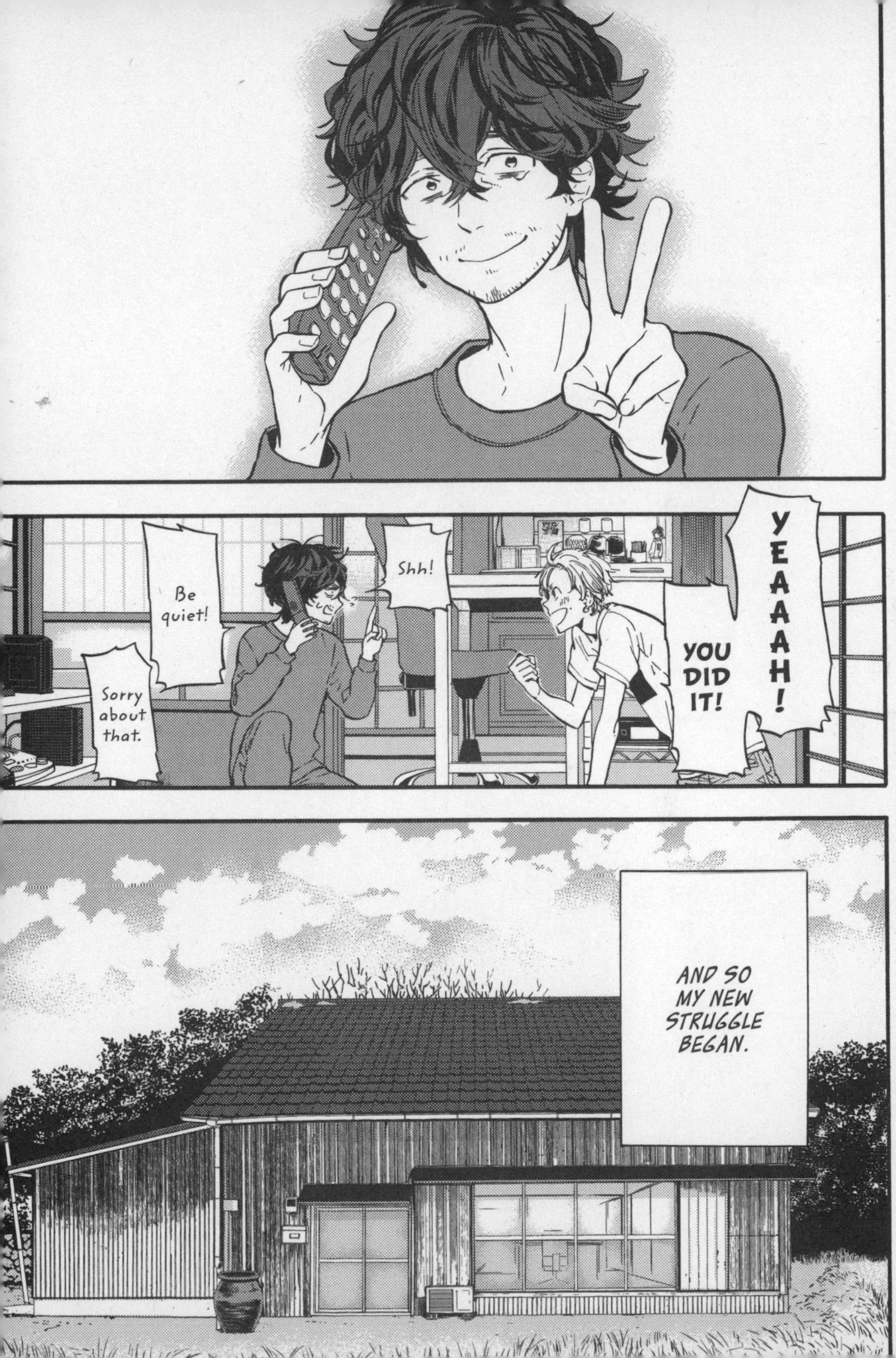
YEAAAH!
YOU DID IT!
Shh!
Be quiet!
Sorry about that.
AND SO MY NEW STRUGGLE BEGAN.

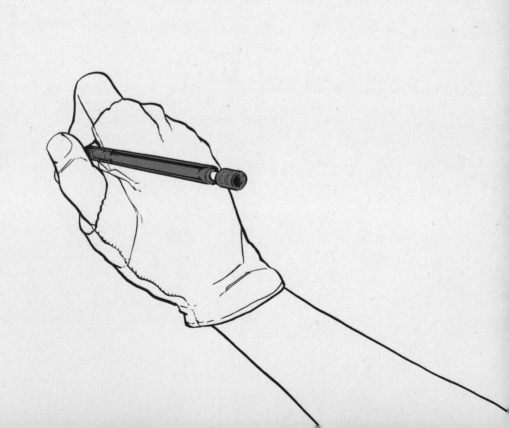

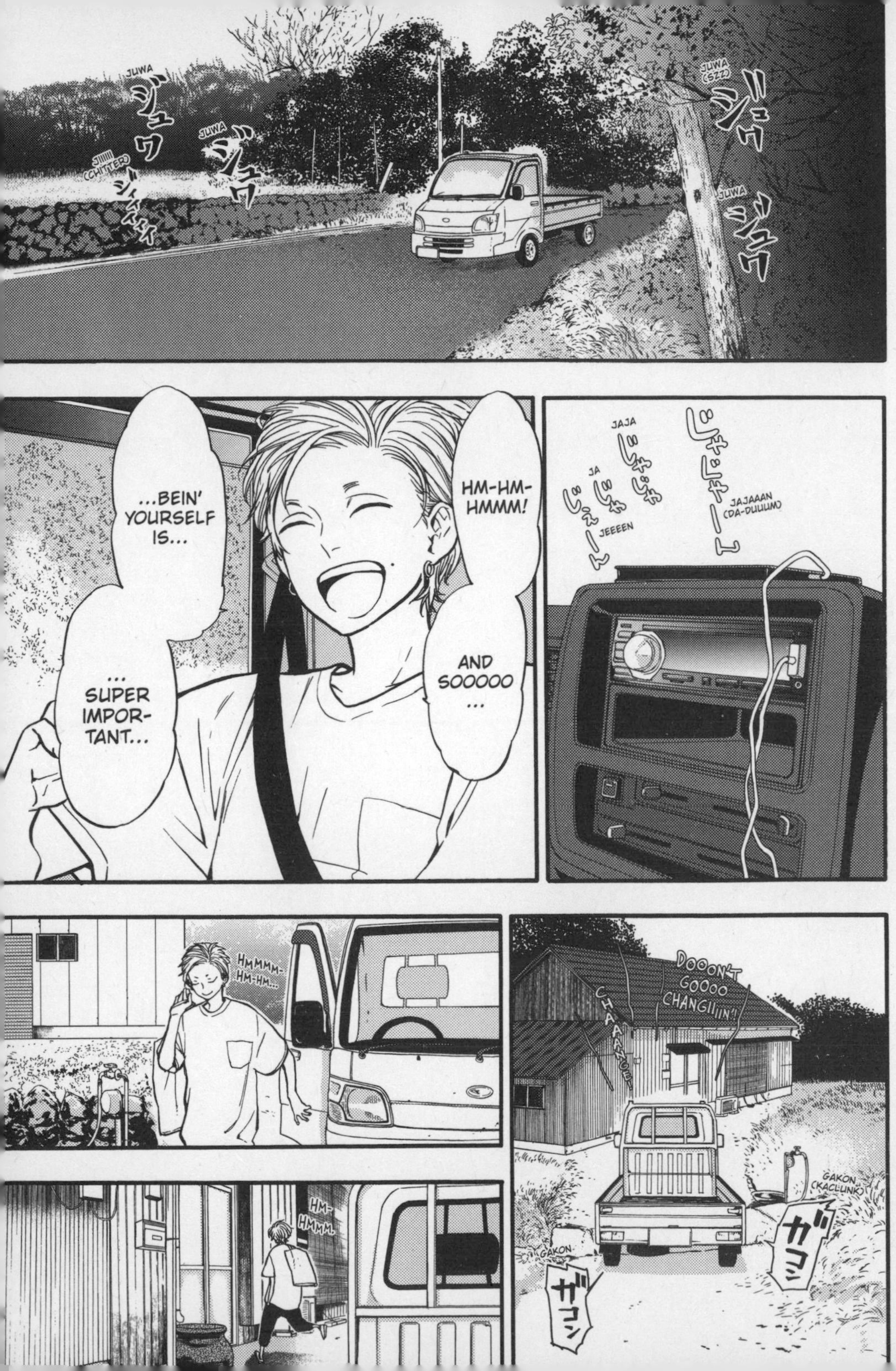

ジュワ
JUWA (SZZ)
ジュワ
JUWA
ジュワ
JUWA
ジュワ
JUWA
JIIIII (CHITTER)
じゃじゃーーん
JAJAAAN (DA-DUUUM)
じゃじゃ
JAJA
じゃ
JA
じぇーん
JEEEEN
HM-HM-HMMM!
AND SOOOOO ...
...BEIN' YOURSELF IS...
... SUPER IMPOR-TANT...
DOOON'T GOOOO CHANGIIIIN'!!
CHAAAANGE!
ガコン
GAKON (KACLUNK)
ガコン
GAKON
HMMMM-HM-HM...
HM-HMMM

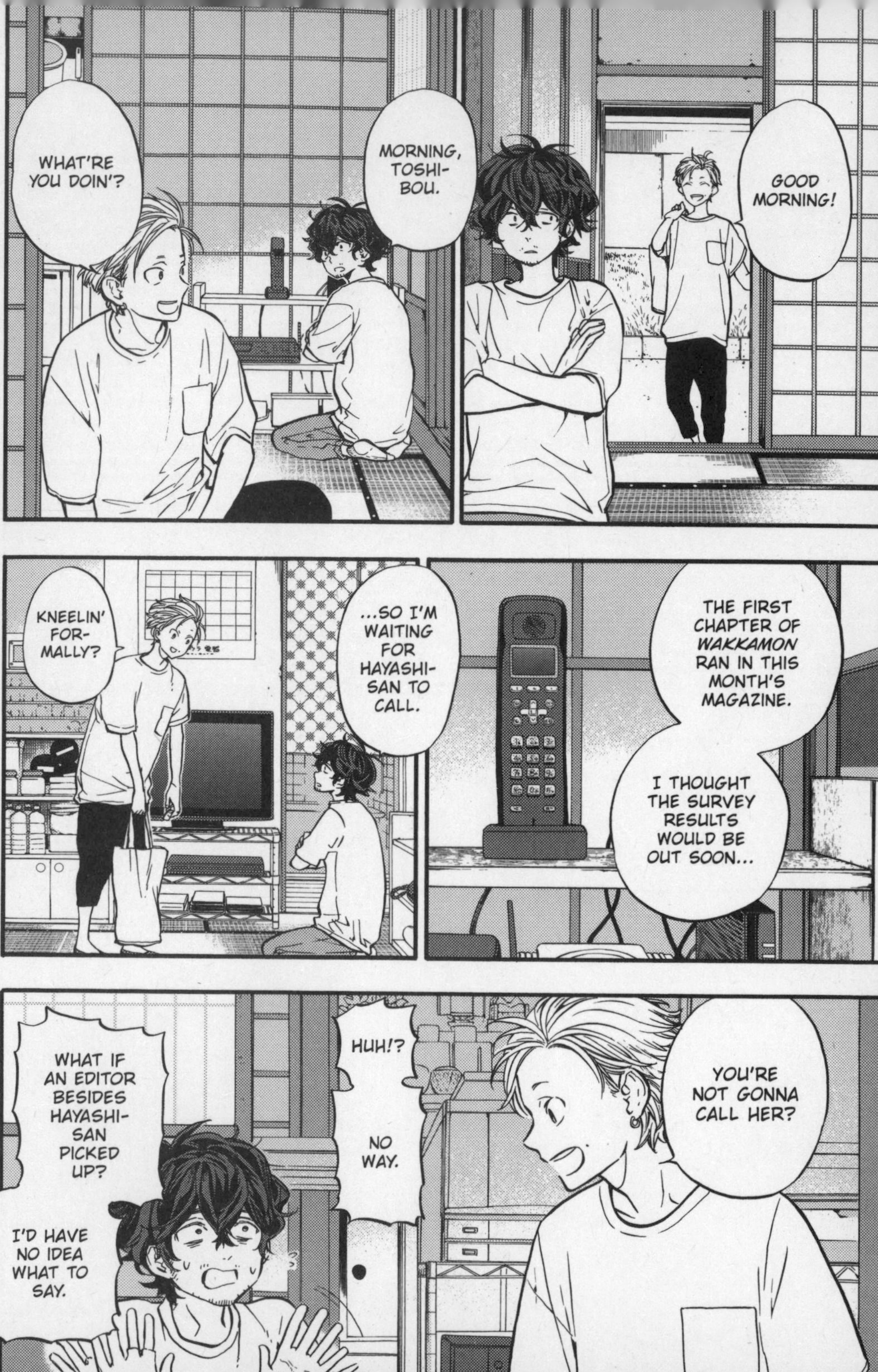
GOOD MORNING!
MORNING, TOSHI-BOU.
WHAT'RE YOU DOIN'?
THE FIRST CHAPTER OF *WAKKAMON* RAN IN THIS MONTH'S MAGAZINE.
I THOUGHT THE SURVEY RESULTS WOULD BE OUT SOON...
...SO I'M WAITING FOR HAYASHI-SAN TO CALL.
KNEELIN' FOR-MALLY?
YOU'RE NOT GONNA CALL HER?
HUH!?
NO WAY.
WHAT IF AN EDITOR BESIDES HAYASHI-SAN PICKED UP?
I'D HAVE NO IDEA WHAT TO SAY.

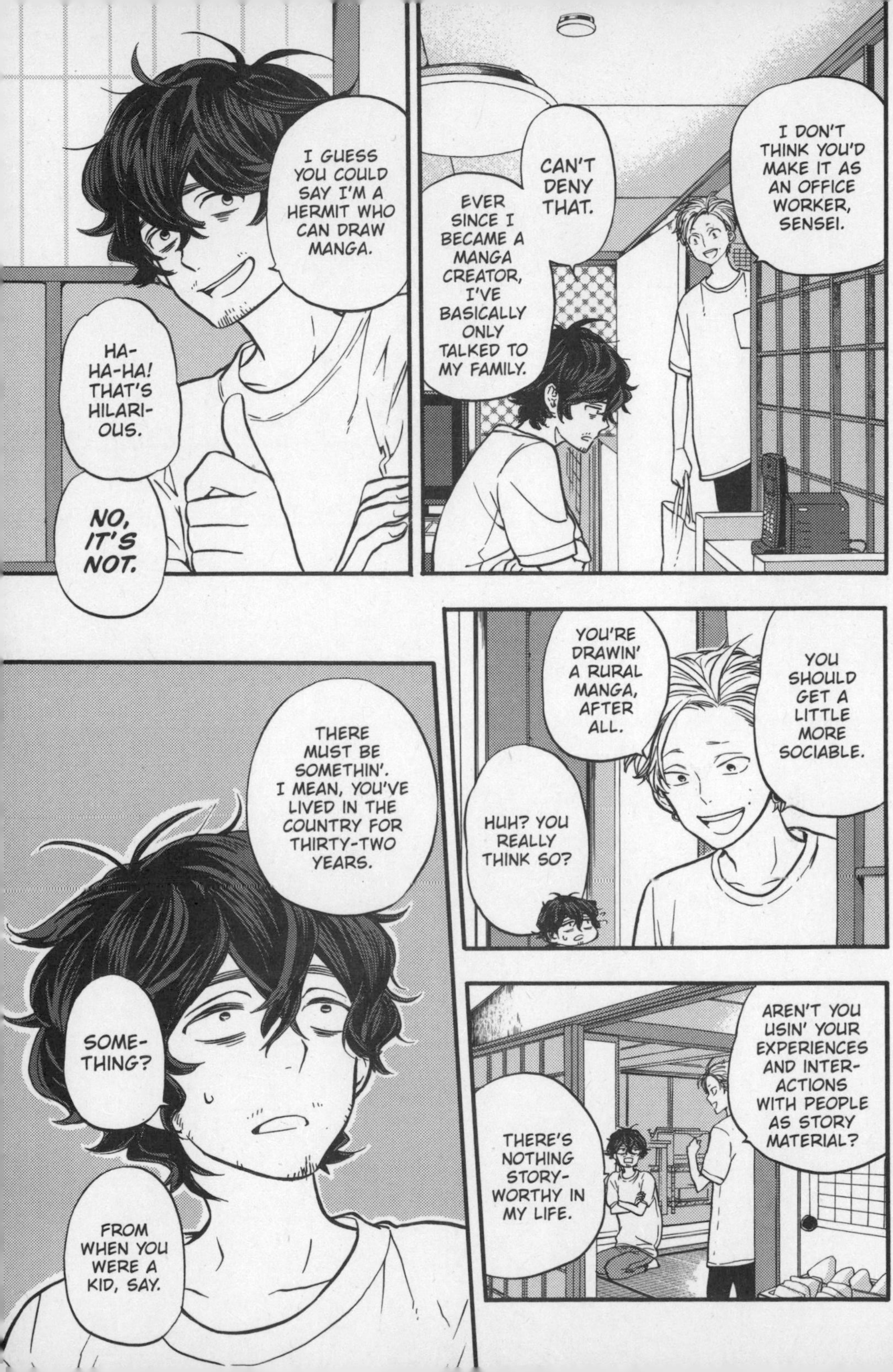
I DON'T THINK YOU'D MAKE IT AS AN OFFICE WORKER, SENSEI.
CAN'T DENY THAT.
EVER SINCE I BECAME A MANGA CREATOR, I'VE BASICALLY ONLY TALKED TO MY FAMILY.
I GUESS YOU COULD SAY I'M A HERMIT WHO CAN DRAW MANGA.
HA-HA-HA! THAT'S HILARI-OUS.
NO, IT'S NOT.
YOU SHOULD GET A LITTLE MORE SOCIABLE.
YOU'RE DRAWIN' A RURAL MANGA, AFTER ALL.
HUH? YOU REALLY THINK SO?
AREN'T YOU USIN' YOUR EXPERIENCES AND INTER-ACTIONS WITH PEOPLE AS STORY MATERIAL?
THERE'S NOTHING STORY-WORTHY IN MY LIFE.
THERE MUST BE SOMETHIN'. I MEAN, YOU'VE LIVED IN THE COUNTRY FOR THIRTY-TWO YEARS.
SOME-THING?
FROM WHEN YOU WERE A KID, SAY.

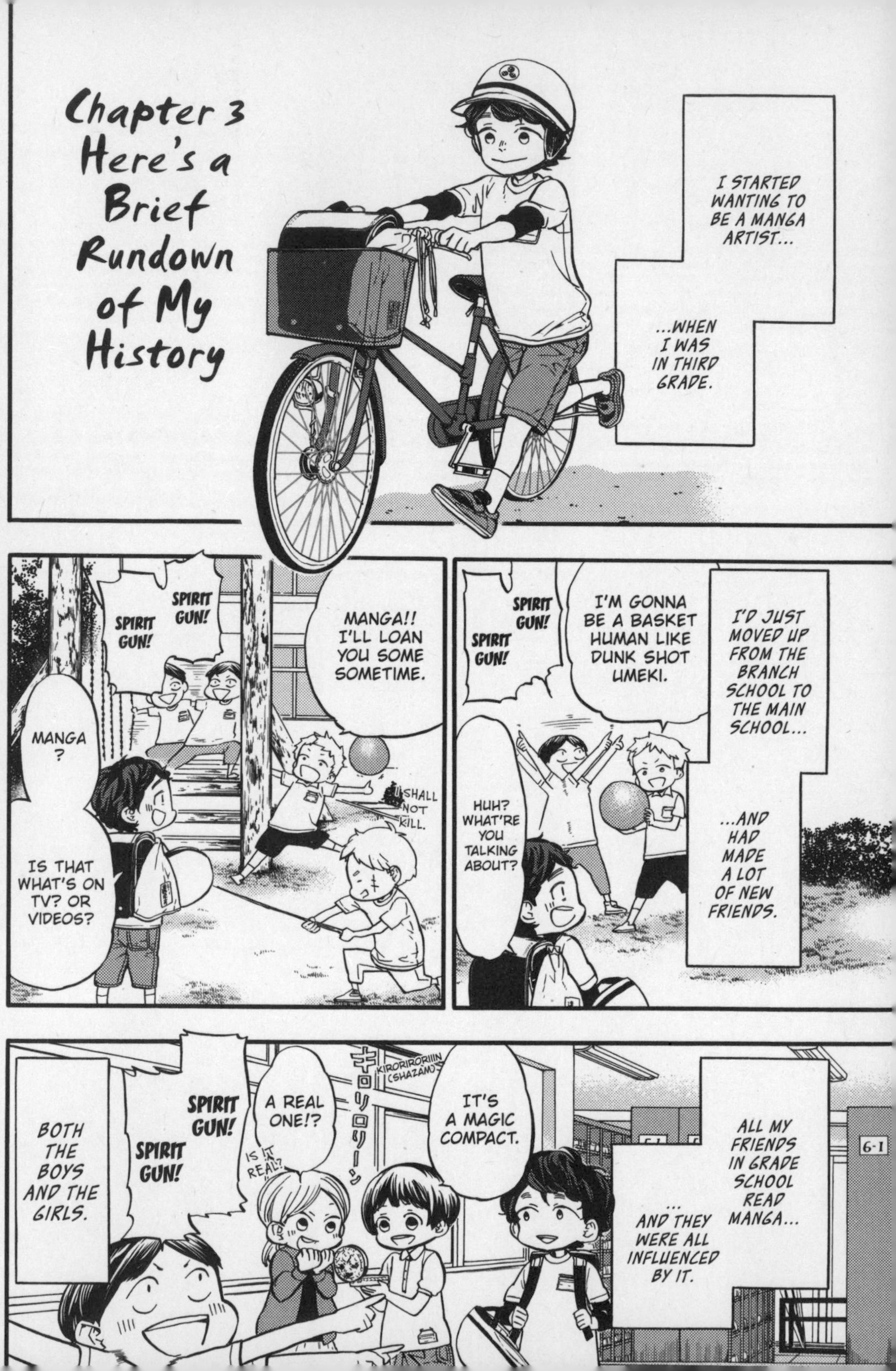
Chapter 3 Here's a Brief Rundown of My History
I STARTED WANTING TO BE A MANGA ARTIST...
...WHEN I WAS IN THIRD GRADE.
I'D JUST MOVED UP FROM THE BRANCH SCHOOL TO THE MAIN SCHOOL...
...AND HAD MADE A LOT OF NEW FRIENDS.
I'M GONNA BE A BASKET HUMAN LIKE DUNK SHOT UMEKI.
SPIRIT GUN!
SPIRIT GUN!
HUH? WHAT'RE YOU TALKING ABOUT?
MANGA!! I'LL LOAN YOU SOME SOMETIME.
SPIRIT GUN!
SPIRIT GUN!
SHALL NOT KILL.
MANGA?
IS THAT WHAT'S ON TV? OR VIDEOS?
ALL MY FRIENDS IN GRADE SCHOOL READ MANGA...
...AND THEY WERE ALL INFLUENCED BY IT.
6-1
IT'S A MAGIC COMPACT.
キロリロリーン
KIRORIRORIIIN (SHAZAM)
A REAL ONE!?
IS IT REAL?
SPIRIT GUN!
SPIRIT GUN!
BOTH THE BOYS AND THE GIRLS.

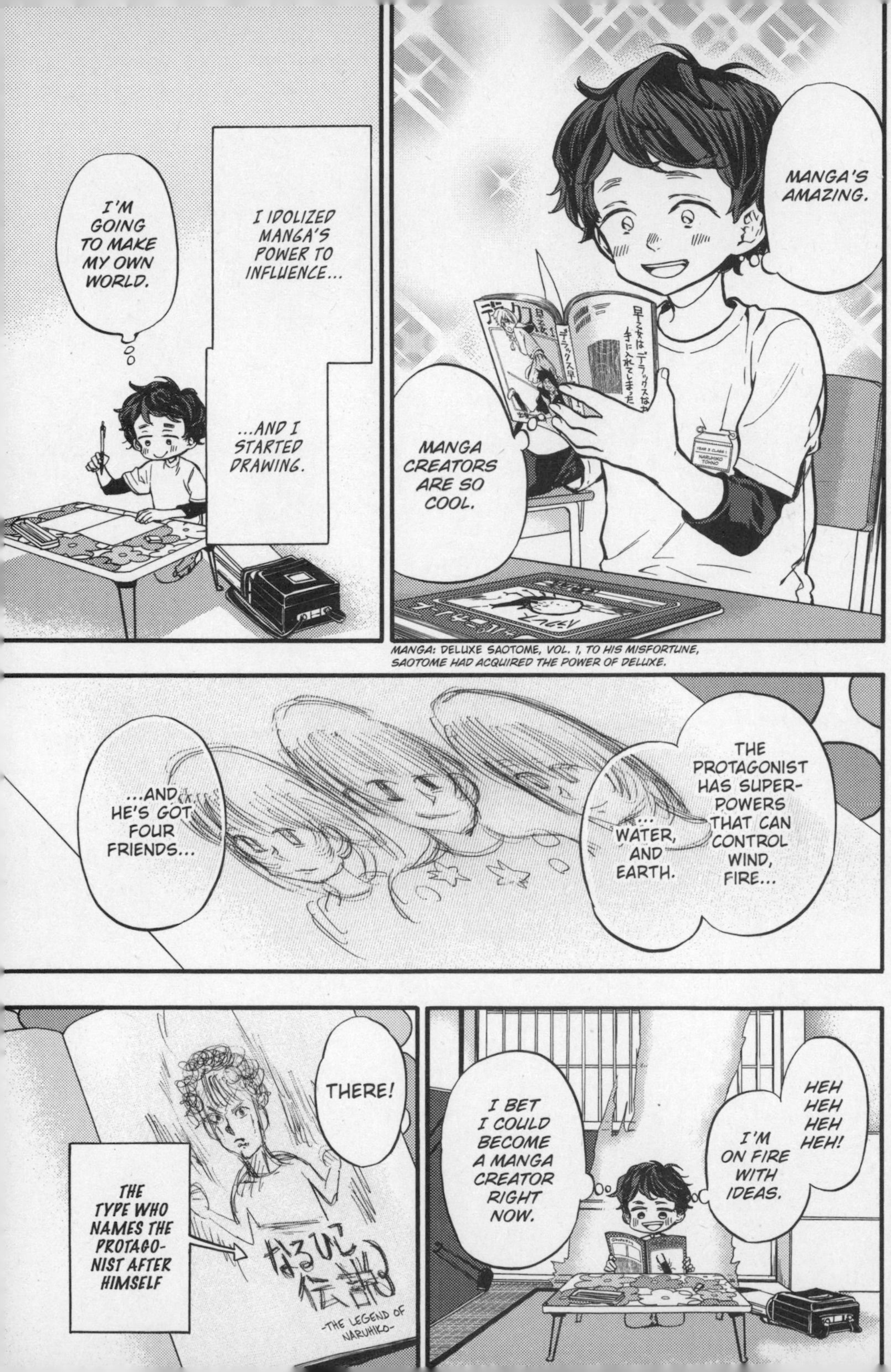
MANGA'S AMAZING.
MANGA CREATORS ARE SO COOL.
MANGA: DELUXE SAOTOME, VOL. 1, TO HIS MISFORTUNE, SAOTOME HAD ACQUIRED THE POWER OF DELUXE.
I IDOLIZED MANGA'S POWER TO INFLUENCE...
...AND I STARTED DRAWING.
I'M GOING TO MAKE MY OWN WORLD.
THE PROTAGONIST HAS SUPER-POWERS THAT CAN CONTROL WIND, FIRE...
...WATER, AND EARTH.
...AND HE'S GOT FOUR FRIENDS...
HEH HEH HEH HEH!
I'M ON FIRE WITH IDEAS.
I BET I COULD BECOME A MANGA CREATOR RIGHT NOW.
THERE!
THE TYPE WHO NAMES THE PROTAGO-NIST AFTER HIMSELF
なるひこ伝説
-THE LEGEND OF NARUHIKO-

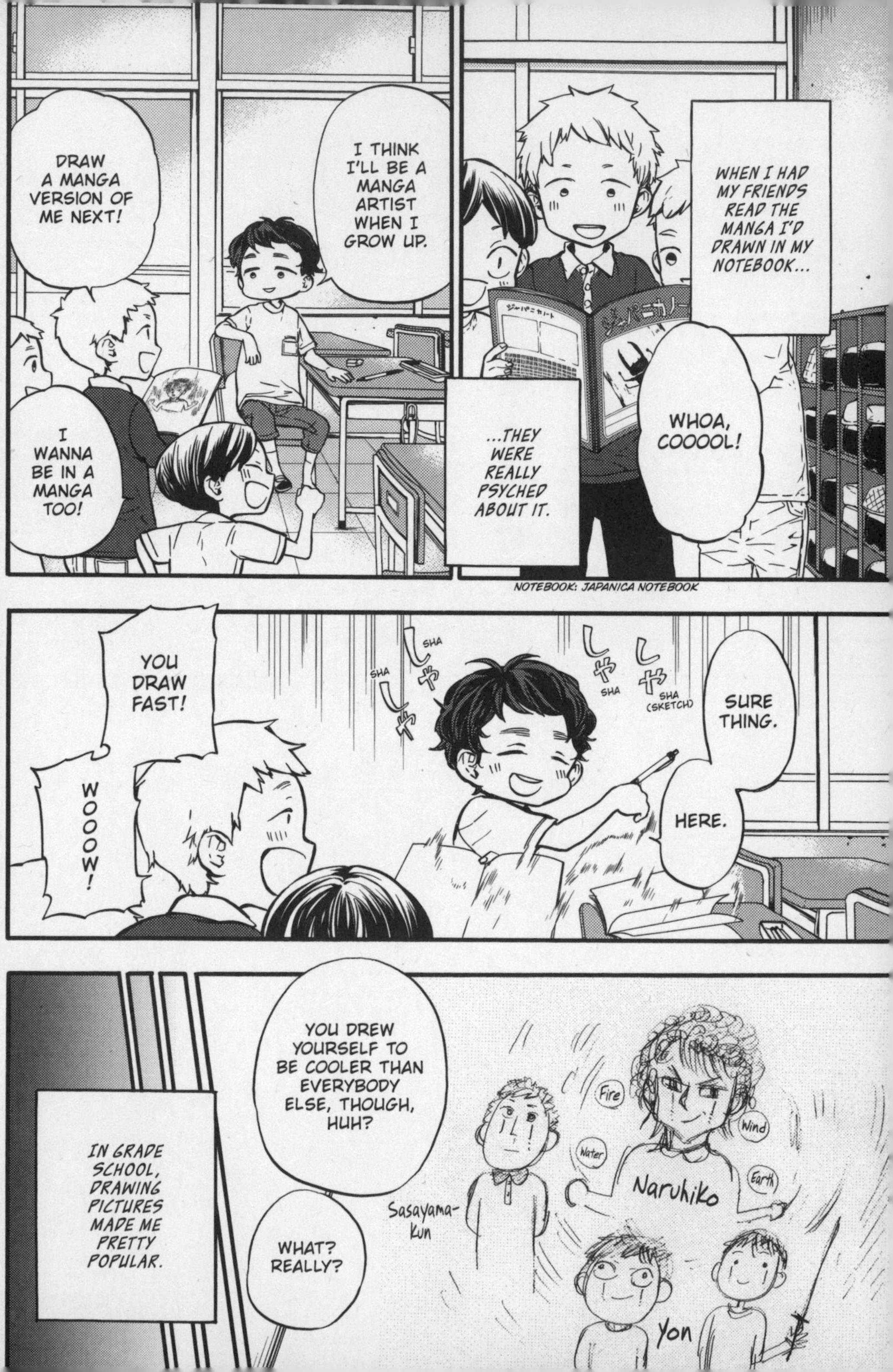
WHEN I HAD MY FRIENDS READ THE MANGA I'D DRAWN IN MY NOTEBOOK...
WHOA, COOOOL!
...THEY WERE REALLY PSYCHED ABOUT IT.
I THINK I'LL BE A MANGA ARTIST WHEN I GROW UP.
DRAW A MANGA VERSION OF ME NEXT!
I WANNA BE IN A MANGA TOO!
NOTEBOOK: JAPANICA NOTEBOOK
SURE THING.
しゃ SHA (SKETCH)
しゃ SHA
しゃ SHA
しゃ SHA
HERE.
YOU DRAW FAST!
WOOOOW!
Fire
Wind
Water
Earth
Naruhiko
Sasayama-Kun
Yon
YOU DREW YOURSELF TO BE COOLER THAN EVERYBODY ELSE, THOUGH, HUH?
WHAT? REALLY?
IN GRADE SCHOOL, DRAWING PICTURES MADE ME PRETTY POPULAR.

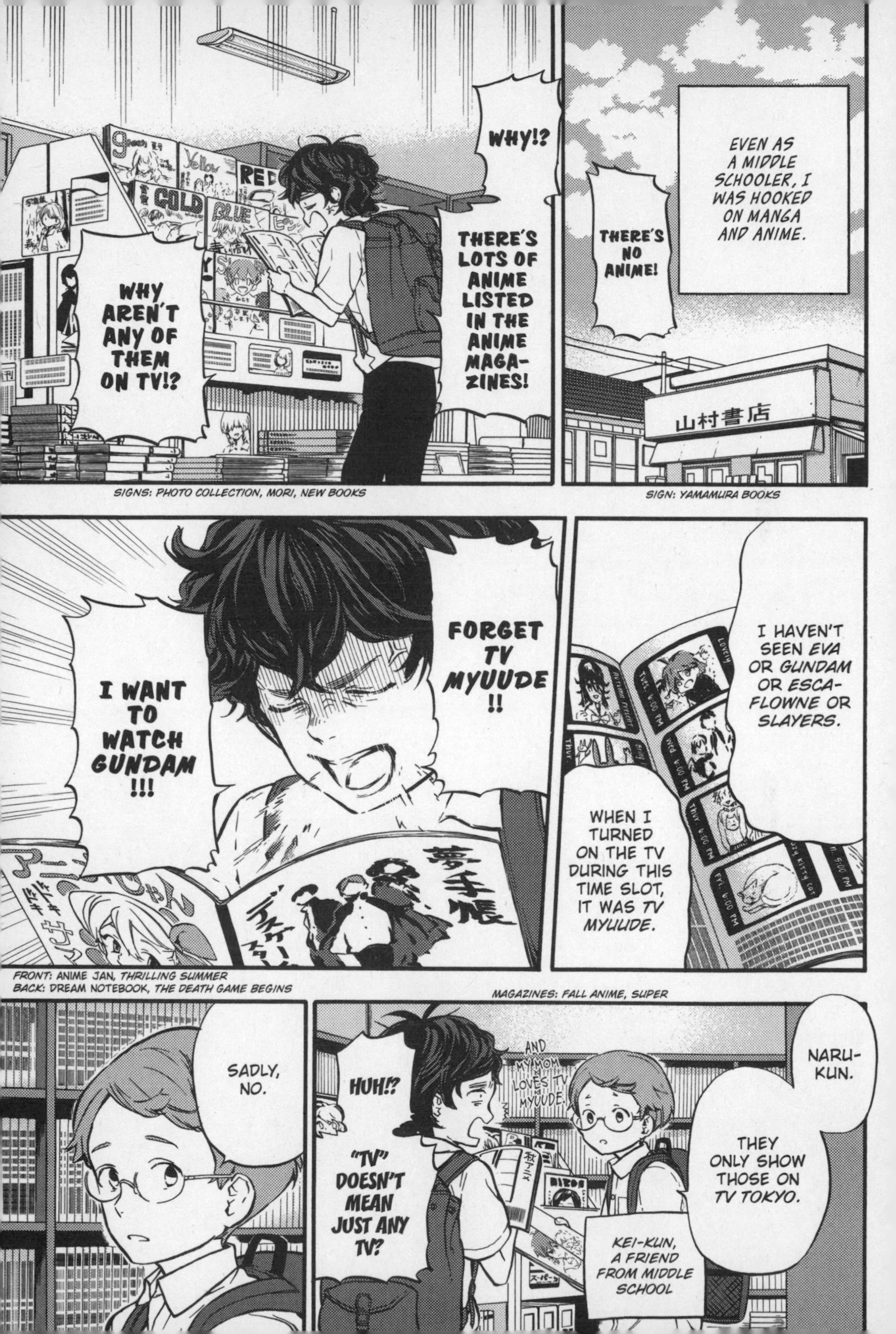
EVEN AS A MIDDLE SCHOOLER, I WAS HOOKED ON MANGA AND ANIME.
山村書店
THERE'S NO ANIME!
WHY!?
THERE'S LOTS OF ANIME LISTED IN THE ANIME MAGAZINES!
WHY AREN'T ANY OF THEM ON TV!?
SIGN: YAMAMURA BOOKS
SIGNS: PHOTO COLLECTION, MORI, NEW BOOKS
I HAVEN'T SEEN *EVA* OR *GUNDAM* OR *ESCAFLOWNE* OR *SLAYERS*.
WHEN I TURNED ON THE TV DURING THIS TIME SLOT, IT WAS *TV MYUUDE*.
FORGET TV MYUUDE!!
I WANT TO WATCH GUNDAM!!!
MAGAZINES: *FALL ANIME, SUPER*
FRONT: *ANIME JAN, THRILLING SUMMER*
BACK: *DREAM NOTEBOOK, THE DEATH GAME BEGINS*
NARU-KUN.
THEY ONLY SHOW THOSE ON *TV TOKYO*.
KEI-KUN, A FRIEND FROM MIDDLE SCHOOL
HUH!?
AND MY MOM LOVES TV MYUUDE.
"TV" DOESN'T MEAN JUST ANY TV?
SADLY, NO.

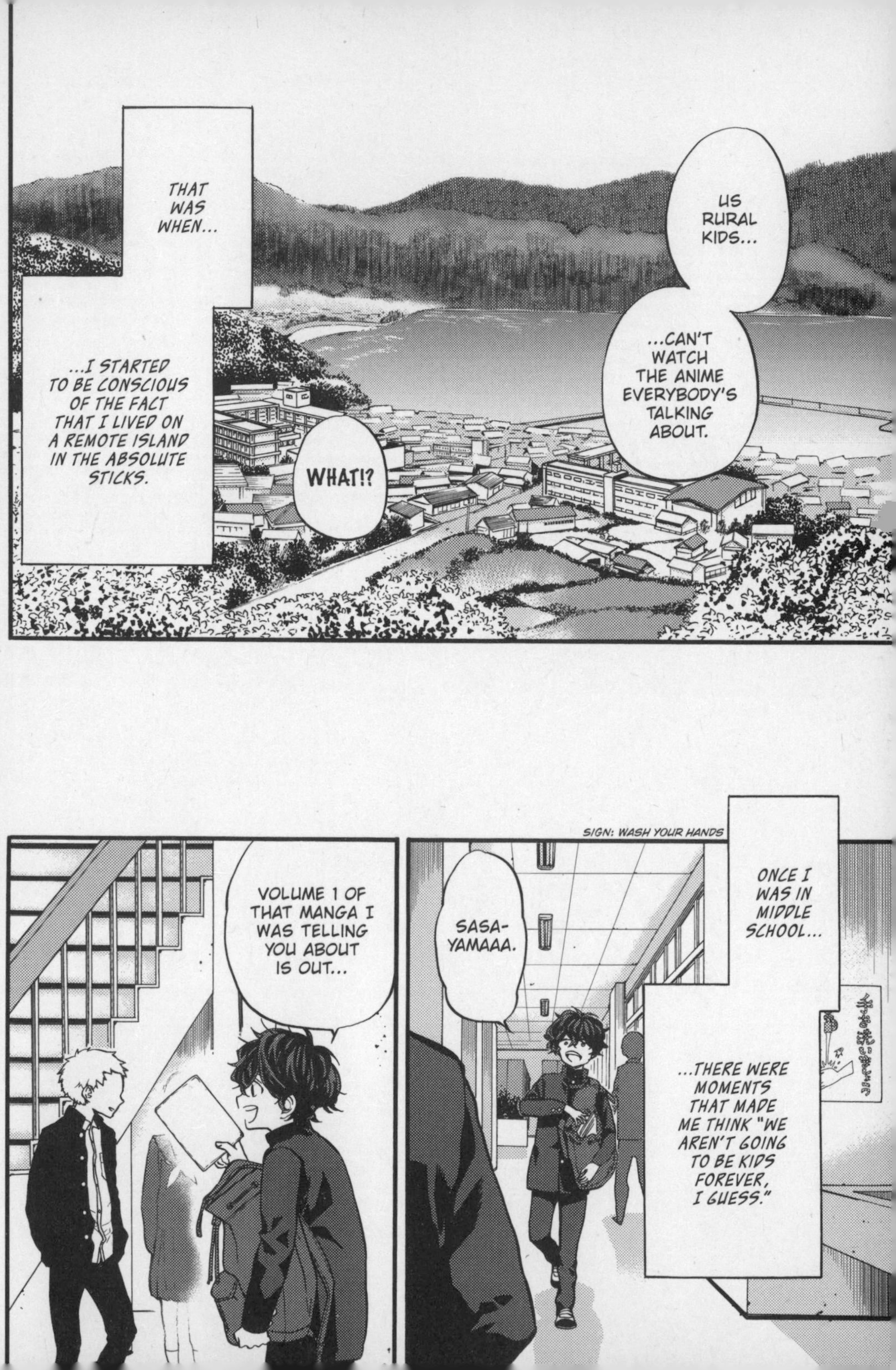
US RURAL KIDS...
...CAN'T WATCH THE ANIME EVERYBODY'S TALKING ABOUT.
WHAT!?
THAT WAS WHEN...
...I STARTED TO BE CONSCIOUS OF THE FACT THAT I LIVED ON A REMOTE ISLAND IN THE ABSOLUTE STICKS.
SIGN: WASH YOUR HANDS
ONCE I WAS IN MIDDLE SCHOOL...
...THERE WERE MOMENTS THAT MADE ME THINK "WE AREN'T GOING TO BE KIDS FOREVER, I GUESS."
SASA-YAMAAA.
VOLUME 1 OF THAT MANGA I WAS TELLING YOU ABOUT IS OUT...

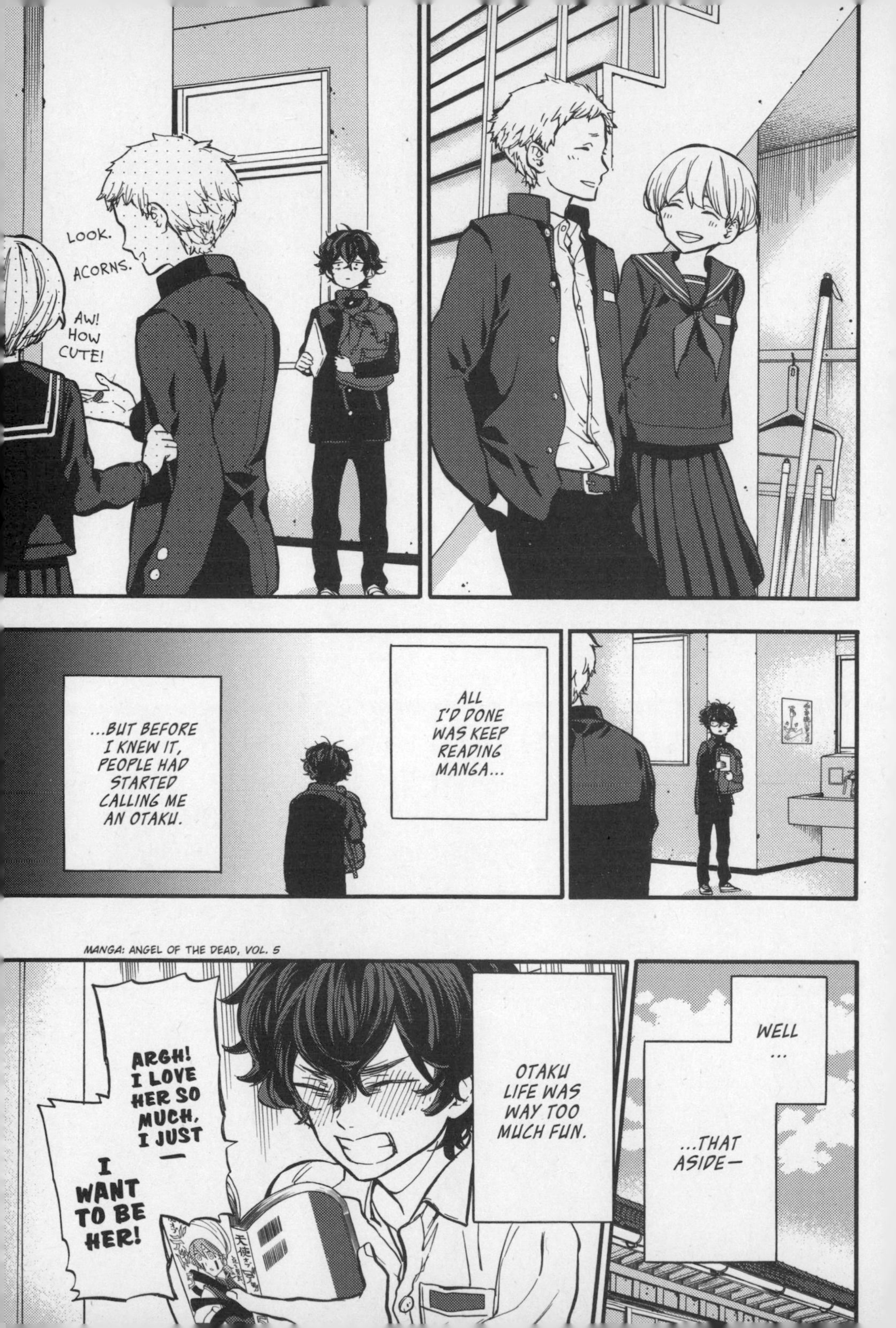
LOOK.
ACORNS.
AW! HOW CUTE!
ALL I'D DONE WAS KEEP READING MANGA...
...BUT BEFORE I KNEW IT, PEOPLE HAD STARTED CALLING ME AN OTAKU.
MANGA: ANGEL OF THE DEAD, VOL. 5
WELL...
...THAT ASIDE—
OTAKU LIFE WAS WAY TOO MUCH FUN.
ARGH! I LOVE HER SO MUCH, I JUST—
I WANT TO BE HER!

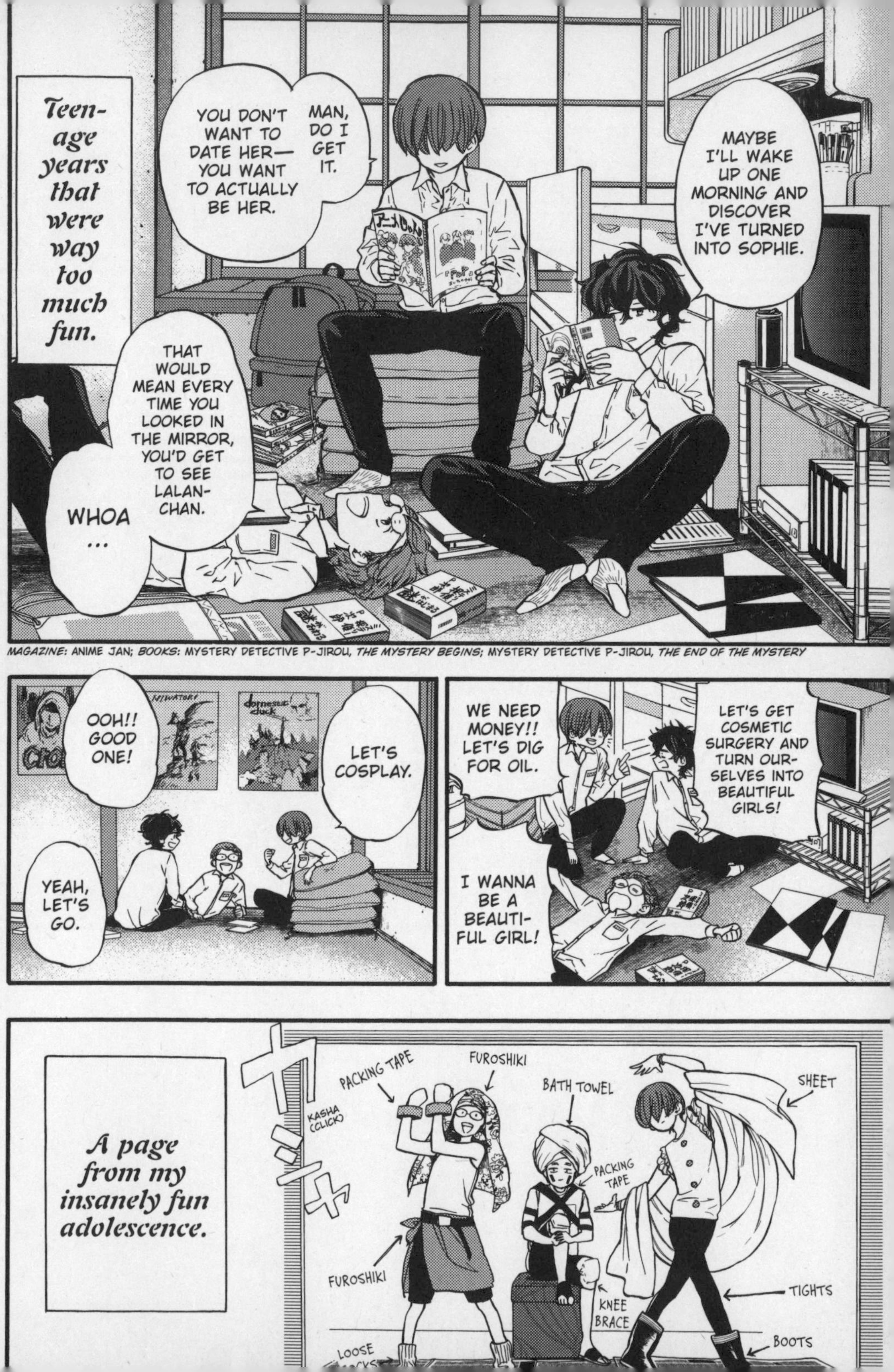
MAYBE I'LL WAKE UP ONE MORNING AND DISCOVER I'VE TURNED INTO SOPHIE.
MAN, DO I GET IT.
YOU DON'T WANT TO DATE HER— YOU WANT TO ACTUALLY BE HER.
THAT WOULD MEAN EVERY TIME YOU LOOKED IN THE MIRROR, YOU'D GET TO SEE LALAN-CHAN.
WHOA...
Teen-age years that were way too much fun.
MAGAZINE: ANIME JAN; BOOKS: MYSTERY DETECTIVE P-JIROU, THE MYSTERY BEGINS; MYSTERY DETECTIVE P-JIROU, THE END OF THE MYSTERY
LET'S GET COSMETIC SURGERY AND TURN OUR-SELVES INTO BEAUTIFUL GIRLS!
WE NEED MONEY!! LET'S DIG FOR OIL.
I WANNA BE A BEAUTI-FUL GIRL!
LET'S COSPLAY.
OOH!! GOOD ONE!
YEAH, LET'S GO.
SHEET
BATH TOWEL
FUROSHIKI
PACKING TAPE
KASHA (CLICK)
PACKING TAPE
TIGHTS
KNEE BRACE
BOOTS
FUROSHIKI
LOOSE
A page from my insanely fun adolescence.

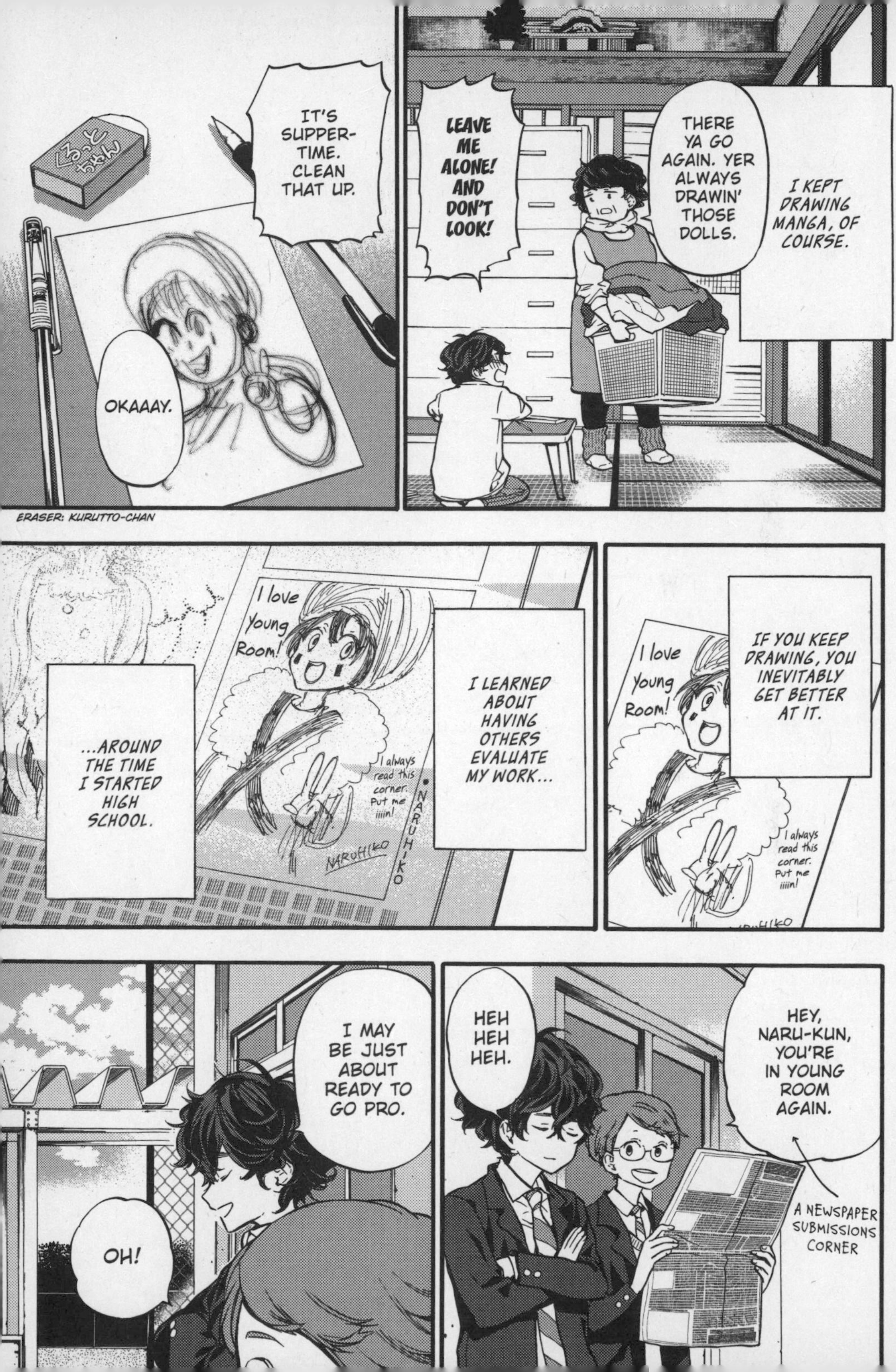
I KEPT DRAWING MANGA, OF COURSE.
THERE YA GO AGAIN. YER ALWAYS DRAWIN' THOSE DOLLS.
LEAVE ME ALONE! AND DON'T LOOK!
IT'S SUPPER-TIME. CLEAN THAT UP.
OKAAAY.
ERASER: KURUTTO-CHAN
IF YOU KEEP DRAWING, YOU INEVITABLY GET BETTER AT IT.
I love Young Room!
I always read this corner. Put me iiiin!
I LEARNED ABOUT HAVING OTHERS EVALUATE MY WORK...
I love Young Room!
I always read this corner. Put me iiiin!
NARUHIKO
NARUHIKO
...AROUND THE TIME I STARTED HIGH SCHOOL.
HEY, NARU-KUN, YOU'RE IN YOUNG ROOM AGAIN.
A NEWSPAPER SUBMISSIONS CORNER
HEH HEH HEH.
I MAY BE JUST ABOUT READY TO GO PRO.
OH!

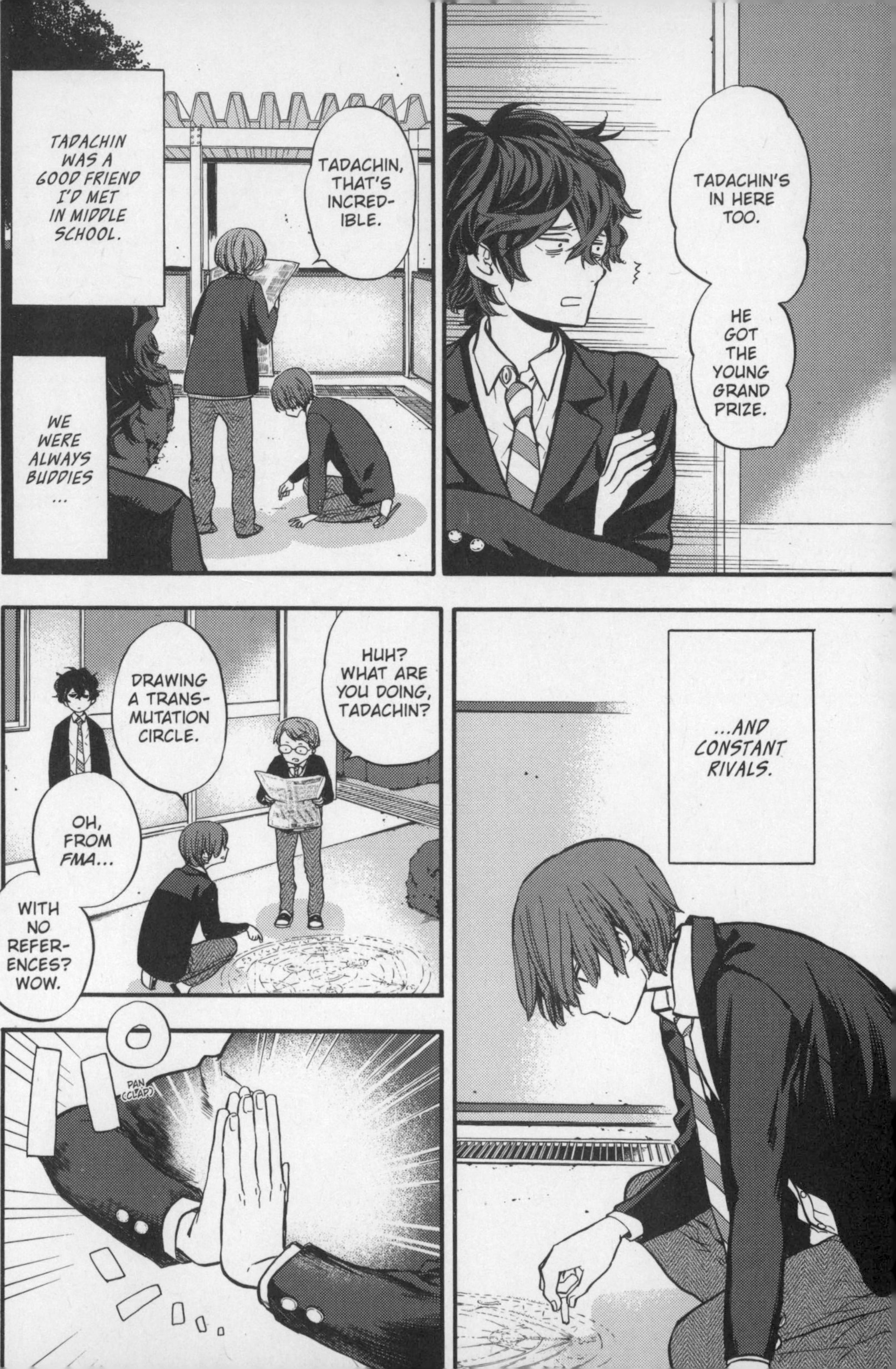
TADACHIN'S IN HERE TOO.
HE GOT THE YOUNG GRAND PRIZE.
TADACHIN, THAT'S INCRED-IBLE.
TADACHIN WAS A GOOD FRIEND I'D MET IN MIDDLE SCHOOL.
WE WERE ALWAYS BUDDIES ...
...AND CONSTANT RIVALS.
HUH? WHAT ARE YOU DOING, TADACHIN?
DRAWING A TRANS-MUTATION CIRCLE.
OH, FROM FMA...
WITH NO REFER-ENCES? WOW.
PAN (CLAP)

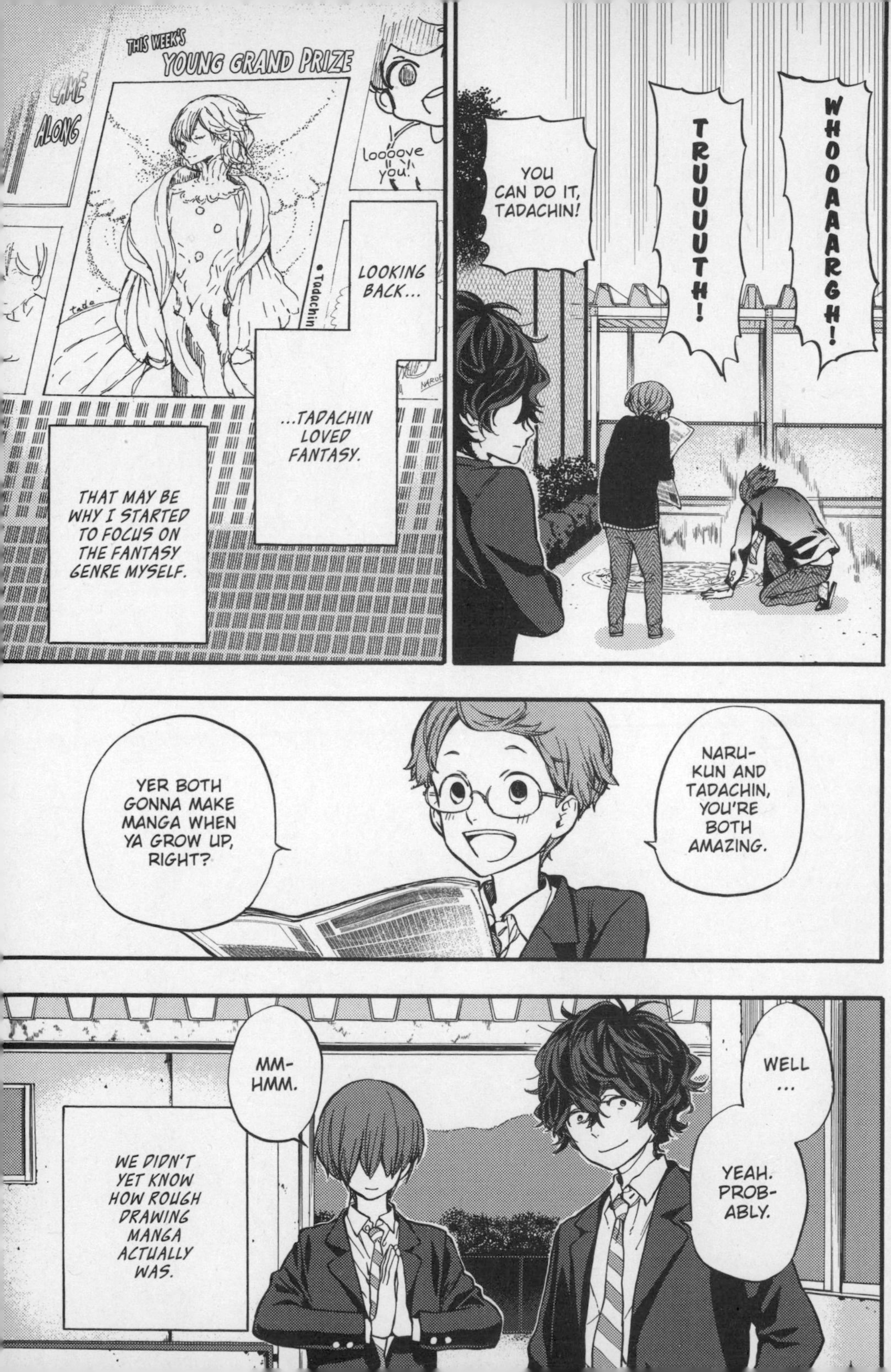
WHOOAAARGH!
TRUUUUTH!
YOU CAN DO IT, TADACHIN!
THIS WEEK'S YOUNG GRAND PRIZE
CAME ALONG
looooove you!
●Tadachin
LOOKING BACK...
...TADACHIN LOVED FANTASY.
THAT MAY BE WHY I STARTED TO FOCUS ON THE FANTASY GENRE MYSELF.
NARU-KUN AND TADACHIN, YOU'RE BOTH AMAZING.
YER BOTH GONNA MAKE MANGA WHEN YA GROW UP, RIGHT?
WELL ...
YEAH. PROBABLY.
MM-HMM.
WE DIDN'T YET KNOW HOW ROUGH DRAWING MANGA ACTUALLY WAS.

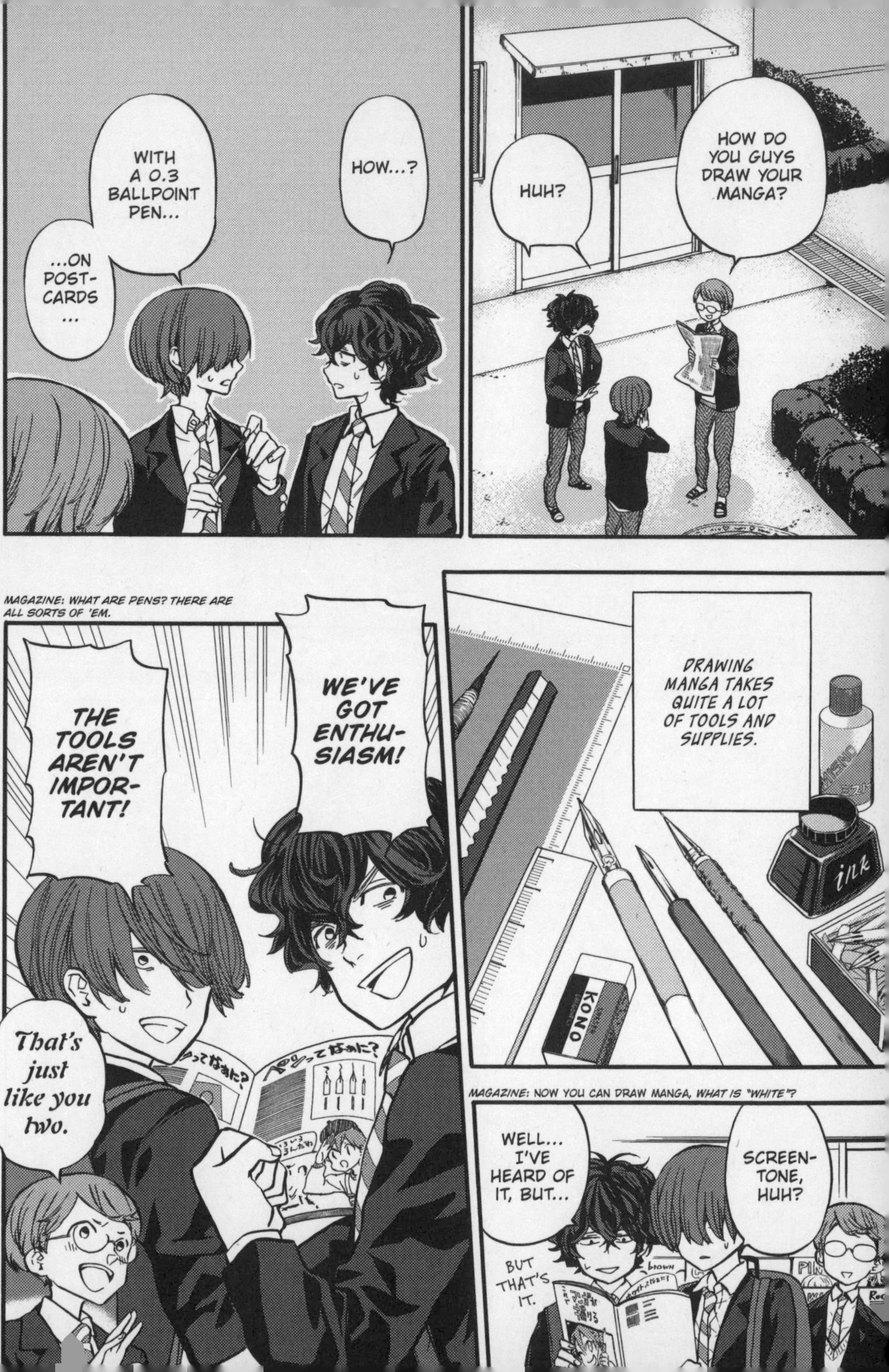
HOW DO YOU GUYS DRAW YOUR MANGA?
HUH?
HOW...?
WITH A 0.3 BALLPOINT PEN...
...ON POST-CARDS...
DRAWING MANGA TAKES QUITE A LOT OF TOOLS AND SUPPLIES.
ink
KONO
MAGAZINE: NOW YOU CAN DRAW MANGA, WHAT IS "WHITE"?
SCREEN-TONE, HUH?
WELL... I'VE HEARD OF IT, BUT...
BUT THAT'S IT.
MAGAZINE: WHAT ARE PENS? THERE ARE ALL SORTS OF 'EM.
WE'VE GOT ENTHU-SIASM!
THE TOOLS AREN'T IMPOR-TANT!
That's just like you two.

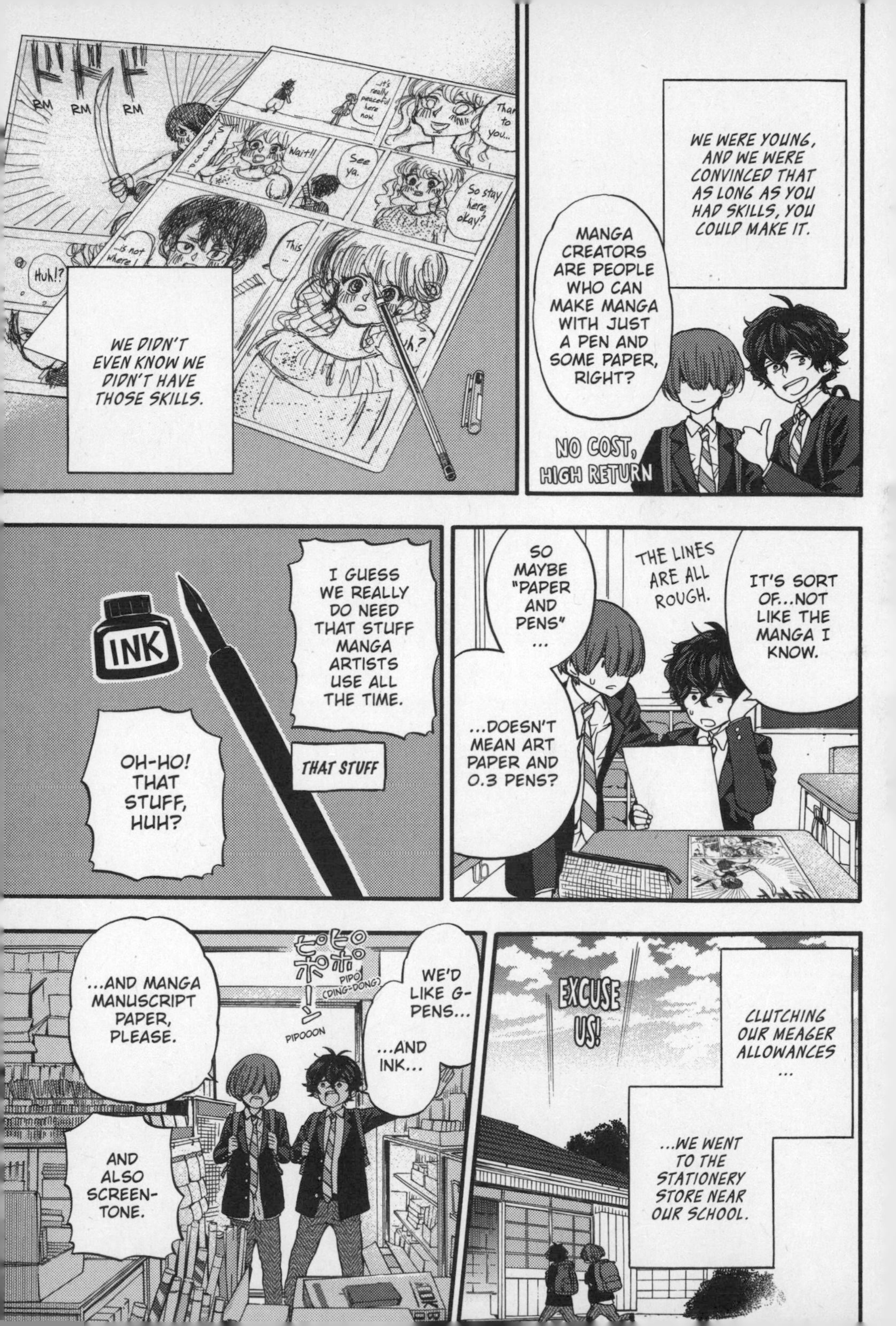
WE WERE YOUNG, AND WE WERE CONVINCED THAT AS LONG AS YOU HAD SKILLS, YOU COULD MAKE IT.
MANGA CREATORS ARE PEOPLE WHO CAN MAKE MANGA WITH JUST A PEN AND SOME PAPER, RIGHT?
NO COST, HIGH RETURN
RM RM RM
...it's really peaceful here now.
Wait!!
See ya.
So stay here, okay?
This...
Huh!?
WE DIDN'T EVEN KNOW WE DIDN'T HAVE THOSE SKILLS.
IT'S SORT OF...NOT LIKE THE MANGA I KNOW.
THE LINES ARE ALL ROUGH.
SO MAYBE "PAPER AND PENS"...
...DOESN'T MEAN ART PAPER AND 0.3 PENS?
I GUESS WE REALLY DO NEED THAT STUFF MANGA ARTISTS USE ALL THE TIME.
INK
THAT STUFF
OH-HO! THAT STUFF, HUH?
CLUTCHING OUR MEAGER ALLOWANCES...
EXCUSE US!
...WE WENT TO THE STATIONERY STORE NEAR OUR SCHOOL.
PIPO (DING-DONG)
PIPOOON
WE'D LIKE G-PENS...
...AND INK...
...AND MANGA MANUSCRIPT PAPER, PLEASE.
AND ALSO SCREEN-TONE.

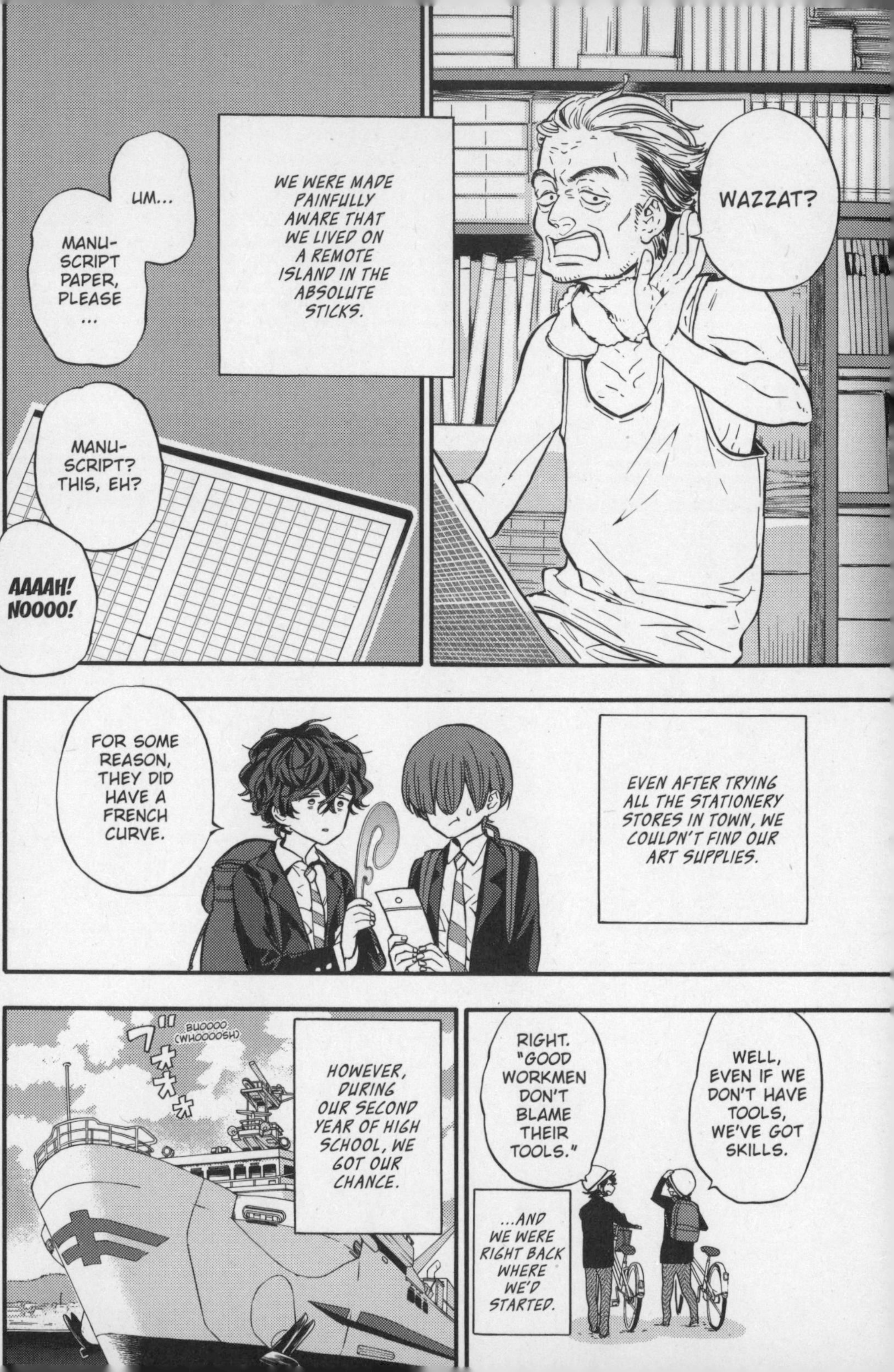
WAZZAT?
WE WERE MADE PAINFULLY AWARE THAT WE LIVED ON A REMOTE ISLAND IN THE ABSOLUTE STICKS.
UM...
MANU-SCRIPT PAPER, PLEASE ...
MANU-SCRIPT? THIS, EH?
AAAAH! NOOOO!
EVEN AFTER TRYING ALL THE STATIONERY STORES IN TOWN, WE COULDN'T FIND OUR ART SUPPLIES.
FOR SOME REASON, THEY DID HAVE A FRENCH CURVE.
WELL, EVEN IF WE DON'T HAVE TOOLS, WE'VE GOT SKILLS.
RIGHT. "GOOD WORKMEN DON'T BLAME THEIR TOOLS."
...AND WE WERE RIGHT BACK WHERE WE'D STARTED.
HOWEVER, DURING OUR SECOND YEAR OF HIGH SCHOOL, WE GOT OUR CHANCE.
BUOOOO (WHOOOOSH)

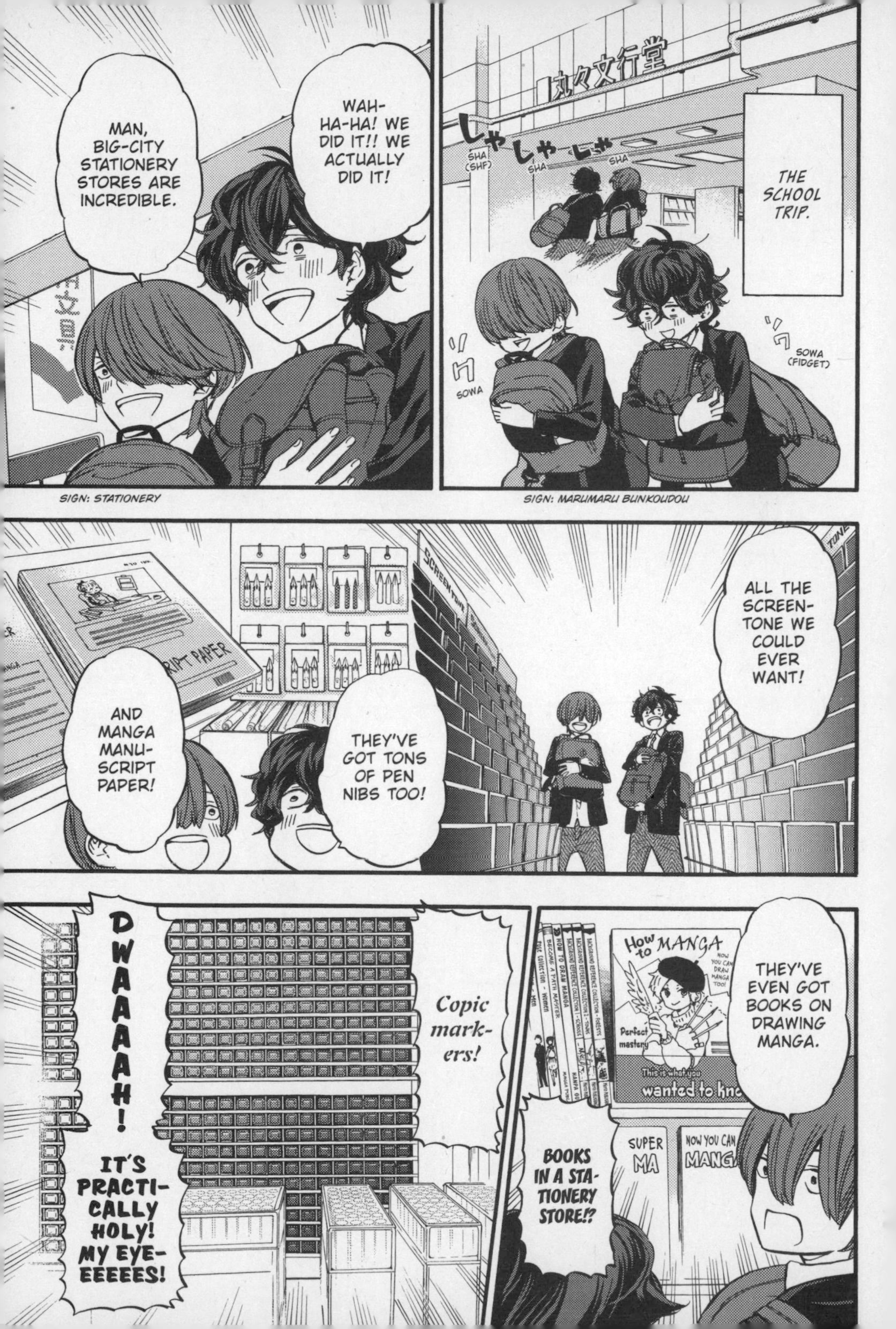
丸々文行堂
SHA (SHF)
SHA
SHA
THE SCHOOL TRIP.
SOWA (FIDGET)
SOWA
SIGN: MARUMARU BUNKOUDOU
WAH-HA-HA! WE DID IT!! WE ACTUALLY DID IT!
MAN, BIG-CITY STATIONERY STORES ARE INCREDIBLE.
SIGN: STATIONERY
ALL THE SCREEN-TONE WE COULD EVER WANT!
THEY'VE GOT TONS OF PEN NIBS TOO!
AND MANGA MANU-SCRIPT PAPER!
THEY'VE EVEN GOT BOOKS ON DRAWING MANGA.
How to MANGA
NOW YOU CAN DRAW MANGA TOO!
Perfect mastery
This is what you wanted to kno
SUPER MA
NOW YOU CAN MANGA
BOOKS IN A STA-TIONERY STORE!?
Copic mark-ers!
DWAAAAAH!
IT'S PRACTI-CALLY HOLY! MY EYE-EEEEES!

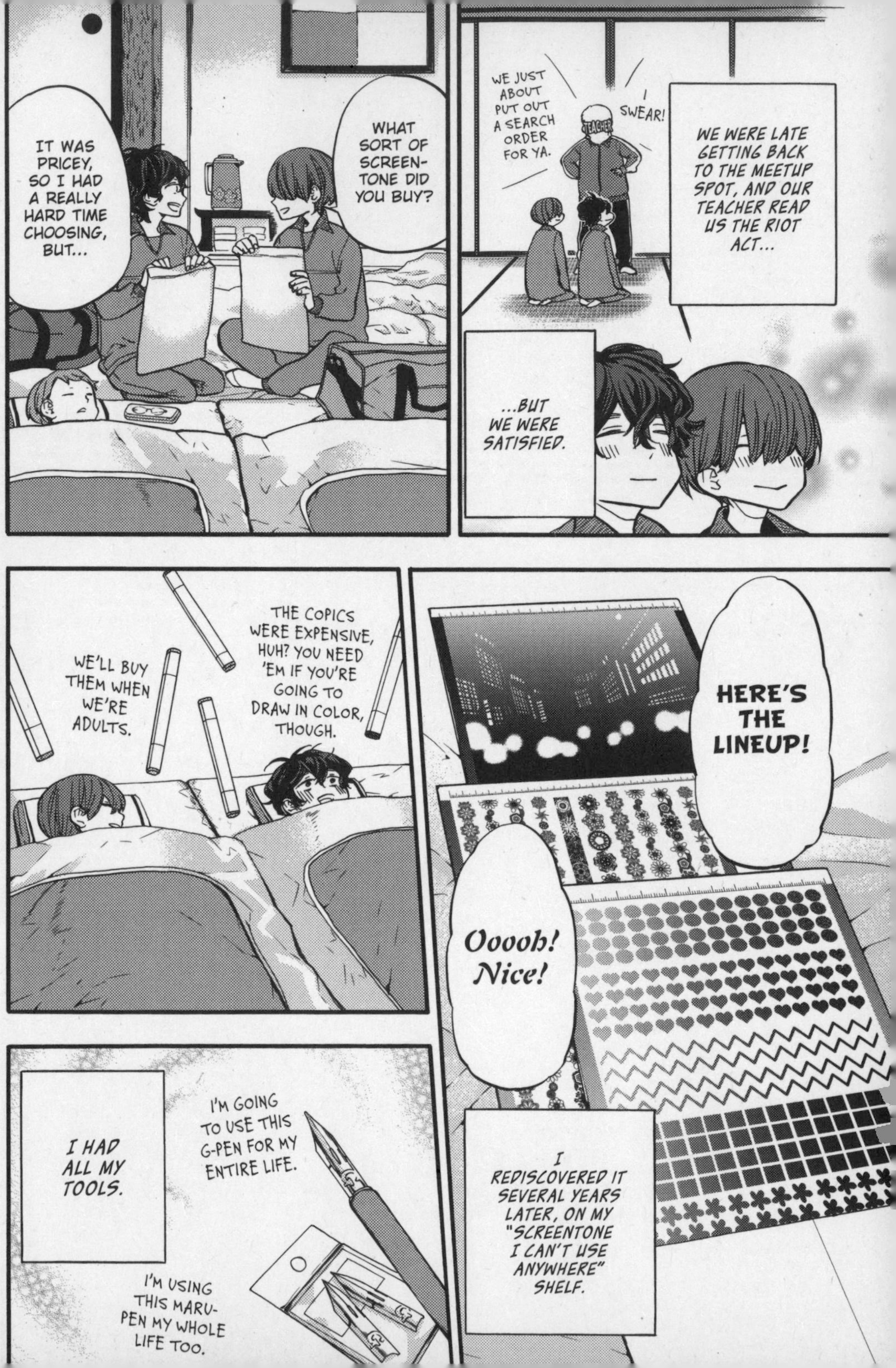
WE WERE LATE GETTING BACK TO THE MEETUP SPOT, AND OUR TEACHER READ US THE RIOT ACT...
I SWEAR!
TEACHER
WE JUST ABOUT PUT OUT A SEARCH ORDER FOR YA.
...BUT WE WERE SATISFIED.
WHAT SORT OF SCREEN-TONE DID YOU BUY?
IT WAS PRICEY, SO I HAD A REALLY HARD TIME CHOOSING, BUT...
HERE'S THE LINEUP!
Ooooh! Nice!
I REDISCOVERED IT SEVERAL YEARS LATER, ON MY "SCREENTONE I CAN'T USE ANYWHERE" SHELF.
THE COPICS WERE EXPENSIVE, HUH? YOU NEED 'EM IF YOU'RE GOING TO DRAW IN COLOR, THOUGH.
WE'LL BUY THEM WHEN WE'RE ADULTS.
I'M GOING TO USE THIS G-PEN FOR MY ENTIRE LIFE.
I HAD ALL MY TOOLS.
I'M USING THIS MARU-PEN MY WHOLE LIFE TOO.

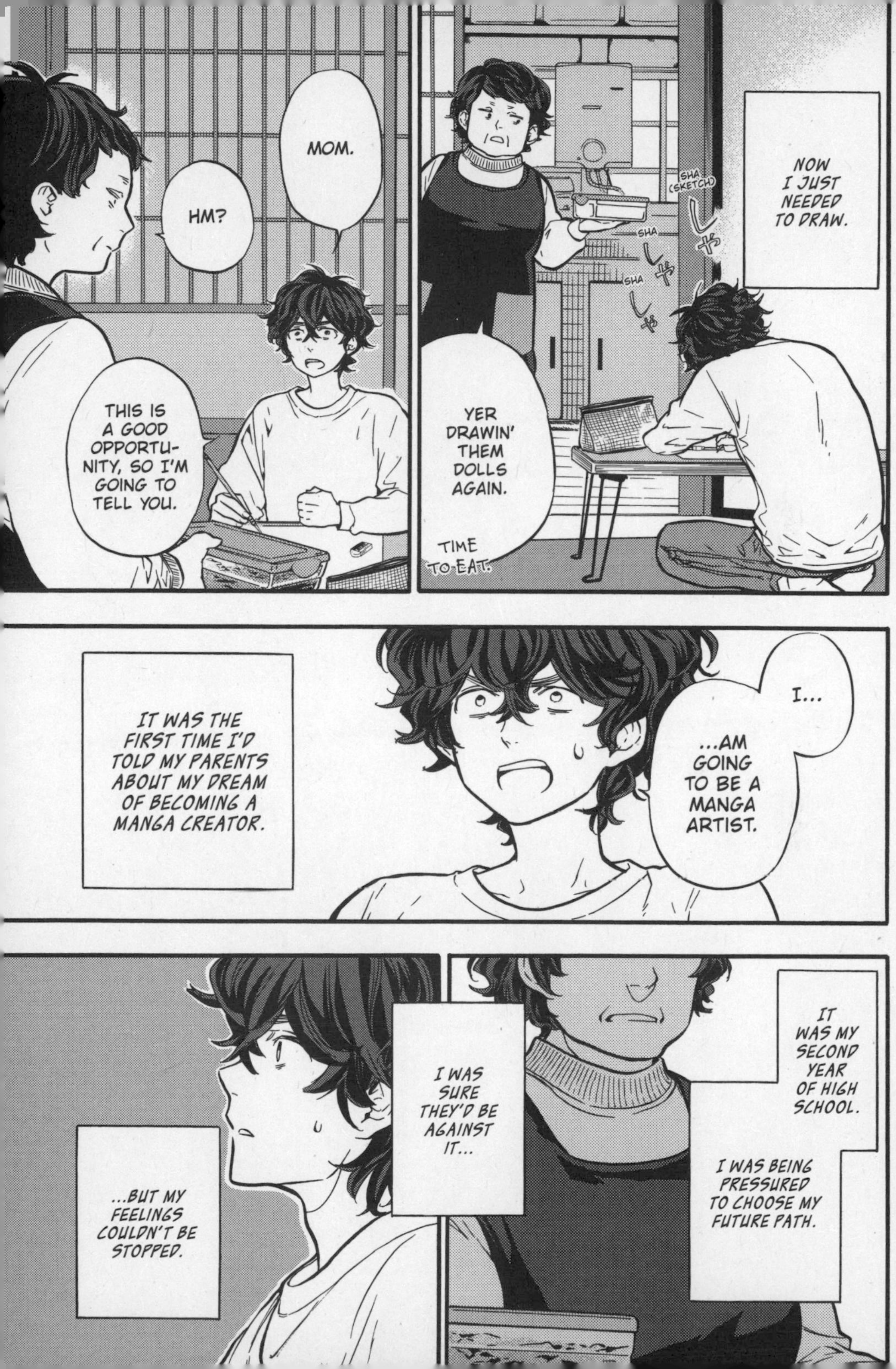
NOW I JUST NEEDED TO DRAW.
しゃ SHA (SKETCH)
しゃ SHA
しゃ SHA
YER DRAWIN' THEM DOLLS AGAIN.
TIME TO EAT.
MOM.
HM?
THIS IS A GOOD OPPORTUNITY, SO I'M GOING TO TELL YOU.
I...
...AM GOING TO BE A MANGA ARTIST.
IT WAS THE FIRST TIME I'D TOLD MY PARENTS ABOUT MY DREAM OF BECOMING A MANGA CREATOR.
IT WAS MY SECOND YEAR OF HIGH SCHOOL.
I WAS BEING PRESSURED TO CHOOSE MY FUTURE PATH.
I WAS SURE THEY'D BE AGAINST IT...
...BUT MY FEELINGS COULDN'T BE STOPPED.

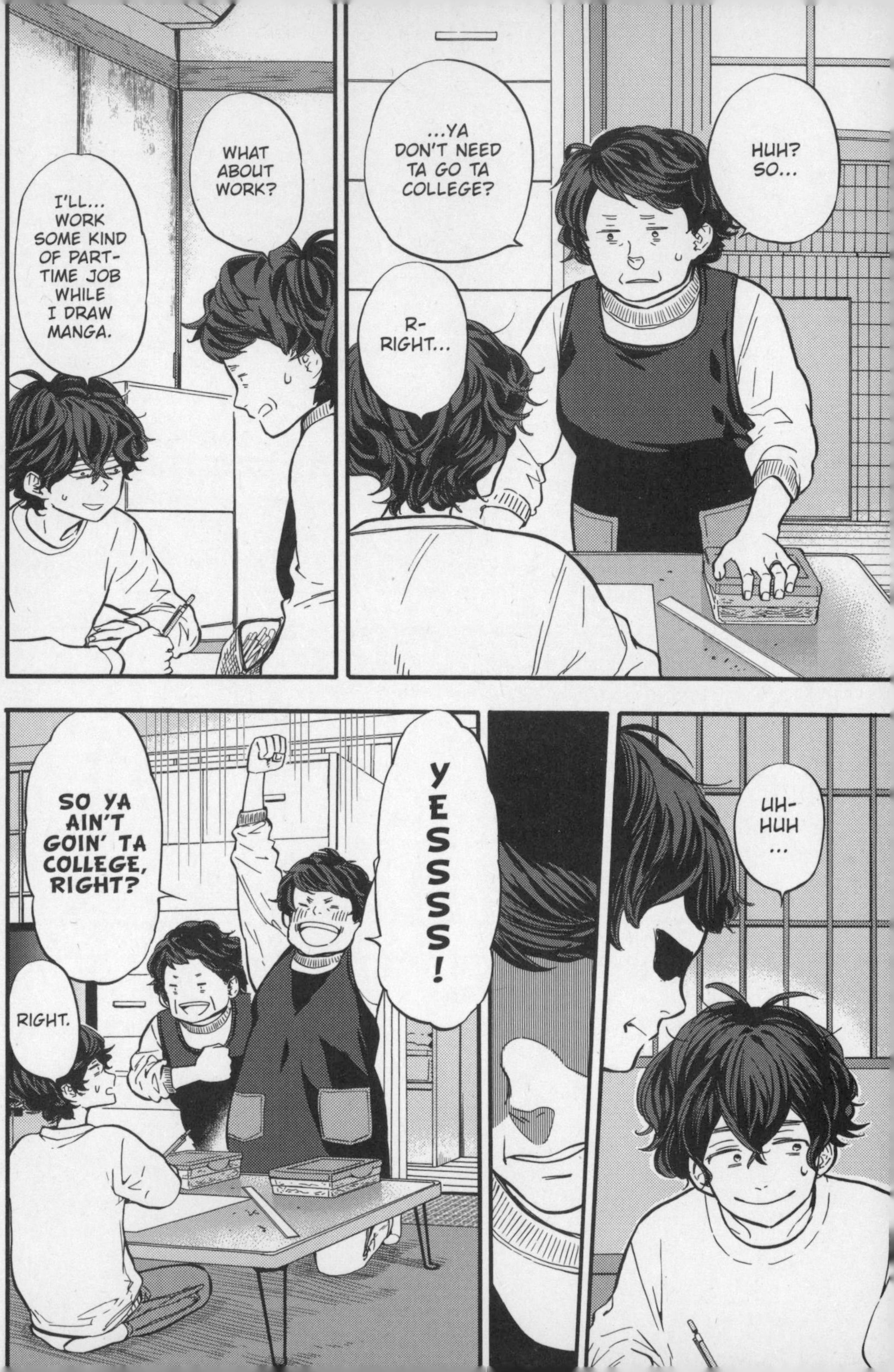
HUH? SO...
...YA DON'T NEED TA GO TA COLLEGE?
R-RIGHT...
WHAT ABOUT WORK?
I'LL... WORK SOME KIND OF PART-TIME JOB WHILE I DRAW MANGA.
UH-HUH...
YESSS!
SO YA AIN'T GOIN' TA COLLEGE, RIGHT?
RIGHT.

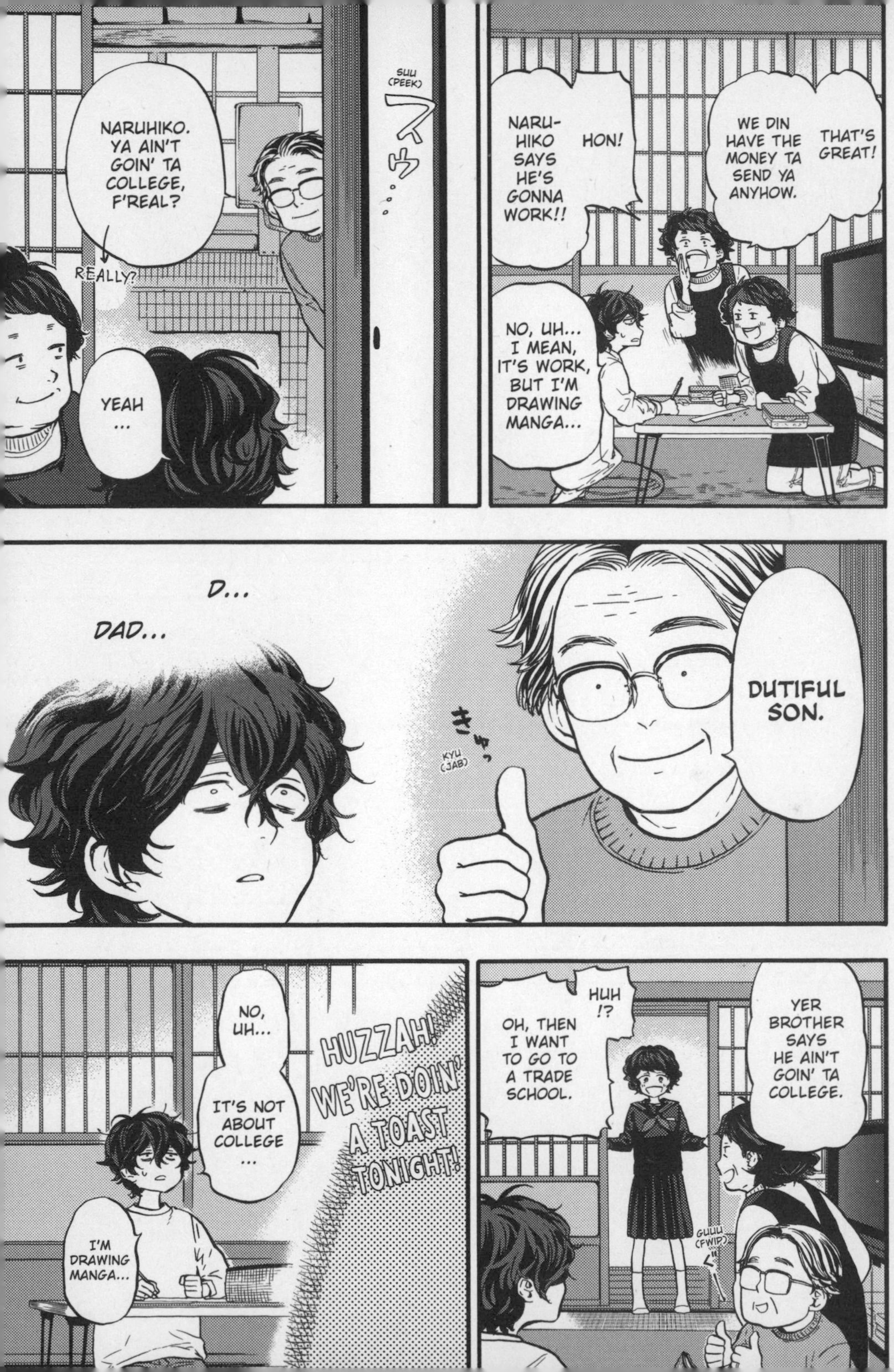
THAT'S GREAT!
WE DIN HAVE THE MONEY TA SEND YA ANYHOW.
HON!
NARUHIKO SAYS HE'S GONNA WORK!!
NO, UH... I MEAN, IT'S WORK, BUT I'M DRAWING MANGA...
SUU (PEEK)
スゥ...
NARUHIKO. YA AIN'T GOIN' TA COLLEGE, F'REAL?
REALLY?
YEAH ...
DUTIFUL SON.
KYU (JAB)
D...
DAD...
YER BROTHER SAYS HE AIN'T GOIN' TA COLLEGE.
GUUU (FWIP)
HUH !?
OH, THEN I WANT TO GO TO A TRADE SCHOOL.
HUZZAH! WE'RE DOIN' A TOAST TONIGHT!
NO, UH...
IT'S NOT ABOUT COLLEGE ...
I'M DRAWING MANGA...

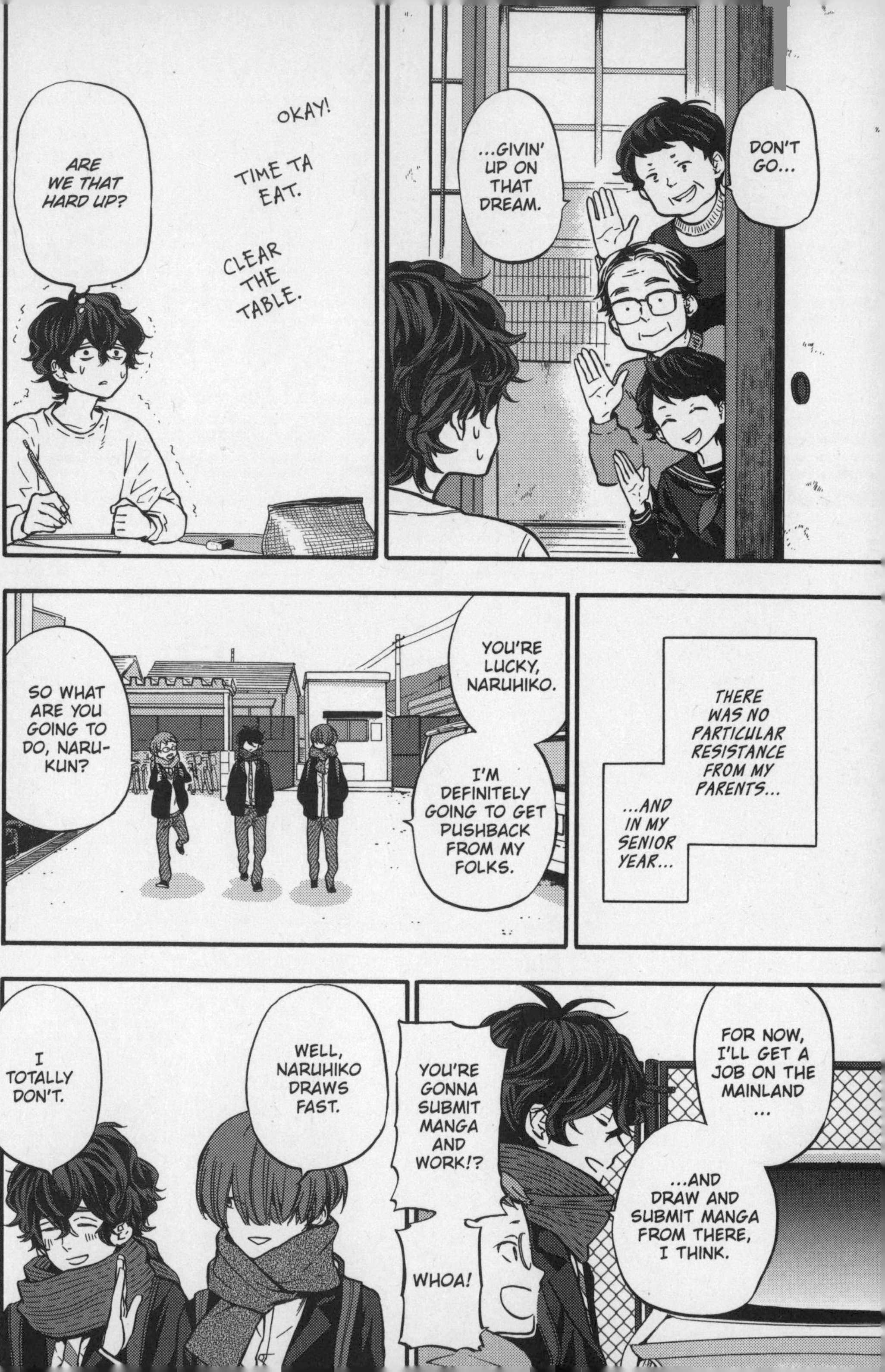
DON'T GO...
...GIVIN' UP ON THAT DREAM.
OKAY!
TIME TA EAT.
CLEAR THE TABLE.
ARE WE THAT HARD UP?
THERE WAS NO PARTICULAR RESISTANCE FROM MY PARENTS...
...AND IN MY SENIOR YEAR...
YOU'RE LUCKY, NARUHIKO.
I'M DEFINITELY GOING TO GET PUSHBACK FROM MY FOLKS.
SO WHAT ARE YOU GOING TO DO, NARU-KUN?
FOR NOW, I'LL GET A JOB ON THE MAINLAND ...
...AND DRAW AND SUBMIT MANGA FROM THERE, I THINK.
YOU'RE GONNA SUBMIT MANGA AND WORK!?
WHOA!
WELL, NARUHIKO DRAWS FAST.
I TOTALLY DON'T.

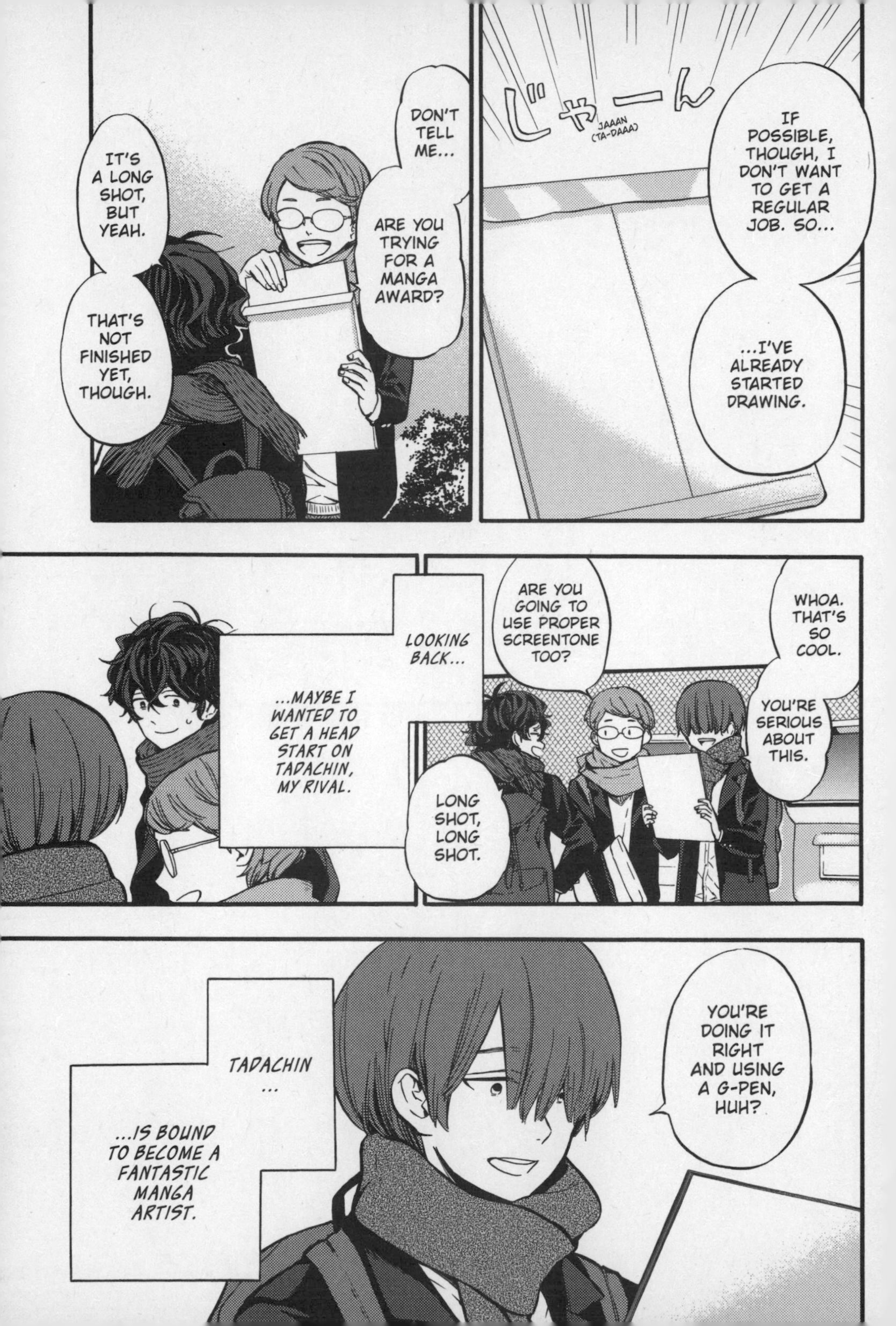
じゃーん
JAAAN (TA-DAAA)
IF POSSIBLE, THOUGH, I DON'T WANT TO GET A REGULAR JOB. SO...
...I'VE ALREADY STARTED DRAWING.
DON'T TELL ME...
ARE YOU TRYING FOR A MANGA AWARD?
IT'S A LONG SHOT, BUT YEAH.
THAT'S NOT FINISHED YET, THOUGH.
WHOA. THAT'S SO COOL.
YOU'RE SERIOUS ABOUT THIS.
ARE YOU GOING TO USE PROPER SCREENTONE TOO?
LONG SHOT, LONG SHOT.
LOOKING BACK...
...MAYBE I WANTED TO GET A HEAD START ON TADACHIN, MY RIVAL.
YOU'RE DOING IT RIGHT AND USING A G-PEN, HUH?
TADACHIN...
...IS BOUND TO BECOME A FANTASTIC MANGA ARTIST.

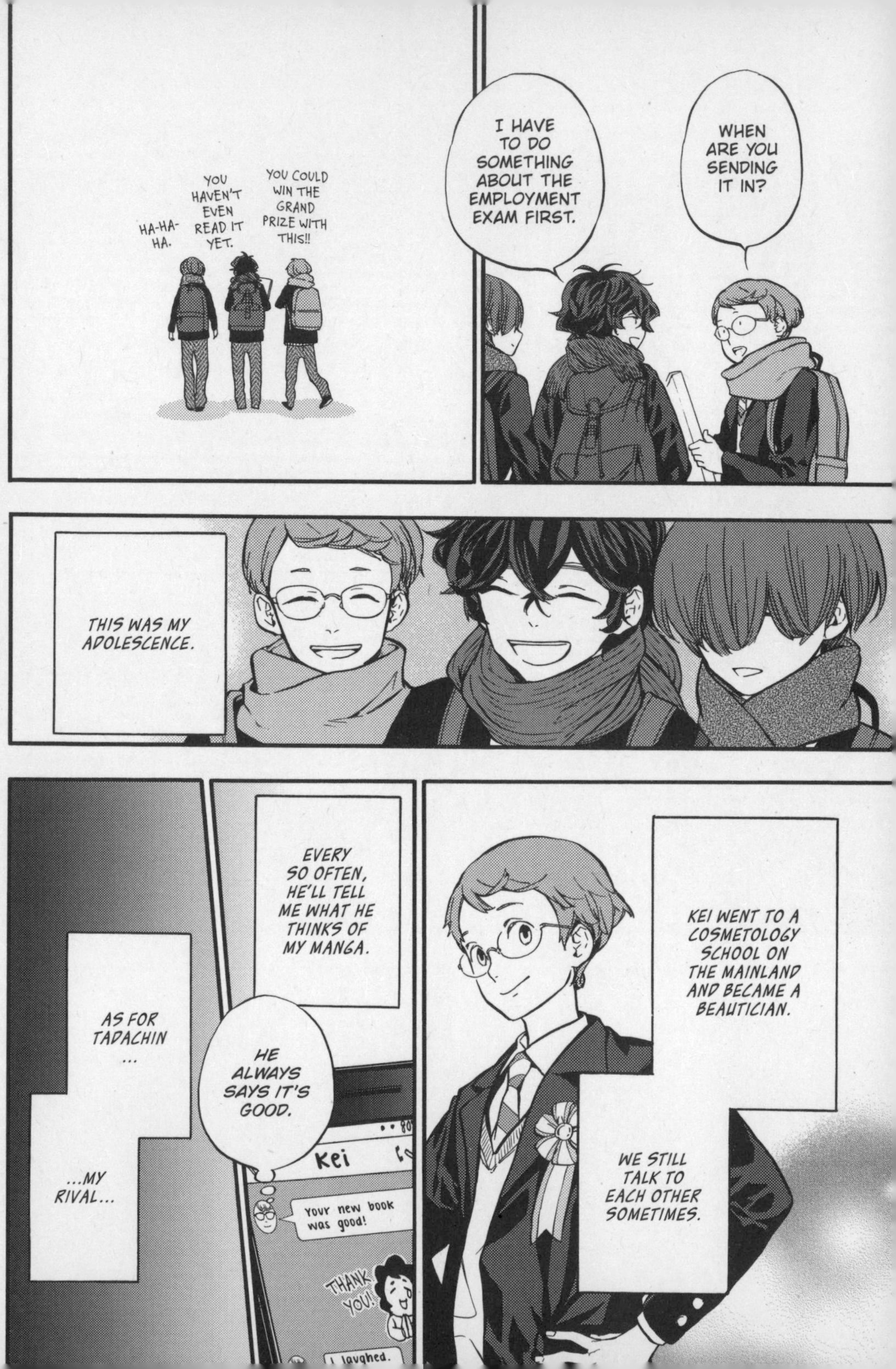
WHEN ARE YOU SENDING IT IN?
I HAVE TO DO SOMETHING ABOUT THE EMPLOYMENT EXAM FIRST.
YOU COULD WIN THE GRAND PRIZE WITH THIS!!
YOU HAVEN'T EVEN READ IT YET.
HA-HA-HA.
THIS WAS MY ADOLESCENCE.
KEI WENT TO A COSMETOLOGY SCHOOL ON THE MAINLAND AND BECAME A BEAUTICIAN.
WE STILL TALK TO EACH OTHER SOMETIMES.
EVERY SO OFTEN, HE'LL TELL ME WHAT HE THINKS OF MY MANGA.
HE ALWAYS SAYS IT'S GOOD.
Kei
Your new book was good!
THANK YOU!
I laughed.
AS FOR TADACHIN ...
...MY RIVAL...

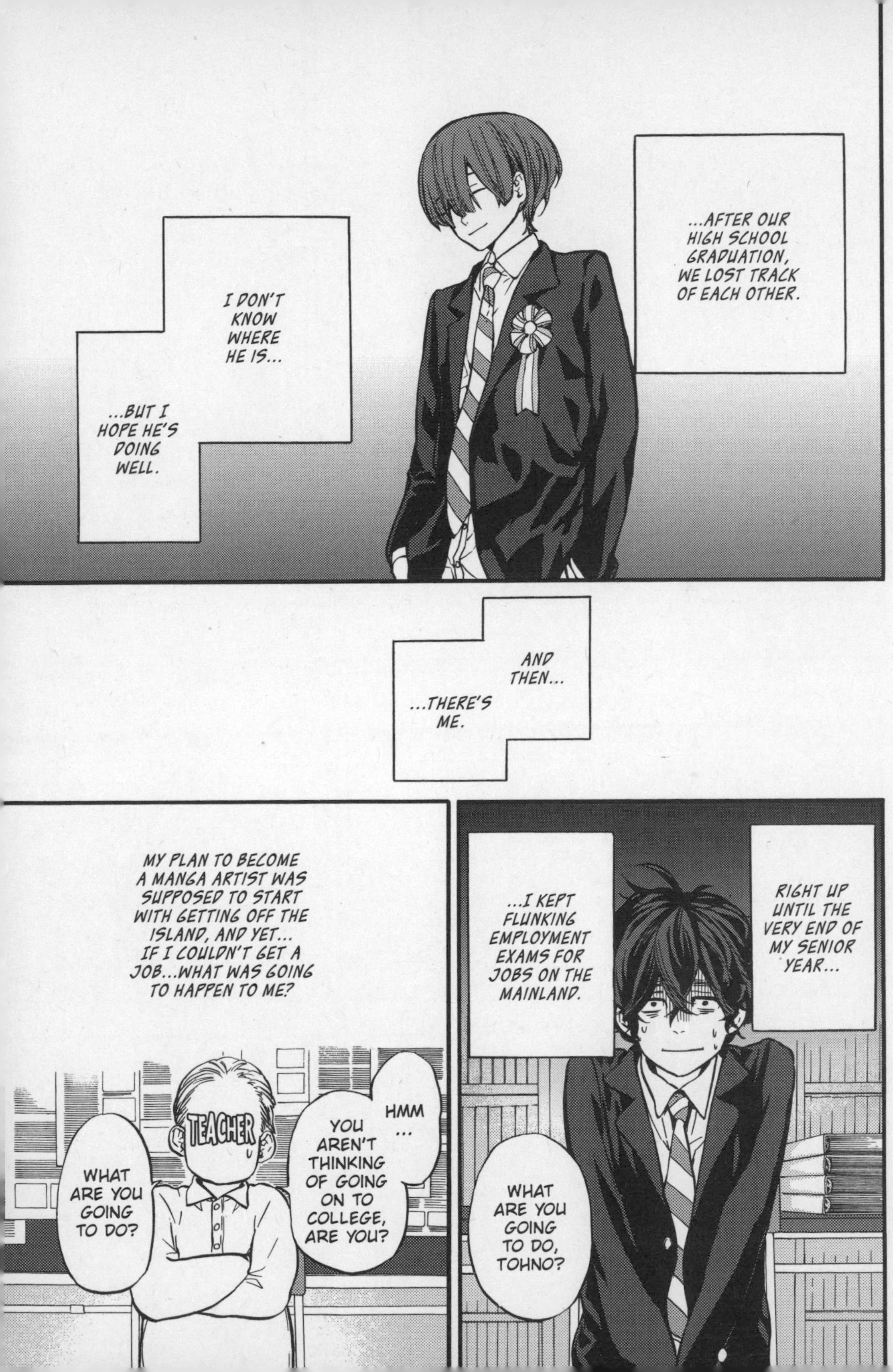
...AFTER OUR HIGH SCHOOL GRADUATION, WE LOST TRACK OF EACH OTHER.
I DON'T KNOW WHERE HE IS...
...BUT I HOPE HE'S DOING WELL.
AND THEN...
...THERE'S ME.
RIGHT UP UNTIL THE VERY END OF MY SENIOR YEAR...
...I KEPT FLUNKING EMPLOYMENT EXAMS FOR JOBS ON THE MAINLAND.
WHAT ARE YOU GOING TO DO, TOHNO?
MY PLAN TO BECOME A MANGA ARTIST WAS SUPPOSED TO START WITH GETTING OFF THE ISLAND, AND YET... IF I COULDN'T GET A JOB...WHAT WAS GOING TO HAPPEN TO ME?
HMM...
YOU AREN'T THINKING OF GOING ON TO COLLEGE, ARE YOU?
TEACHER
WHAT ARE YOU GOING TO DO?

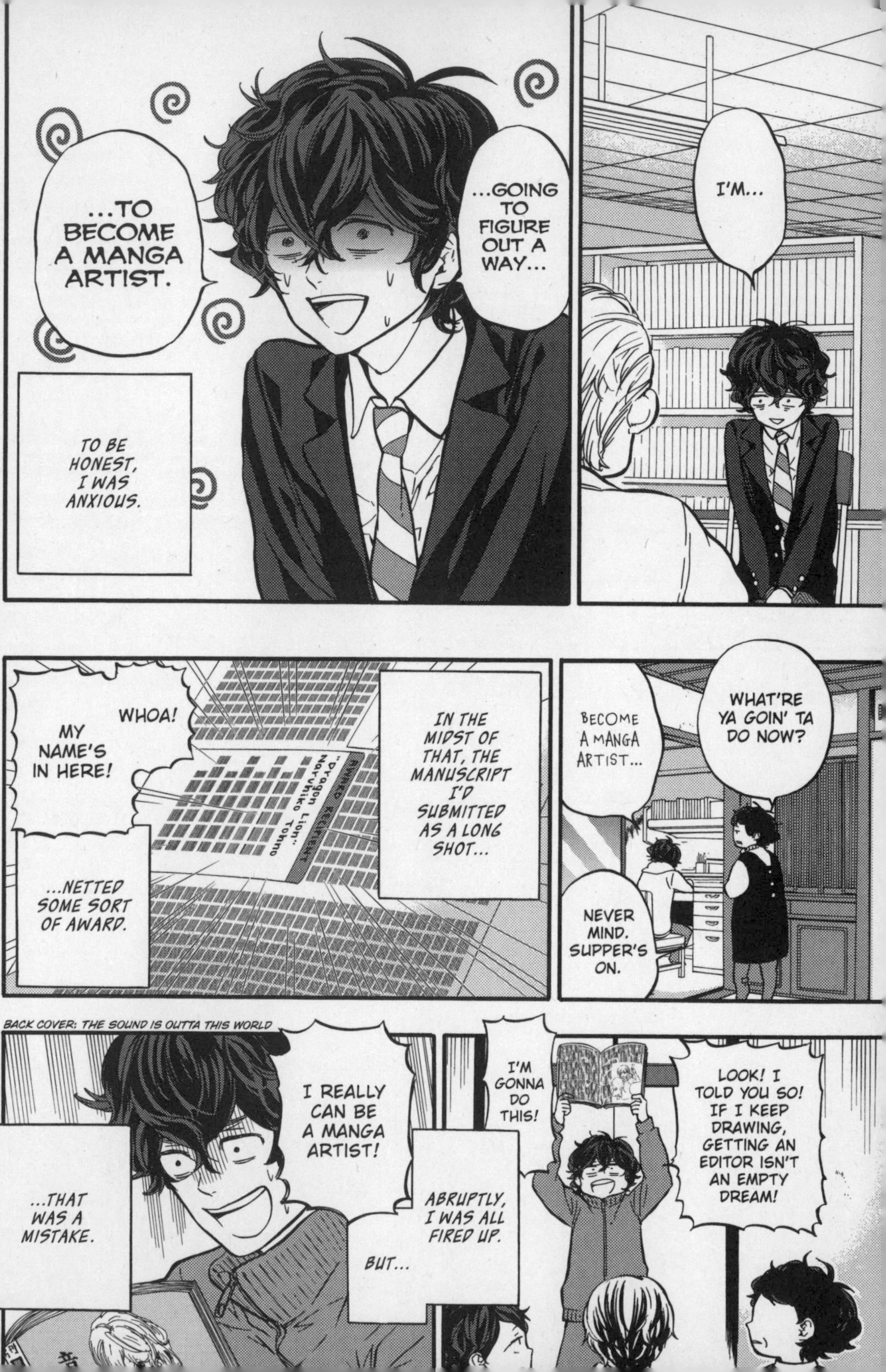
I'M...
...GOING TO FIGURE OUT A WAY...
...TO BECOME A MANGA ARTIST.
TO BE HONEST, I WAS ANXIOUS.
WHAT'RE YA GOIN' TA DO NOW?
BECOME A MANGA ARTIST...
NEVER MIND. SUPPER'S ON.
IN THE MIDST OF THAT, THE MANUSCRIPT I'D SUBMITTED AS A LONG SHOT...
WHOA!
MY NAME'S IN HERE!
...NETTED SOME SORT OF AWARD.
BACK COVER: THE SOUND IS OUTTA THIS WORLD
LOOK! I TOLD YOU SO! IF I KEEP DRAWING, GETTING AN EDITOR ISN'T AN EMPTY DREAM!
I'M GONNA DO THIS!
I REALLY CAN BE A MANGA ARTIST!
ABRUPTLY, I WAS ALL FIRED UP.
BUT...
...THAT WAS A MISTAKE.

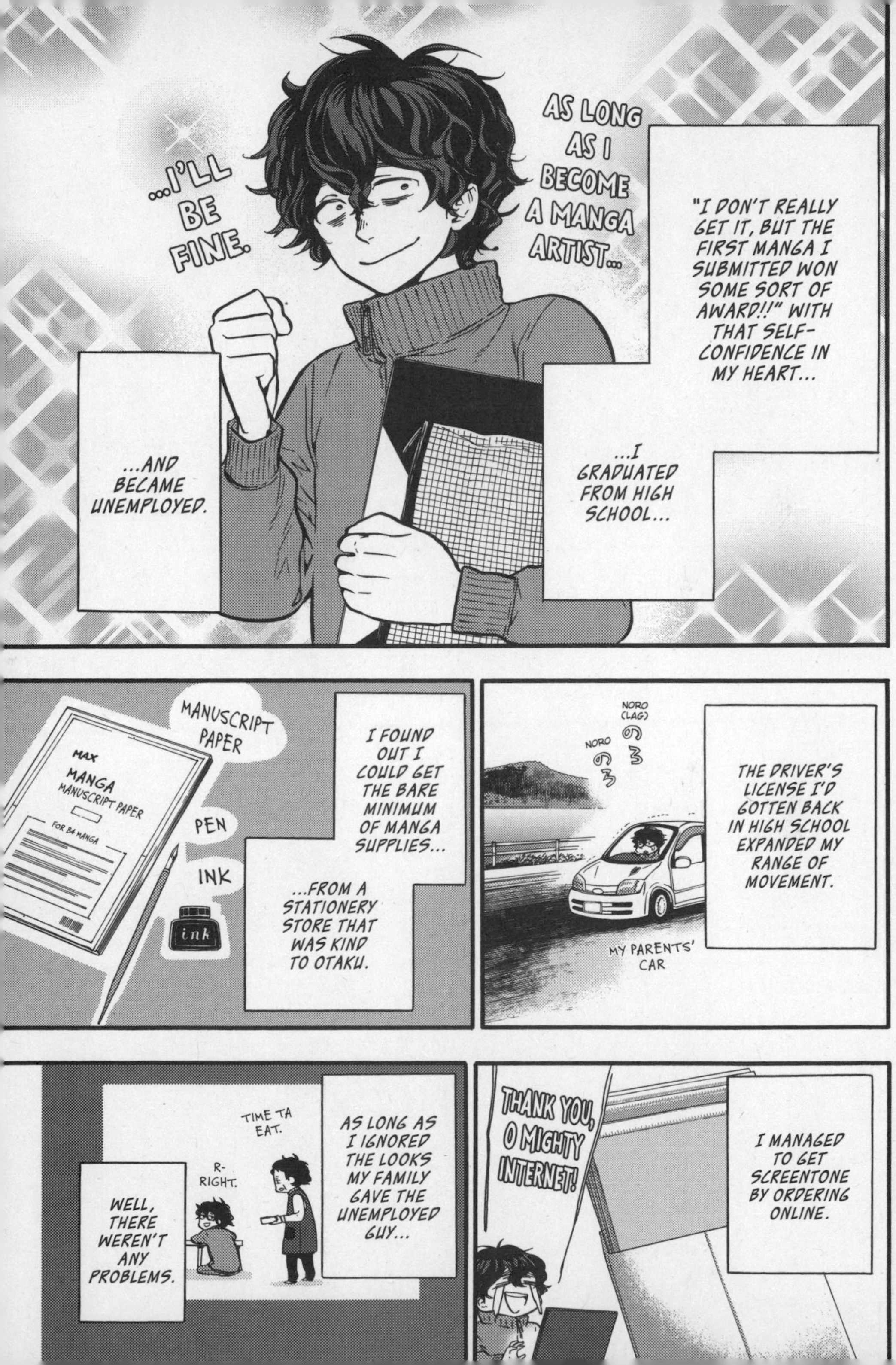
"I DON'T REALLY GET IT, BUT THE FIRST MANGA I SUBMITTED WON SOME SORT OF AWARD!!" WITH THAT SELF-CONFIDENCE IN MY HEART...
AS LONG AS I BECOME A MANGA ARTIST...
...I'LL BE FINE.
...I GRADUATED FROM HIGH SCHOOL...
...AND BECAME UNEMPLOYED.
THE DRIVER'S LICENSE I'D GOTTEN BACK IN HIGH SCHOOL EXPANDED MY RANGE OF MOVEMENT.
NORO (LAG)
NORO
MY PARENTS' CAR
I FOUND OUT I COULD GET THE BARE MINIMUM OF MANGA SUPPLIES...
...FROM A STATIONERY STORE THAT WAS KIND TO OTAKU.
MANUSCRIPT PAPER
MAX
MANGA
MANUSCRIPT PAPER
FOR B4 MANGA
PEN
INK
ink
I MANAGED TO GET SCREENTONE BY ORDERING ONLINE.
THANK YOU, O MIGHTY INTERNET!
AS LONG AS I IGNORED THE LOOKS MY FAMILY GAVE THE UNEMPLOYED GUY...
TIME TA EAT.
R-RIGHT.
WELL, THERE WEREN'T ANY PROBLEMS.

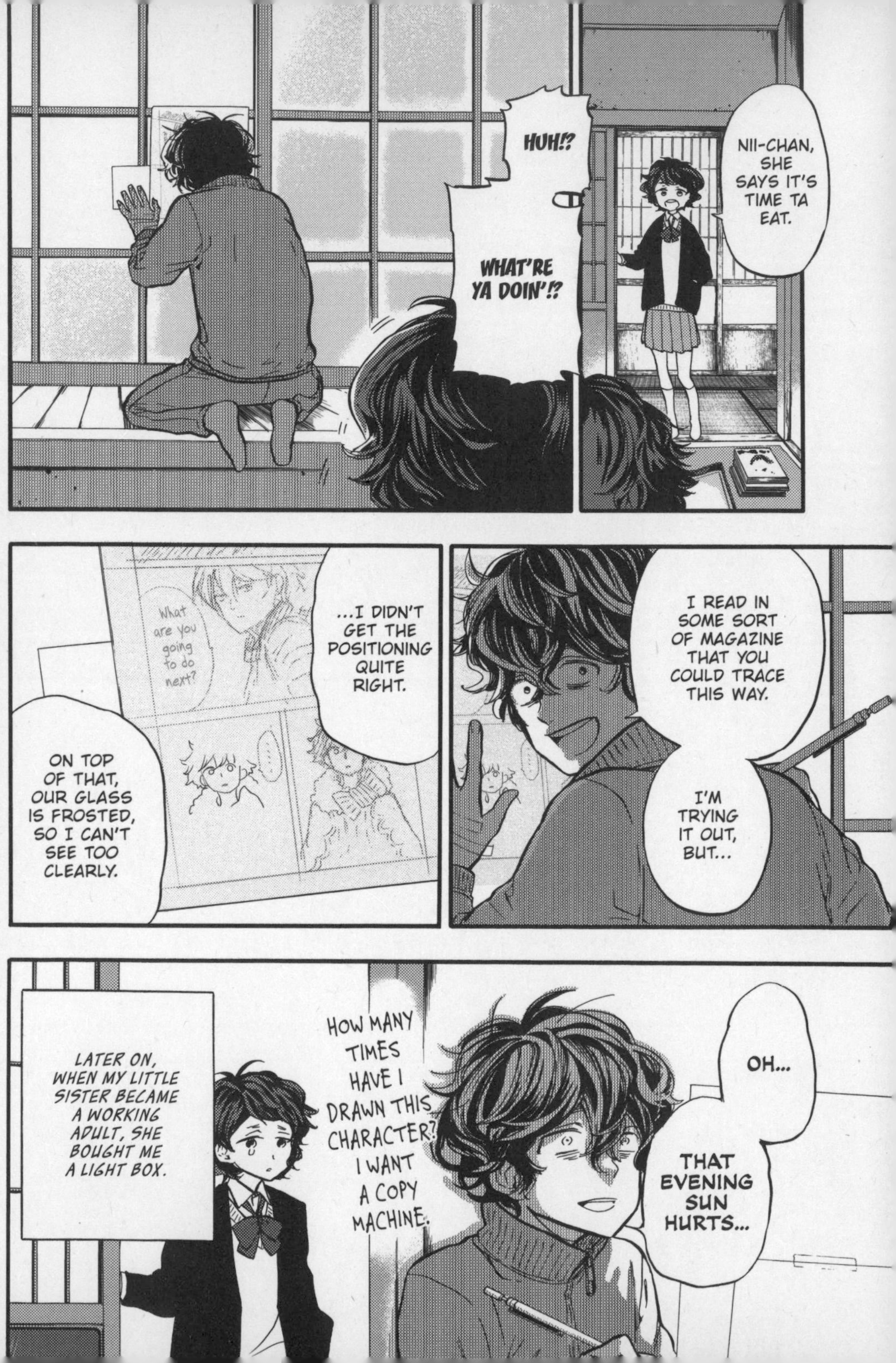
NII-CHAN, SHE SAYS IT'S TIME TA EAT.
HUH!?
WHAT'RE YA DOIN'!?
I READ IN SOME SORT OF MAGAZINE THAT YOU COULD TRACE THIS WAY.
I'M TRYING IT OUT, BUT...
...I DIDN'T GET THE POSITIONING QUITE RIGHT.
What are you going to do next?
ON TOP OF THAT, OUR GLASS IS FROSTED, SO I CAN'T SEE TOO CLEARLY.
OH...
THAT EVENING SUN HURTS...
HOW MANY TIMES HAVE I DRAWN THIS CHARACTER? I WANT A COPY MACHINE.
LATER ON, WHEN MY LITTLE SISTER BECAME A WORKING ADULT, SHE BOUGHT ME A LIGHT BOX.

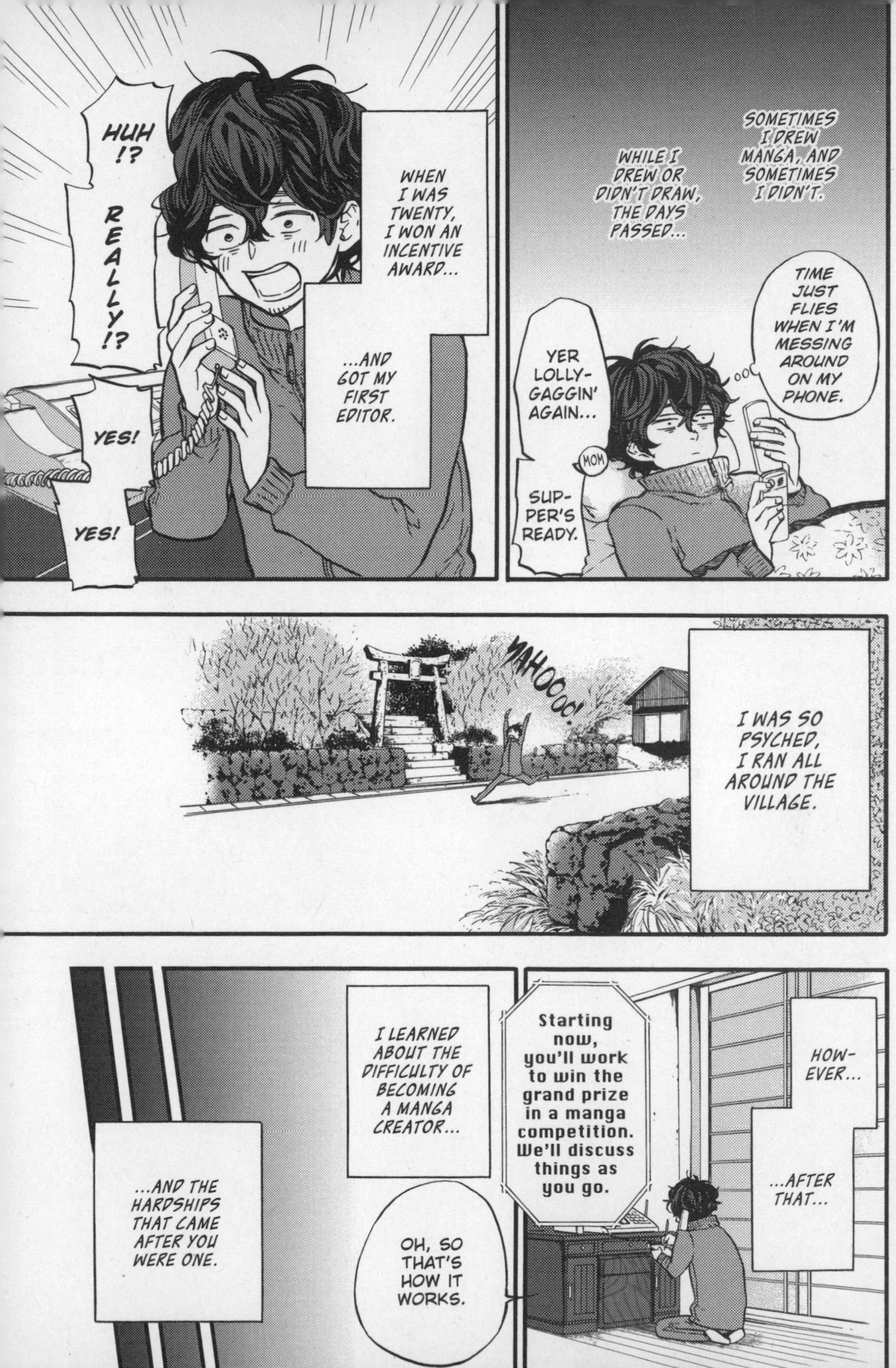
SOMETIMES I DREW MANGA, AND SOMETIMES I DIDN'T.
WHILE I DREW OR DIDN'T DRAW, THE DAYS PASSED...
TIME JUST FLIES WHEN I'M MESSING AROUND ON MY PHONE.
YER LOLLY-GAGGIN' AGAIN...
MOM
SUP-PER'S READY.
WHEN I WAS TWENTY, I WON AN INCENTIVE AWARD...
HUH!? REALLY!?
...AND GOT MY FIRST EDITOR.
YES!
YES!
I WAS SO PSYCHED, I RAN ALL AROUND THE VILLAGE.
WAHOOOO!
HOW-EVER...
...AFTER THAT...
Starting now, you'll work to win the grand prize in a manga competition. We'll discuss things as you go.
OH, SO THAT'S HOW IT WORKS.
I LEARNED ABOUT THE DIFFICULTY OF BECOMING A MANGA CREATOR...
...AND THE HARDSHIPS THAT CAME AFTER YOU WERE ONE.

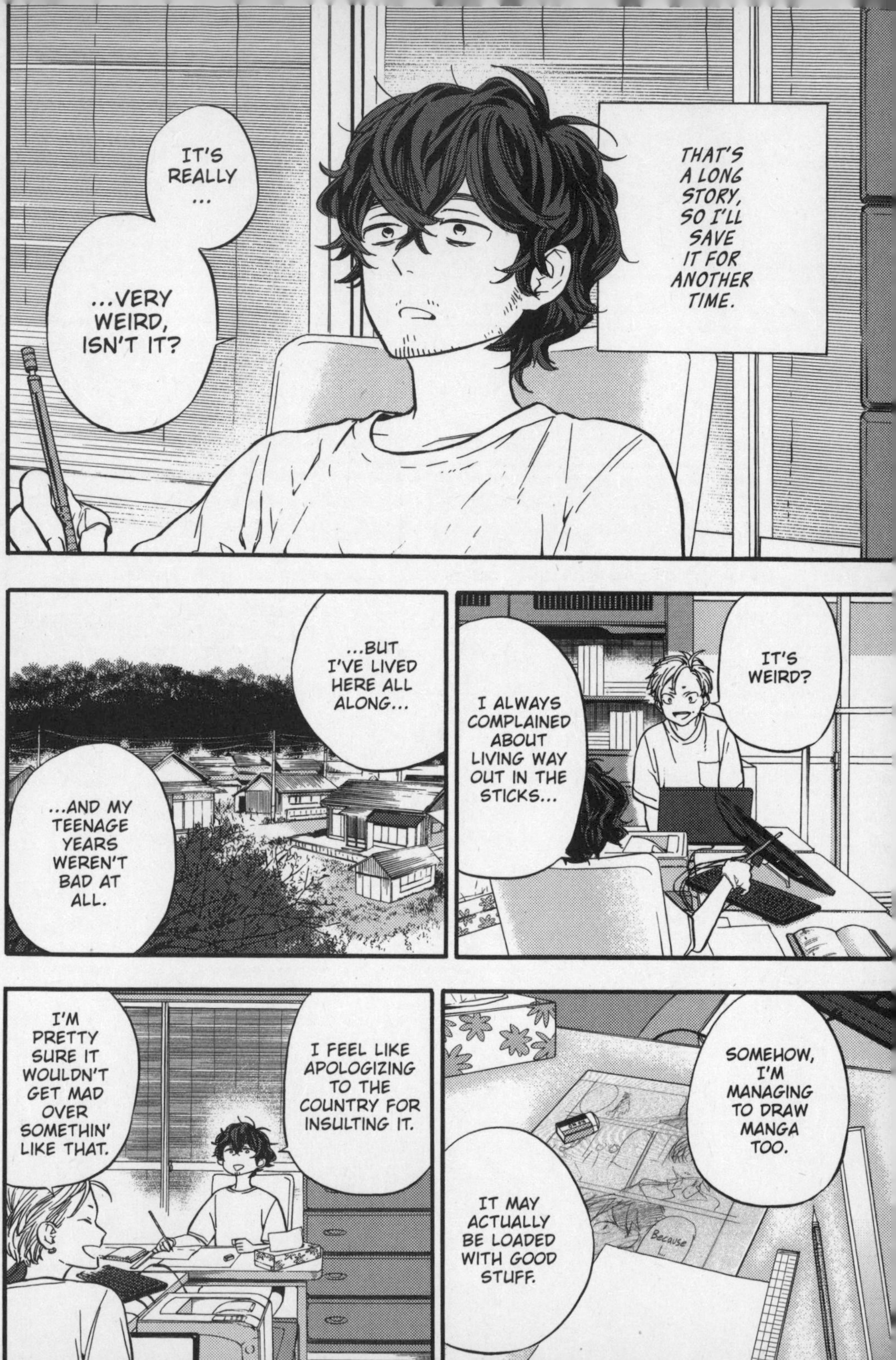
THAT'S A LONG STORY, SO I'LL SAVE IT FOR ANOTHER TIME.
IT'S REALLY ...
...VERY WEIRD, ISN'T IT?
IT'S WEIRD?
I ALWAYS COMPLAINED ABOUT LIVING WAY OUT IN THE STICKS...
...BUT I'VE LIVED HERE ALL ALONG...
...AND MY TEENAGE YEARS WEREN'T BAD AT ALL.
SOMEHOW, I'M MANAGING TO DRAW MANGA TOO.
IT MAY ACTUALLY BE LOADED WITH GOOD STUFF.
Because
I FEEL LIKE APOLOGIZING TO THE COUNTRY FOR INSULTING IT.
I'M PRETTY SURE IT WOULDN'T GET MAD OVER SOMETHIN' LIKE THAT.

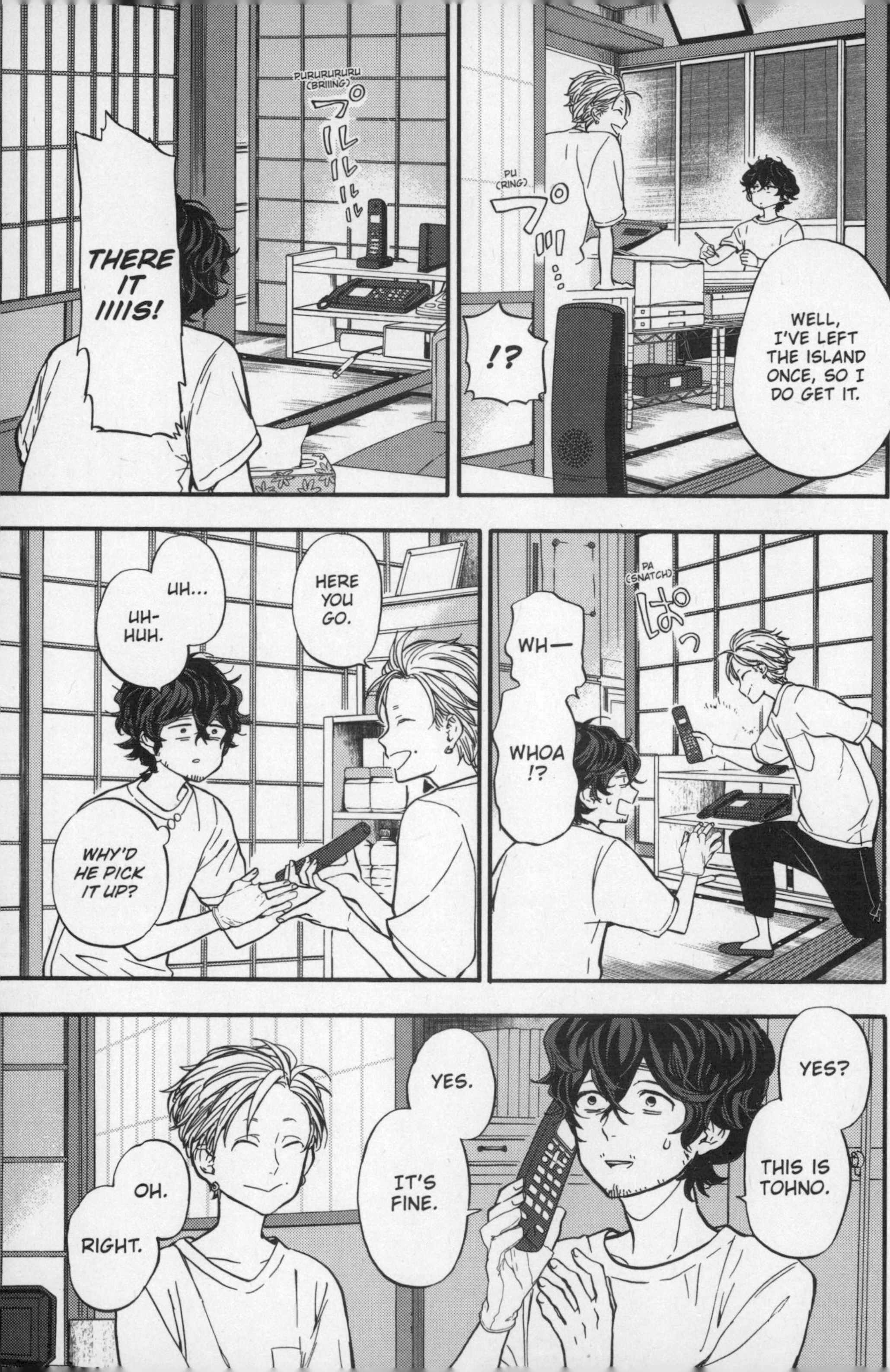
PU
(RING)
プッ
WELL, I'VE LEFT THE ISLAND ONCE, SO I DO GET IT.
!?
PURURURURU
(BRIIING)
プルルルル
THERE IT IIIIS!
PA
(SNATCH)
ぱっ
WH—
WHOA !?
HERE YOU GO.
UH...
UH-HUH.
WHY'D HE PICK IT UP?
YES?
THIS IS TOHNO.
YES.
IT'S FINE.
OH.
RIGHT.

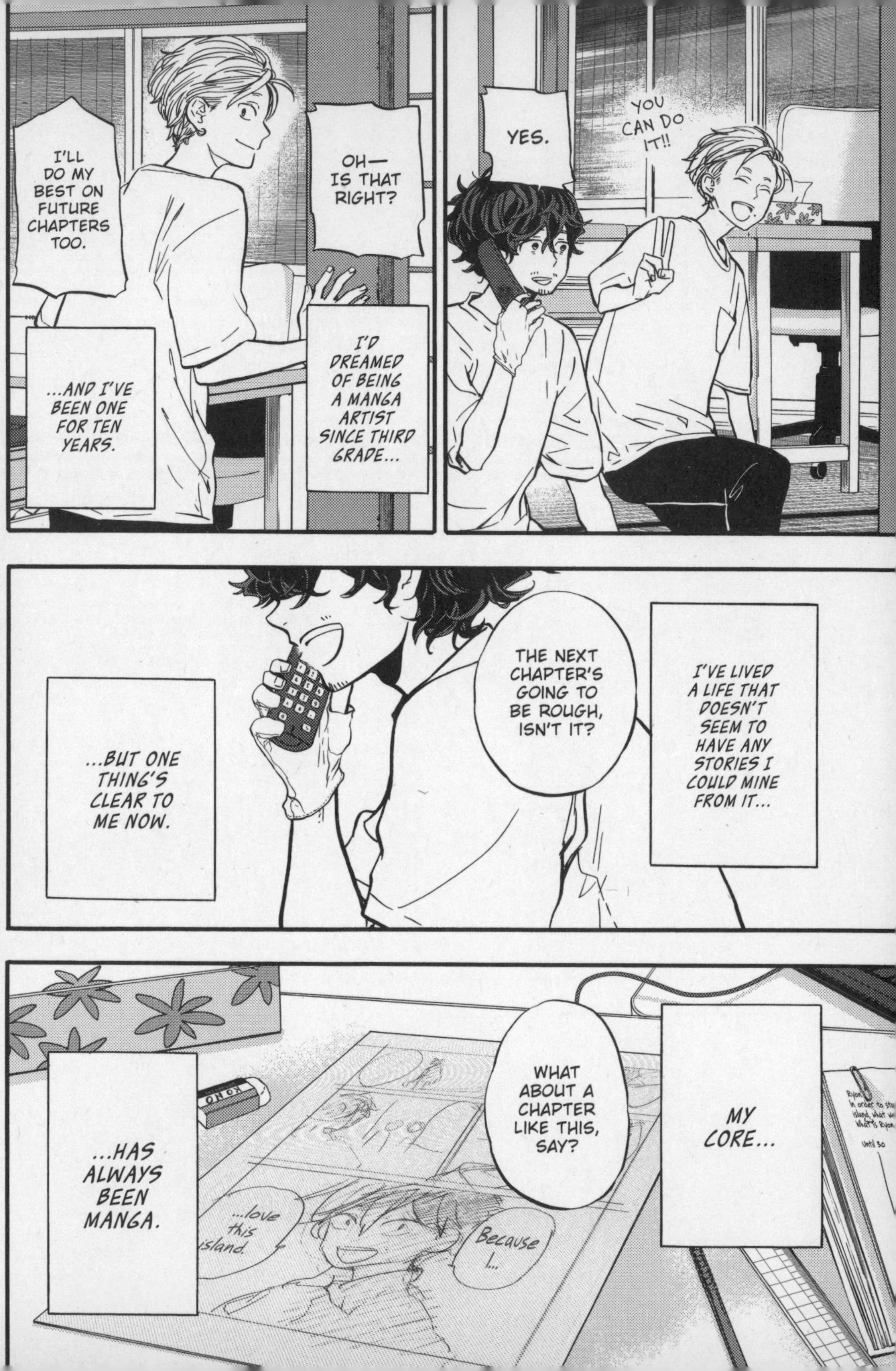
YOU CAN DO IT!!
YES.
OH— IS THAT RIGHT?
I'LL DO MY BEST ON FUTURE CHAPTERS TOO.
I'D DREAMED OF BEING A MANGA ARTIST SINCE THIRD GRADE...
...AND I'VE BEEN ONE FOR TEN YEARS.
I'VE LIVED A LIFE THAT DOESN'T SEEM TO HAVE ANY STORIES I COULD MINE FROM IT...
THE NEXT CHAPTER'S GOING TO BE ROUGH, ISN'T IT?
...BUT ONE THING'S CLEAR TO ME NOW.
MY CORE...
WHAT ABOUT A CHAPTER LIKE THIS, SAY?
Because I...
...love this island.
...HAS ALWAYS BEEN MANGA.

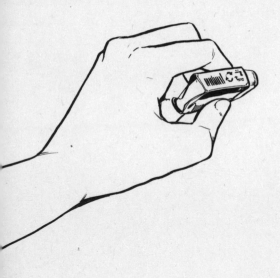

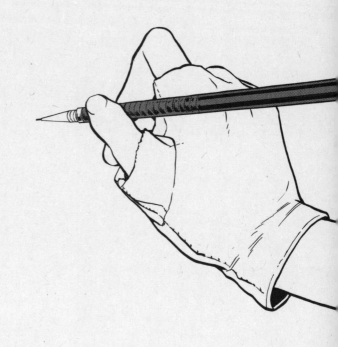

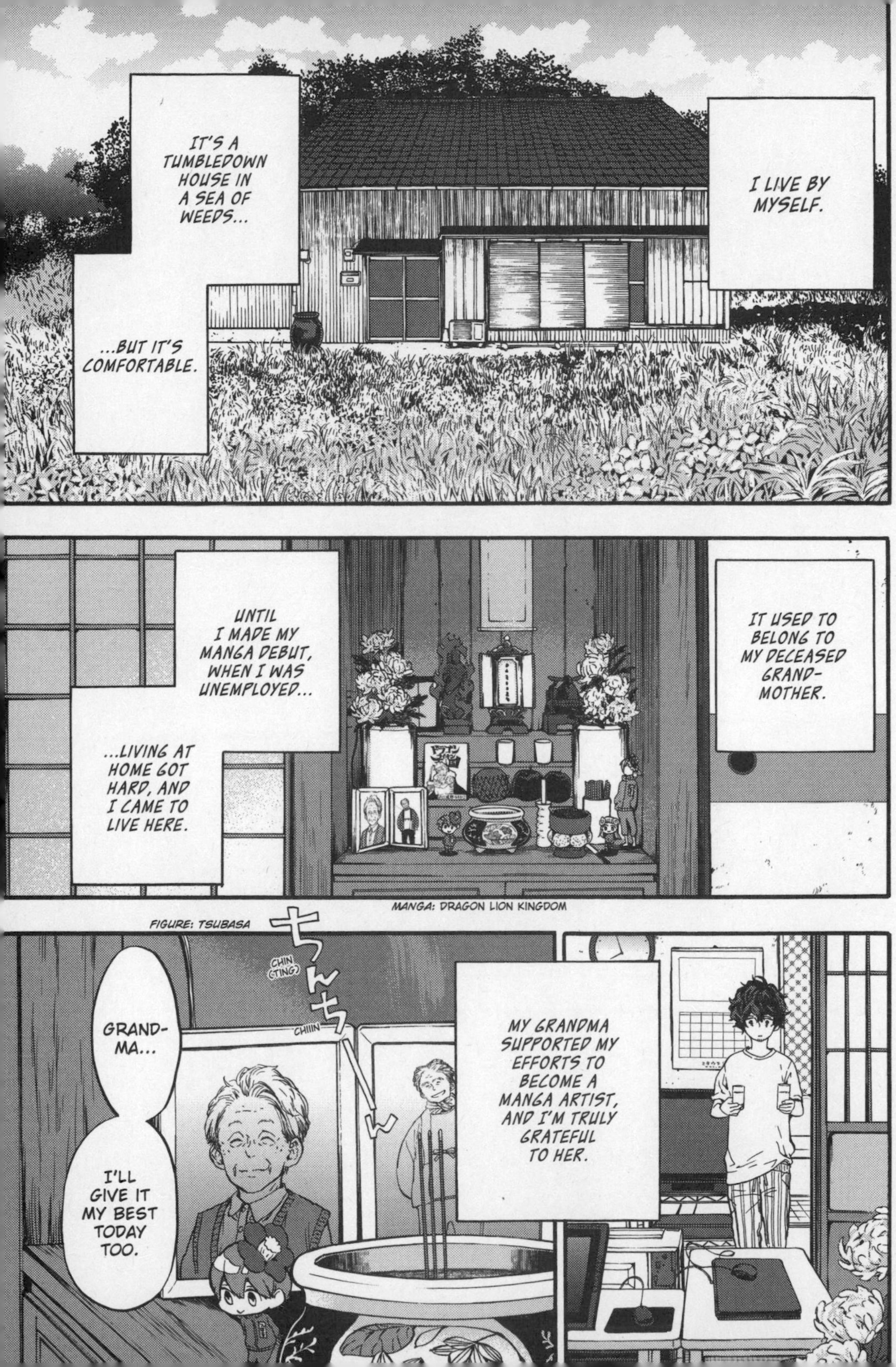
I LIVE BY MYSELF.
IT'S A TUMBLEDOWN HOUSE IN A SEA OF WEEDS...
...BUT IT'S COMFORTABLE.
IT USED TO BELONG TO MY DECEASED GRAND-MOTHER.
UNTIL I MADE MY MANGA DEBUT, WHEN I WAS UNEMPLOYED...
...LIVING AT HOME GOT HARD, AND I CAME TO LIVE HERE.
MANGA: DRAGON LION KINGDOM
FIGURE: TSUBASA
MY GRANDMA SUPPORTED MY EFFORTS TO BECOME A MANGA ARTIST, AND I'M TRULY GRATEFUL TO HER.
CHIN (TING)
CHIIIN
GRAND-MA...
I'LL GIVE IT MY BEST TODAY TOO.

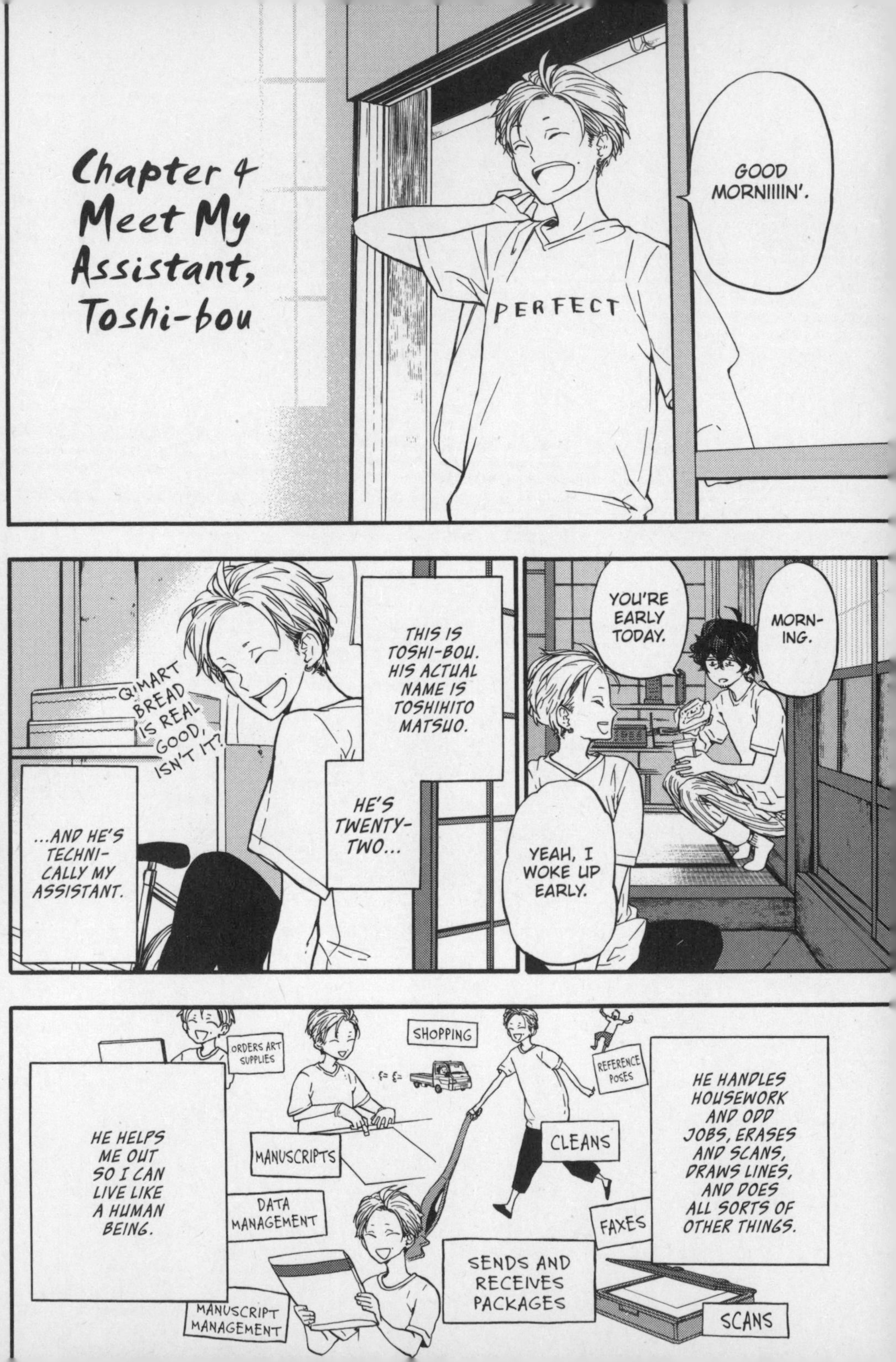
GOOD MORNIIIIN'.
Chapter 4
Meet My Assistant, Toshi-bou
PERFECT
MORN-ING.
YOU'RE EARLY TODAY.
YEAH, I WOKE UP EARLY.
THIS IS TOSHI-BOU. HIS ACTUAL NAME IS TOSHIHITO MATSUO.
QIMART BREAD IS REAL GOOD, ISN'T IT?
HE'S TWENTY-TWO...
...AND HE'S TECHNI-CALLY MY ASSISTANT.
HE HANDLES HOUSEWORK AND ODD JOBS, ERASES AND SCANS, DRAWS LINES, AND DOES ALL SORTS OF OTHER THINGS.
REFERENCE POSES
SHOPPING
ORDERS ART SUPPLIES
CLEANS
MANUSCRIPTS
FAXES
DATA MANAGEMENT
SCANS
SENDS AND RECEIVES PACKAGES
MANUSCRIPT MANAGEMENT
HE HELPS ME OUT SO I CAN LIVE LIKE A HUMAN BEING.

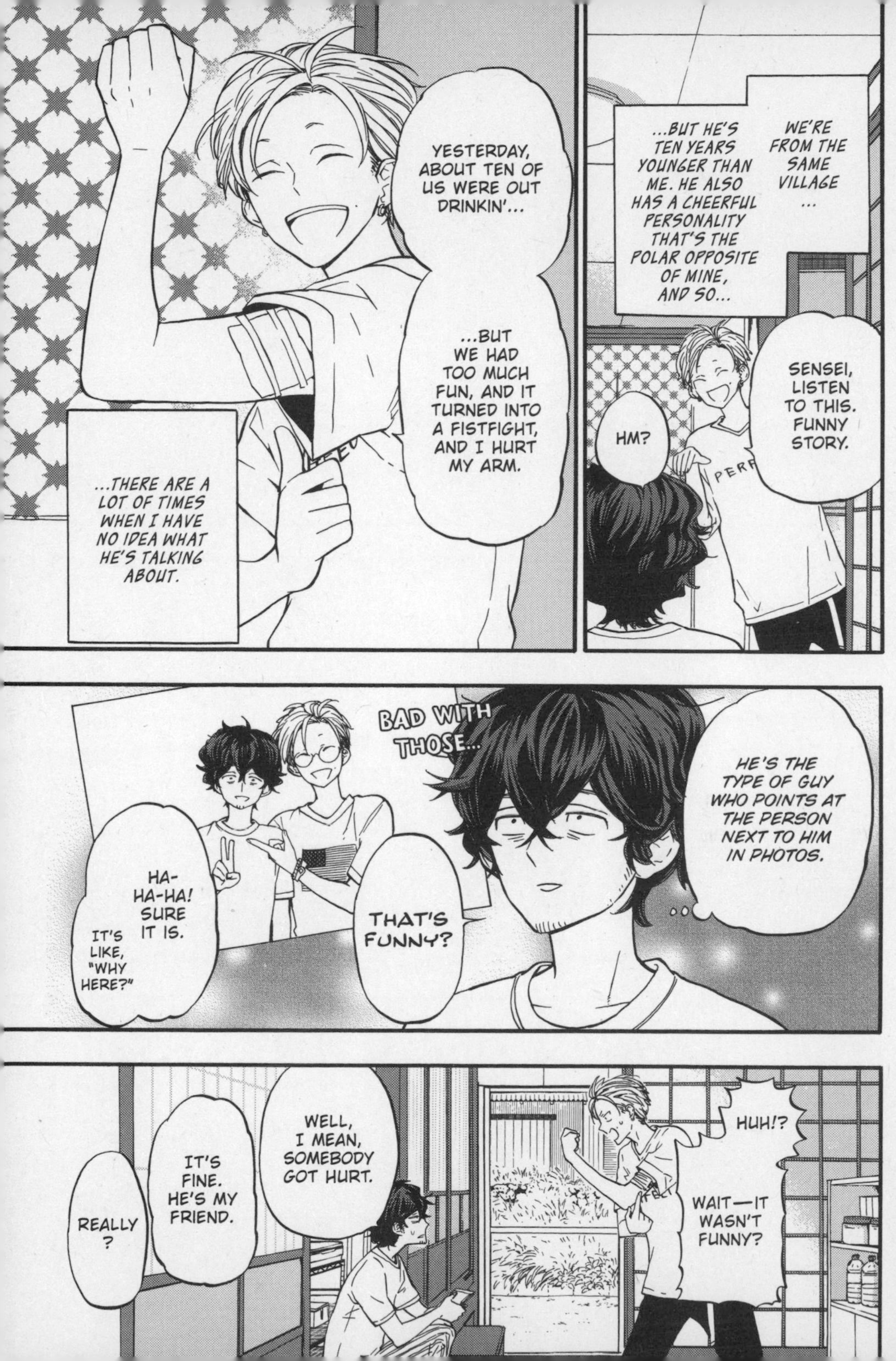
WE'RE FROM THE SAME VILLAGE ...
...BUT HE'S TEN YEARS YOUNGER THAN ME. HE ALSO HAS A CHEERFUL PERSONALITY THAT'S THE POLAR OPPOSITE OF MINE, AND SO...
SENSEI, LISTEN TO THIS. FUNNY STORY.
HM?
YESTERDAY, ABOUT TEN OF US WERE OUT DRINKIN'...
...BUT WE HAD TOO MUCH FUN, AND IT TURNED INTO A FISTFIGHT, AND I HURT MY ARM.
...THERE ARE A LOT OF TIMES WHEN I HAVE NO IDEA WHAT HE'S TALKING ABOUT.
HE'S THE TYPE OF GUY WHO POINTS AT THE PERSON NEXT TO HIM IN PHOTOS.
BAD WITH THOSE...
THAT'S FUNNY?
HA-HA-HA! SURE IT IS.
IT'S LIKE, "WHY HERE?"
HUH!?
WAIT—IT WASN'T FUNNY?
WELL, I MEAN, SOMEBODY GOT HURT.
IT'S FINE. HE'S MY FRIEND.
REALLY ?

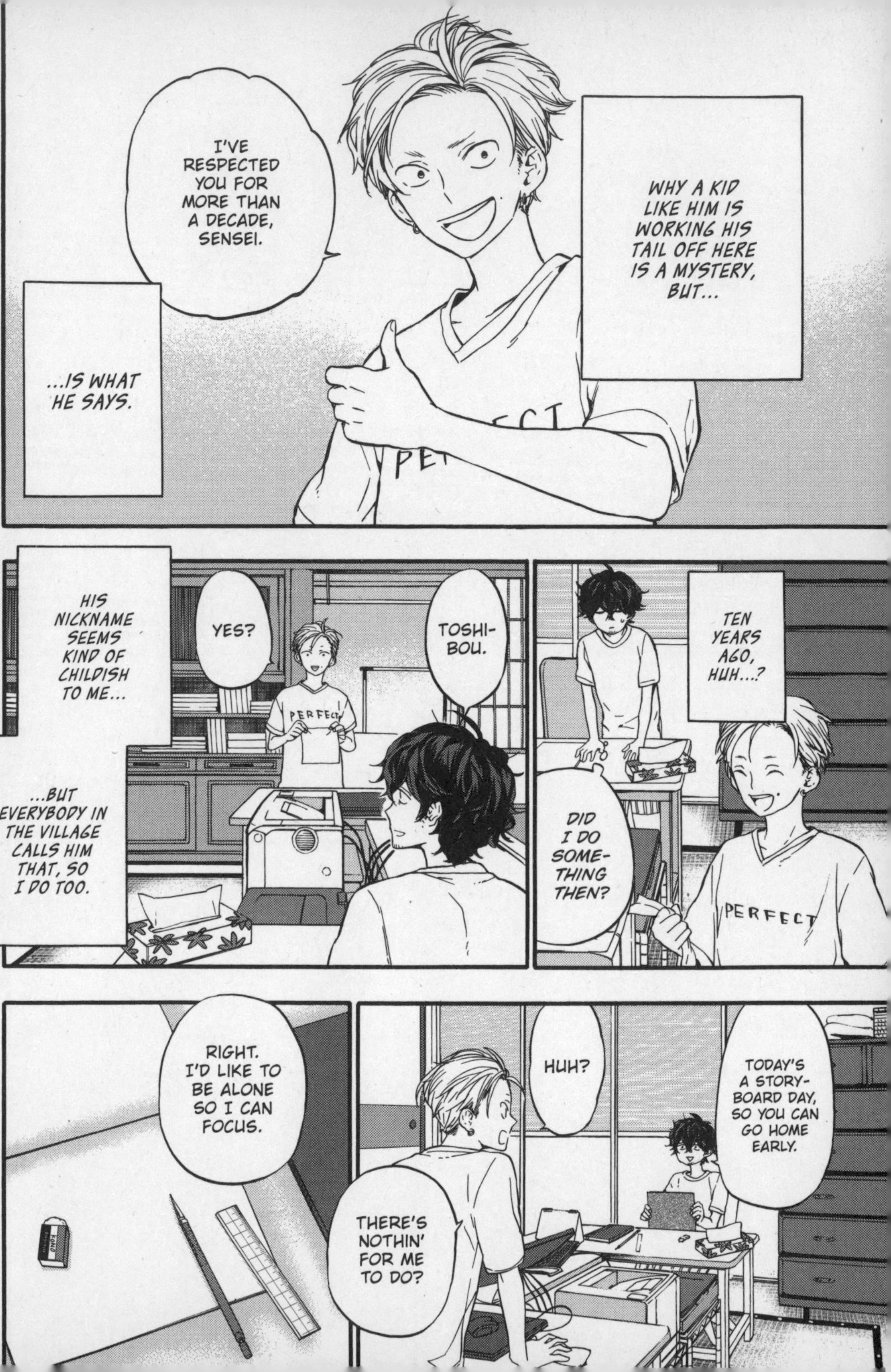
WHY A KID LIKE HIM IS WORKING HIS TAIL OFF HERE IS A MYSTERY, BUT...
I'VE RESPECTED YOU FOR MORE THAN A DECADE, SENSEI.
...IS WHAT HE SAYS.
TEN YEARS AGO, HUH...?
DID I DO SOME-THING THEN?
TOSHI-BOU.
YES?
HIS NICKNAME SEEMS KIND OF CHILDISH TO ME...
...BUT EVERYBODY IN THE VILLAGE CALLS HIM THAT, SO I DO TOO.
TODAY'S A STORY-BOARD DAY, SO YOU CAN GO HOME EARLY.
HUH?
THERE'S NOTHIN' FOR ME TO DO?
RIGHT. I'D LIKE TO BE ALONE SO I CAN FOCUS.

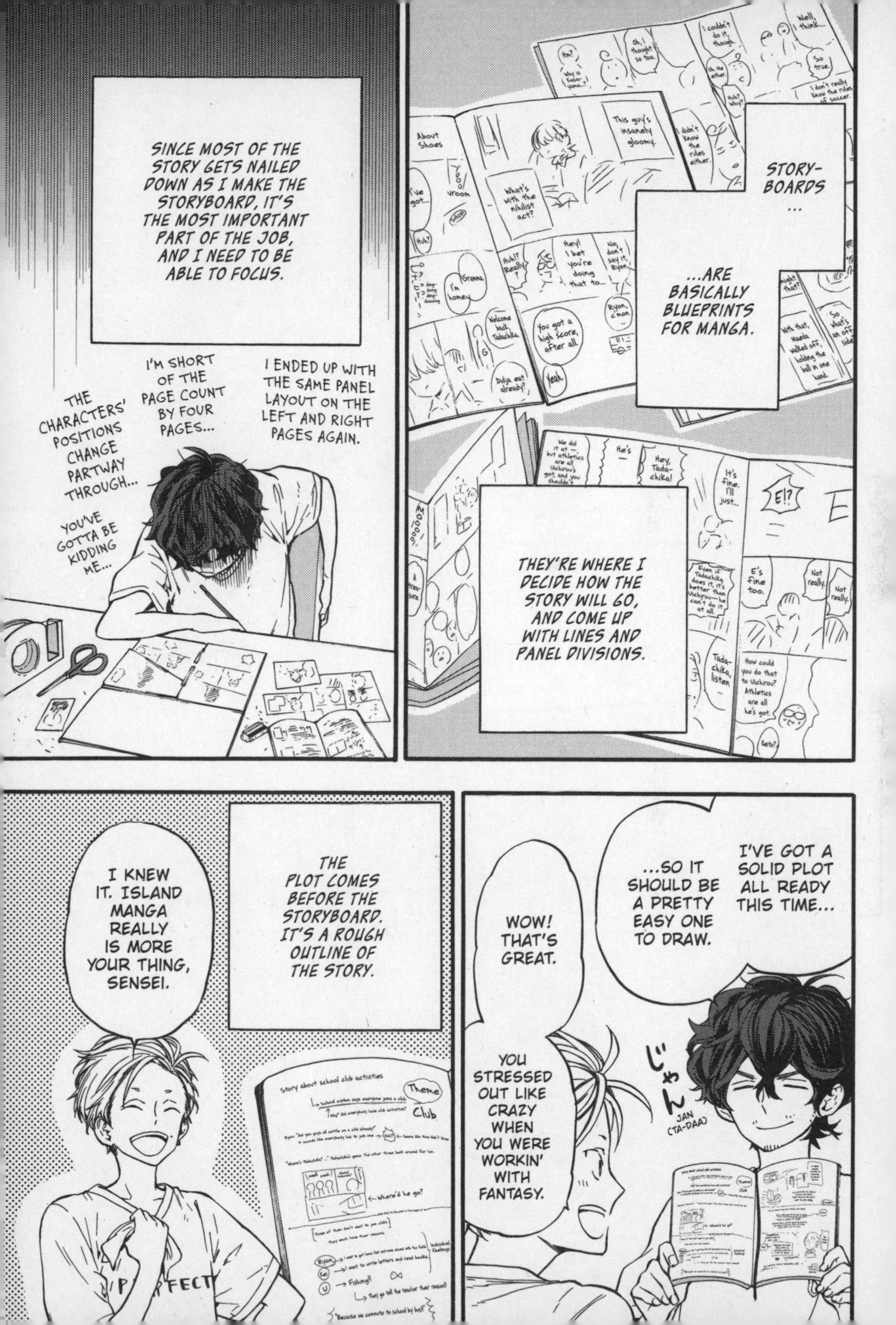
STORY-BOARDS ...
...ARE BASICALLY BLUEPRINTS FOR MANGA.
THEY'RE WHERE I DECIDE HOW THE STORY WILL GO, AND COME UP WITH LINES AND PANEL DIVISIONS.
SINCE MOST OF THE STORY GETS NAILED DOWN AS I MAKE THE STORYBOARD, IT'S THE MOST IMPORTANT PART OF THE JOB, AND I NEED TO BE ABLE TO FOCUS.
I ENDED UP WITH THE SAME PANEL LAYOUT ON THE LEFT AND RIGHT PAGES AGAIN.
I'M SHORT OF THE PAGE COUNT BY FOUR PAGES...
THE CHARACTERS' POSITIONS CHANGE PARTWAY THROUGH...
YOU'VE GOTTA BE KIDDING ME...
I'VE GOT A SOLID PLOT ALL READY THIS TIME...
...SO IT SHOULD BE A PRETTY EASY ONE TO DRAW.
じゃん
JAN (TA-DAA)
WOW! THAT'S GREAT.
YOU STRESSED OUT LIKE CRAZY WHEN YOU WERE WORKIN' WITH FANTASY.
THE PLOT COMES BEFORE THE STORYBOARD. IT'S A ROUGH OUTLINE OF THE STORY.
I KNEW IT. ISLAND MANGA REALLY IS MORE YOUR THING, SENSEI.
Story about school club activities
Theme
Club
Where'd he go?
Fishing!!
PERFECT

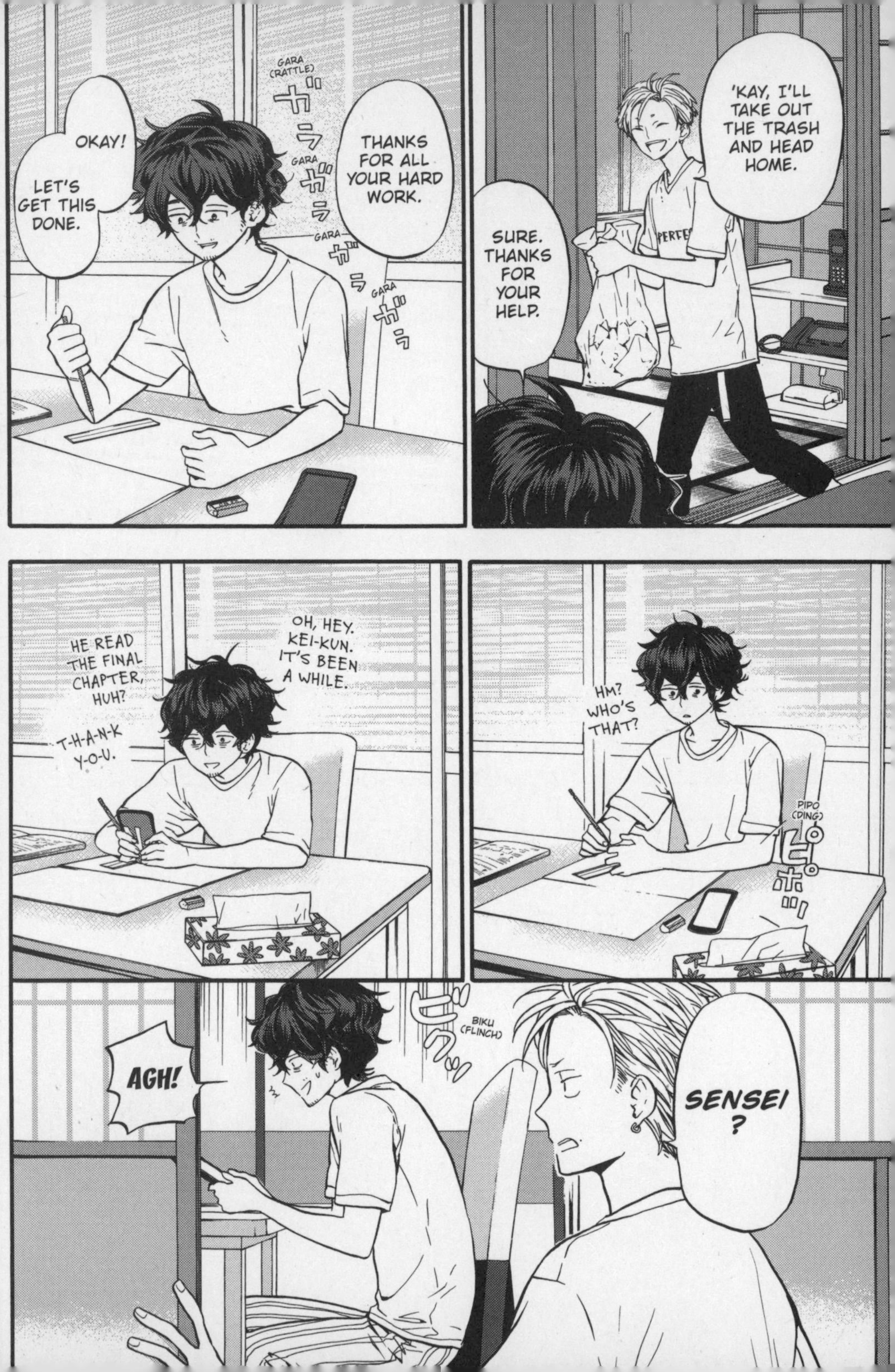
'KAY, I'LL TAKE OUT THE TRASH AND HEAD HOME.
SURE. THANKS FOR YOUR HELP.
PERFE
THANKS FOR ALL YOUR HARD WORK.
GARA (RATTLE)
GARA
GARA
GARA
OKAY!
LET'S GET THIS DONE.
PIPO (DING)
HM? WHO'S THAT?
OH, HEY. KEI-KUN. IT'S BEEN A WHILE.
HE READ THE FINAL CHAPTER, HUH?
T-H-A-N-K Y-O-U.
SENSEI?
BIKU (FLINCH)
AGH!

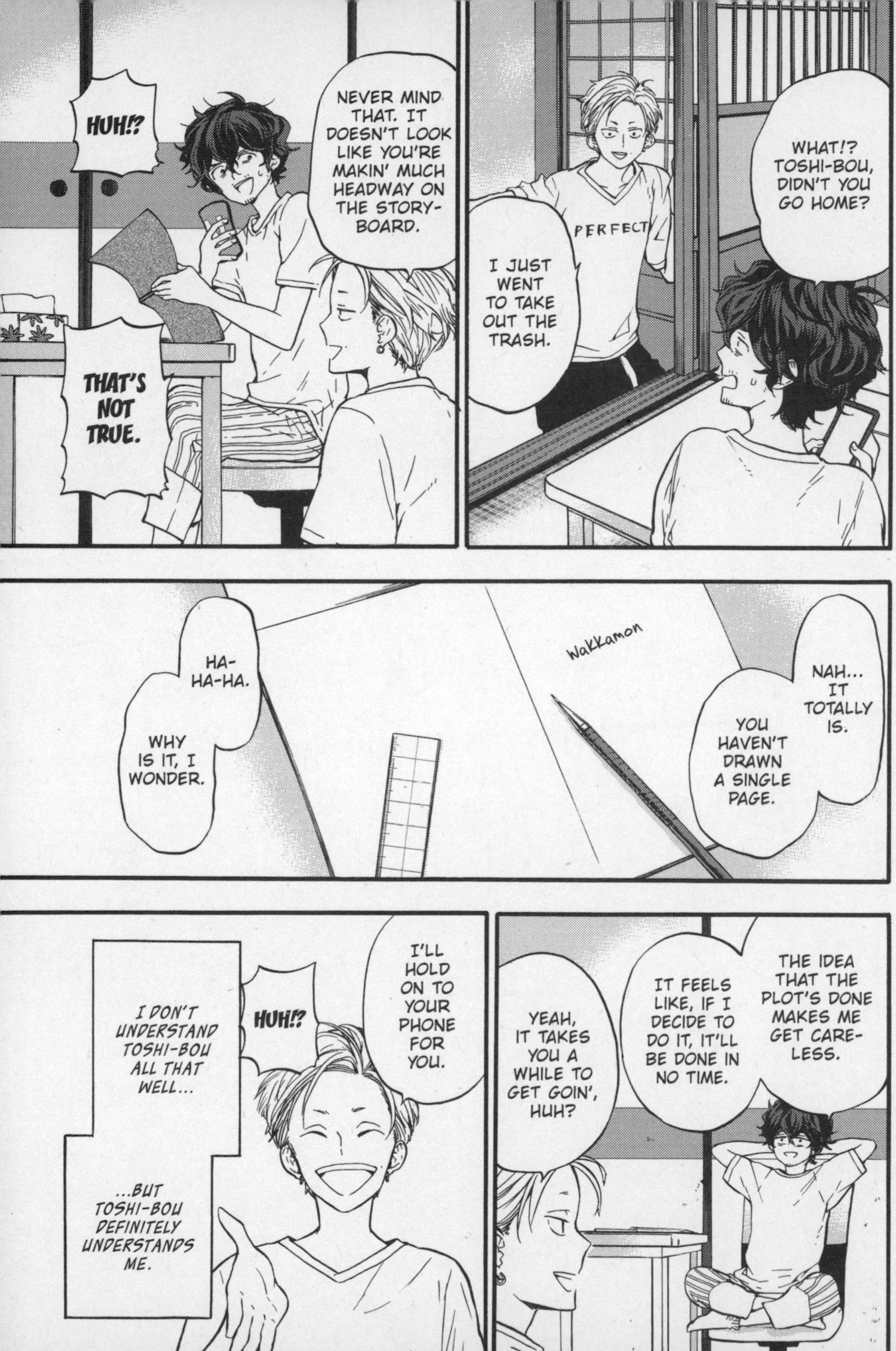
WHAT!? TOSHI-BOU, DIDN'T YOU GO HOME?
I JUST WENT TO TAKE OUT THE TRASH.
NEVER MIND THAT. IT DOESN'T LOOK LIKE YOU'RE MAKIN' MUCH HEADWAY ON THE STORY-BOARD.
HUH!?
THAT'S NOT TRUE.
NAH... IT TOTALLY IS.
YOU HAVEN'T DRAWN A SINGLE PAGE.
WaKKamon
HA-HA-HA.
WHY IS IT, I WONDER.
THE IDEA THAT THE PLOT'S DONE MAKES ME GET CARE-LESS.
IT FEELS LIKE, IF I DECIDE TO DO IT, IT'LL BE DONE IN NO TIME.
YEAH, IT TAKES YOU A WHILE TO GET GOIN', HUH?
I'LL HOLD ON TO YOUR PHONE FOR YOU.
HUH!?
I DON'T UNDERSTAND TOSHI-BOU ALL THAT WELL...
...BUT TOSHI-BOU DEFINITELY UNDERSTANDS ME.

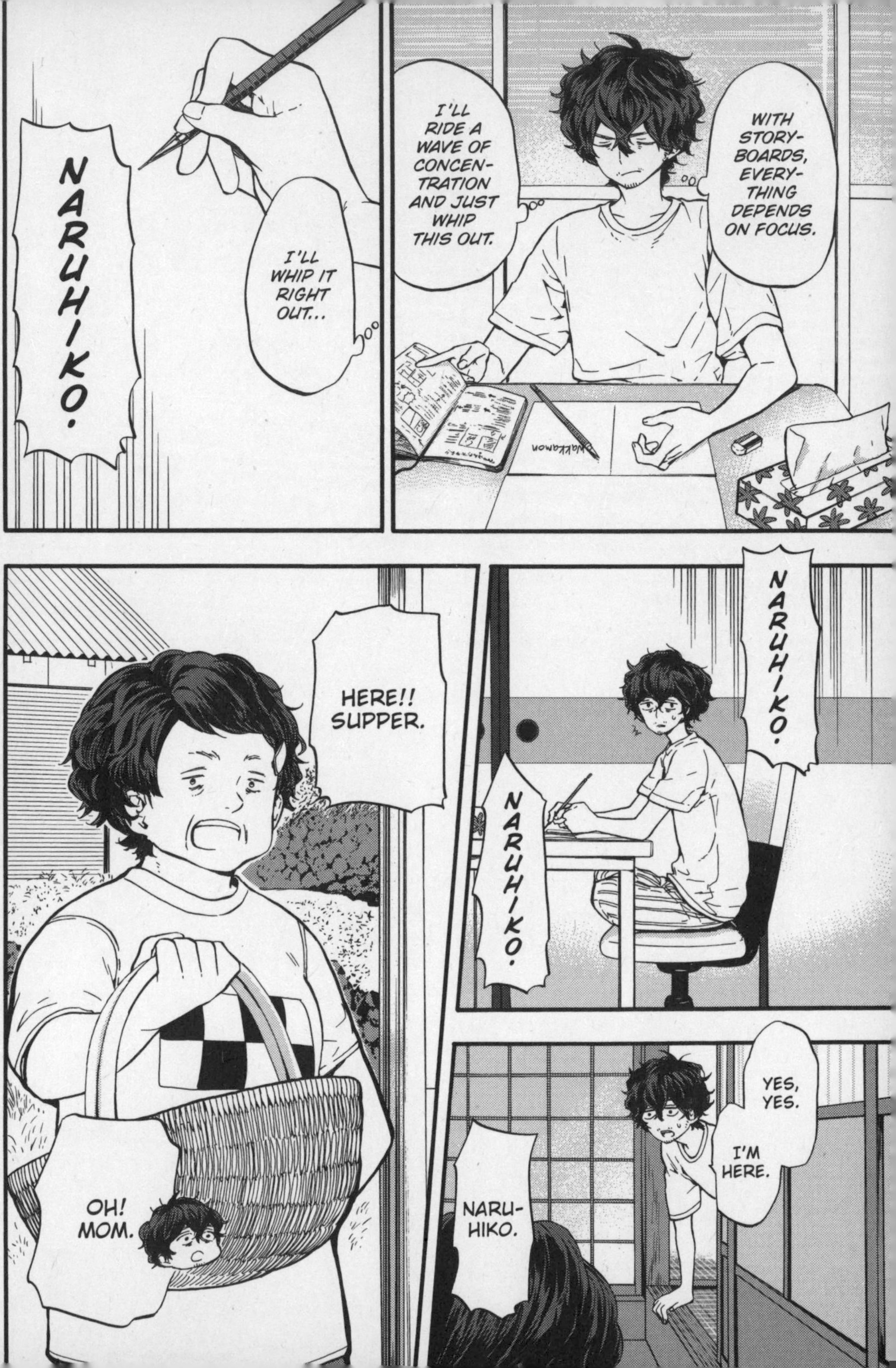
WITH STORY-BOARDS, EVERY-THING DEPENDS ON FOCUS.
I'LL RIDE A WAVE OF CONCEN-TRATION AND JUST WHIP THIS OUT.
I'LL WHIP IT RIGHT OUT...
NARUHIKO.
NARUHIKO.
NARUHIKO.
YES, YES.
I'M HERE.
NARU-HIKO.
HERE!! SUPPER.
OH! MOM.

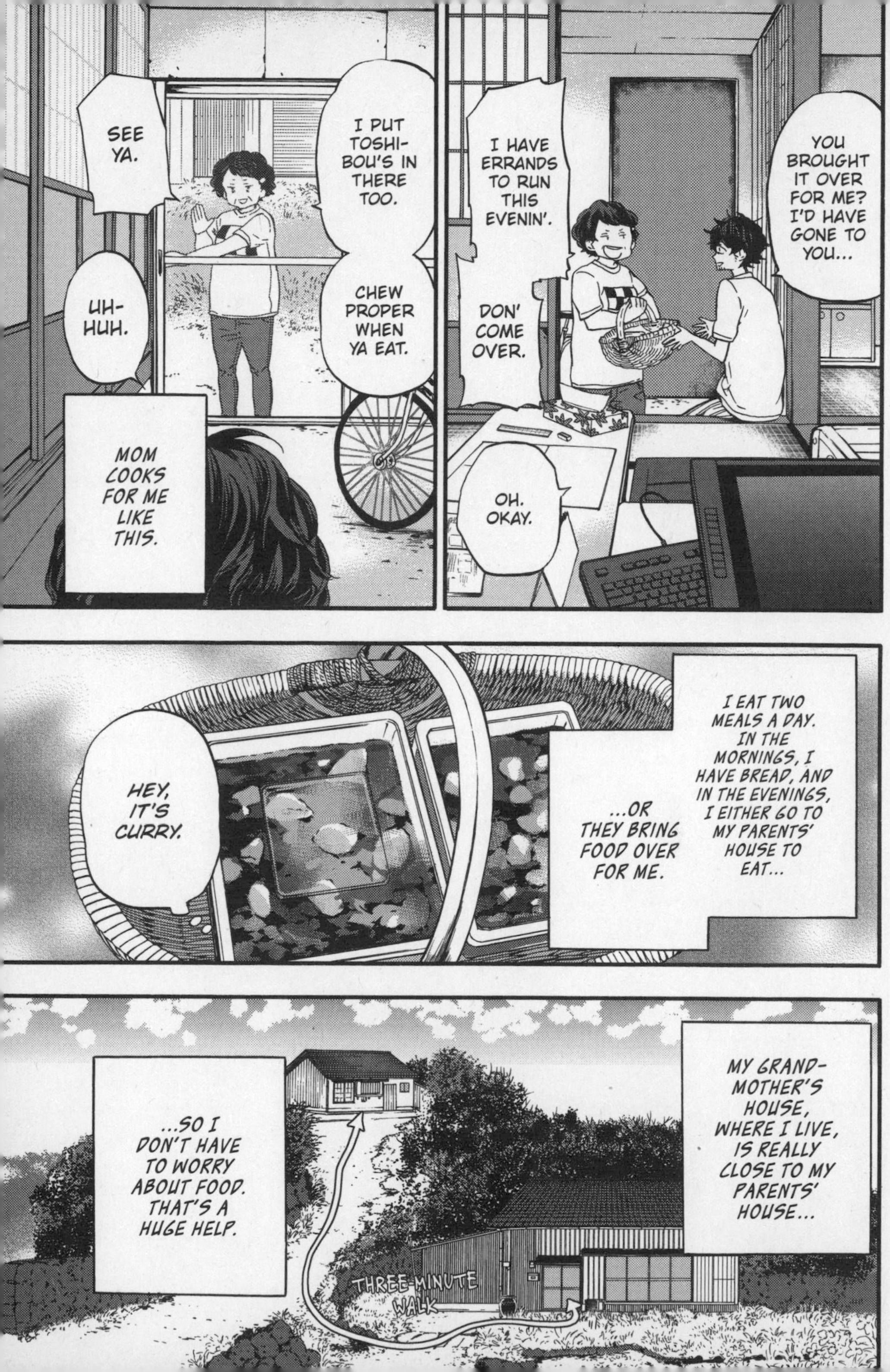
YOU BROUGHT IT OVER FOR ME? I'D HAVE GONE TO YOU...
I HAVE ERRANDS TO RUN THIS EVENIN'.
DON' COME OVER.
OH. OKAY.
I PUT TOSHI-BOU'S IN THERE TOO.
CHEW PROPER WHEN YA EAT.
SEE YA.
UH-HUH.
MOM COOKS FOR ME LIKE THIS.
I EAT TWO MEALS A DAY. IN THE MORNINGS, I HAVE BREAD, AND IN THE EVENINGS, I EITHER GO TO MY PARENTS' HOUSE TO EAT...
...OR THEY BRING FOOD OVER FOR ME.
HEY, IT'S CURRY.
MY GRAND-MOTHER'S HOUSE, WHERE I LIVE, IS REALLY CLOSE TO MY PARENTS' HOUSE...
THREE MINUTE WALK
...SO I DON'T HAVE TO WORRY ABOUT FOOD. THAT'S A HUGE HELP.

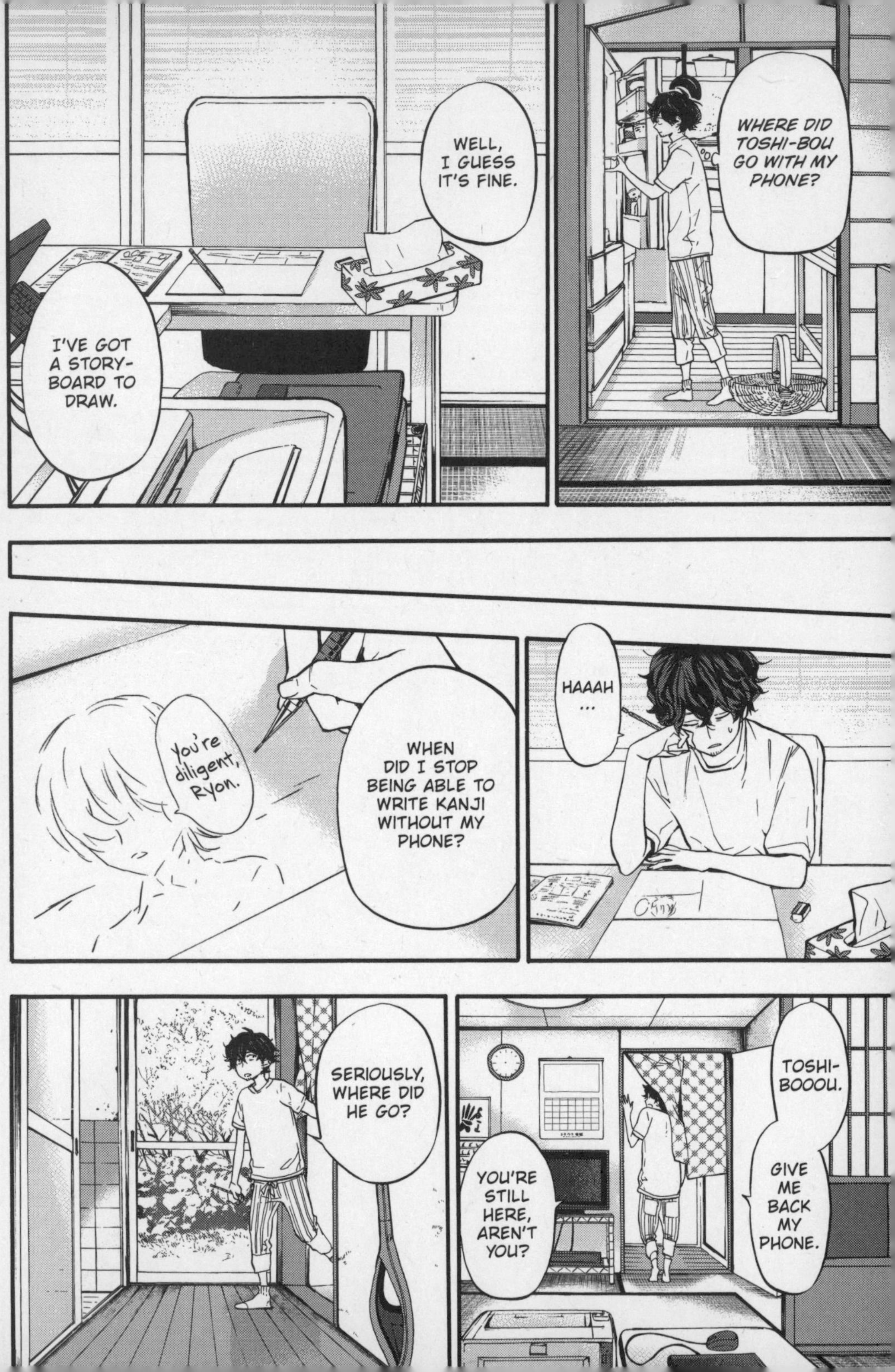
WHERE DID TOSHI-BOU GO WITH MY PHONE?
WELL, I GUESS IT'S FINE.
I'VE GOT A STORY-BOARD TO DRAW.
HAAAH ...
WHEN DID I STOP BEING ABLE TO WRITE KANJI WITHOUT MY PHONE?
You're diligent, Ryon.
TOSHI-BOOOU.
GIVE ME BACK MY PHONE.
YOU'RE STILL HERE, AREN'T YOU?
SERIOUSLY, WHERE DID HE GO?

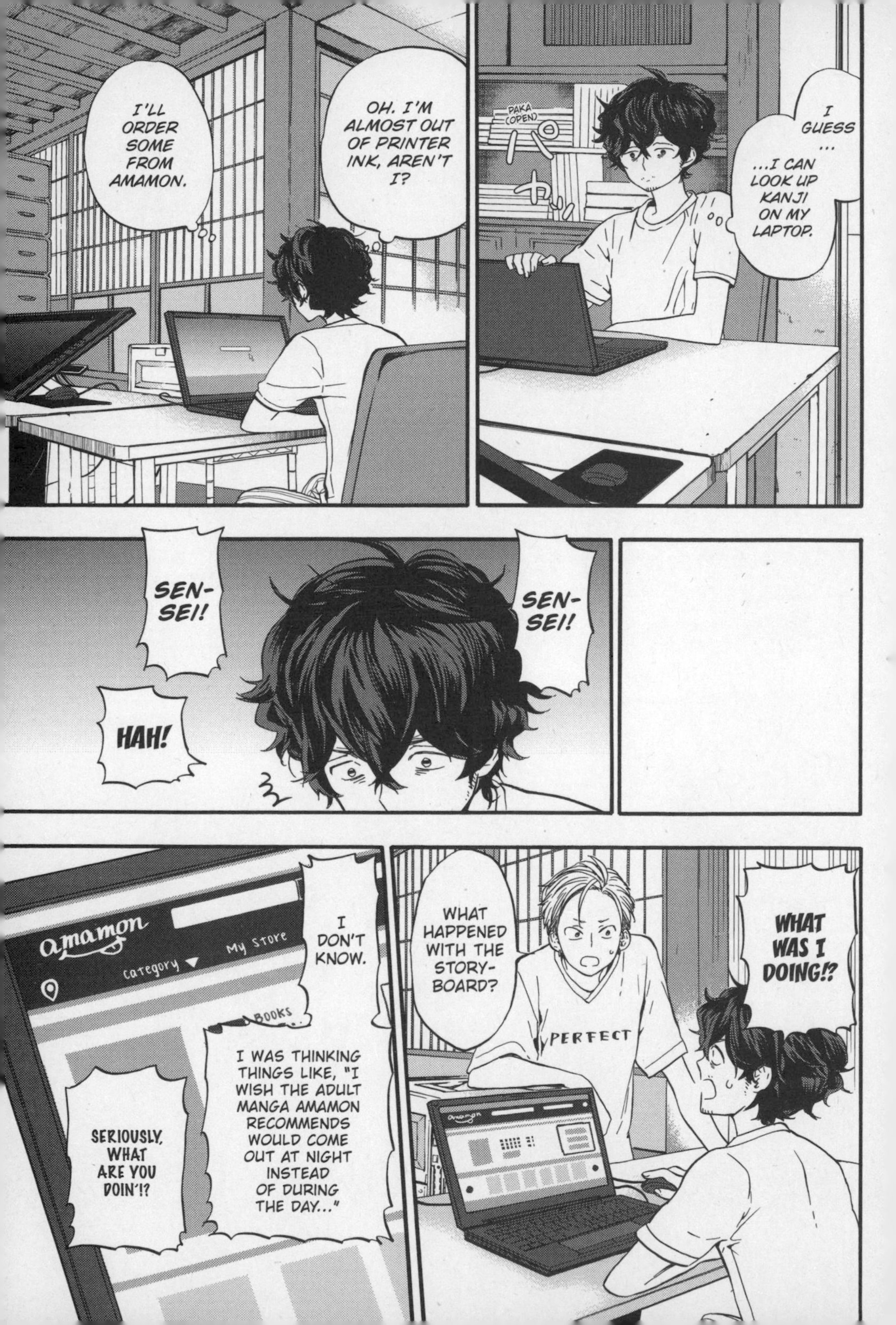
PAKA (OPEN)
I GUESS ...
...I CAN LOOK UP KANJI ON MY LAPTOP.
OH. I'M ALMOST OUT OF PRINTER INK, AREN'T I?
I'LL ORDER SOME FROM AMAMON.
SEN-SEI!
SEN-SEI!
HAH!
WHAT WAS I DOING!?
WHAT HAPPENED WITH THE STORY-BOARD?
PERFECT
I DON'T KNOW.
amamon
My Store
Category
BOOKS
I WAS THINKING THINGS LIKE, "I WISH THE ADULT MANGA AMAMON RECOMMENDS WOULD COME OUT AT NIGHT INSTEAD OF DURING THE DAY..."
SERIOUSLY, WHAT ARE YOU DOIN'!?

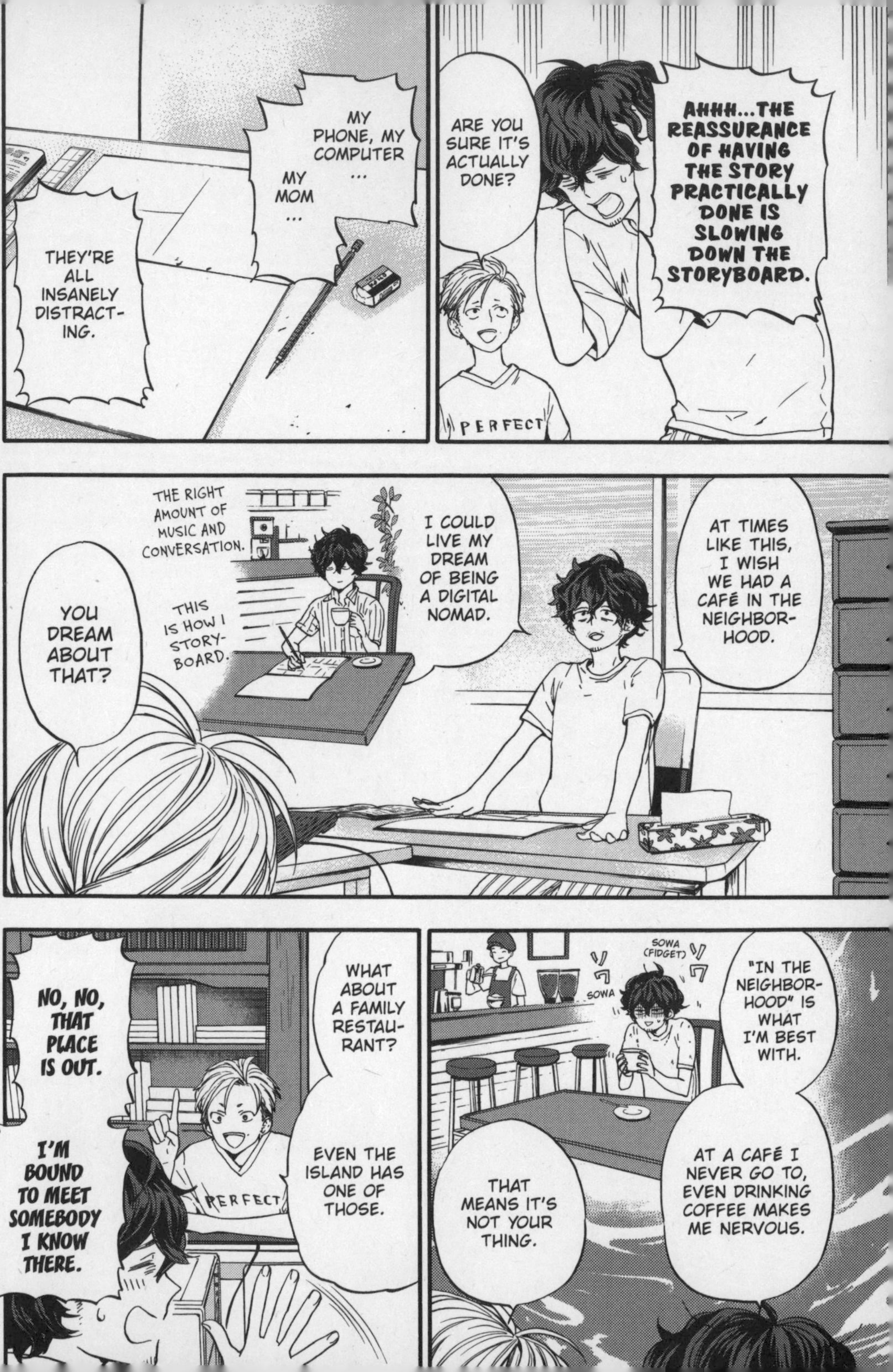
AHHH...THE REASSURANCE OF HAVING THE STORY PRACTICALLY DONE IS SLOWING DOWN THE STORYBOARD.
ARE YOU SURE IT'S ACTUALLY DONE?
PERFECT
MY PHONE, MY COMPUTER ...
MY MOM ...
THEY'RE ALL INSANELY DISTRACT-ING.
AT TIMES LIKE THIS, I WISH WE HAD A CAFÉ IN THE NEIGHBOR-HOOD.
I COULD LIVE MY DREAM OF BEING A DIGITAL NOMAD.
THE RIGHT AMOUNT OF MUSIC AND CONVERSATION.
THIS IS HOW I STORY-BOARD.
YOU DREAM ABOUT THAT?
SOWA (FIDGET)
SOWA
"IN THE NEIGHBOR-HOOD" IS WHAT I'M BEST WITH.
AT A CAFÉ I NEVER GO TO, EVEN DRINKING COFFEE MAKES ME NERVOUS.
THAT MEANS IT'S NOT YOUR THING.
WHAT ABOUT A FAMILY RESTAU-RANT?
EVEN THE ISLAND HAS ONE OF THOSE.
PERFECT
NO, NO, THAT PLACE IS OUT.
I'M BOUND TO MEET SOMEBODY I KNOW THERE.

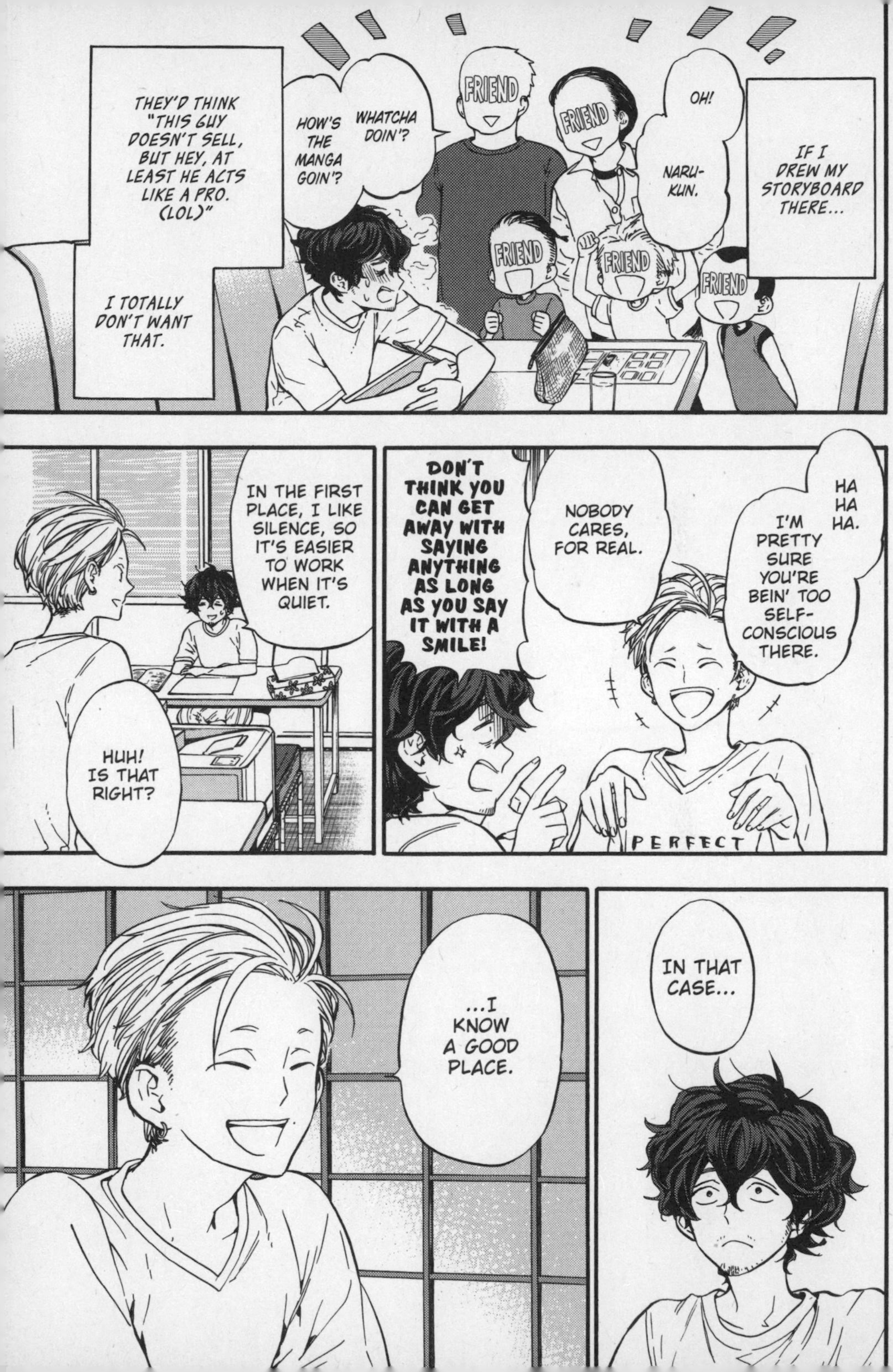
IF I DREW MY STORYBOARD THERE...
OH!
NARU-KUN.
FRIEND
FRIEND
WHATCHA DOIN'?
HOW'S THE MANGA GOIN'?
FRIEND
FRIEND
FRIEND
THEY'D THINK "THIS GUY DOESN'T SELL, BUT HEY, AT LEAST HE ACTS LIKE A PRO. (LOL)"
I TOTALLY DON'T WANT THAT.
HA HA HA.
I'M PRETTY SURE YOU'RE BEIN' TOO SELF-CONSCIOUS THERE.
NOBODY CARES, FOR REAL.
DON'T THINK YOU CAN GET AWAY WITH SAYING ANYTHING AS LONG AS YOU SAY IT WITH A SMILE!
PERFECT
IN THE FIRST PLACE, I LIKE SILENCE, SO IT'S EASIER TO WORK WHEN IT'S QUIET.
HUH! IS THAT RIGHT?
IN THAT CASE...
...I KNOW A GOOD PLACE.

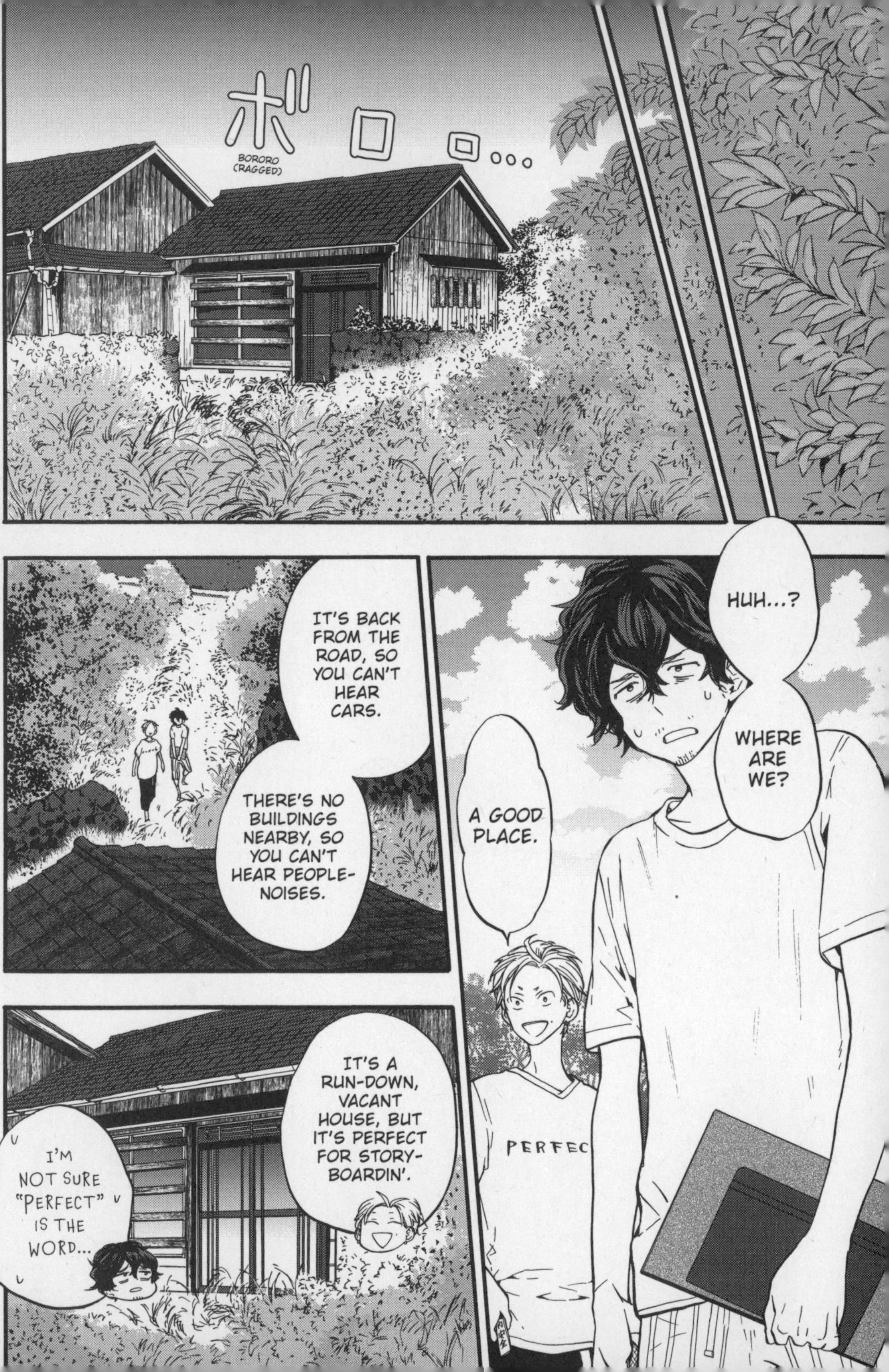
ボロロ…
BORORO (RAGGED)
HUH...?
WHERE ARE WE?
A GOOD PLACE.
PERFEC
IT'S BACK FROM THE ROAD, SO YOU CAN'T HEAR CARS.
THERE'S NO BUILDINGS NEARBY, SO YOU CAN'T HEAR PEOPLE-NOISES.
IT'S A RUN-DOWN, VACANT HOUSE, BUT IT'S PERFECT FOR STORY-BOARDIN'.
I'M NOT SURE "PERFECT" IS THE WORD...

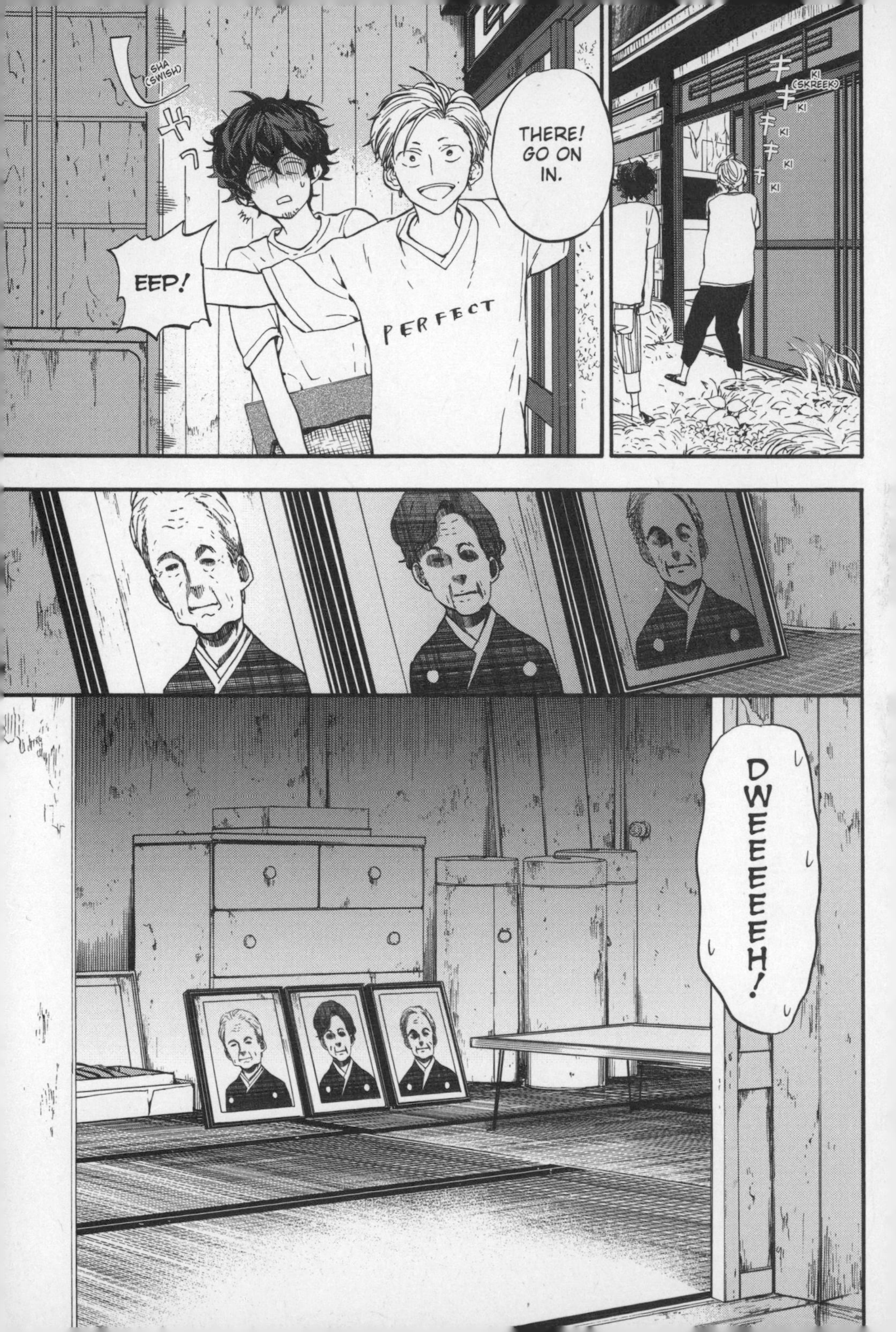

KI (SKREEK) KI KI KI KI
THERE! GO ON IN.
SHA (SWISH)
EEP!
PERFECT
DWEEEEEEH!

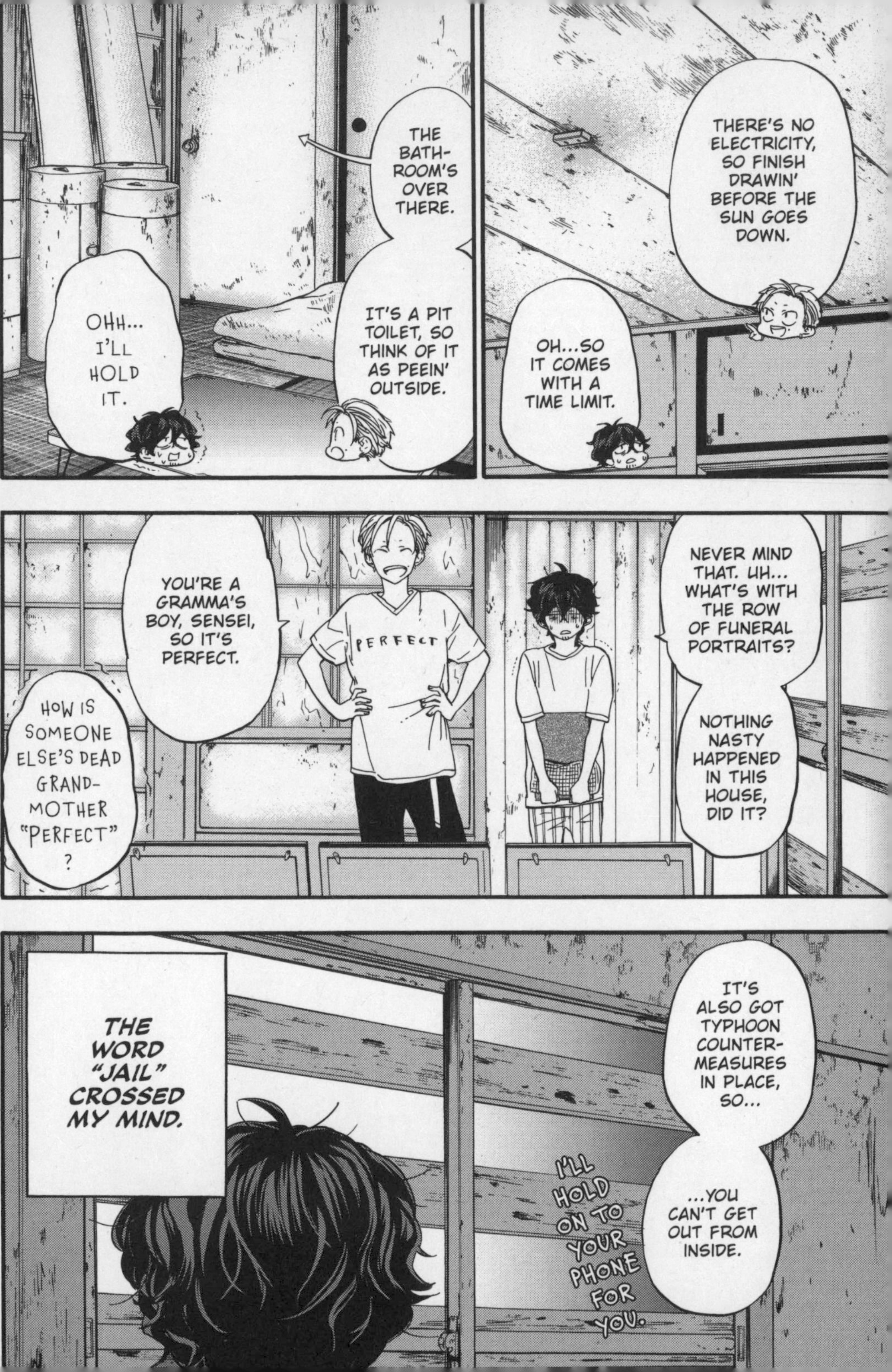
THERE'S NO ELECTRICITY, SO FINISH DRAWIN' BEFORE THE SUN GOES DOWN.
OH...SO IT COMES WITH A TIME LIMIT.
THE BATH-ROOM'S OVER THERE.
IT'S A PIT TOILET, SO THINK OF IT AS PEEIN' OUTSIDE.
OHH... I'LL HOLD IT.
NEVER MIND THAT. UH... WHAT'S WITH THE ROW OF FUNERAL PORTRAITS?
NOTHING NASTY HAPPENED IN THIS HOUSE, DID IT?
YOU'RE A GRAMMA'S BOY, SENSEI, SO IT'S PERFECT.
PERFECT
HOW IS SOMEONE ELSE'S DEAD GRAND-MOTHER "PERFECT"?
IT'S ALSO GOT TYPHOON COUNTER-MEASURES IN PLACE, SO...
...YOU CAN'T GET OUT FROM INSIDE.
I'LL HOLD ON TO YOUR PHONE FOR YOU.
THE WORD "JAIL" CROSSED MY MIND.

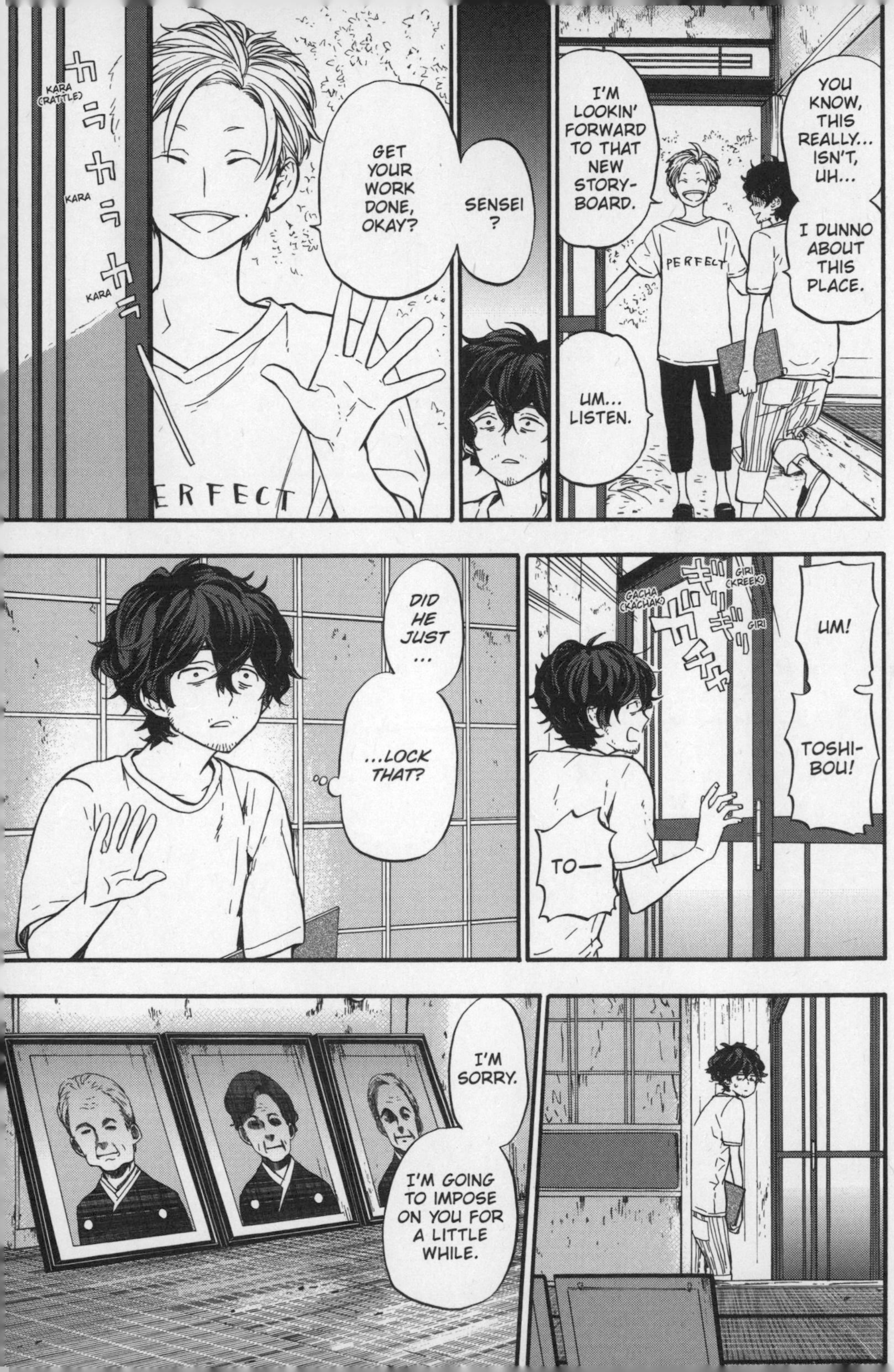
YOU KNOW, THIS REALLY... ISN'T, UH...
I DUNNO ABOUT THIS PLACE.
I'M LOOKIN' FORWARD TO THAT NEW STORY-BOARD.
UM... LISTEN.
SENSEI ?
GET YOUR WORK DONE, OKAY?
KARA (RATTLE)
KARA
KARA
GIRI (KREEK)
GIRI
GACHA (KACHAK)
UM!
TOSHI-BOU!
TO—
DID HE JUST ...
...LOCK THAT?
I'M SORRY.
I'M GOING TO IMPOSE ON YOU FOR A LITTLE WHILE.

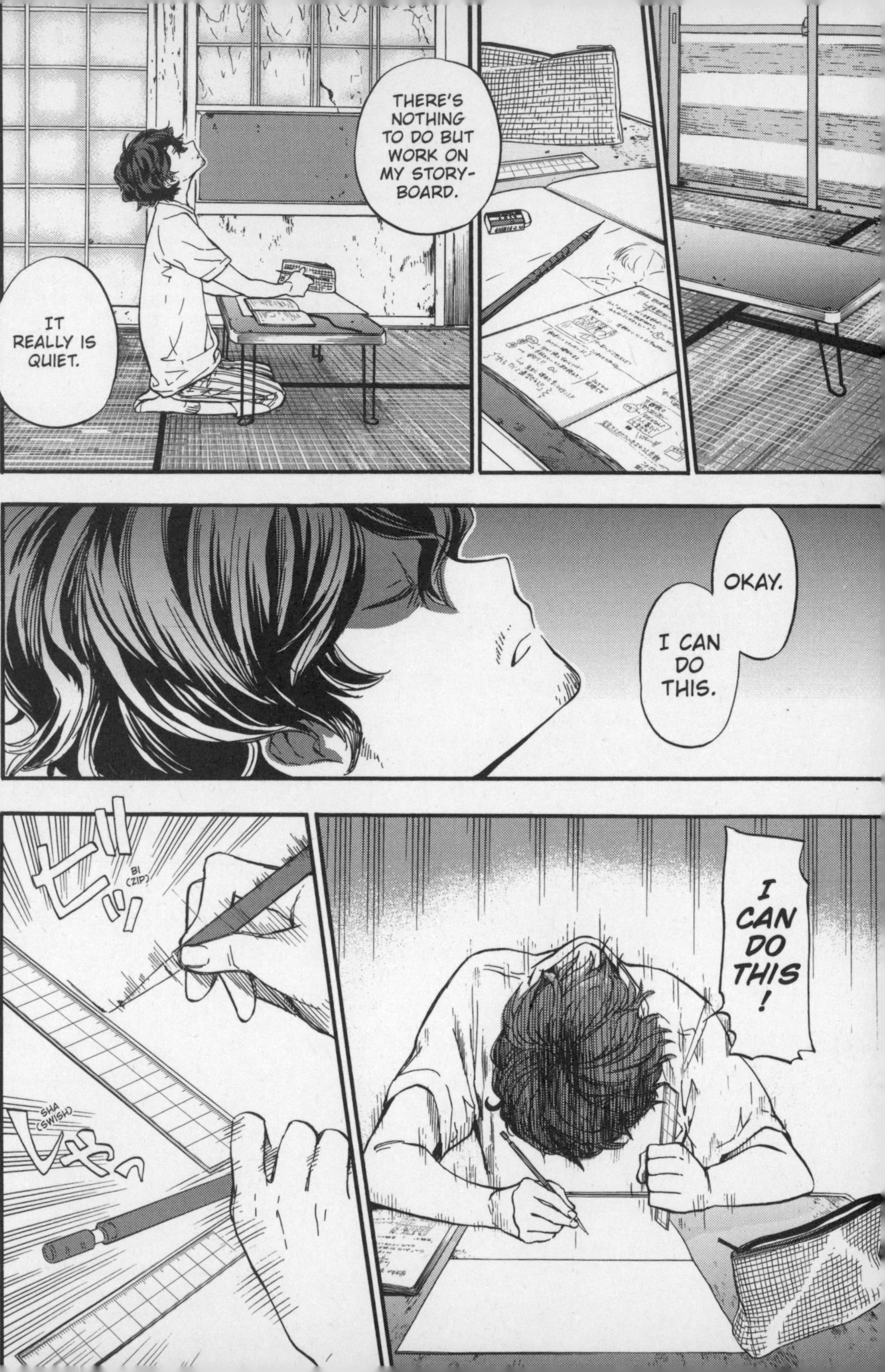
THERE'S NOTHING TO DO BUT WORK ON MY STORY-BOARD.
IT REALLY IS QUIET.
OKAY.
I CAN DO THIS.
I CAN DO THIS!
ビッ
BI (ZIP)
シャッ
SHA (SWISH)

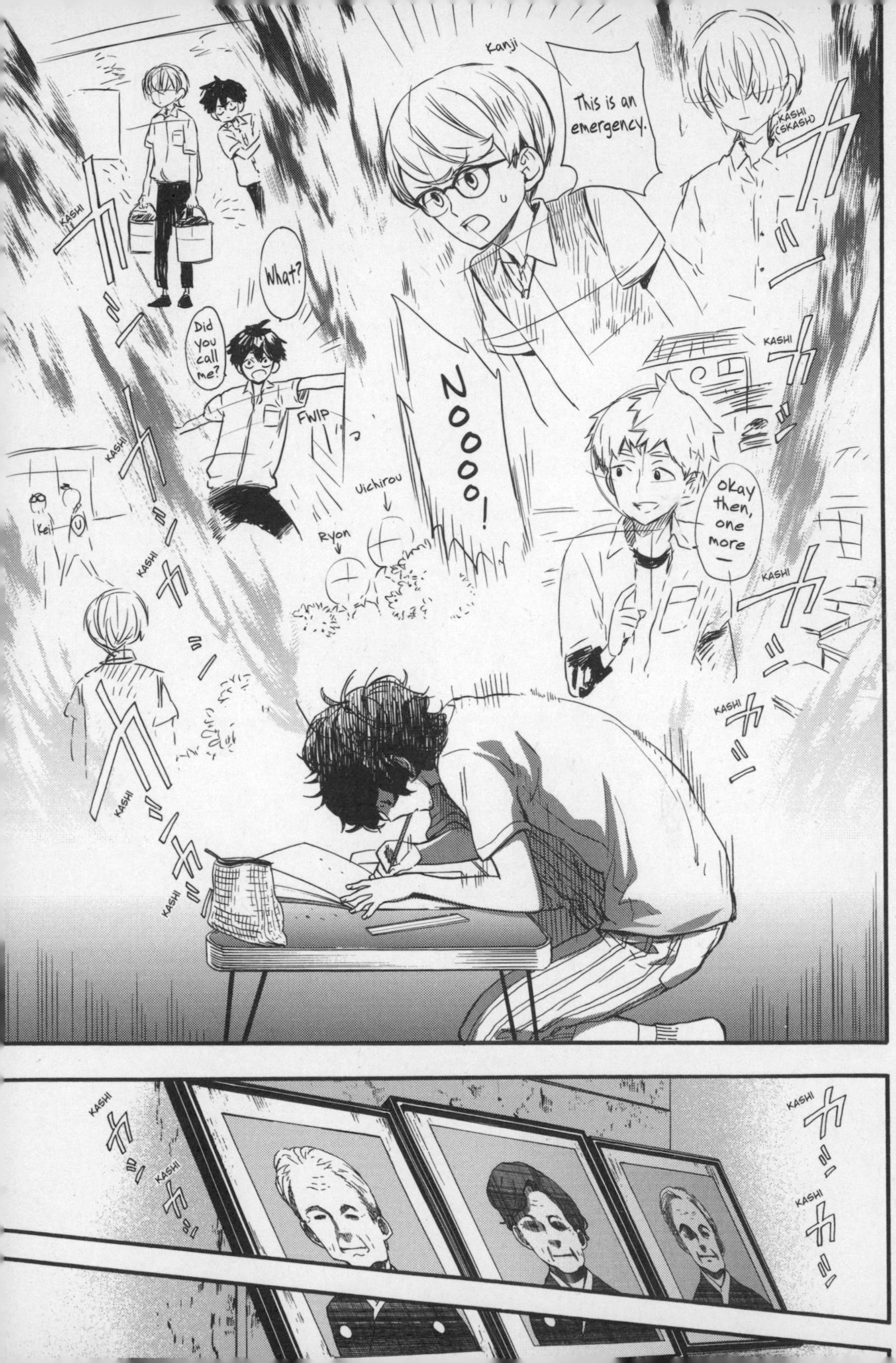
KASHI (SKASH)
Kanji
This is an emergency.
KASHI
Okay then, one more—
KASHI
NOOOO!
Uichirou
Ryon
What?
KASHI
Did you call me?
FWIP
KASHI
KASHI
Kei
KASHI
KASHI
KASHI
KASHI
KASHI
KASHI
KASHI

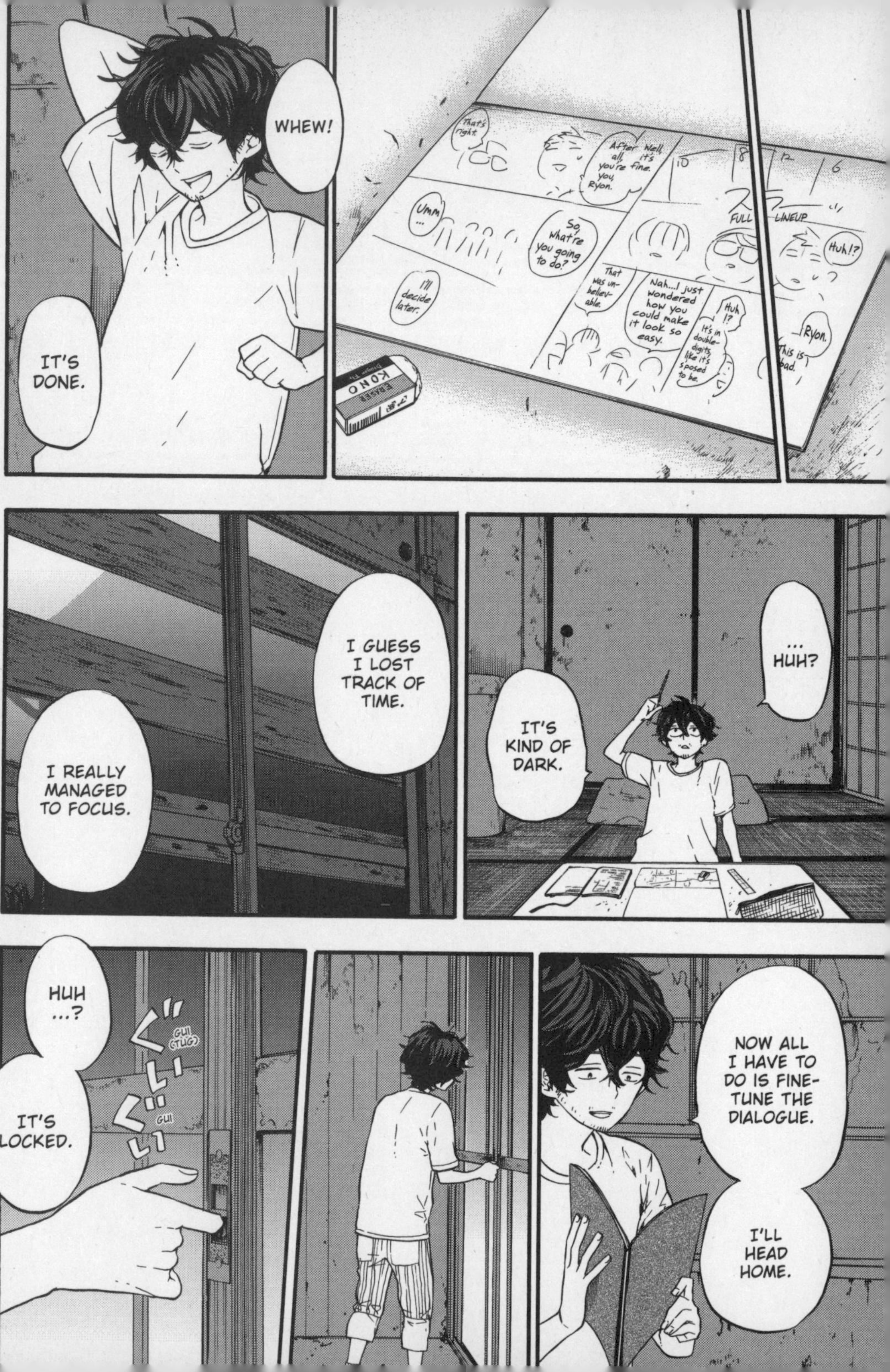
Huh!?
FULL LINEUP
Ryon.
This is bad.
Huh!?
It's in double-digits, like it's s'posed to be.
Nah...I just wondered how you could make it look so easy.
That was un-believ-able.
Well, it's fine.
After all, you, Ryon.
That's right.
So, what're you going to do?
Umm...
I'll decide later.
KONO
ERASER
WHEW!
IT'S DONE.
... HUH?
IT'S KIND OF DARK.
I GUESS I LOST TRACK OF TIME.
I REALLY MANAGED TO FOCUS.
NOW ALL I HAVE TO DO IS FINE-TUNE THE DIALOGUE.
I'LL HEAD HOME.
HUH ...?
GUI (TUG)
GUI
IT'S LOCKED.

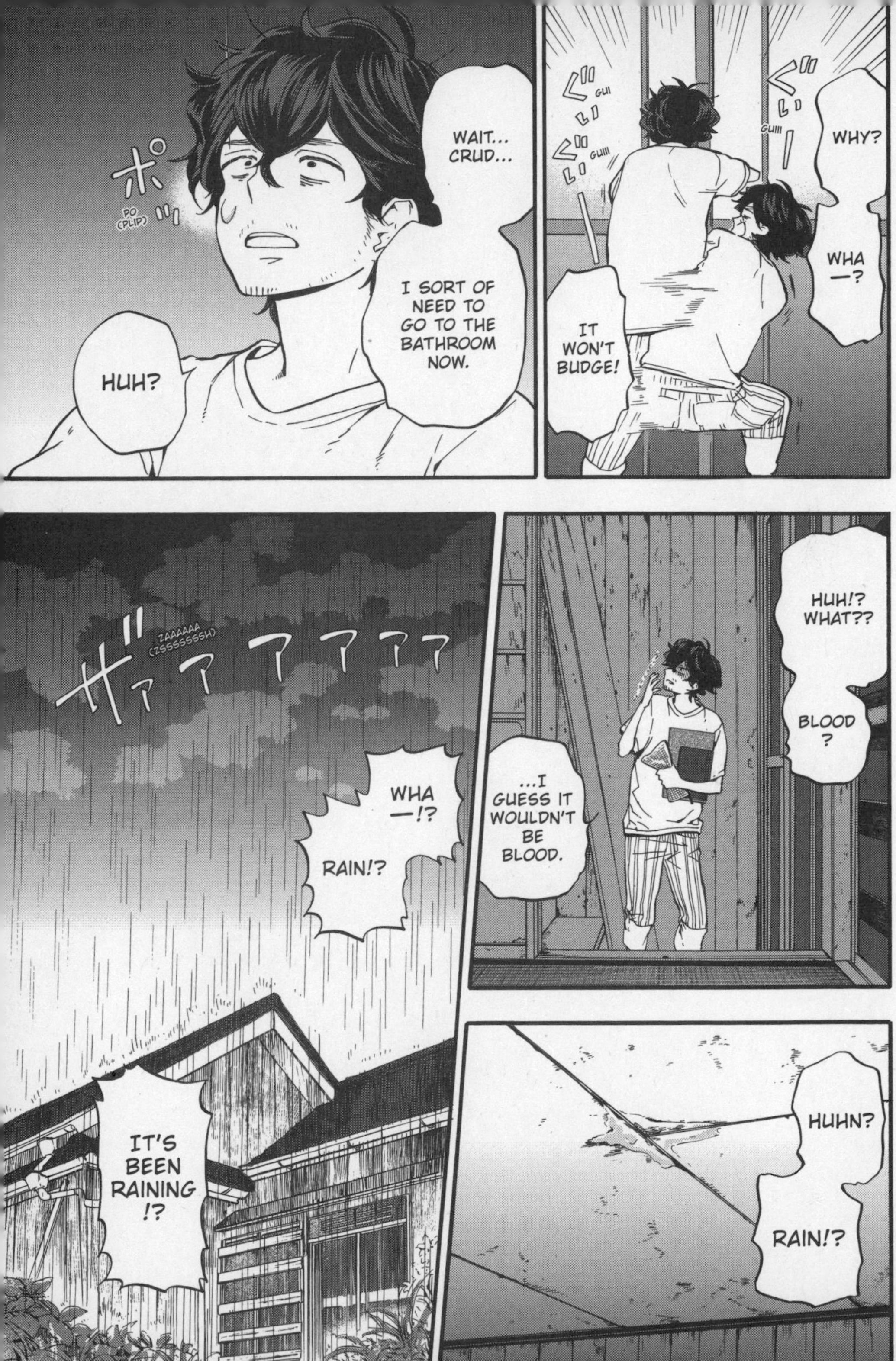
GUI
GUIII
GUIII
WHY?
WHA—?
IT WON'T BUDGE!
WAIT... CRUD...
I SORT OF NEED TO GO TO THE BATHROOM NOW.
PO (PLIP)
HUH?
HUH!? WHAT??
BLOOD?
...I GUESS IT WOULDN'T BE BLOOD.
HUHN?
RAIN!?
ZAAAAAA (ZSSSSSSSH)
WHA—!?
RAIN!?
IT'S BEEN RAINING!?

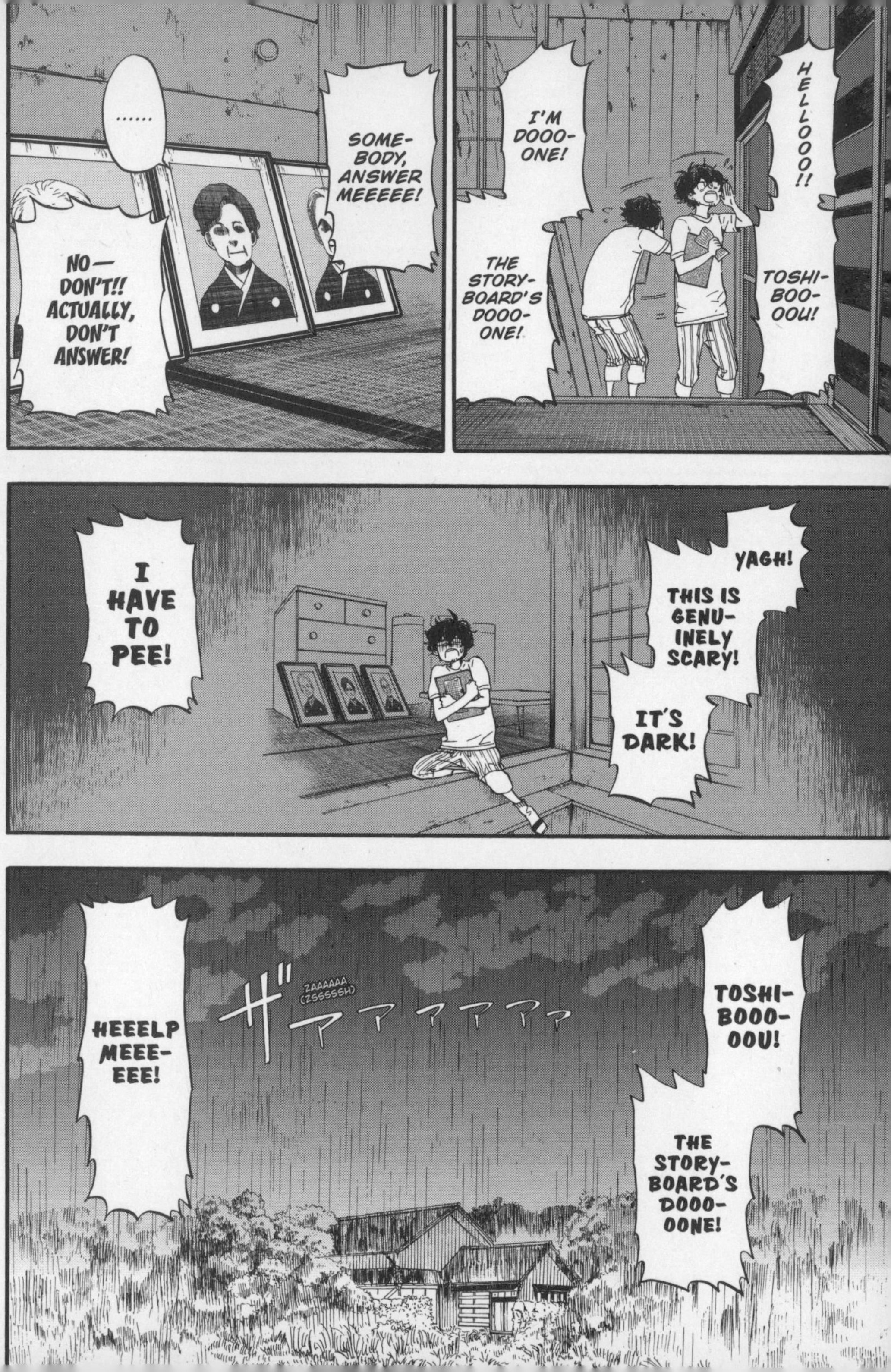
HELLOOOO!!
TOSHIBOOOOU!
I'M DOOOONE!
THE STORYBOARD'S DOOOONE!
SOMEBODY, ANSWER MEEEEEE!
......
NO—DON'T!! ACTUALLY, DON'T ANSWER!
YAGH!
THIS IS GENUINELY SCARY!
IT'S DARK!
I HAVE TO PEE!
TOSHIBOOOOU!
THE STORYBOARD'S DOOOOONE!
ザアアアアァ
ZAAAAAA (ZSSSSSH)
HEEELP MEEEEEE!

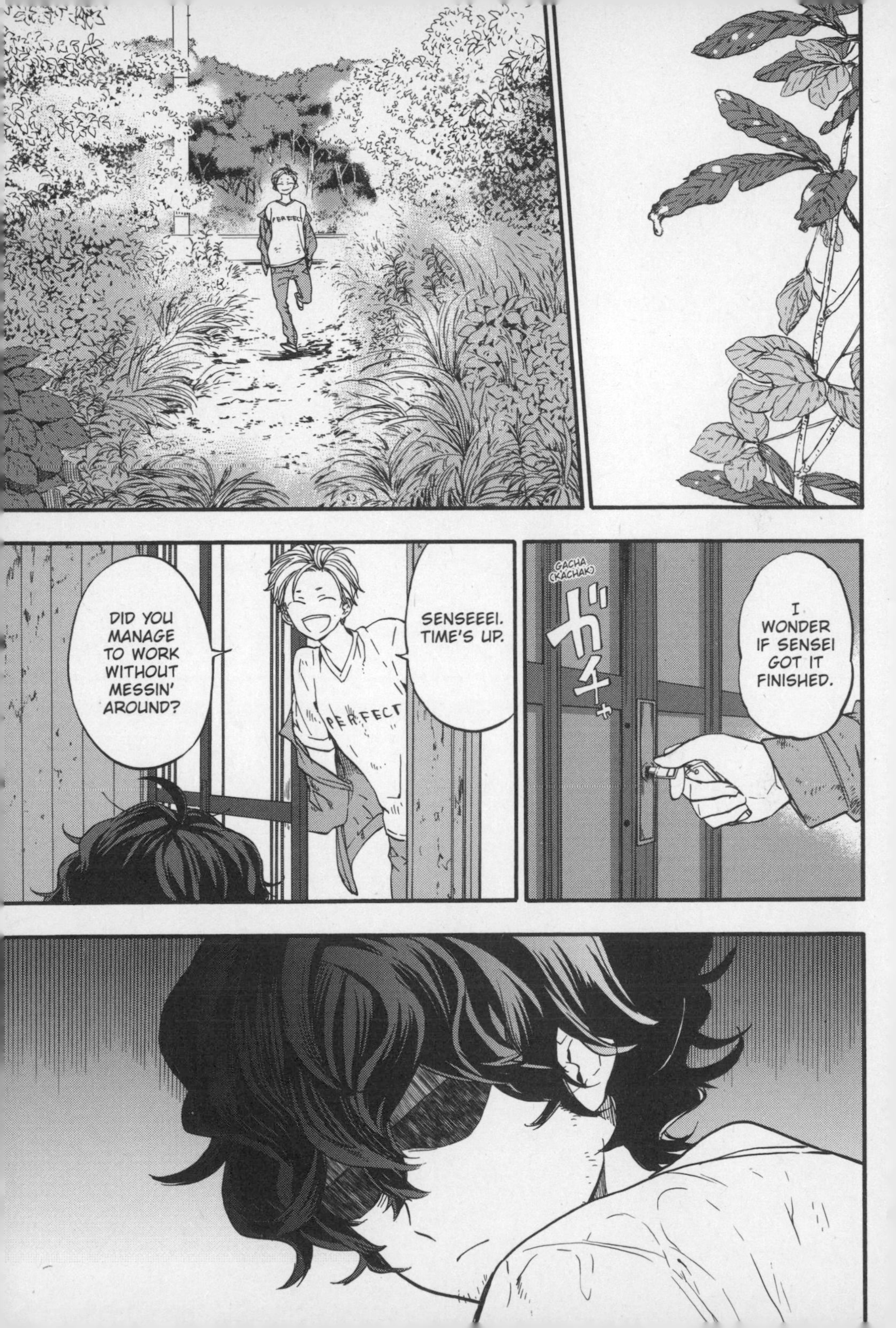
GACHA (KACHAK)
ガチャ
I WONDER IF SENSEI GOT IT FINISHED.
SENSEEEI. TIME'S UP.
DID YOU MANAGE TO WORK WITHOUT MESSIN' AROUND?

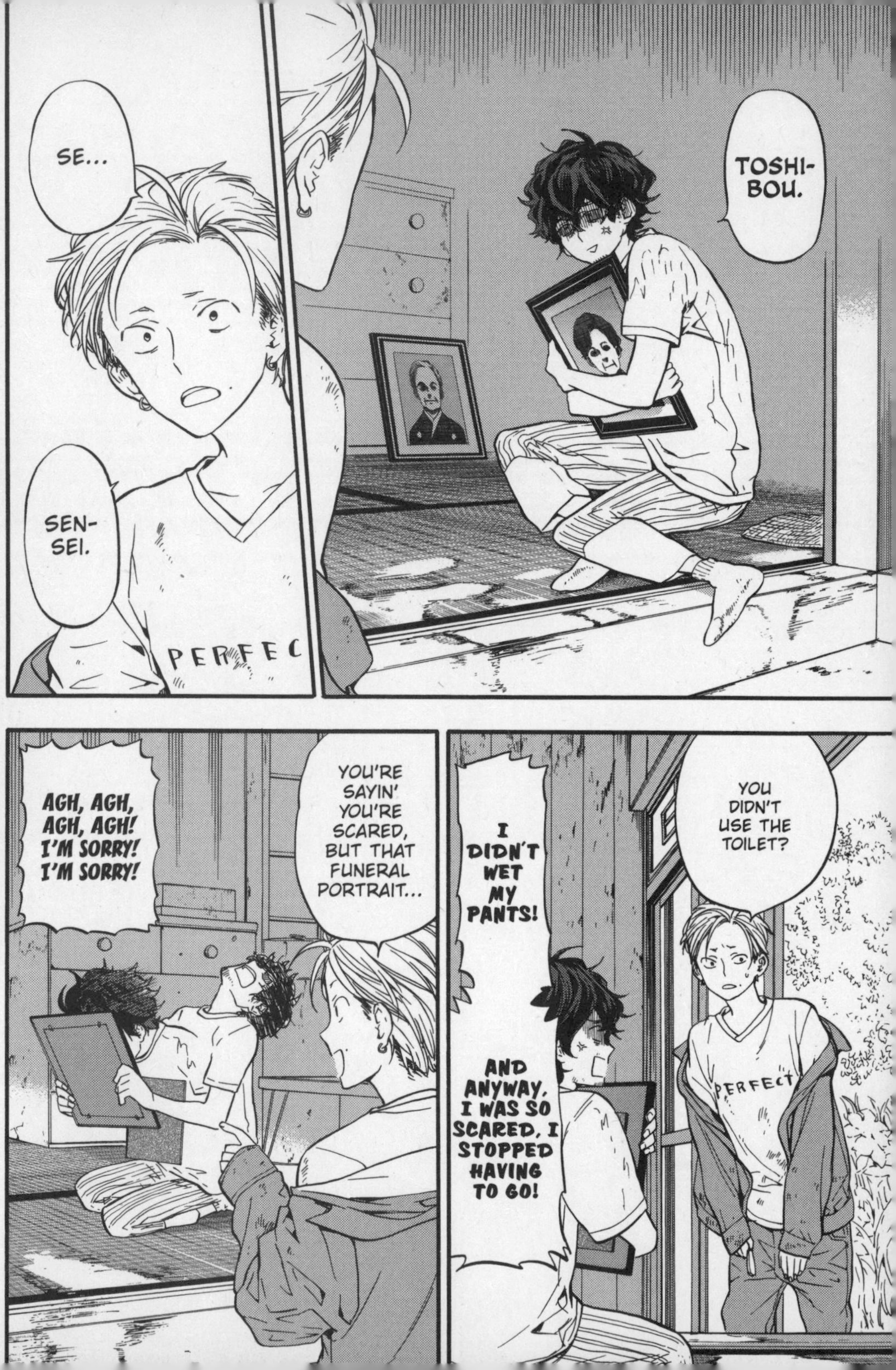
TOSHI-BOU.
SE...
SEN-SEI.
PERFEC
YOU DIDN'T USE THE TOILET?
PERFECT
I DIDN'T WET MY PANTS!
AND ANYWAY, I WAS SO SCARED, I STOPPED HAVING TO GO!
YOU'RE SAYIN' YOU'RE SCARED, BUT THAT FUNERAL PORTRAIT...
AGH, AGH, AGH, AGH! I'M SORRY! I'M SORRY!

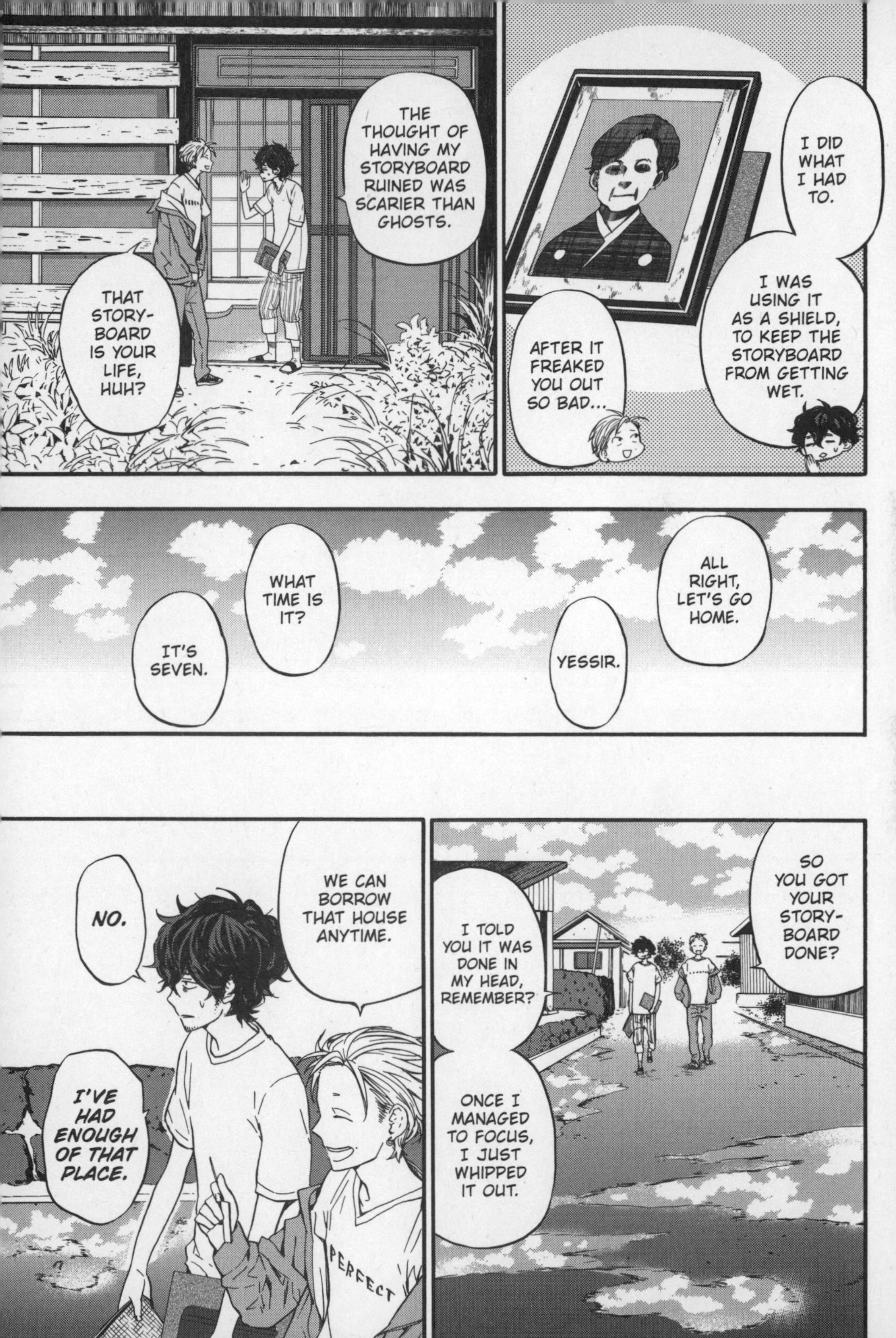
I DID WHAT I HAD TO.
I WAS USING IT AS A SHIELD, TO KEEP THE STORYBOARD FROM GETTING WET.
AFTER IT FREAKED YOU OUT SO BAD...
THE THOUGHT OF HAVING MY STORYBOARD RUINED WAS SCARIER THAN GHOSTS.
THAT STORY-BOARD IS YOUR LIFE, HUH?
ALL RIGHT, LET'S GO HOME.
YESSIR.
WHAT TIME IS IT?
IT'S SEVEN.
SO YOU GOT YOUR STORY-BOARD DONE?
I TOLD YOU IT WAS DONE IN MY HEAD, REMEMBER?
ONCE I MANAGED TO FOCUS, I JUST WHIPPED IT OUT.
WE CAN BORROW THAT HOUSE ANYTIME.
NO.
I'VE HAD ENOUGH OF THAT PLACE.
PERFECT

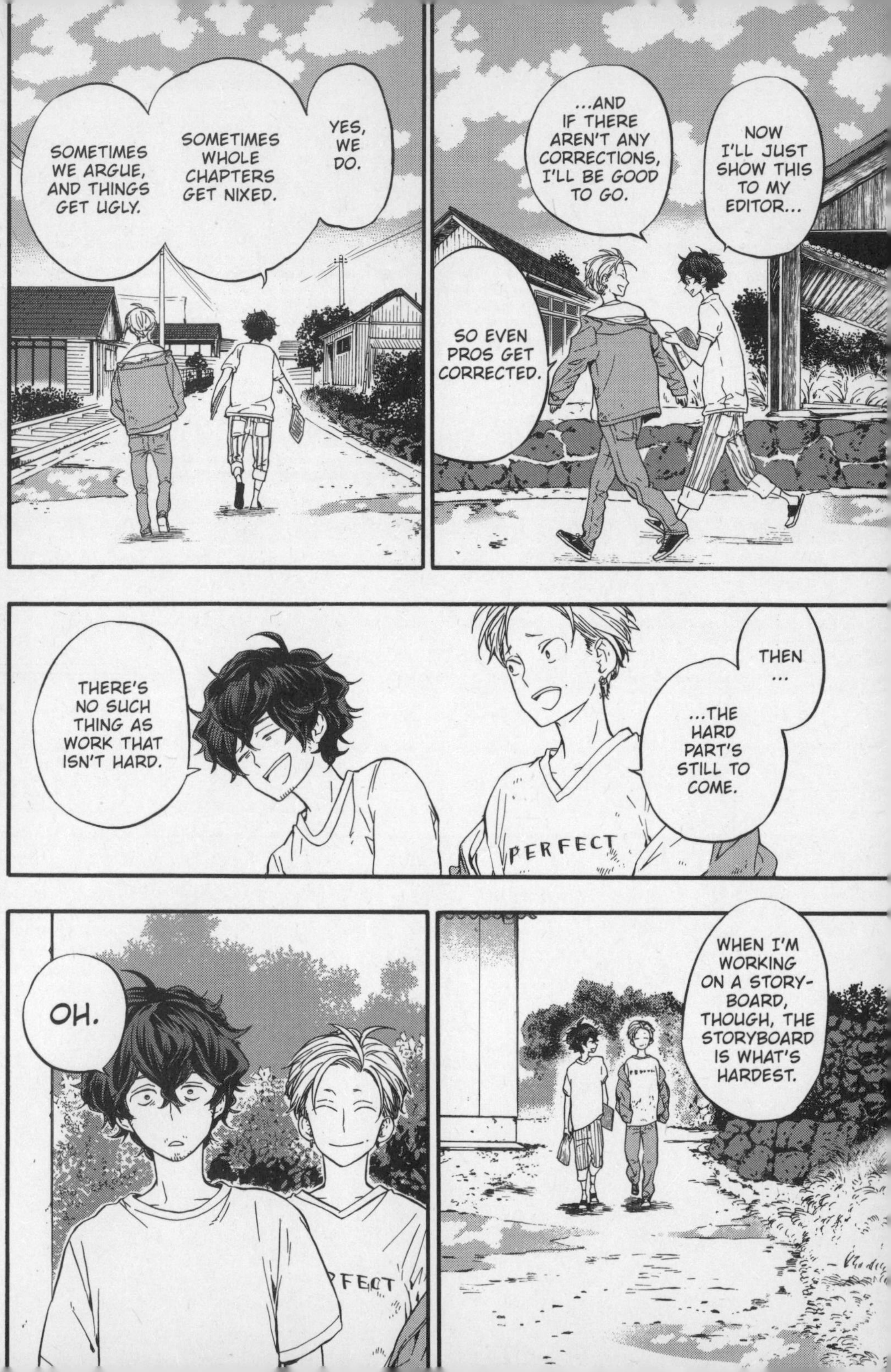
NOW I'LL JUST SHOW THIS TO MY EDITOR...
...AND IF THERE AREN'T ANY CORRECTIONS, I'LL BE GOOD TO GO.
SO EVEN PROS GET CORRECTED.
YES, WE DO.
SOMETIMES WHOLE CHAPTERS GET NIXED.
SOMETIMES WE ARGUE, AND THINGS GET UGLY.
THEN ...
...THE HARD PART'S STILL TO COME.
PERFECT
THERE'S NO SUCH THING AS WORK THAT ISN'T HARD.
WHEN I'M WORKING ON A STORY-BOARD, THOUGH, THE STORYBOARD IS WHAT'S HARDEST.
OH.

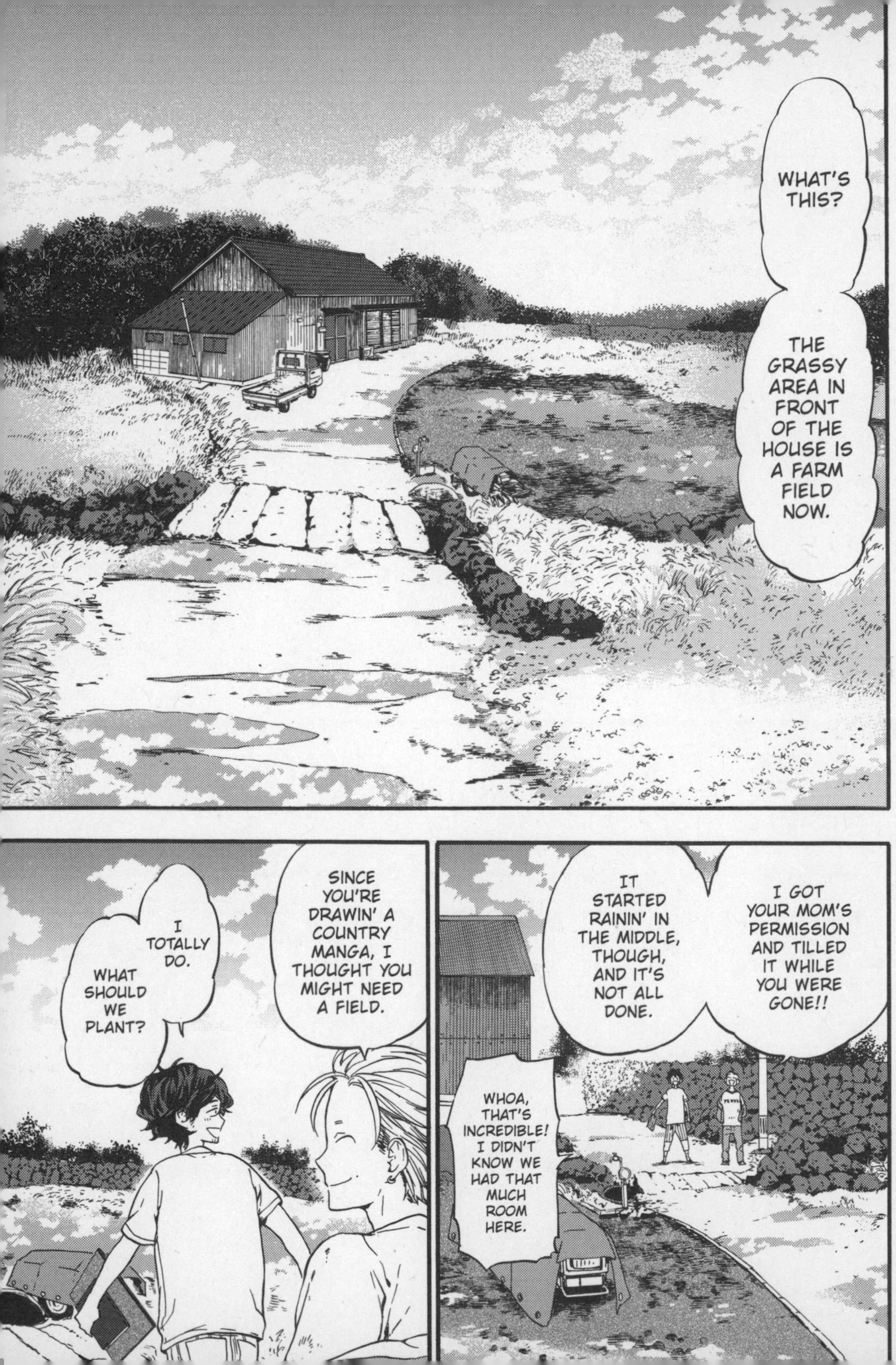
WHAT'S THIS?
THE GRASSY AREA IN FRONT OF THE HOUSE IS A FARM FIELD NOW.
I GOT YOUR MOM'S PERMISSION AND TILLED IT WHILE YOU WERE GONE!!
IT STARTED RAININ' IN THE MIDDLE, THOUGH, AND IT'S NOT ALL DONE.
WHOA, THAT'S INCREDIBLE! I DIDN'T KNOW WE HAD THAT MUCH ROOM HERE.
SINCE YOU'RE DRAWIN' A COUNTRY MANGA, I THOUGHT YOU MIGHT NEED A FIELD.
I TOTALLY DO. WHAT SHOULD WE PLANT?

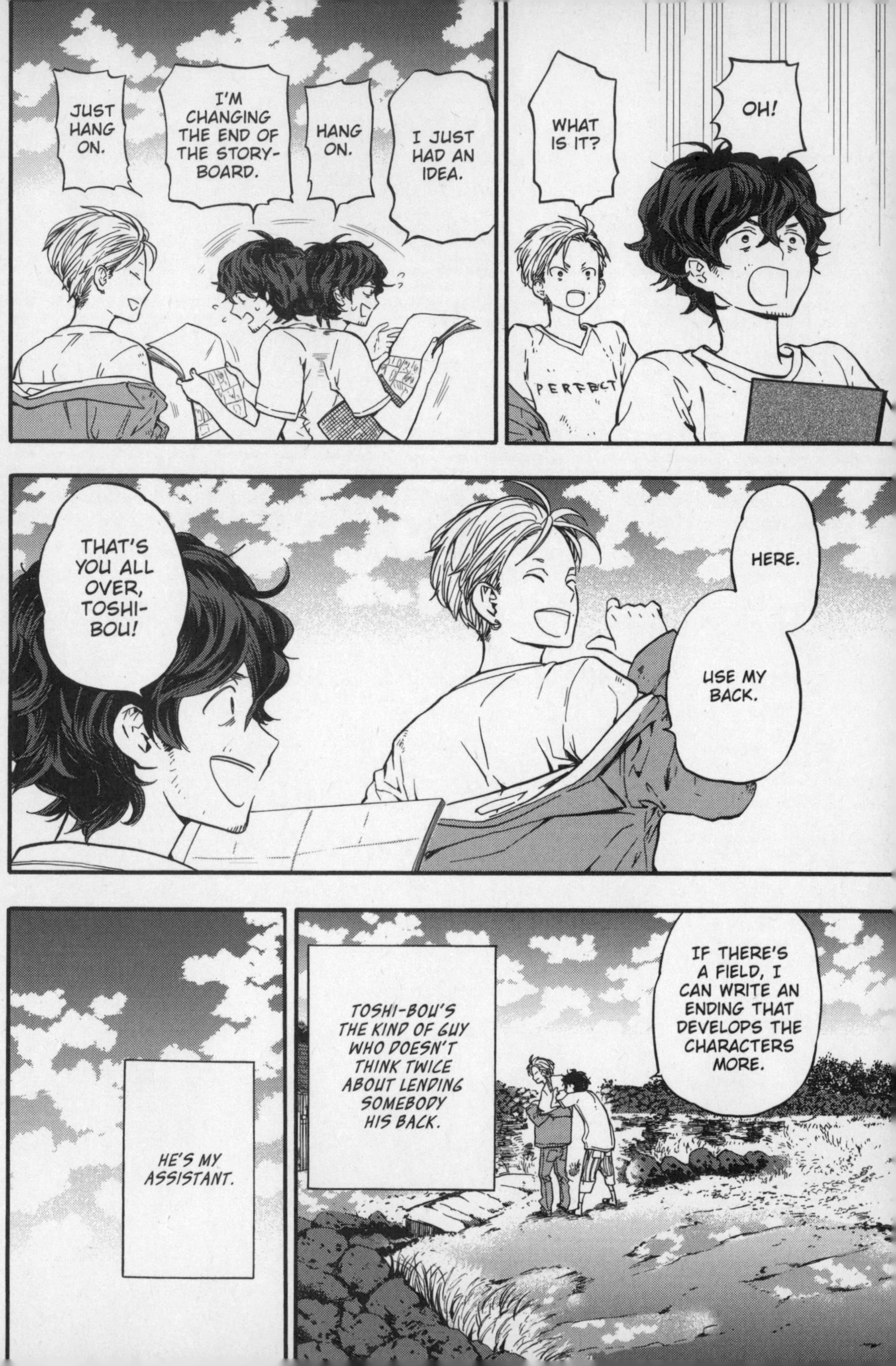
OH!
WHAT IS IT?
I JUST HAD AN IDEA.
HANG ON.
I'M CHANGING THE END OF THE STORY-BOARD.
JUST HANG ON.
HERE.
USE MY BACK.
THAT'S YOU ALL OVER, TOSHI-BOU!
IF THERE'S A FIELD, I CAN WRITE AN ENDING THAT DEVELOPS THE CHARACTERS MORE.
TOSHI-BOU'S THE KIND OF GUY WHO DOESN'T THINK TWICE ABOUT LENDING SOMEBODY HIS BACK.
HE'S MY ASSISTANT.

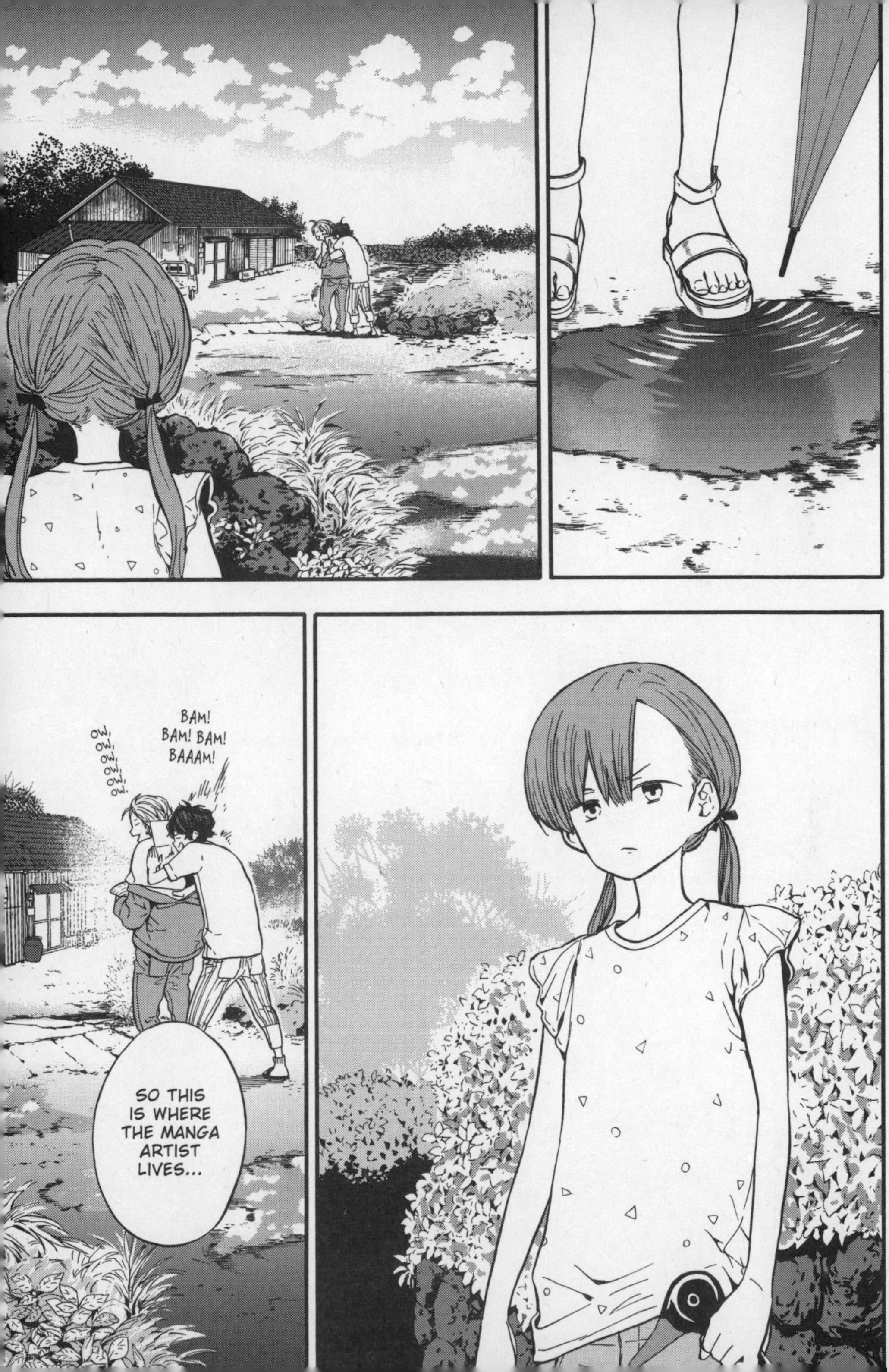
BAM! BAM! BAM! BAAAM!
OW, OW, OW, OW, OW, OW.
SO THIS IS WHERE THE MANGA ARTIST LIVES...

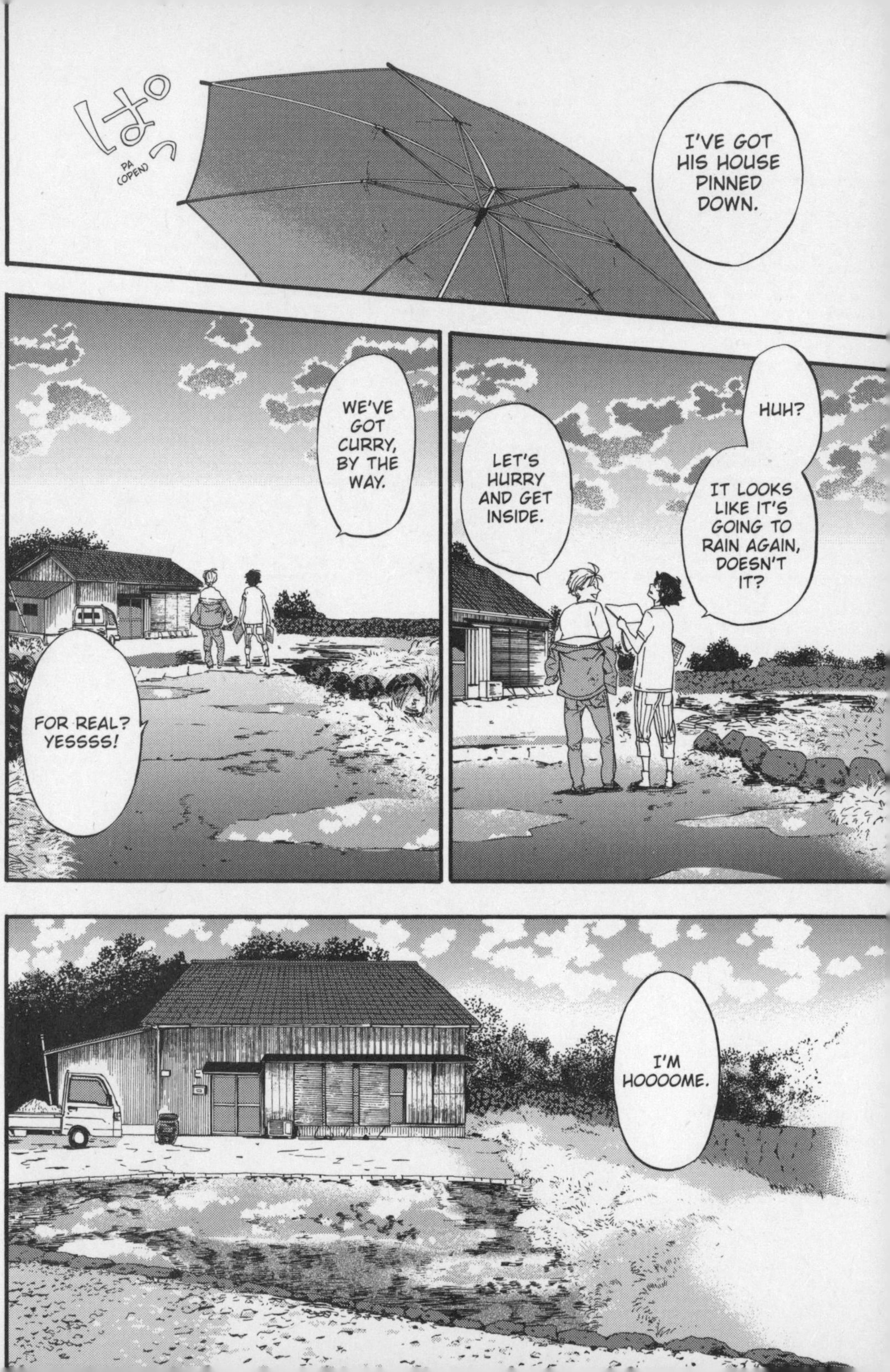
I'VE GOT HIS HOUSE PINNED DOWN.
ぱっ
PA (OPEN)
HUH?
IT LOOKS LIKE IT'S GOING TO RAIN AGAIN, DOESN'T IT?
LET'S HURRY AND GET INSIDE.
WE'VE GOT CURRY, BY THE WAY.
FOR REAL? YESSSS!
I'M HOOOOME.

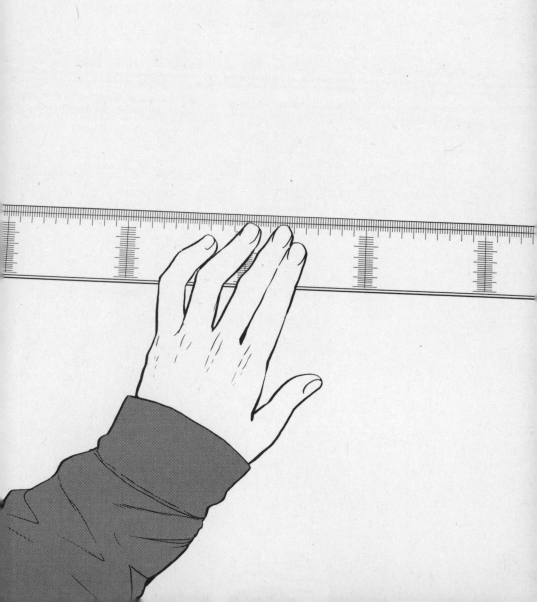

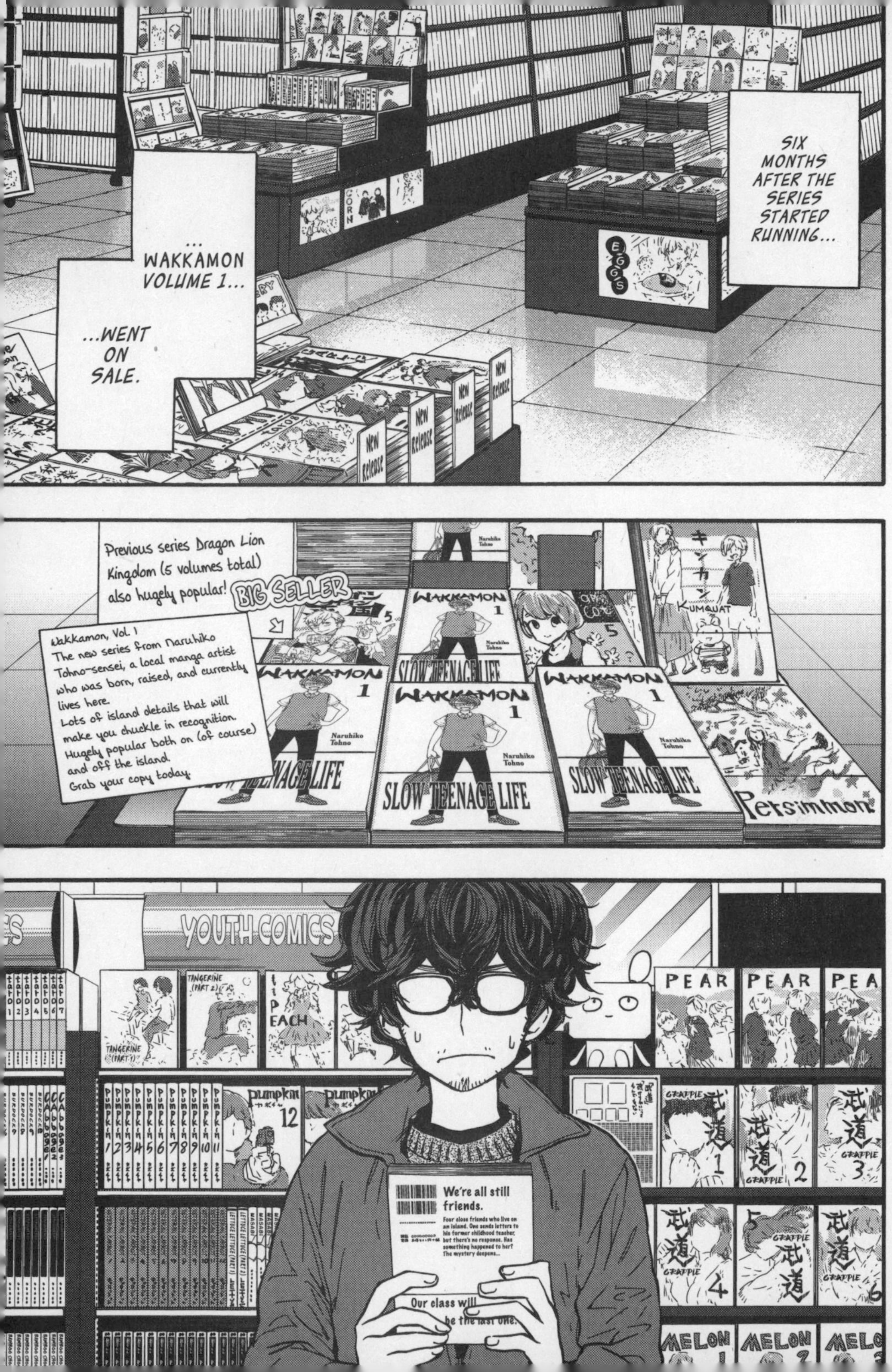
SIX MONTHS AFTER THE SERIES STARTED RUNNING...
EGGS
CORN
New release
New release
New release
New release
...WAKKAMON VOLUME 1...
...WENT ON SALE.
KUMQUAT
Persimmon
WAKKAMON 1
Naruhiko Tohno
SLOW TEENAGE LIFE
BIG SELLER
Previous series Dragon Lion Kingdom (5 volumes total) also hugely popular!
Wakkamon, Vol. 1
The new series from Naruhiko Tohno-sensei, a local manga artist who was born, raised, and currently lives here.
Lots of island details that will make you chuckle in recognition.
Hugely popular both on (of course) and off the island.
Grab your copy today.
YOUTH COMICS
PEAR
PEAR
TANGERINE (PART 2)
PEACH
TANGERINE (PART 1)
pumpkin 12
GRAPPLE
We're all still friends.
Four close friends who live on an island. One sends letters to his former childhood teacher, but there's no response. Has something happened to her? The mystery deepens...
Our class will be the last one.
MELON
MELON

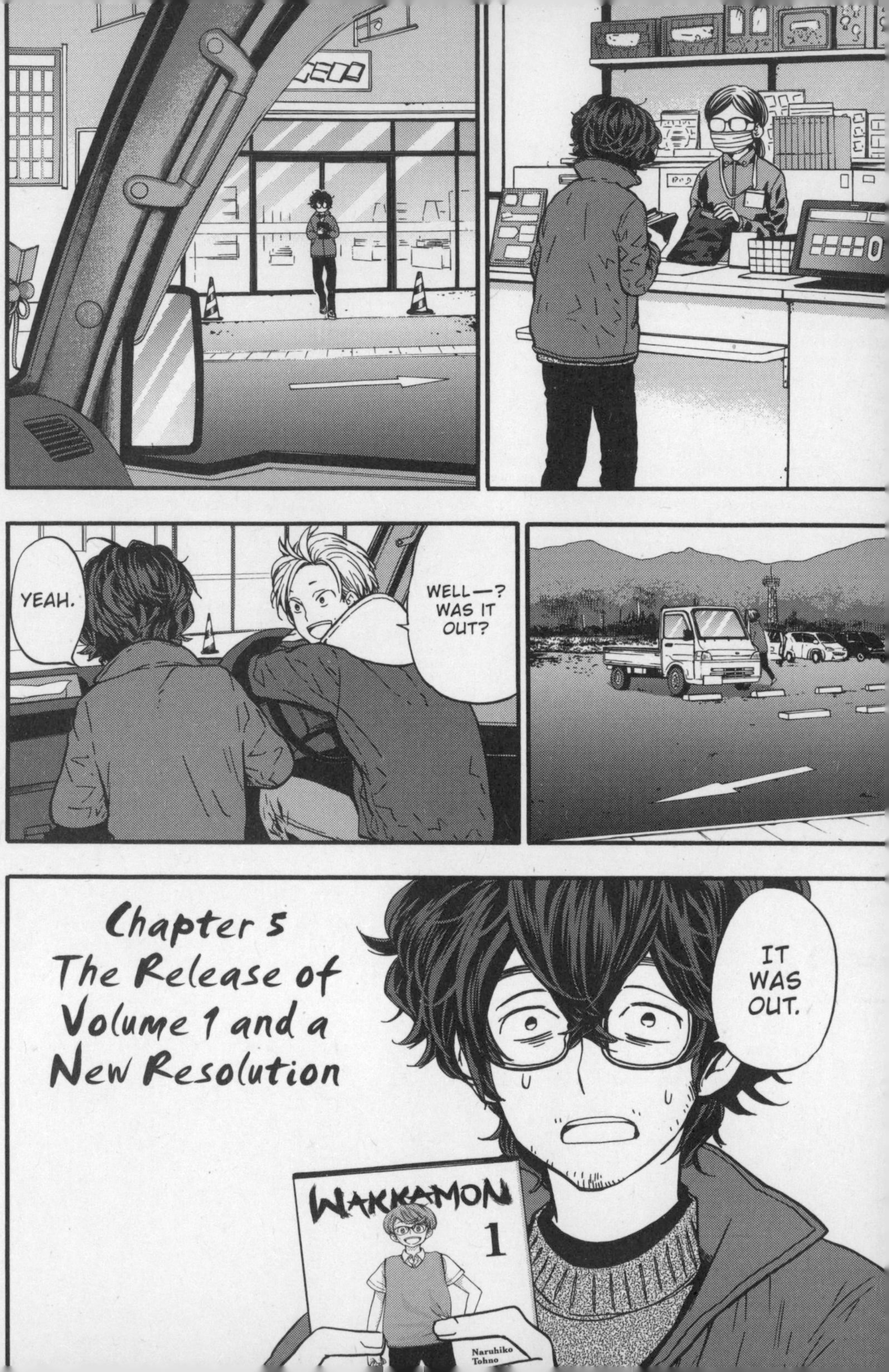
WELL—? WAS IT OUT?
YEAH.
IT WAS OUT.
Chapter 5 The Release of Volume 1 and a New Resolution
WAKKAMON
1
Naruhiko Tohno

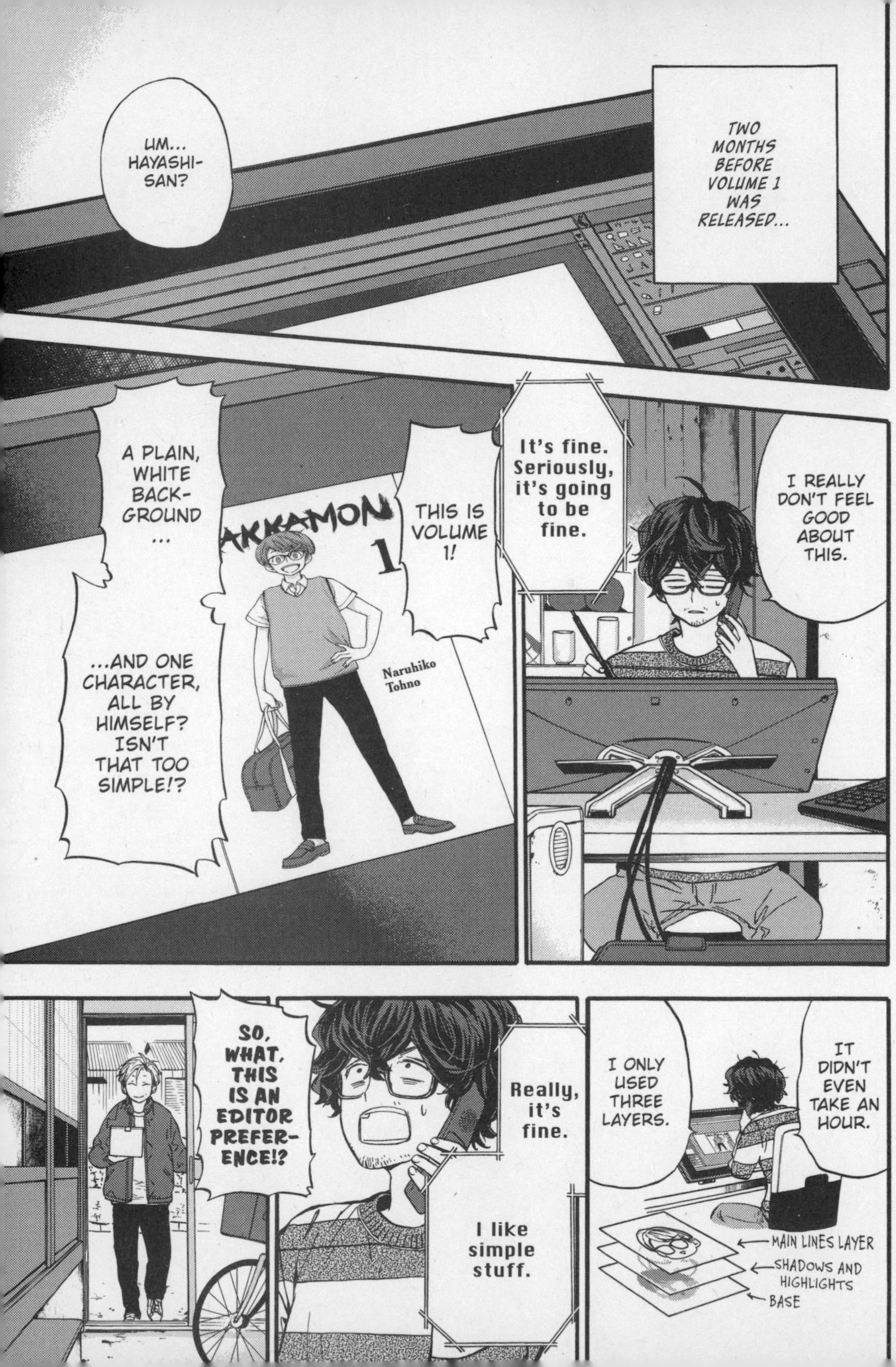
TWO MONTHS BEFORE VOLUME 1 WAS RELEASED...
UM... HAYASHI-SAN?
I REALLY DON'T FEEL GOOD ABOUT THIS.
It's fine. Seriously, it's going to be fine.
THIS IS VOLUME 1!
AKKAMON 1
Naruhiko Tohno
A PLAIN, WHITE BACK-GROUND...
...AND ONE CHARACTER, ALL BY HIMSELF? ISN'T THAT TOO SIMPLE!?
IT DIDN'T EVEN TAKE AN HOUR.
I ONLY USED THREE LAYERS.
MAIN LINES LAYER
SHADOWS AND HIGHLIGHTS
BASE
Really, it's fine.
SO, WHAT, THIS IS AN EDITOR PREFER-ENCE!?
I like simple stuff.

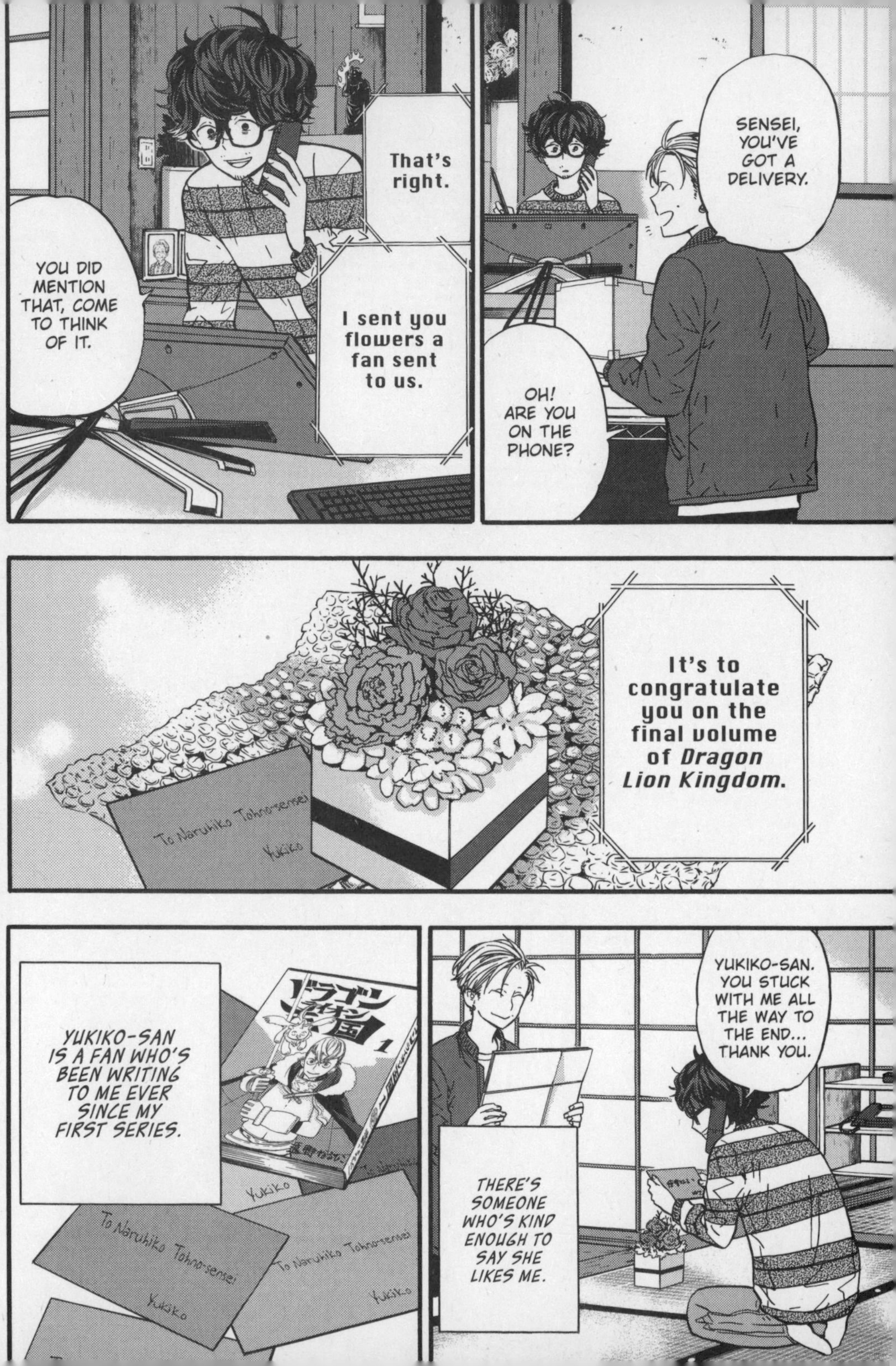
SENSEI, YOU'VE GOT A DELIVERY.
OH! ARE YOU ON THE PHONE?
That's right.
I sent you flowers a fan sent to us.
YOU DID MENTION THAT, COME TO THINK OF IT.
It's to congratulate you on the final volume of *Dragon Lion Kingdom*.
To Naruhiko Tohno-sensei
Yukiko
YUKIKO-SAN. YOU STUCK WITH ME ALL THE WAY TO THE END... THANK YOU.
THERE'S SOMEONE WHO'S KIND ENOUGH TO SAY SHE LIKES ME.
YUKIKO-SAN IS A FAN WHO'S BEEN WRITING TO ME EVER SINCE MY FIRST SERIES.
To Naruhiko Tohno-sensei
Yukiko
To Naruhiko Tohno-sensei
Yukiko

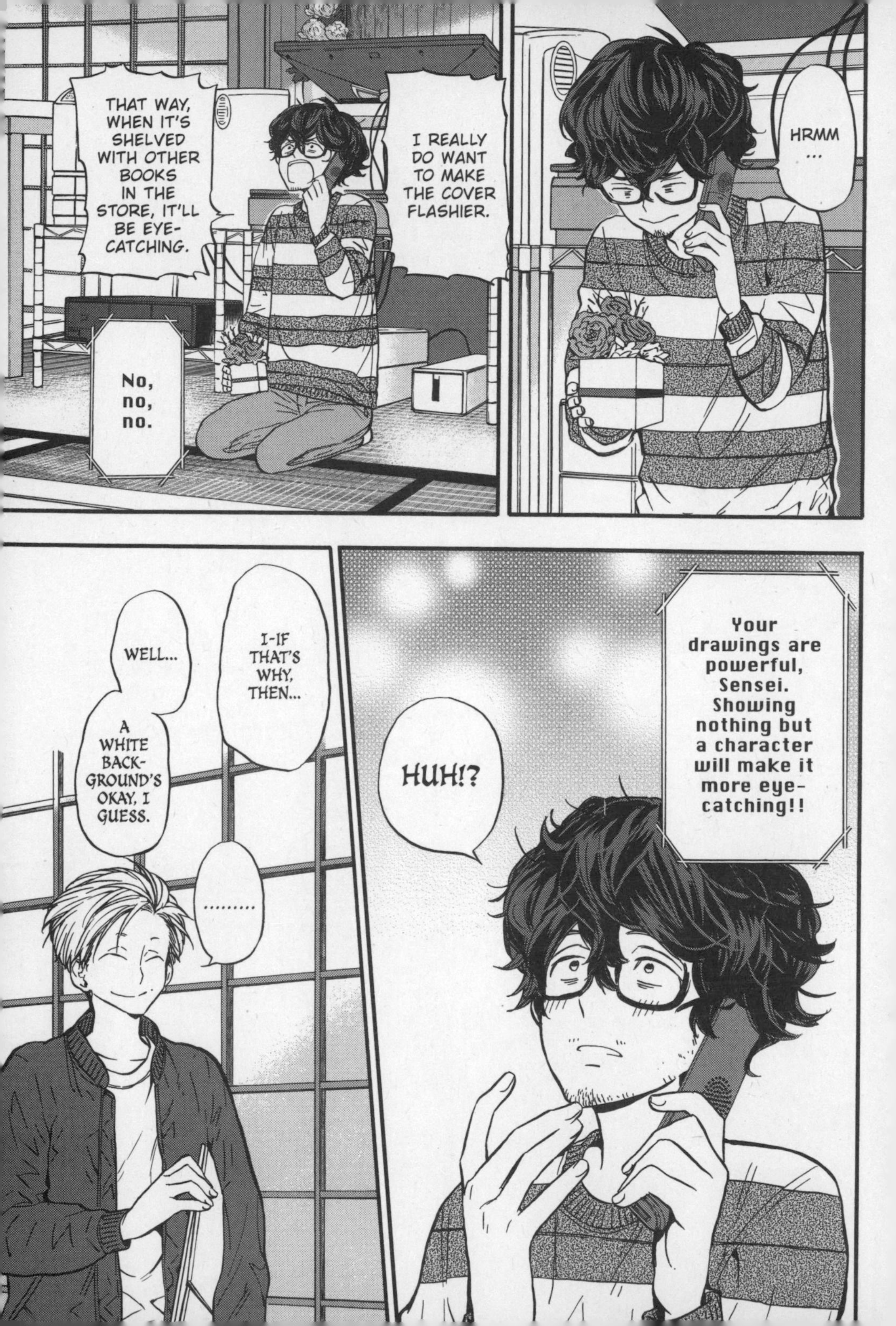
HRMM...
I REALLY DO WANT TO MAKE THE COVER FLASHIER.
THAT WAY, WHEN IT'S SHELVED WITH OTHER BOOKS IN THE STORE, IT'LL BE EYE-CATCHING.
No, no, no.
Your drawings are powerful, Sensei. Showing nothing but a character will make it more eye-catching!!
HUH!?
I-IF THAT'S WHY, THEN...
WELL...
A WHITE BACK-GROUND'S OKAY, I GUESS.
....

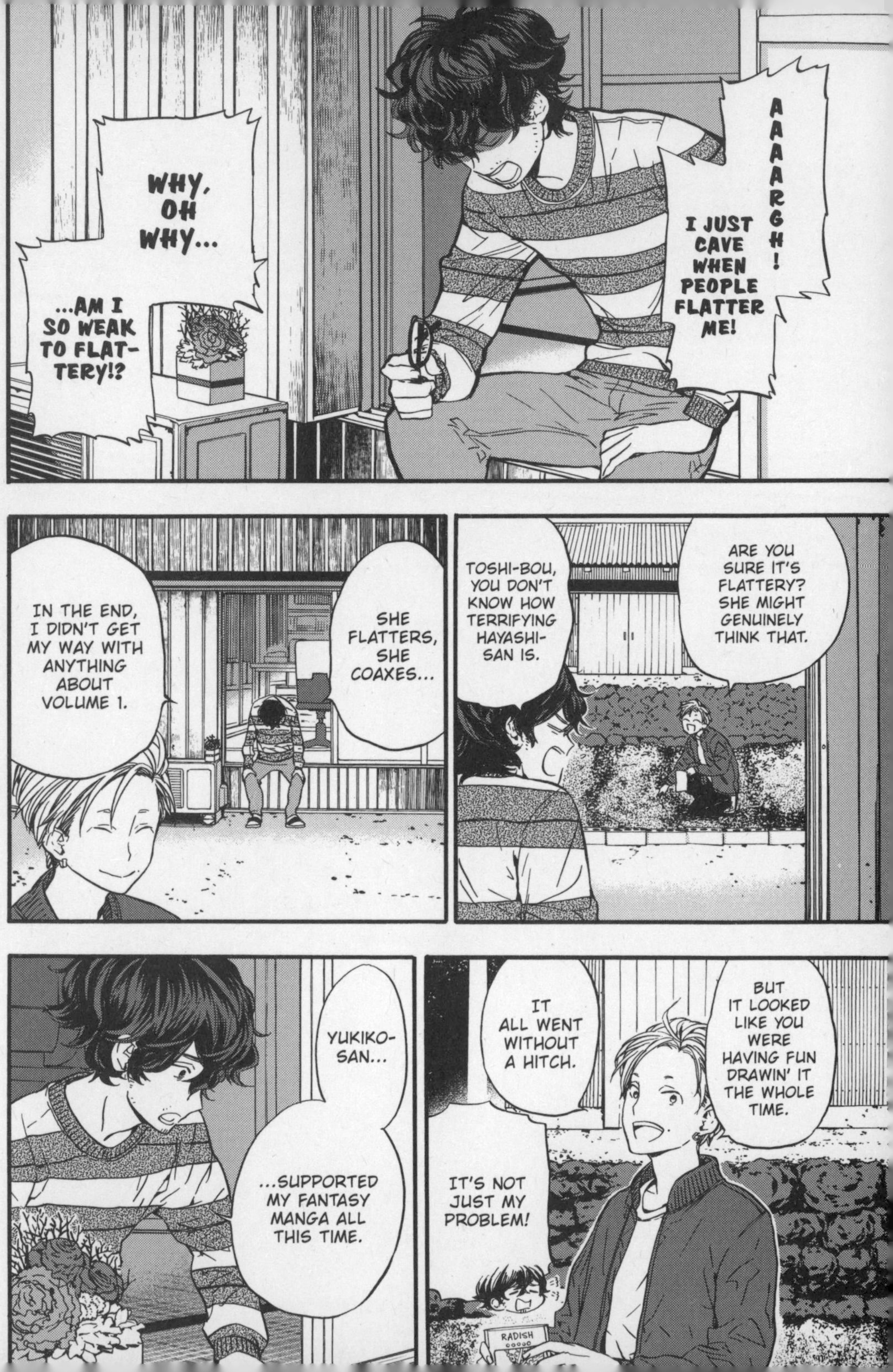
AAAARGH!
I JUST CAVE WHEN PEOPLE FLATTER ME!
WHY, OH WHY...
...AM I SO WEAK TO FLATTERY!?
ARE YOU SURE IT'S FLATTERY? SHE MIGHT GENUINELY THINK THAT.
TOSHI-BOU, YOU DON'T KNOW HOW TERRIFYING HAYASHI-SAN IS.
SHE FLATTERS, SHE COAXES...
IN THE END, I DIDN'T GET MY WAY WITH ANYTHING ABOUT VOLUME 1.
BUT IT LOOKED LIKE YOU WERE HAVING FUN DRAWIN' IT THE WHOLE TIME.
IT ALL WENT WITHOUT A HITCH.
IT'S NOT JUST MY PROBLEM!
RADISH
YUKIKO-SAN...
...SUPPORTED MY FANTASY MANGA ALL THIS TIME.

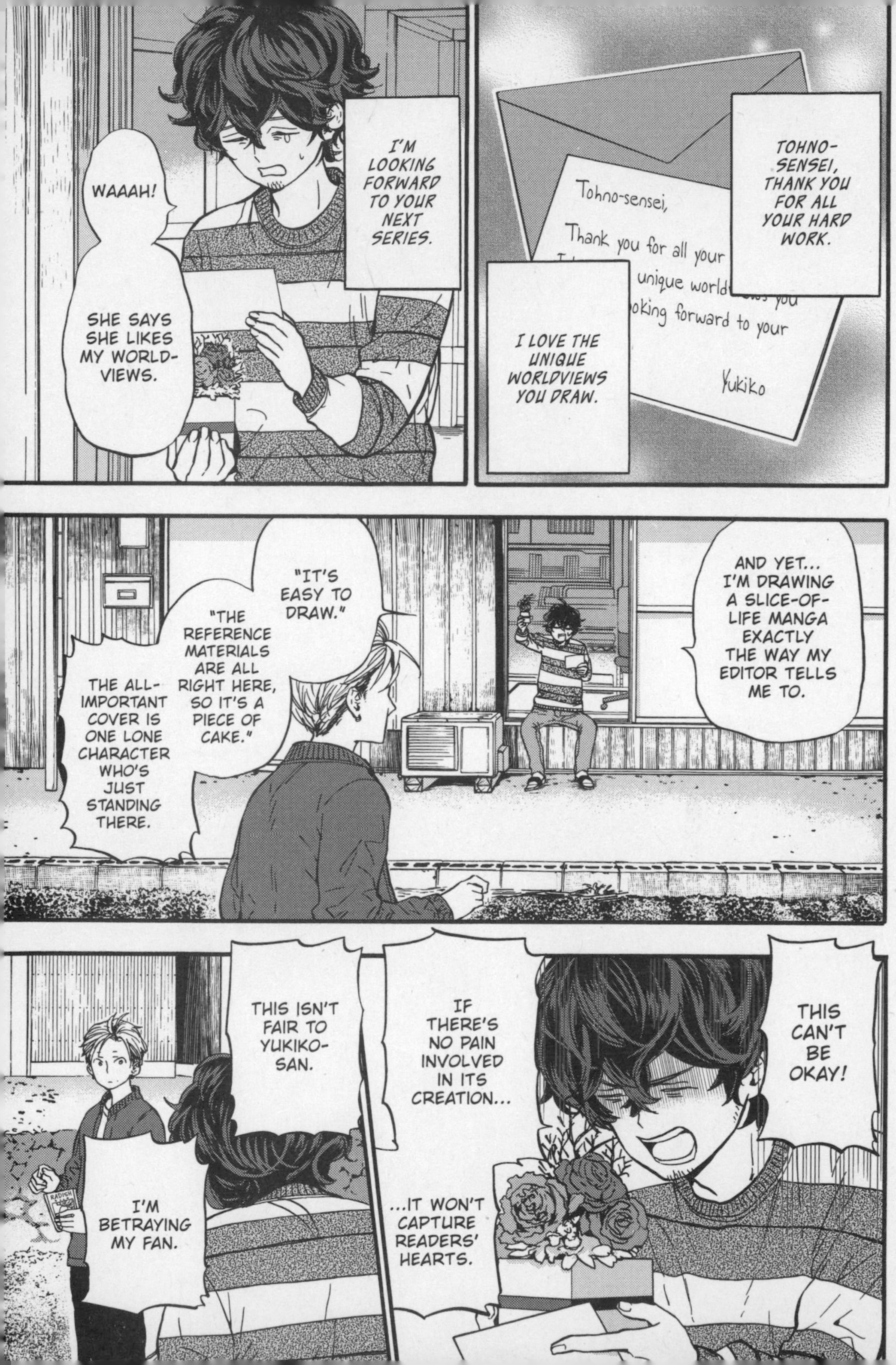
TOHNO-SENSEI, THANK YOU FOR ALL YOUR HARD WORK.
Tohno-sensei,
Thank you for all your
unique worldviews you
oking forward to your
Yukiko
I LOVE THE UNIQUE WORLDVIEWS YOU DRAW.
I'M LOOKING FORWARD TO YOUR NEXT SERIES.
WAAAH!
SHE SAYS SHE LIKES MY WORLD-VIEWS.
AND YET... I'M DRAWING A SLICE-OF-LIFE MANGA EXACTLY THE WAY MY EDITOR TELLS ME TO.
"IT'S EASY TO DRAW."
"THE REFERENCE MATERIALS ARE ALL RIGHT HERE, SO IT'S A PIECE OF CAKE."
THE ALL-IMPORTANT COVER IS ONE LONE CHARACTER WHO'S JUST STANDING THERE.
THIS CAN'T BE OKAY!
IF THERE'S NO PAIN INVOLVED IN ITS CREATION...
...IT WON'T CAPTURE READERS' HEARTS.
THIS ISN'T FAIR TO YUKIKO-SAN.
I'M BETRAYING MY FAN.

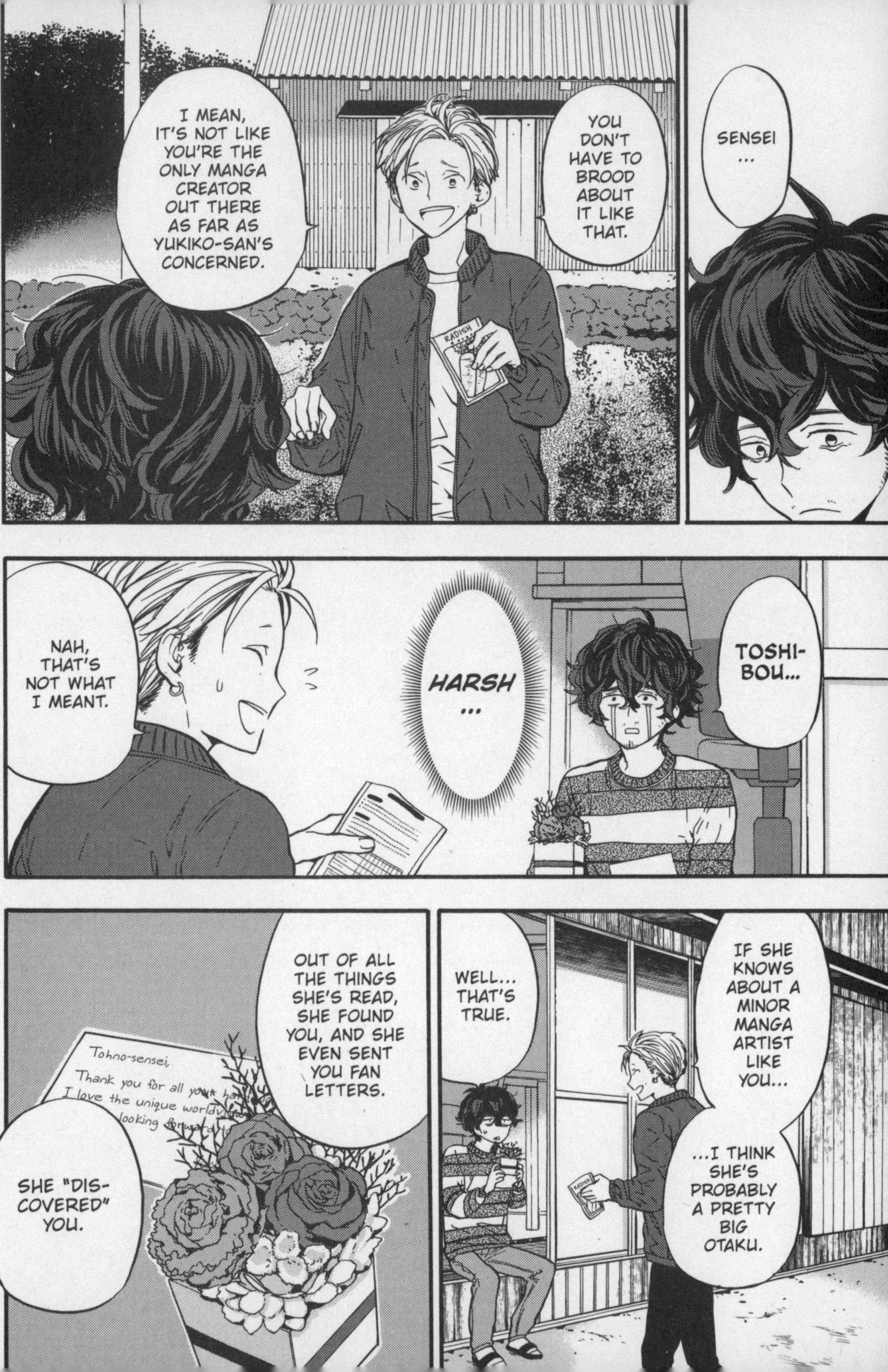
SENSEI ...
YOU DON'T HAVE TO BROOD ABOUT IT LIKE THAT.
I MEAN, IT'S NOT LIKE YOU'RE THE ONLY MANGA CREATOR OUT THERE AS FAR AS YUKIKO-SAN'S CONCERNED.
RADISH
TOSHI-BOU...
HARSH ...
NAH, THAT'S NOT WHAT I MEANT.
IF SHE KNOWS ABOUT A MINOR MANGA ARTIST LIKE YOU...
...I THINK SHE'S PROBABLY A PRETTY BIG OTAKU.
WELL... THAT'S TRUE.
RADISH
OUT OF ALL THE THINGS SHE'S READ, SHE FOUND YOU, AND SHE EVEN SENT YOU FAN LETTERS.
Tohno-sensei,
Thank you for all your
I love the unique world
SHE "DIS-COVERED" YOU.

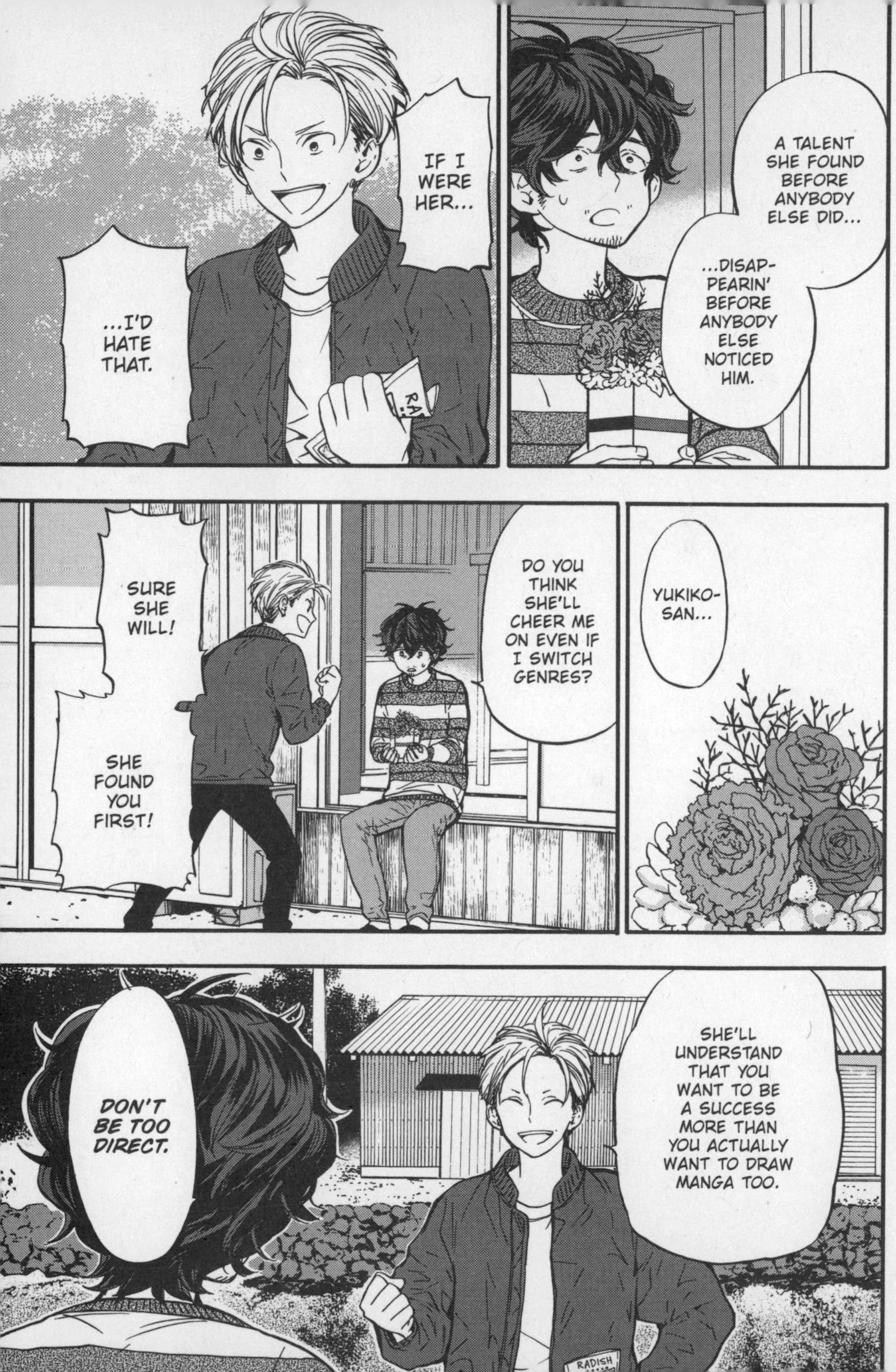
A TALENT SHE FOUND BEFORE ANYBODY ELSE DID...
...DISAP-PEARIN' BEFORE ANYBODY ELSE NOTICED HIM.
IF I WERE HER...
...I'D HATE THAT.
YUKIKO-SAN...
DO YOU THINK SHE'LL CHEER ME ON EVEN IF I SWITCH GENRES?
SURE SHE WILL!
SHE FOUND YOU FIRST!
SHE'LL UNDERSTAND THAT YOU WANT TO BE A SUCCESS MORE THAN YOU ACTUALLY WANT TO DRAW MANGA TOO.
DON'T BE TOO DIRECT.
RADISH

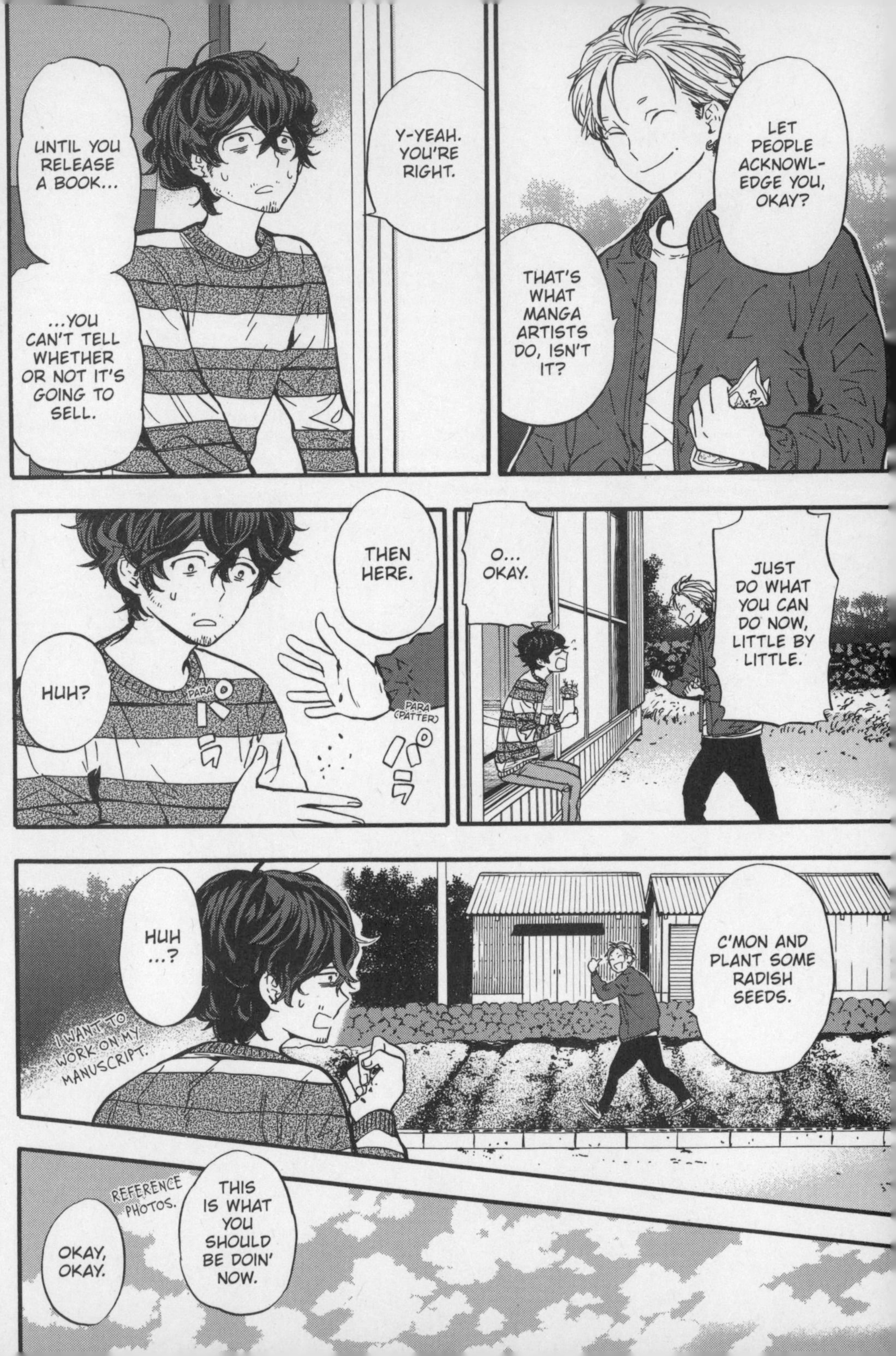
LET PEOPLE ACKNOWL-EDGE YOU, OKAY?
THAT'S WHAT MANGA ARTISTS DO, ISN'T IT?
Y-YEAH. YOU'RE RIGHT.
UNTIL YOU RELEASE A BOOK...
...YOU CAN'T TELL WHETHER OR NOT IT'S GOING TO SELL.
JUST DO WHAT YOU CAN DO NOW, LITTLE BY LITTLE.
O... OKAY.
THEN HERE.
PARA (PATTER)
HUH?
PARA
C'MON AND PLANT SOME RADISH SEEDS.
HUH ...?
I WANT TO WORK ON MY MANUSCRIPT.
THIS IS WHAT YOU SHOULD BE DOIN' NOW.
REFERENCE PHOTOS.
OKAY, OKAY.

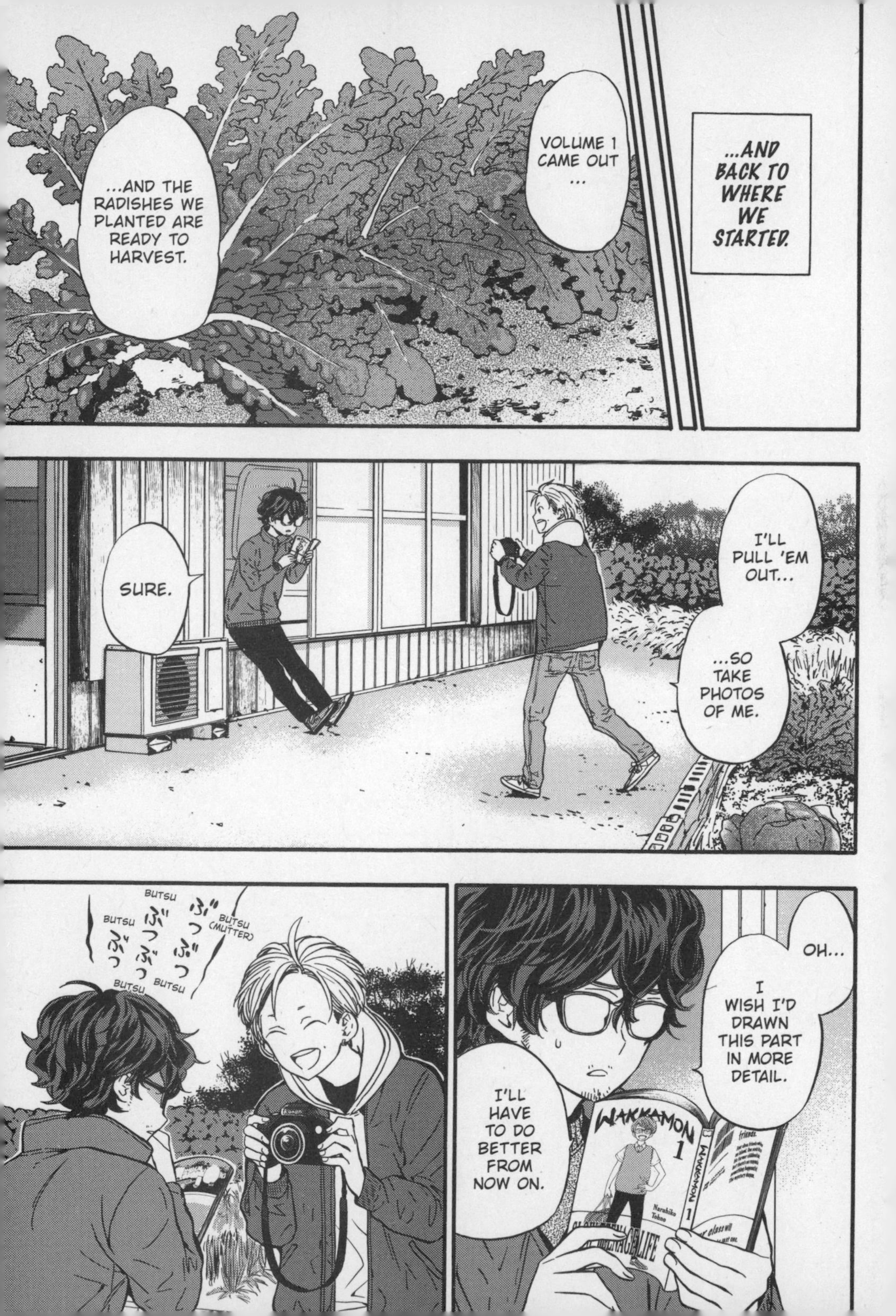
...AND BACK TO WHERE WE STARTED.
VOLUME 1 CAME OUT ...
...AND THE RADISHES WE PLANTED ARE READY TO HARVEST.
I'LL PULL 'EM OUT...
...SO TAKE PHOTOS OF ME.
SURE.
OH...
I WISH I'D DRAWN THIS PART IN MORE DETAIL.
I'LL HAVE TO DO BETTER FROM NOW ON.
WAKKAMON 1
Naruhiko Tohno
ぶつ BUTSU (MUTTER)
ぶつ BUTSU
ぶつ BUTSU
ぶつ BUTSU
ぶつ BUTSU
ぶつ BUTSU

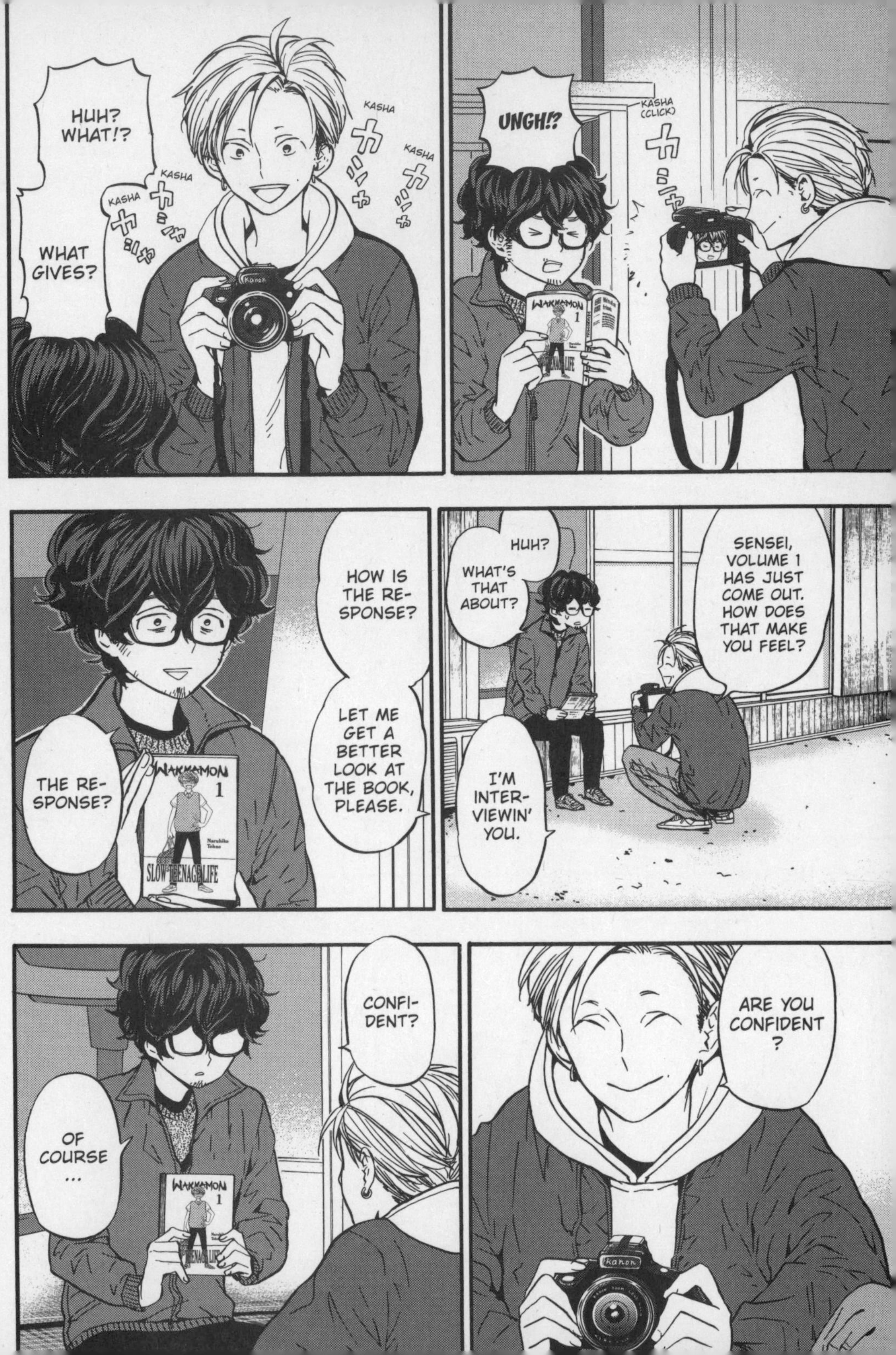
UNGH!?
KASHA (CLICK)
WAKKAMON 1
HUH? WHAT!?
KASHA
KASHA
KASHA
KASHA
WHAT GIVES?
SENSEI, VOLUME 1 HAS JUST COME OUT. HOW DOES THAT MAKE YOU FEEL?
HUH?
WHAT'S THAT ABOUT?
I'M INTERVIEWIN' YOU.
HOW IS THE RESPONSE?
LET ME GET A BETTER LOOK AT THE BOOK, PLEASE.
THE RESPONSE?
WAKKAMON 1
SLOW TEENAGE LIFE
ARE YOU CONFIDENT?
CONFIDENT?
OF COURSE...
WAKKAMON 1

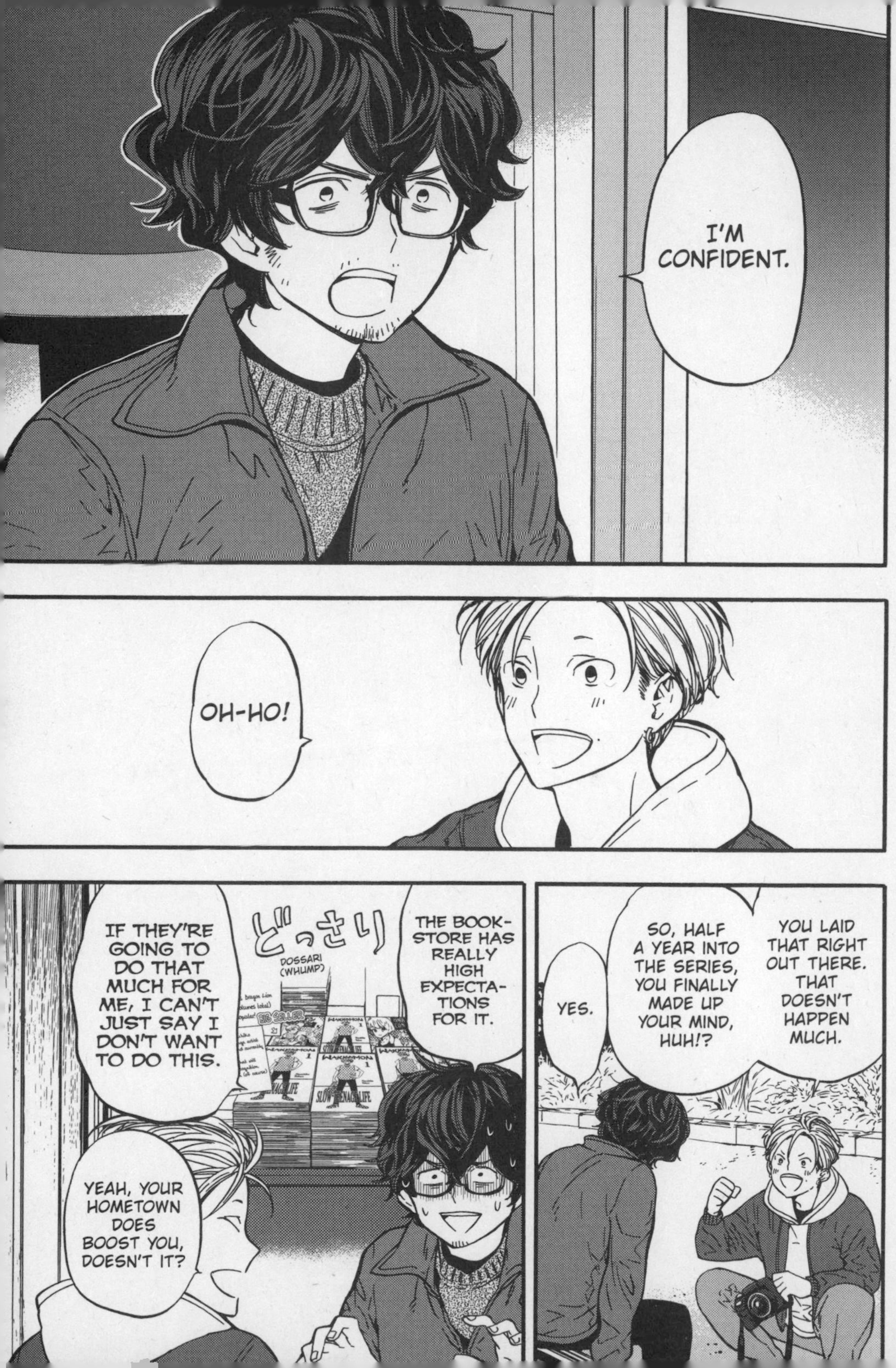
I'M CONFIDENT.
OH-HO!
YOU LAID THAT RIGHT OUT THERE. THAT DOESN'T HAPPEN MUCH.
SO, HALF A YEAR INTO THE SERIES, YOU FINALLY MADE UP YOUR MIND, HUH!?
YES.
THE BOOK-STORE HAS REALLY HIGH EXPECTA-TIONS FOR IT.
どっさり
DOSSARI (WHUMP)
IF THEY'RE GOING TO DO THAT MUCH FOR ME, I CAN'T JUST SAY I DON'T WANT TO DO THIS.
YEAH, YOUR HOMETOWN DOES BOOST YOU, DOESN'T IT?

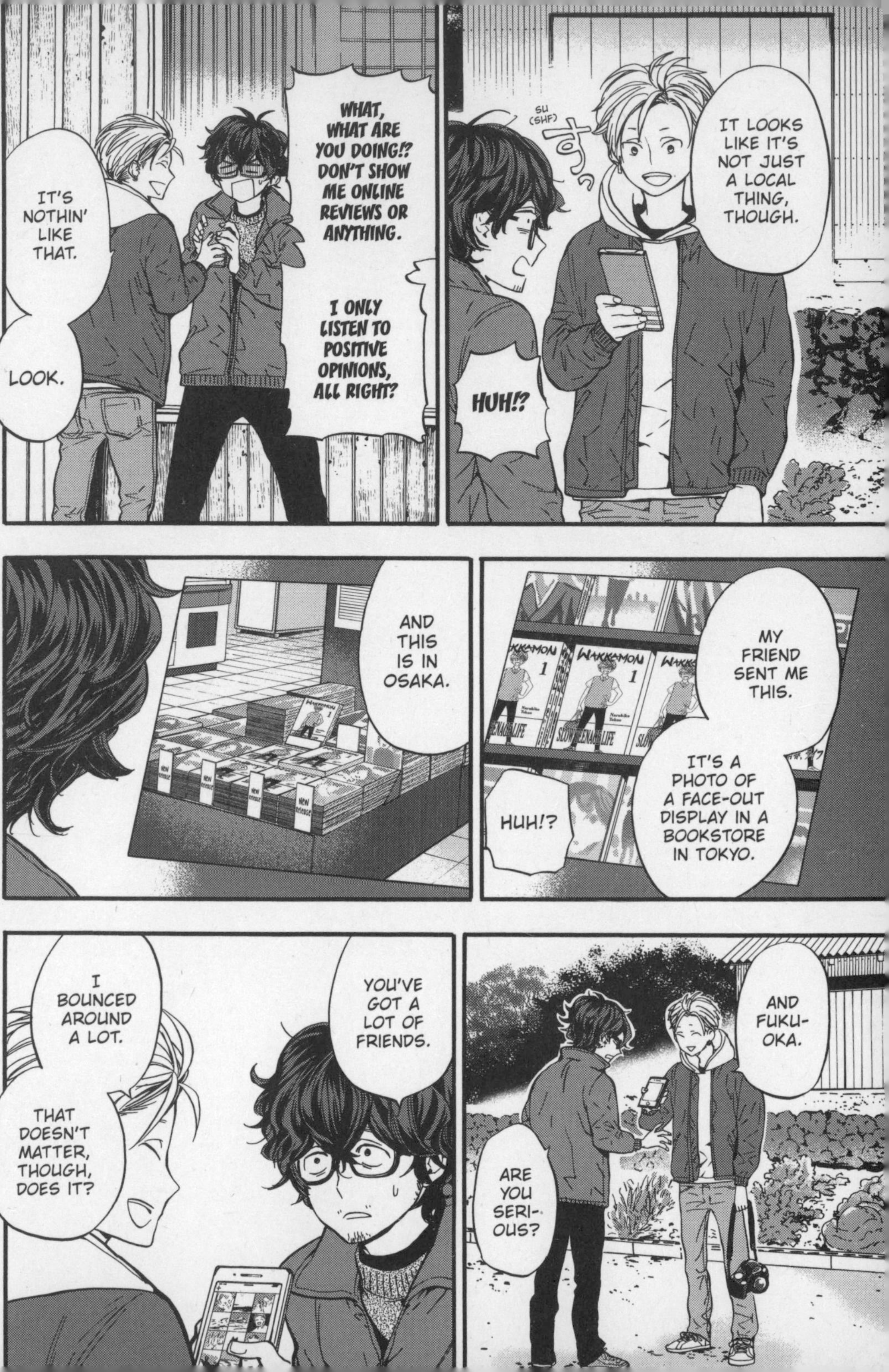
SU (SHF)
IT LOOKS LIKE IT'S NOT JUST A LOCAL THING, THOUGH.
HUH!?
WHAT, WHAT ARE YOU DOING!? DON'T SHOW ME ONLINE REVIEWS OR ANYTHING.
I ONLY LISTEN TO POSITIVE OPINIONS, ALL RIGHT?
IT'S NOTHIN' LIKE THAT.
LOOK.
MY FRIEND SENT ME THIS.
IT'S A PHOTO OF A FACE-OUT DISPLAY IN A BOOKSTORE IN TOKYO.
HUH!?
WAKKAMON
AND THIS IS IN OSAKA.
AND FUKU-OKA.
ARE YOU SERI-OUS?
YOU'VE GOT A LOT OF FRIENDS.
I BOUNCED AROUND A LOT.
THAT DOESN'T MATTER, THOUGH, DOES IT?

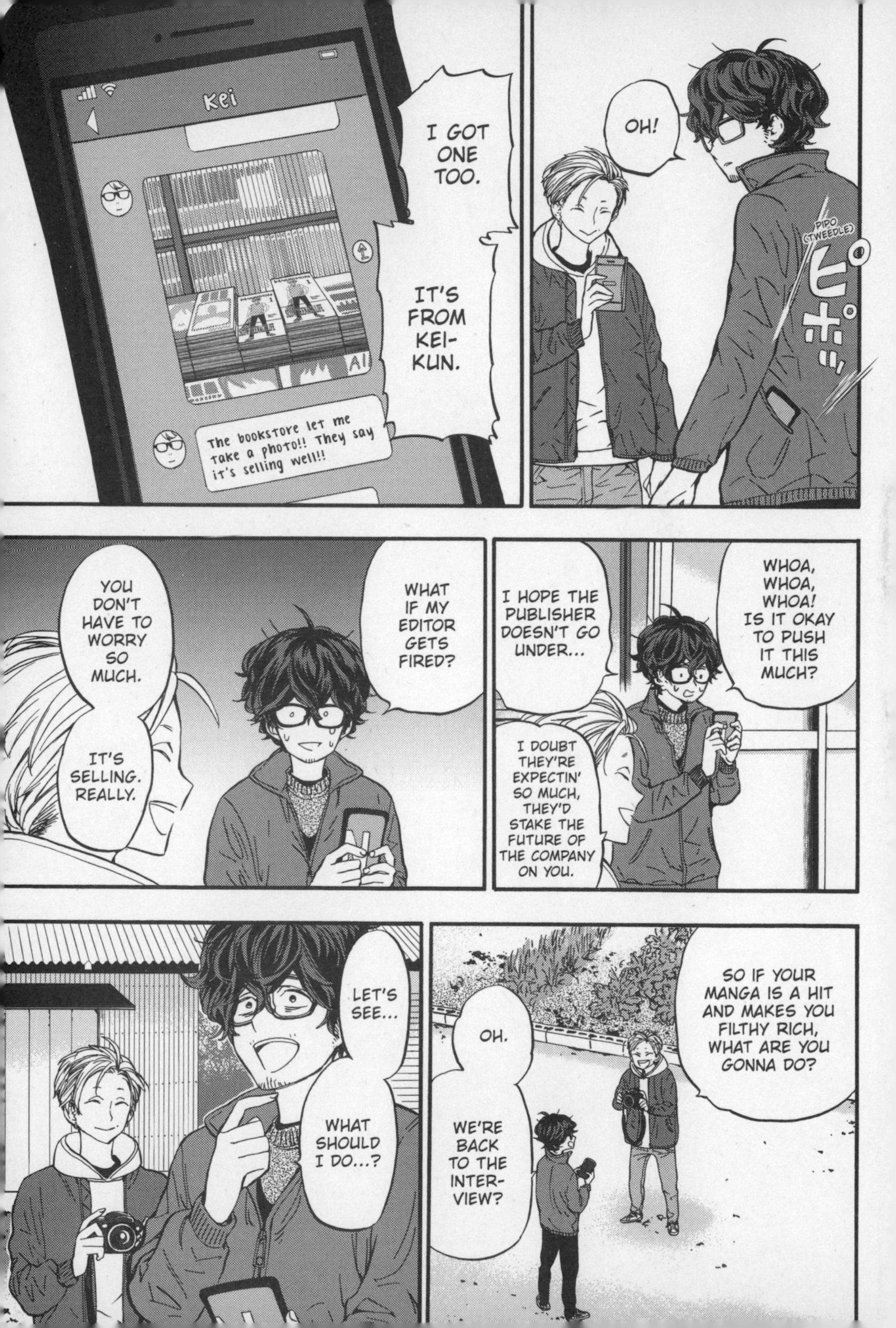
OH!
PIPO (TWEEDLE)
ピポッ
I GOT ONE TOO.
IT'S FROM KEI-KUN.
Kei
The bookstore let me take a photo!! They say it's selling well!!
WHOA, WHOA, WHOA! IS IT OKAY TO PUSH IT THIS MUCH?
I HOPE THE PUBLISHER DOESN'T GO UNDER...
I DOUBT THEY'RE EXPECTIN' SO MUCH, THEY'D STAKE THE FUTURE OF THE COMPANY ON YOU.
WHAT IF MY EDITOR GETS FIRED?
YOU DON'T HAVE TO WORRY SO MUCH.
IT'S SELLING. REALLY.
SO IF YOUR MANGA IS A HIT AND MAKES YOU FILTHY RICH, WHAT ARE YOU GONNA DO?
OH.
WE'RE BACK TO THE INTERVIEW?
LET'S SEE...
WHAT SHOULD I DO...?

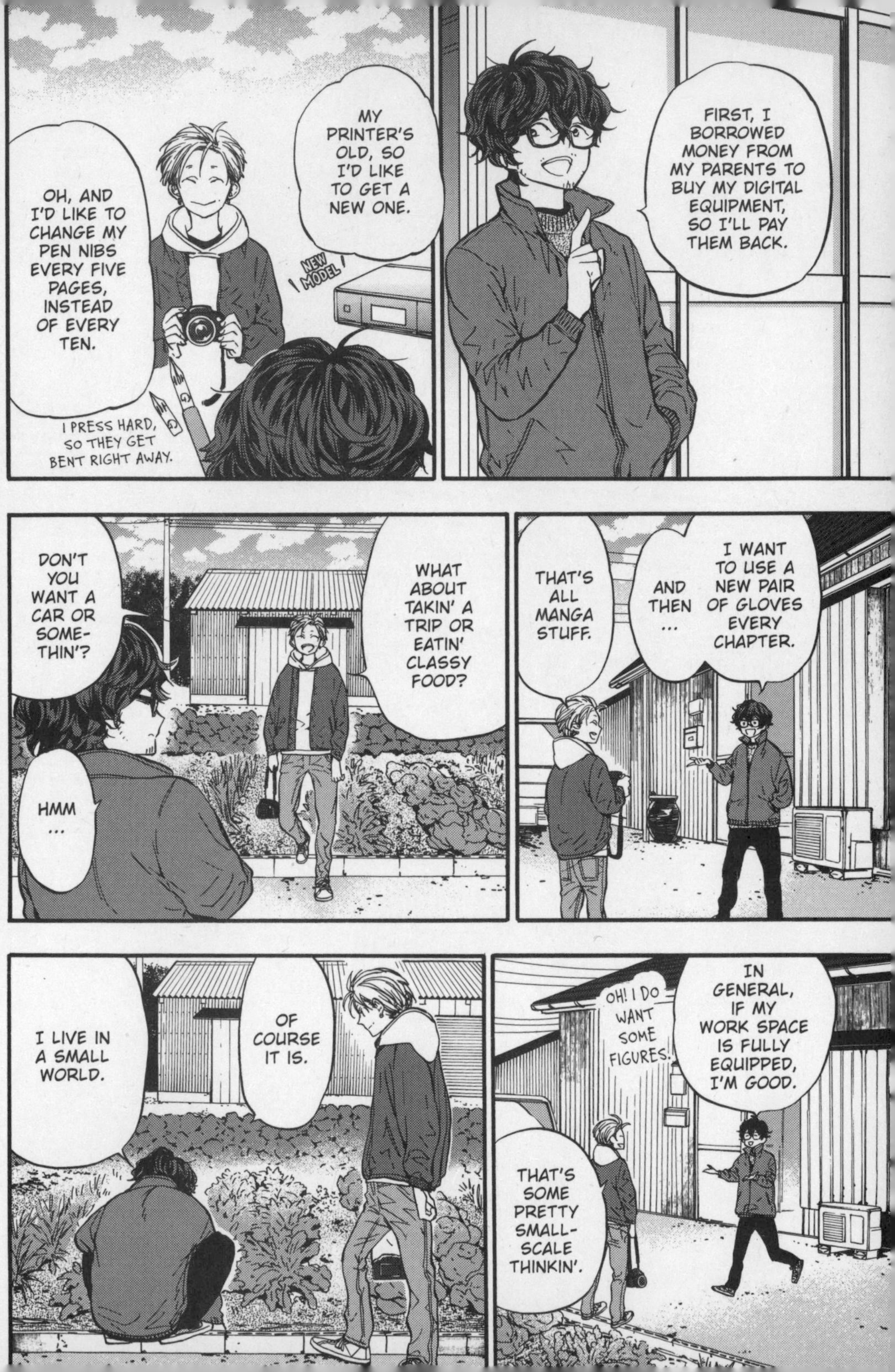
FIRST, I BORROWED MONEY FROM MY PARENTS TO BUY MY DIGITAL EQUIPMENT, SO I'LL PAY THEM BACK.
MY PRINTER'S OLD, SO I'D LIKE TO GET A NEW ONE.
NEW MODEL!
OH, AND I'D LIKE TO CHANGE MY PEN NIBS EVERY FIVE PAGES, INSTEAD OF EVERY TEN.
I PRESS HARD, SO THEY GET BENT RIGHT AWAY.
I WANT TO USE A NEW PAIR OF GLOVES EVERY CHAPTER.
AND THEN ...
THAT'S ALL MANGA STUFF.
WHAT ABOUT TAKIN' A TRIP OR EATIN' CLASSY FOOD?
DON'T YOU WANT A CAR OR SOME-THIN'?
HMM ...
IN GENERAL, IF MY WORK SPACE IS FULLY EQUIPPED, I'M GOOD.
OH! I DO WANT SOME FIGURES.
THAT'S SOME PRETTY SMALL-SCALE THINKIN'.
OF COURSE IT IS.
I LIVE IN A SMALL WORLD.

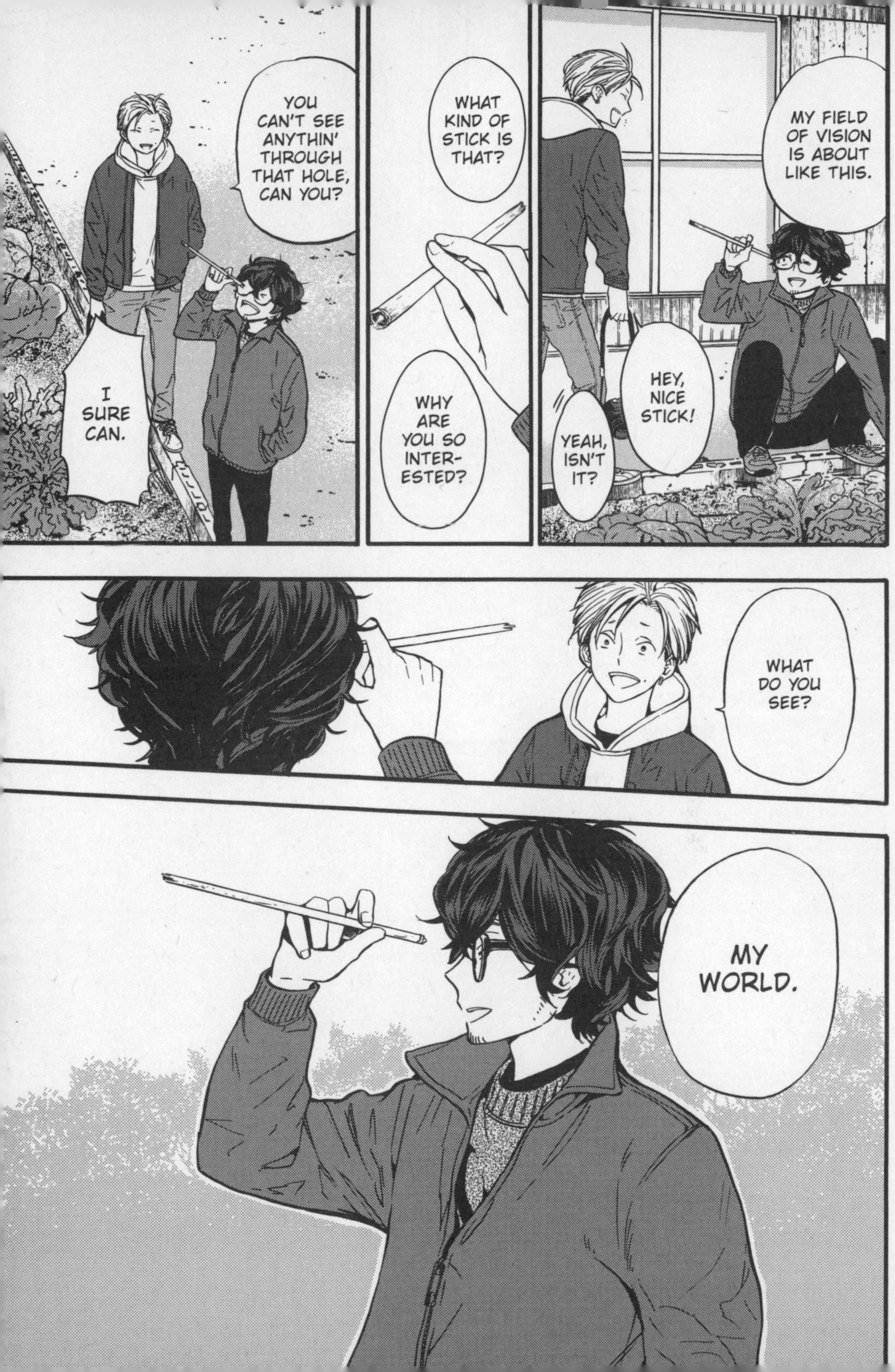
MY FIELD OF VISION IS ABOUT LIKE THIS.
HEY, NICE STICK!
YEAH, ISN'T IT?
WHAT KIND OF STICK IS THAT?
WHY ARE YOU SO INTER-ESTED?
YOU CAN'T SEE ANYTHIN' THROUGH THAT HOLE, CAN YOU?
I SURE CAN.
WHAT DO YOU SEE?
MY WORLD.

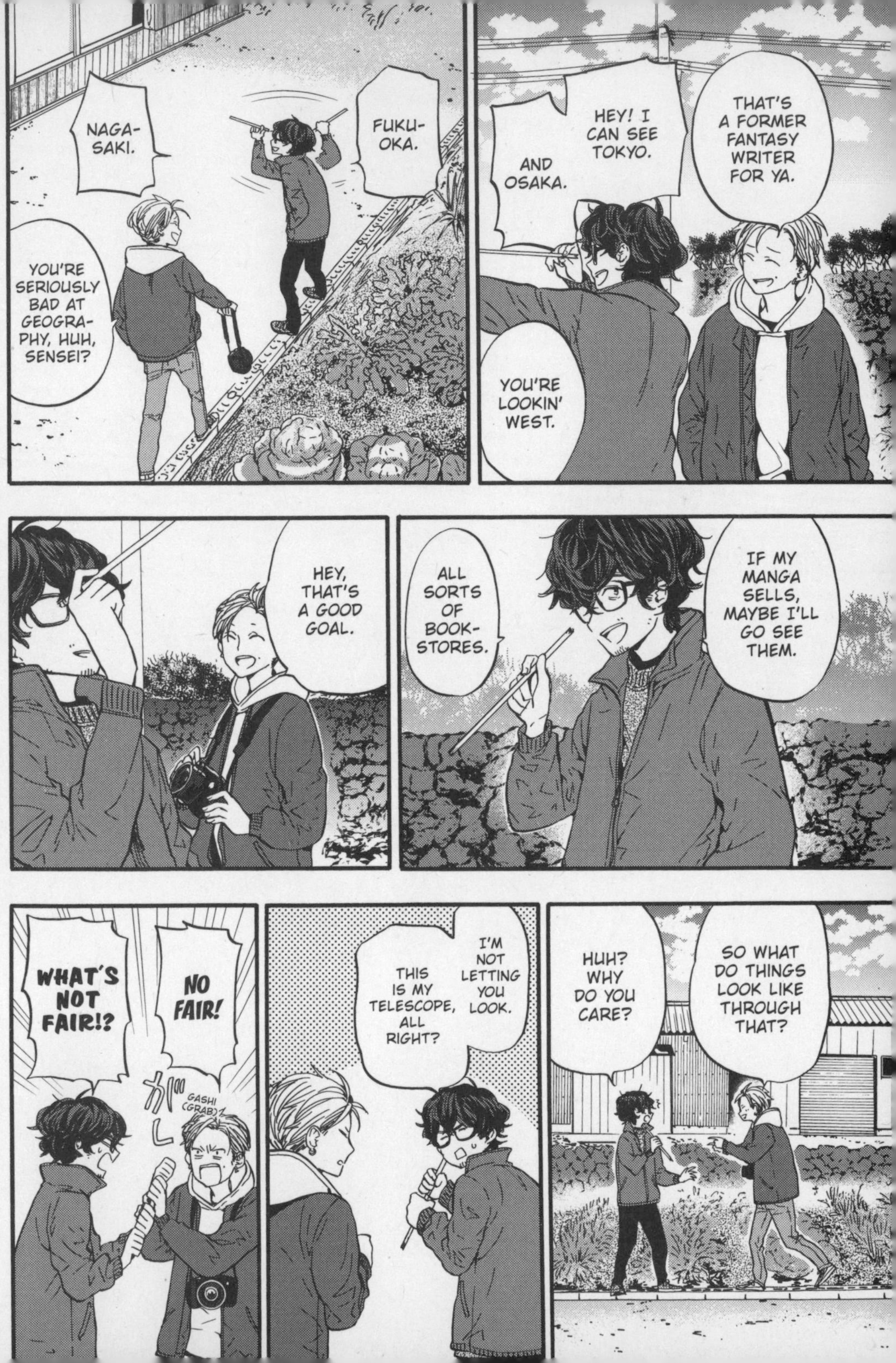
THAT'S A FORMER FANTASY WRITER FOR YA.
HEY! I CAN SEE TOKYO.
AND OSAKA.
YOU'RE LOOKIN' WEST.
FUKU-OKA.
NAGA-SAKI.
YOU'RE SERIOUSLY BAD AT GEOGRA-PHY, HUH, SENSEI?
IF MY MANGA SELLS, MAYBE I'LL GO SEE THEM.
ALL SORTS OF BOOK-STORES.
HEY, THAT'S A GOOD GOAL.
SO WHAT DO THINGS LOOK LIKE THROUGH THAT?
HUH? WHY DO YOU CARE?
I'M NOT LETTING YOU LOOK.
THIS IS MY TELESCOPE, ALL RIGHT?
NO FAIR!
GASHI (GRAB)
WHAT'S NOT FAIR!?

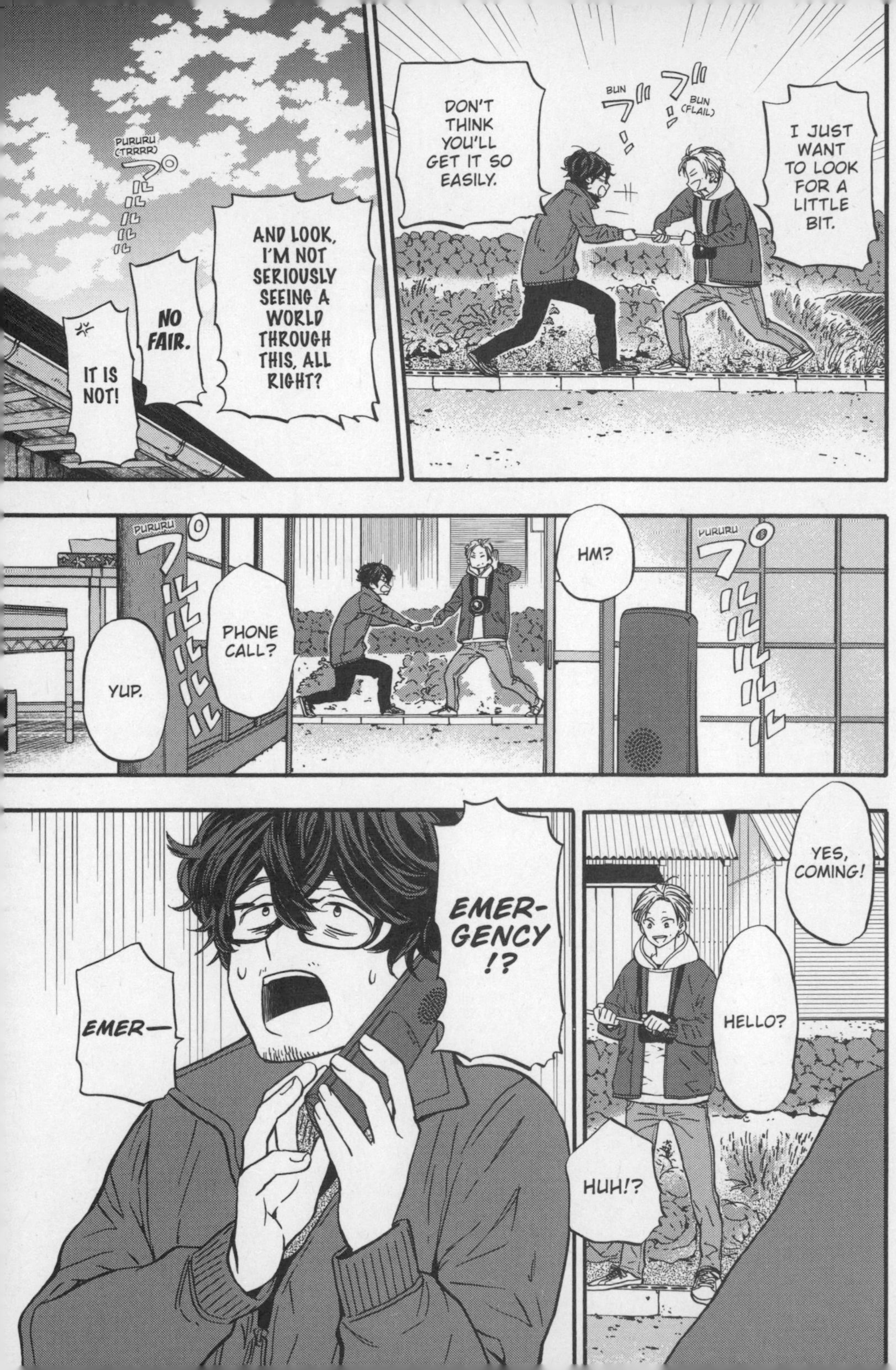
BUN
BUN (FLAIL)
I JUST WANT TO LOOK FOR A LITTLE BIT.
DON'T THINK YOU'LL GET IT SO EASILY.
AND LOOK, I'M NOT SERIOUSLY SEEING A WORLD THROUGH THIS, ALL RIGHT?
NO FAIR.
IT IS NOT!
PURURU (TRRRR)
PURURU
HM?
PHONE CALL?
YUP.
PURURU
YES, COMING!
HELLO?
HUH!?
EMER-GENCY!?
EMER—

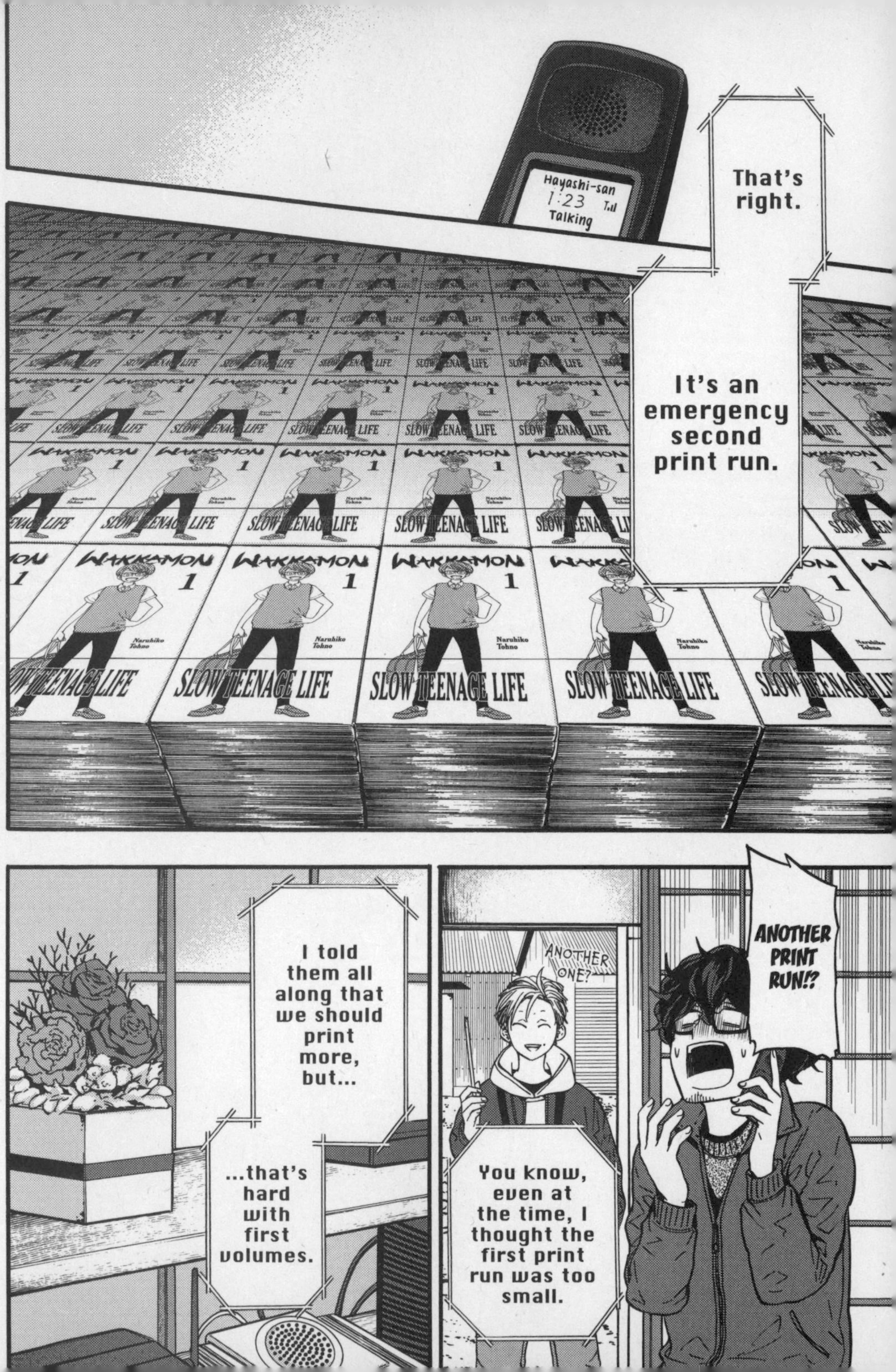

Hayashi-san
1:23
Talking
That's right.
It's an emergency second print run.
WAKKAMON 1
Naruhiko Tohno
SLOW TEENAGE LIFE
ANOTHER PRINT RUN!?
ANOTHER ONE?
You know, even at the time, I thought the first print run was too small.
I told them all along that we should print more, but...
...that's hard with first volumes.

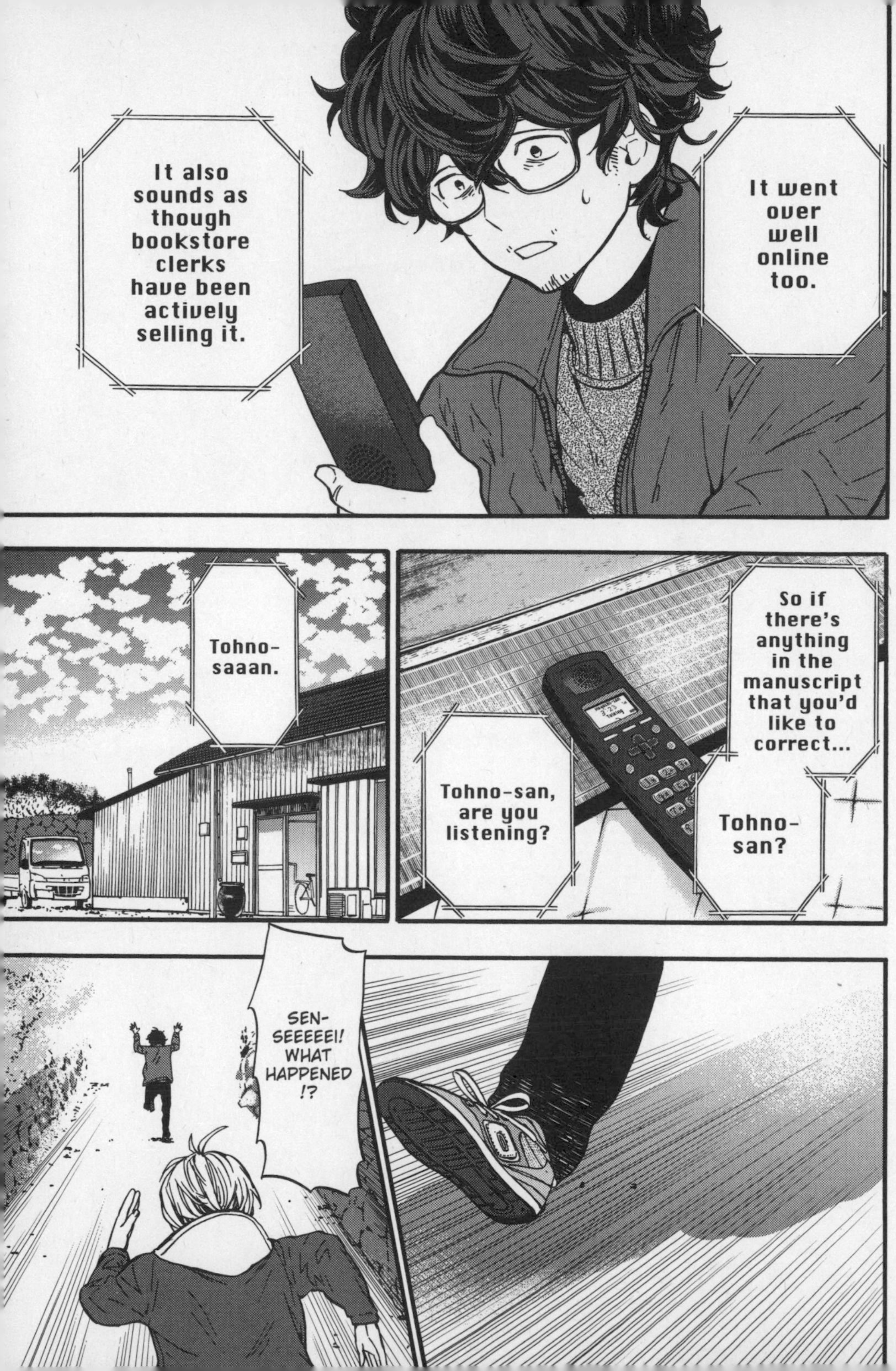
It went over well online too.
It also sounds as though bookstore clerks have been actively selling it.
So if there's anything in the manuscript that you'd like to correct...
Tohno-san?
Tohno-san, are you listening?
Tohno-saaan.
SEN-SEEEEEI! WHAT HAPPENED!?

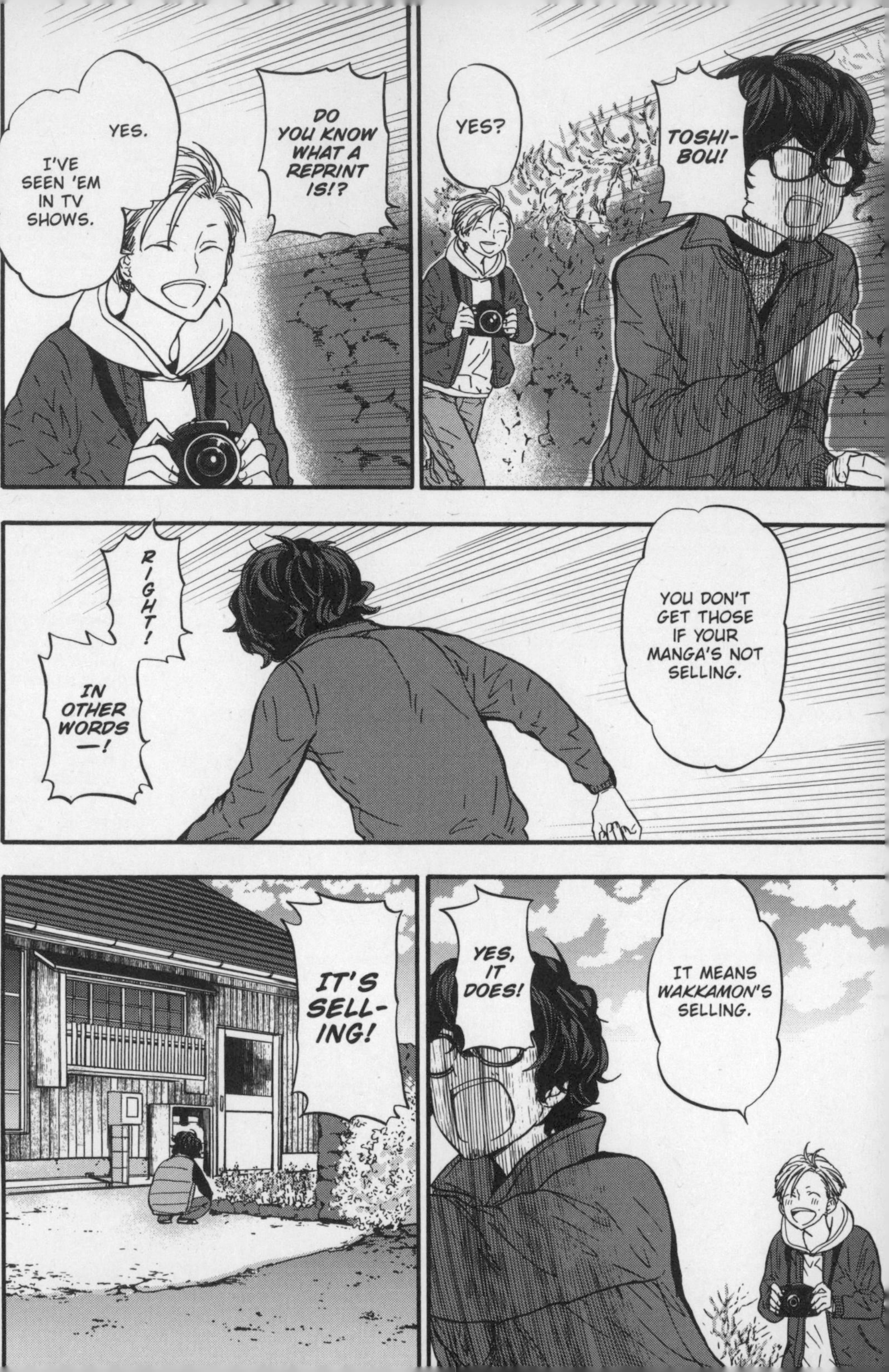
TOSHI-BOU!
YES?
DO YOU KNOW WHAT A REPRINT IS!?
YES.
I'VE SEEN 'EM IN TV SHOWS.
YOU DON'T GET THOSE IF YOUR MANGA'S NOT SELLING.
RIGHT!
IN OTHER WORDS—!
IT MEANS WAKKAMON'S SELLING.
YES, IT DOES!
IT'S SELL-ING!

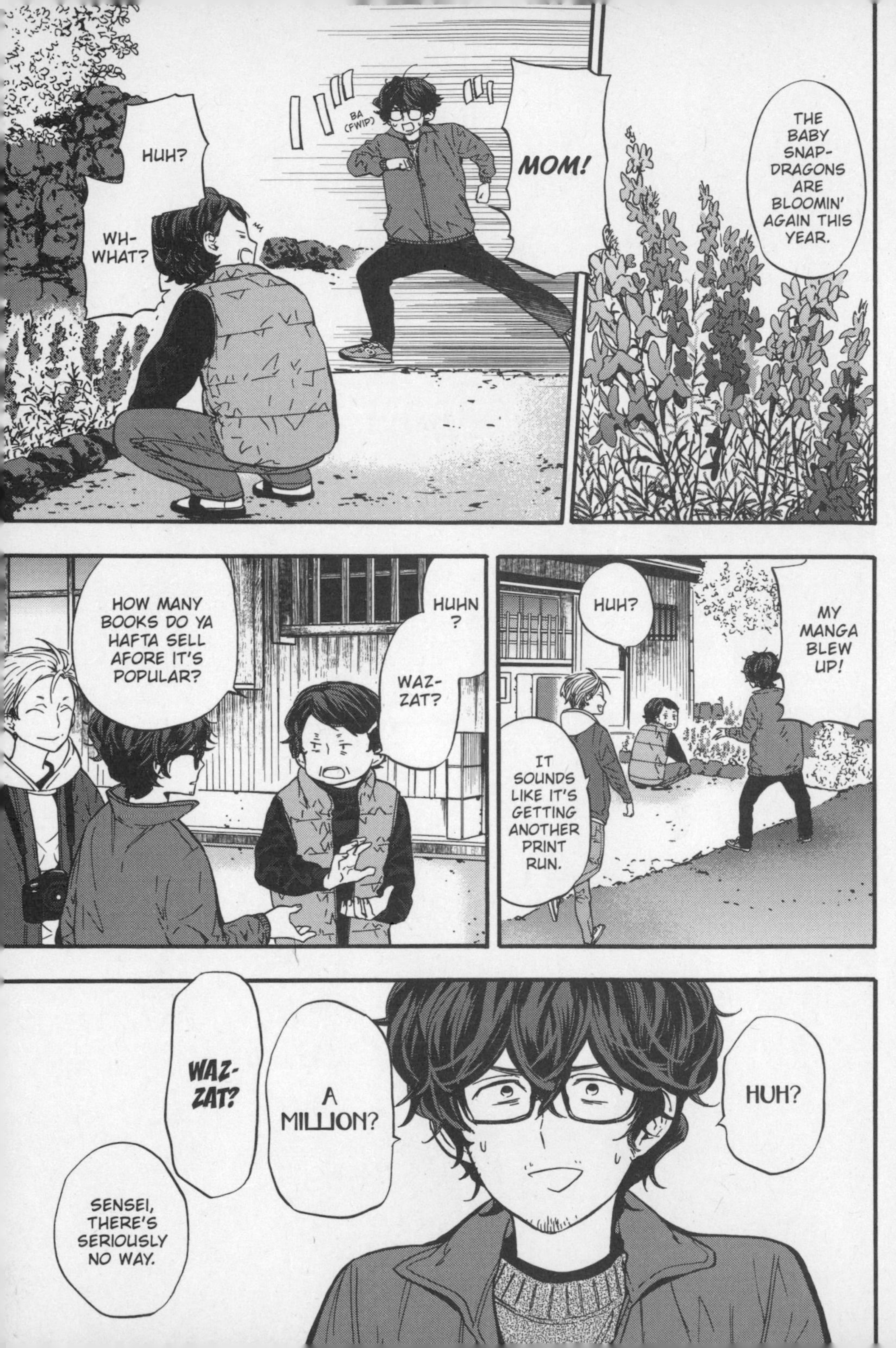
THE BABY SNAP-DRAGONS ARE BLOOMIN' AGAIN THIS YEAR.
MOM!
BA (FWIP)
HUH?
WH-WHAT?
MY MANGA BLEW UP!
HUH?
IT SOUNDS LIKE IT'S GETTING ANOTHER PRINT RUN.
HUHN?
WAZ-ZAT?
HOW MANY BOOKS DO YA HAFTA SELL AFORE IT'S POPULAR?
HUH?
A MILLION?
WAZ-ZAT?
SENSEI, THERE'S SERIOUSLY NO WAY.

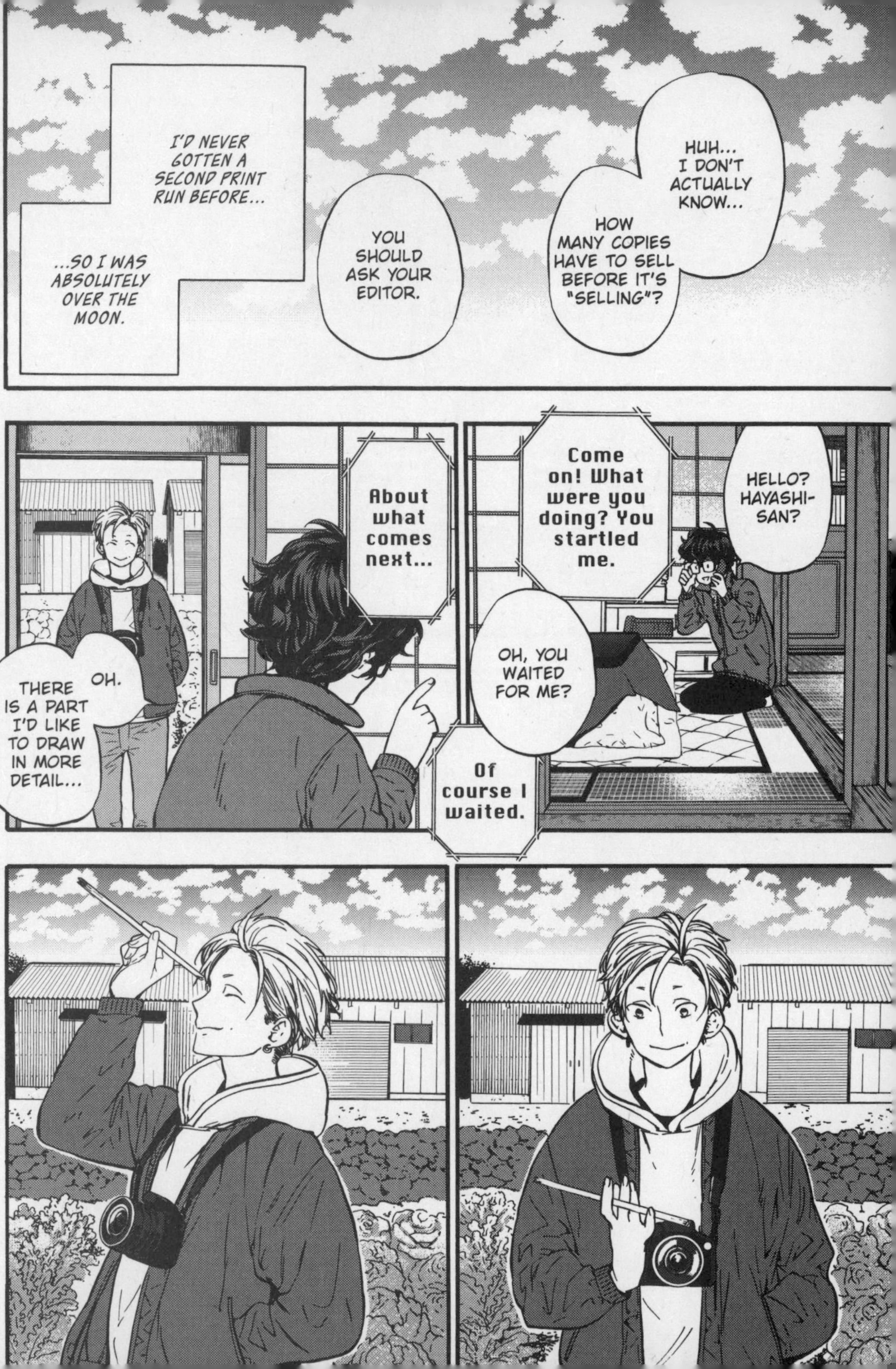
HUH... I DON'T ACTUALLY KNOW...
HOW MANY COPIES HAVE TO SELL BEFORE IT'S "SELLING"?
YOU SHOULD ASK YOUR EDITOR.
I'D NEVER GOTTEN A SECOND PRINT RUN BEFORE...
...SO I WAS ABSOLUTELY OVER THE MOON.
HELLO? HAYASHI-SAN?
Come on! What were you doing? You startled me.
OH, YOU WAITED FOR ME?
Of course I waited.
About what comes next...
OH.
THERE IS A PART I'D LIKE TO DRAW IN MORE DETAIL...

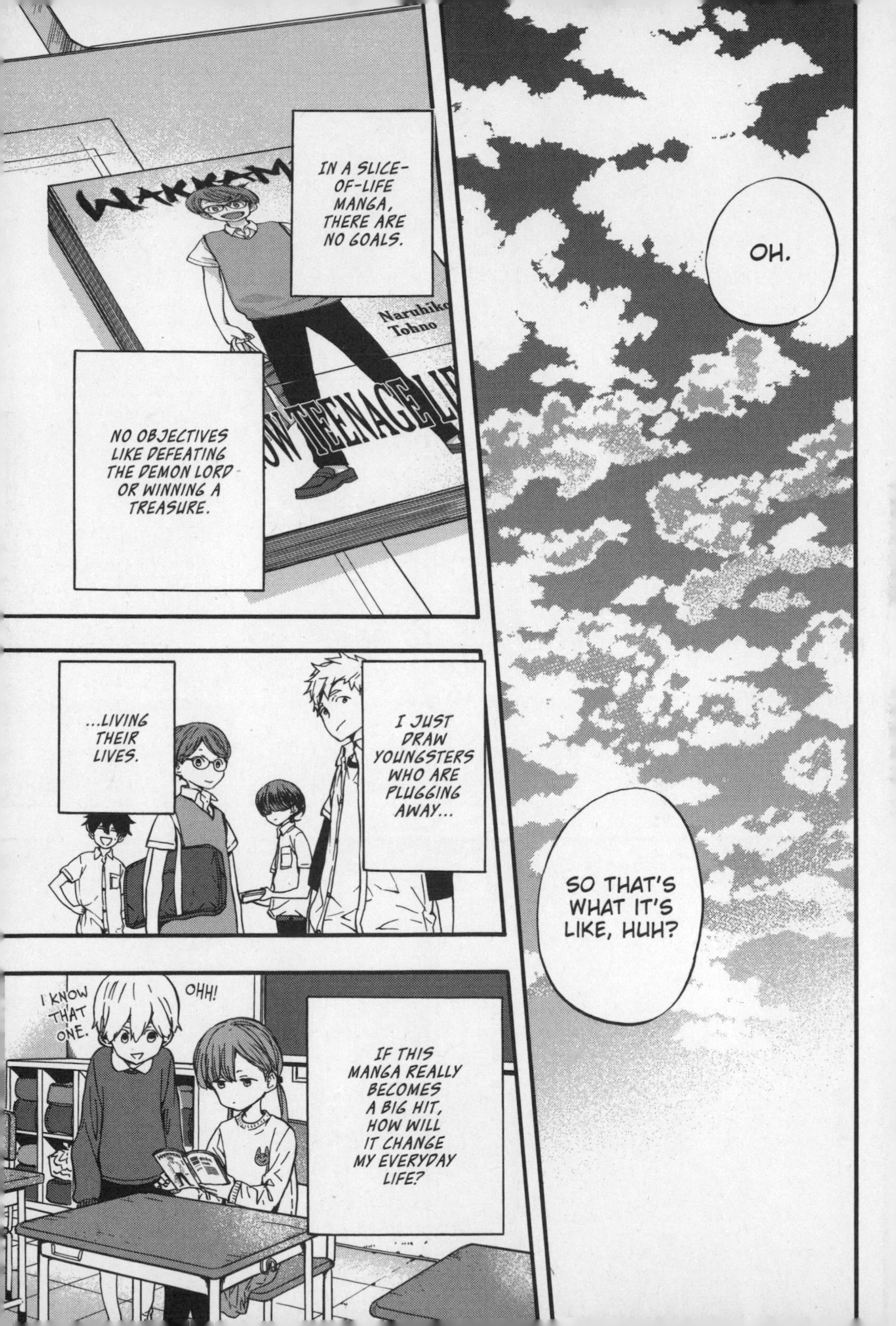
OH.
SO THAT'S WHAT IT'S LIKE, HUH?
IN A SLICE-OF-LIFE MANGA, THERE ARE NO GOALS.
Naruhiko Tohno
NO OBJECTIVES LIKE DEFEATING THE DEMON LORD OR WINNING A TREASURE.
I JUST DRAW YOUNGSTERS WHO ARE PLUGGING AWAY...
...LIVING THEIR LIVES.
IF THIS MANGA REALLY BECOMES A BIG HIT, HOW WILL IT CHANGE MY EVERYDAY LIFE?
OHH!
I KNOW THAT ONE.

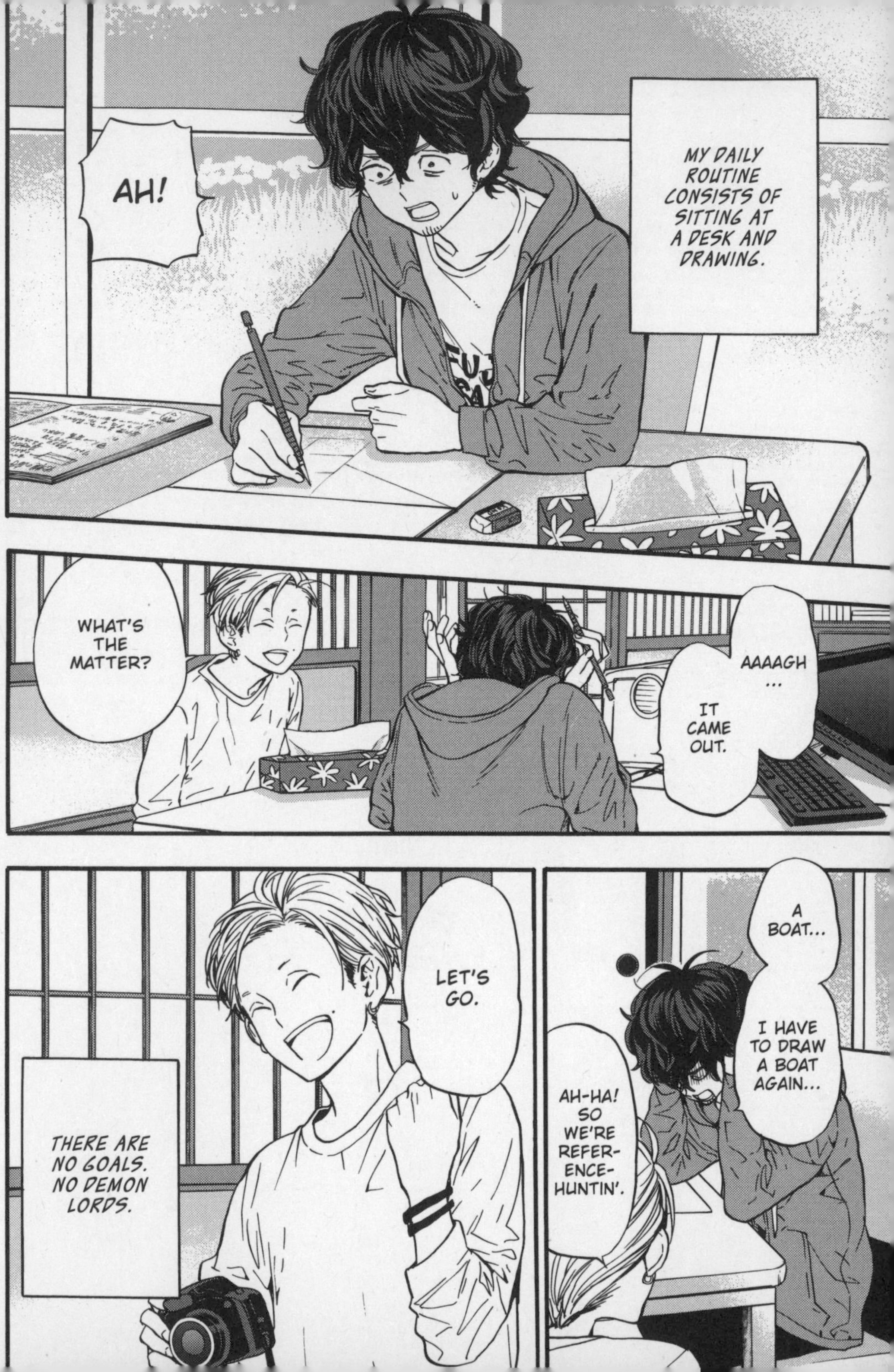
MY DAILY ROUTINE CONSISTS OF SITTING AT A DESK AND DRAWING.
AH!
AAAAGH...
IT CAME OUT.
WHAT'S THE MATTER?
A BOAT...
I HAVE TO DRAW A BOAT AGAIN...
AH-HA! SO WE'RE REFERENCE-HUNTIN'.
LET'S GO.
THERE ARE NO GOALS. NO DEMON LORDS.

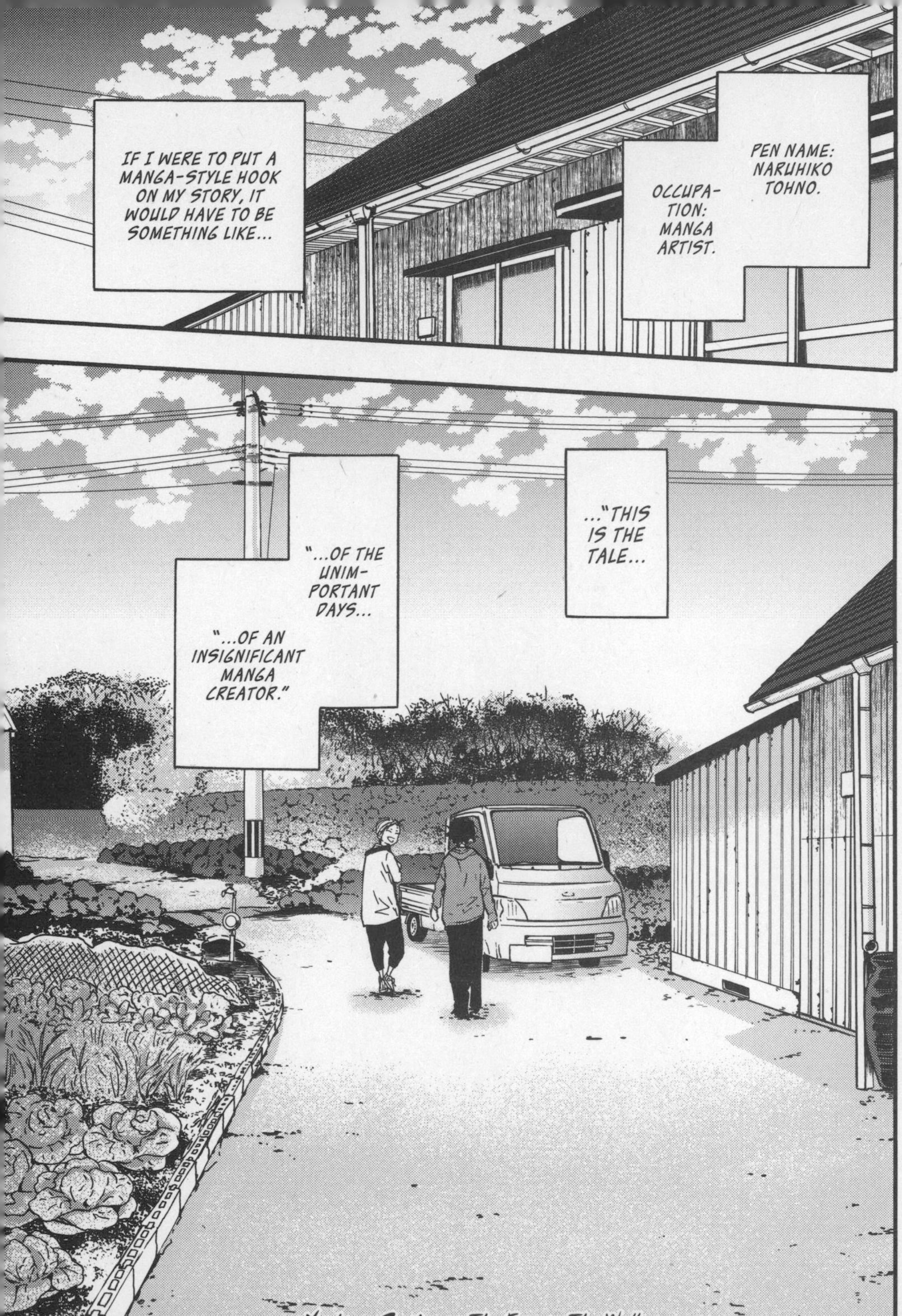
PEN NAME: NARUHIKO TOHNO.
OCCUPATION: MANGA ARTIST.
IF I WERE TO PUT A MANGA-STYLE HOOK ON MY STORY, IT WOULD HAVE TO BE SOMETHING LIKE...
..."THIS IS THE TALE...
"...OF THE UNIMPORTANT DAYS...
"...OF AN INSIGNIFICANT MANGA CREATOR."
Yoshi no Zuikara: The Frog in The Well Does not Know the Ocean 1 End

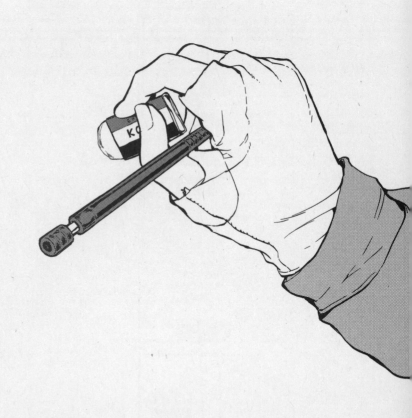

YOSHI NO ZUIKARA

- EVERYDAY STORIES -

THE "TOHNO DOESN'T EXERCISE ENOUGH" VOLUME

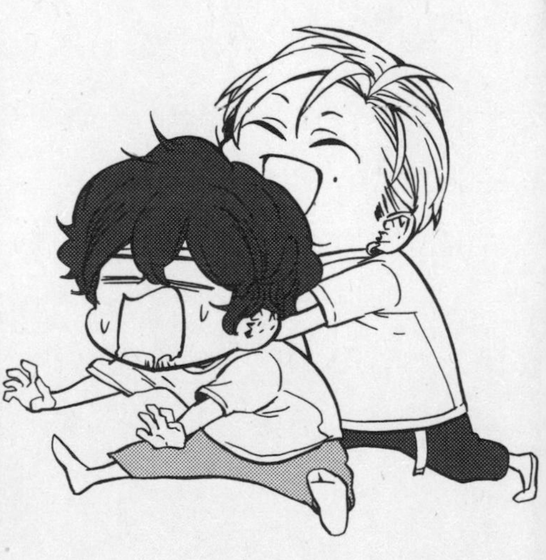

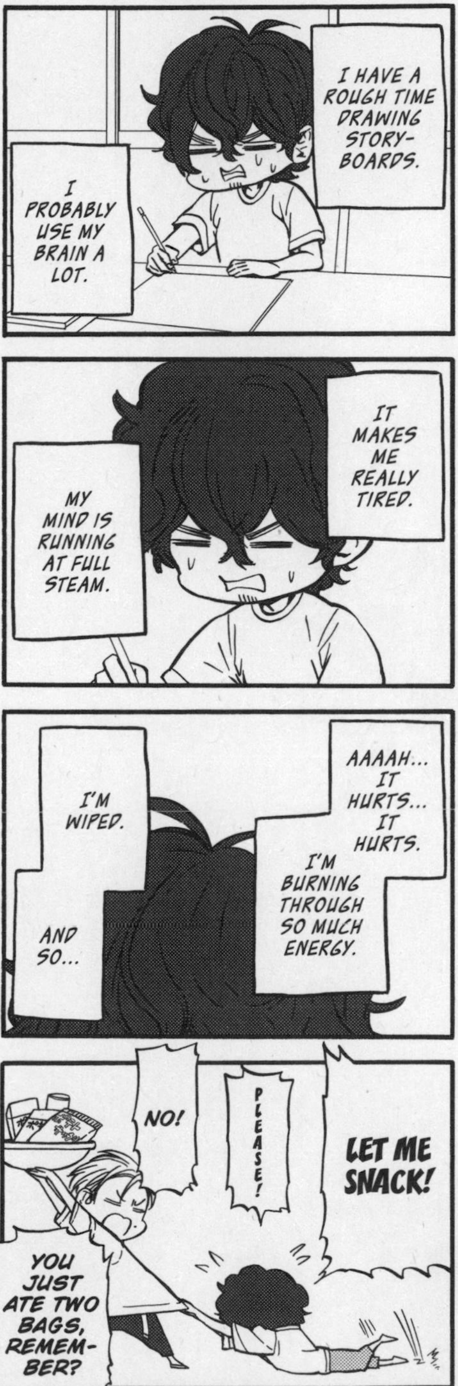
I HAVE A ROUGH TIME DRAWING STORY-BOARDS.
I PROBABLY USE MY BRAIN A LOT.
IT MAKES ME REALLY TIRED.
MY MIND IS RUNNING AT FULL STEAM.
AAAAH... IT HURTS... IT HURTS.
I'M BURNING THROUGH SO MUCH ENERGY.
I'M WIPED.
AND SO...
LET ME SNACK!
PLEASE!
NO!
YOU JUST ATE TWO BAGS, REMEMBER?

BAGS: CRUNCHY POTATO

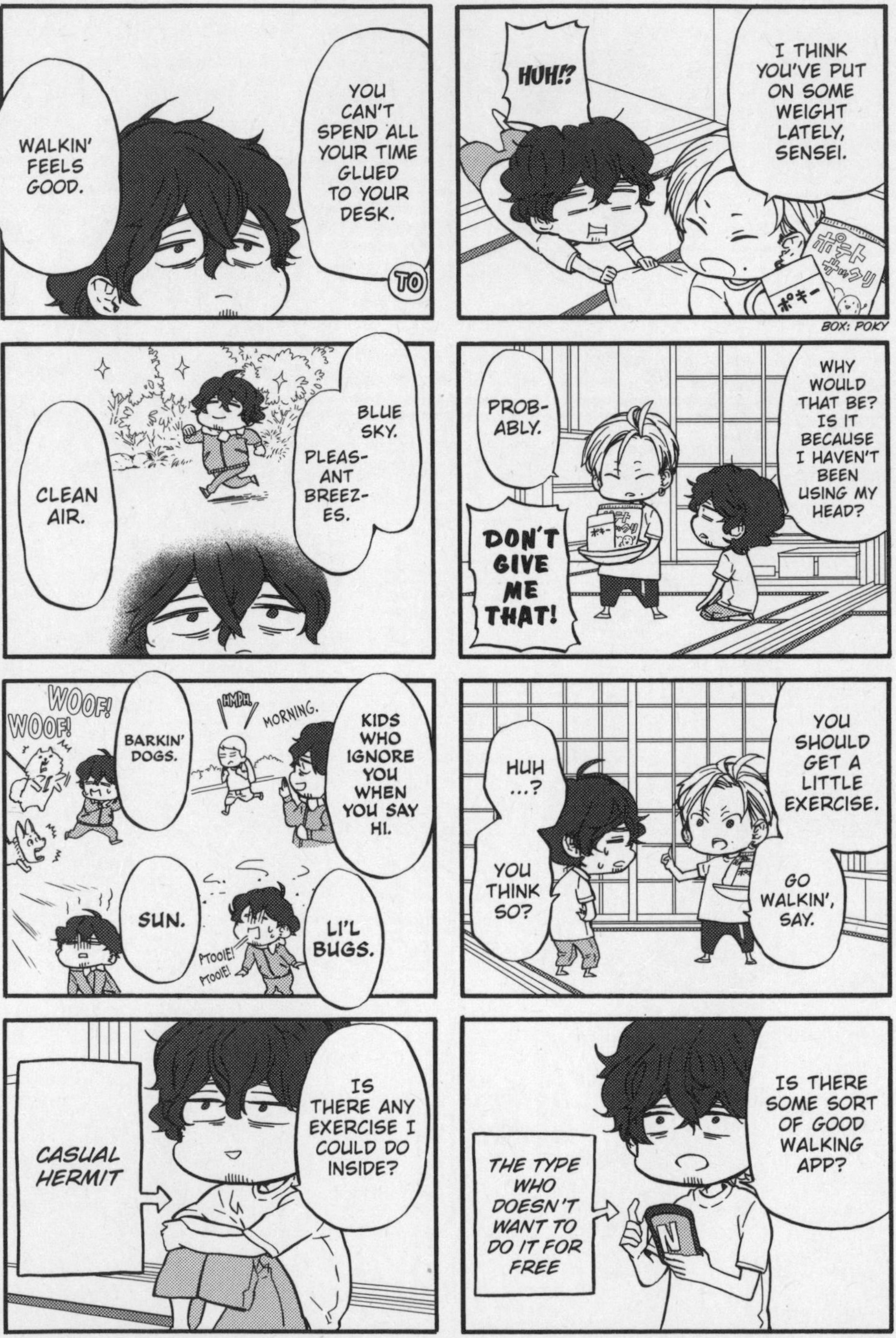
I THINK YOU'VE PUT ON SOME WEIGHT LATELY, SENSEI.
HUH!?
BOX: POKY
WHY WOULD THAT BE? IS IT BECAUSE I HAVEN'T BEEN USING MY HEAD?
PROB-ABLY.
DON'T GIVE ME THAT!
YOU SHOULD GET A LITTLE EXERCISE.
GO WALKIN', SAY.
HUH ...?
YOU THINK SO?
IS THERE SOME SORT OF GOOD WALKING APP?
THE TYPE WHO DOESN'T WANT TO DO IT FOR FREE
YOU CAN'T SPEND ALL YOUR TIME GLUED TO YOUR DESK.
TO
WALKIN' FEELS GOOD.
BLUE SKY.
PLEAS-ANT BREEZ-ES.
CLEAN AIR.
KIDS WHO IGNORE YOU WHEN YOU SAY HI.
MORNING.
HMPH.
BARKIN' DOGS.
WOOF!
WOOF!
LI'L BUGS.
PTOOIE!
PTOOIE!
SUN.
IS THERE ANY EXERCISE I COULD DO INSIDE?
CASUAL HERMIT

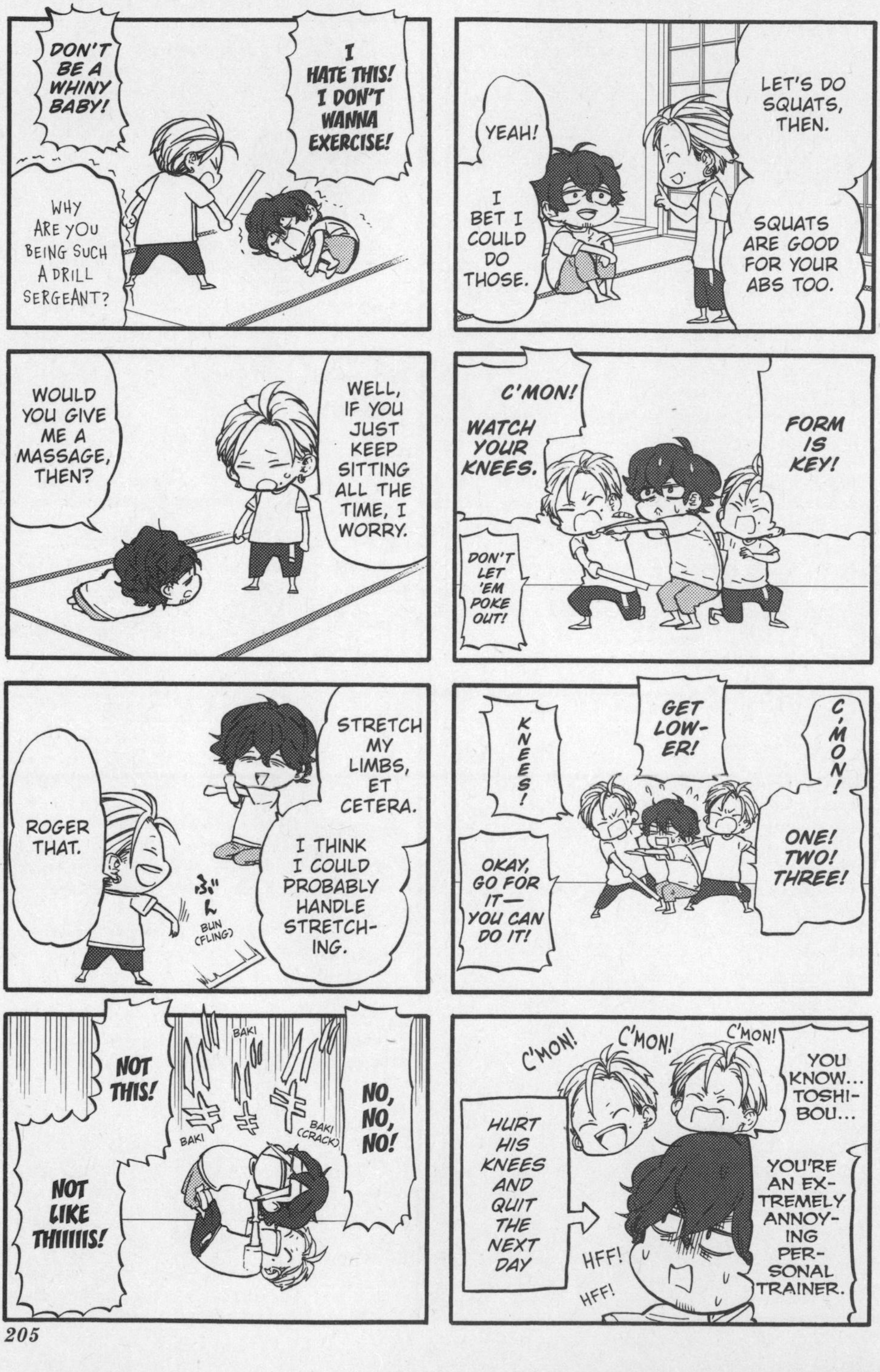
LET'S DO SQUATS, THEN.
SQUATS ARE GOOD FOR YOUR ABS TOO.
YEAH!
I BET I COULD DO THOSE.
FORM IS KEY!
C'MON!
WATCH YOUR KNEES.
DON'T LET 'EM POKE OUT!
C'MON!
ONE! TWO! THREE!
GET LOWER!
KNEES!
OKAY, GO FOR IT— YOU CAN DO IT!
YOU KNOW... TOSHI-BOU...
YOU'RE AN EX-TREMELY ANNOY-ING PER-SONAL TRAINER.
C'MON!
C'MON!
C'MON!
HURT HIS KNEES AND QUIT THE NEXT DAY
HFF!
HFF!
I HATE THIS! I DON'T WANNA EXERCISE!
DON'T BE A WHINY BABY!
WHY ARE YOU BEING SUCH A DRILL SERGEANT?
WELL, IF YOU JUST KEEP SITTING ALL THE TIME, I WORRY.
WOULD YOU GIVE ME A MASSAGE, THEN?
STRETCH MY LIMBS, ET CETERA.
I THINK I COULD PROBABLY HANDLE STRETCH-ING.
ぶん
BUN (FLING)
ROGER THAT.
NO, NO, NO!
BAKI
BAKI (CRACK)
BAKI
NOT THIS!
NOT LIKE THIIIIIS!

COMMON HONORIFICS

no honorific: Indicates familiarity or closeness; if used without permission or reason, addressing someone in this manner would constitute an insult.

-san: The Japanese equivalent of Mr./Mrs./Miss. If a situation calls for politeness, this is the fail-safe honorific.

-sama: Conveys great respect; may also indicate that the social status of the speaker is lower than that of the addressee.

-kun: Used most often when referring to boys, this indicates affection or familiarity. Occasionally used by older men among their peers, but it may also be used by anyone referring to a person of lower standing.

-chan: An affectionate honorific indicating familiarity used mostly in reference to girls; also used in reference to cute persons or animals of either gender.

-sensei: A Japanese term of respect commonly used for teachers, but can also refer to doctors, writers, and artists.

PAGE 5

A **branch school** is a satellite facility set up in a remote area to serve children who would have a very hard time getting to the main school. It's noted later that the kids have a half-hour bus ride to the main school from where they live, which would be hard for six- or seven-year-olds to handle every day. Although the reason for demolishing the branch school isn't stated, it's likely that, since these four were the only kids going there seven years ago, due to depopulation, there just aren't enough kids in the area to make having a branch school worthwhile, at this point. Since the island has a population of five thousand, the reasons behind the closure of the high school are probably similar.

PAGE 11

The Rokutou islands bring to mind the Gotou islands from *Barakamon*. *Tou* means "island," and *go* and *roku* mean "five" and "six," respectively.

PAGE 28

Shochu is a distilled Japanese liquor that tends to have an alcohol content upward of 25%. Unlike *sake*, it can be made from not only rice but barley and sugar cane, among other ingredients.

PAGE 36

Sushi grass, or *baran*, is generally placed between different kinds of sushi, to keep the flavors from mixing.

PAGE 57

No guarantees, but since there aren't any other kinds of school shoes that look like these, it's likely that Ryon's found the set of kids' bathroom slippers.

PAGE 75

"-bou" is a suffix meaning "kid"; Toshi-bou is about a decade younger than Tohno.

PAGE 86

This guy's shirt echoes Yoshino-sensei's previous series, *Barakamon*. "*Baraka*" means "energetic" or "vigorous" in the Gotou dialect.

PAGE 87

"-ban" is a dialect suffix meaning "big brother" or "uncle." It doesn't necessarily mean Iwao is actually Toshi-bou's uncle.

PAGE 91

Tohno's talking about **screentone** types here. The first numbers (60 and 50) refer to the line number, which specifies the size of the dots in the tone. The higher the line number, the more dots per inch, and the subtler the effect. The percentages refer to how densely those dots are printed in the pattern. For example, at 50%, if all the dots were gathered together, they would fill 50% of the area.

PAGE 112

Spirit Gun

Yusuke Urameshi's signature move from *Yu Yu Hakusho*. It's actually "*Rei* 'spirit' Gun" — a play on "ray gun" — in Japanese.

PAGE 113

"The type who names the protagonist after himself"

Note Tohno also did this, in a less obtrusive way, in *Wakkamon* with Tohno-sensei...and Tonoshima.

PAGE 115

TV Myuude was a local evening program that was broadcast on the Television Nagasaki network from 1997 to 2002. Although the Gotou islands are about sixty-two miles from the port of Nagasaki and it takes three hours to reach them by ferry, they're technically part of Nagasaki Prefecture.

Eva is short for *Neon Genesis Evangelion*, one of the most influential and well-known anime of all time.

The *Gundam* series is a massive media franchise that spans over a dozen TV shows and movies. Models of the titular *Gundam* robots are very popular among the series's fans.

Escaflowne refers to *The Vision of Escaflowne*, a 26-episode anime series that debuted in 1996. It features elements of fantasy and mecha, and follows a high school girl named Hitomi who finds herself transported to another planet, getting caught up in a war in the process.

Slayers is a light novel series that received its first anime adaptation in 1995. One of the biggest anime series of the 1990s, the story follows a young sorceress named Lina Inverse and her comrades as they fight their way past bandits, dragons, demons, and other baddies.

TV Tokyo is one of Tokyo's major television stations and one of the biggest distributors of anime in Japan, featuring hugely popular titles like *Yu-Gi-Oh!* and *Naruto*.

PAGE 118

Furoshiki are square pieces of fabric traditionally used to transport clothes or goods (by wrapping them in the cloth and tying a knot at the top) or wrap gifts.

PAGE 120

FMA refers to *Fullmetal Alchemist*, a manga series adapted into one of the most popular anime of all time. The plot follows brothers Edward and Alphonse as they search for a way to restore their bodies after a botched attempt to resurrect their late mother.

PAGE 123

G-pens are pens commonly used in manga for their flexibility — depending on how hard one presses, one can create thick, defined lines or thin, contoured lines.

PAGE 124
What he's being offered is the Japanese version of lined notebook paper; the boxes make it easier to space your *kanji* correctly.

PAGE 126
Maru-pens are typically used to draw fine lines and are very useful for tracing.

PAGE 152
Kanji, or Chinese characters, comprise the primary writing system of the Japanese language. With most text being on computers and phones these days, it's not uncommon for people to forget how to write a particularly uncommon or difficult character.

PAGE 175
Grapple
The title is actually *Budou,* or *"Way of the Warrior,"* but when written with different *kanji,* it's the word for "grape."

PAGE 192
Both **Tokyo** and **Osaka** are northeast of the Gotou islands. Tohno would be looking at China, or at Korea's Jeju Island if he's lucky.

PAGE 207
There's a Japanese reality TV show called **The First Errand** about little kids (preschool or so) being sent on their first errands by themselves, and the "do-re-mi" melody is the show's theme song. It's been running since 1991.

BONUS
Blue light is the light from digital displays. Some glasses are designed to block blue light, and sellers claim they help reduce potential retinal damage. Since most screen-related eye trouble is due to a condition known as computer vision syndrome, not blue-light exposure itself, the glasses may not provide much benefit.

Yoshi no Zuikara
The Frog in the Well Does Not Know the Ocean

SATSUKI YOSHINO

TRANSLATOR:
Taylor Engel

LETTERER:
Lys Blakeslee

YOSHINOZUIKARA vol. 1
© 2019 Satsuki Yoshino/SQUARE ENIX CO., LTD.
First published in Japan in 2019 by SQUARE ENIX CO., LTD. English translation rights arranged with SQUARE ENIX CO., LTD. and Yen Press, LLC through Tuttle-Mori Agency, Inc.

English translation © 2020 by SQUARE ENIX CO., LTD.

Yen Press
150 West 30th Street, 19th Floor
New York, NY 10001

Visit us at yenpress.com
facebook.com/yenpress
twitter.com/yenpress
yenpress.tumblr.com
instagram.com/yenpress

First Yen Press Edition: September 2020

Yen Press is an imprint of Yen Press, LLC.
The Yen Press name and logo are trademarks of Yen Press, LLC.

The publisher is not responsible for websites (or their content) that are not owned by the publisher.

Library of Congress Control Number: 2020940867

ISBNs: 978-1-9753-1624-2 (paperback)
978-1-9753-1625-9 (ebook)

10 9 8 7 6 5 4 3 2 1

WOR

Printed in the United States of America